Hard Living on Clay Street

JOSEPH T. HOWELL was raised in Nashville, Tennessee. He graduated from Davidson College in Davidson, North Carolina, and received master's degrees from Union Theological Seminary in New York and the School of City and Regional Planning at the University of North Carolina at Chapel Hill. Mr. Howell presently works with an economic consulting firm in Washington, D.C. He and his family have maintained contact with the families described in *Hard Living on Clay Street*.

Hard Living on Clay Street

PORTRAITS OF BLUE COLLAR FAMILIES

Joseph T. Howell

WAVELAND
PRESS, INC.

Prospect Heights, Illinois

For information about this book, write or call:

Waveland Press, Inc.
P.O. Box 400
Prospect Heights, Illinois 60070
(708) 634-0081

This monograph was prepared at the Center for Urban and Regional Studies, University of North Carolina at Chaper Hill; the project was funded by a research grant from the Center for Studies of Metropolitan Problems NIMH (Grant No. MH 17858). No official endorsement by the Public Health Service is intended or should be inferred.

ISBN 0-88133-526-6

Printed in the United States of America

7 6

This book is dedicated
to the memory of our daughter, Katherine

Contents

Preface 1991

Twenty years ago—almost to the day—I and my wife and infant son pulled up in a U-Haul truck in front of a deteriorating two-story house which was to become our home on Clay street for exactly one year. It did not take us long to get to know two families, one living next door, and the other about four houses away. These two families—the Moseby's and the Shackleford's—ended up being the families this book is about.

When we moved in, I had no idea I was going to write a book. Rather, my role was simply one member of a team of researchers whose primary objective was to study a lower income, white working class community, a group which in the 1970s was considered somewhat neglected in terms of sociological research since the focus of the 1960s was on the black ghetto. My job as participant observer was to keep the researchers honest. In a sense I guess I was a reality check, a sounding board, someone to test ideas on and to keep the sociologists from making assertions that any normal person would know were stupid.

I can remember when it began to dawn on us—to me and to F. Stuart Chapin, Jr., the director of the research effort—that I might be on to something beyond being a reality check. I would routinely dictate all of my observations and send the tapes back to Chapel Hill to be typed. When I would go for more than a week or two without sending back a tape, I would invariably get a call from one of a group of people who became known as "Clay Street weekly reader's club" demanding to know how Barry got out of the mess he was in last week and what was happening with June's grown children. And, by the way, how come I was a week late on the last installment? I knew I was on to something.

That something was quite simply the story of human lives unfolding over the course of a year. For this, full credit goes to the people on Clay street. For the life of me, I did not understand then—nor do I fully understand now — how these people could welcome a stranger into their homes and share with him virtually all parts of their lives. Nothing was off limits. They knew (because I told them) my primary reason for being in the community was somehow to write about them. But beyond that, what I was *really* doing there was fuzzy both to them and to me.

Perhaps it had something to do with non-judgmental acceptance; when people are genuinely accepting of other people — warts and all — strange things happen. In the busy world we live in, we rarely have much time for other people; and when we do, it is more often than not, not for who they are as people, but for what they can do for us. This was an opportunity simply to accept people as people. It was the opportunity of a lifetime.

Looking back on the experience twenty years later, what stands out to me most is not the peculiarity or uniqueness of the lives of the people on Clay Street but rather their universality. The problems that they were struggling with in 1970 are the same problems most people struggle with at one point or another throughout their lives — human relationships, love, children, work, financial security, health, survival. The difference is that on Clay Street there was no veneer of respectability, no pretense that everything is under control, no insistence on sweeping the dust under the carpet. As June Moseby would say, they let it all hang out, the dirty linen with the clean. And they did so because they were (and are) proud people and because deep down I believe they somehow felt as I did that their story was worth telling. The acceptance of the original Anchor paperback and this reprinting twenty years after the fact suggests we were right.

Of course, the beginning of the decade of the 1990s is not the beginning of the 1970s. Despite the Vietnam War, the national mood in 1970 was generally optimistic. Many (including me) really believed that with adequate funding and a true national commitment, the country could solve its tough social problems. In the early 1990s, in many respects, as a nation we are sadder, wiser and, indeed, poorer. The national deficit is a millstone around our neck. (Can you imagine the federal government funding a research project like this today?) The disparity between the rich and poor is much greater now than in 1970. And the working poor, the group which many in Clay Street were part of, have fared even worse. The big difference between the 1990s and the 1970s, however, is not so much that nationally nothing is being done now to address America's nagging social problems. In 1990 neither political party even talked about it.

So how have the Mosebys, the Shackelfords, the other families on Clay Street, and their neighborhood fared over this twenty-year period? This reprinting includes a new epilogue which provides some answers to this question. Fortunately, my wife and I ended up settling in the Washington area; while we did not live on Clay Street, we have managed to maintain ties with the families—especially the Shackelfords. We hear from them at times of joy and sadness and see them from time to time and on special occasions. While the book still stands on its own as a year in the life of these families, being able to follow the lives of these people over twenty years provides, I think, an important perspective on the meaning of what happened in that year.

I am grateful to many people who helped me get the epilogue in shape: to Jared Mintz who provided up-to-date research on the changes in the Clay Street neighborhood, to Linda Leonard who typed the final draft, to my wife, Embry, who shared the original Clay Street experience as well as the ups and downs of the last twenty years and who has provided important insight on this 20-year perspective on Clay Street. And, of course, to the folks on Clay Street. Those who have survived (and there have been many who have not) are as resilient as ever and are just as tough, ornery, cantankerous, and hell bent—and as loving, gentle, kind and proud—as you might expect.

Joseph T. Howell
Washington, D.C.

Preface

In May 1970, just before I was to get a planning degree from the School of City and Regional Planning at the University of North Carolina at Chapel Hill, I received a note from Professor F. Stuart Chapin, Jr., informing me that he wanted to talk to me about a job. At the time I was busily racing about having job interviews with such organizations as the Rouse Company, the Atlanta Model Cities Agency, and the Research Triangle Planning Commission. I wanted to take a job in planning, hopefully in some way related to helping the poor or minority groups.

That afternoon my plans suddenly changed. Chapin said he had just received a grant from the National Institute of Mental Health to undertake a study of a white, working-class community in metropolitan Washington, D.C., and he wanted me to consider being the participant observer. I would live in the community with my family for one year, after which time I would have another year to produce a report on life in that community.

At first I was somewhat cool to the idea. After all, it was not exactly in line with my career interests in urban planning, nor did I feel my academic background was adequate for such a job. I had had few courses in sociology or anthropology and had no desire to pursue an academic career. Later, however, a sociologist, who had just completed his own participant observation study of a ghetto area in Washington, assured me that an academic background in sociology was not an important requirement and that I was probably better off without one. Also, I realized that an opportunity such as this would probably never come along again. So I decided to take the job. I have not yet regretted that decision.

Since a study such as this is the result of how one particular individual observes life, background information regarding the observer is appropriate here. Like many of the people on Clay Street, I am a Southerner. But unlike them I am not the son of a farmer, miner, mason, or carpenter but, rather, of a banker; and while I grew up in the mecca of their culture, Nashville, Tennessee, most of the people from the part of Nashville I grew up in scorned the Grand Ole Opry and prided themselves in having never attended it. Furthermore, by attending a private high school in Nashville, I had very little contact with the kinds of people in Nashville who were like the people who lived on Clay Street.

My first exposure to living with people whose life styles were different from my own came during my college years. Though I attended a southern school with a relatively homogeneous student body—Davidson College—I spent my summers participating in various work projects in Mexico, rural Japan, and the Lower East Side of New York City. These experiences continued during the four years I attended Union Theological Seminary, when I worked with blacks and Puerto Ricans on the Lower East Side and in Harlem. In 1966, the summer just after my marriage to Embry Martin, we lived with a poor black family on their farm in southwest Georgia. While these experiences helped to compensate for an otherwise sheltered upbringing, my exposure had been to blacks and Puerto Ricans, not to lower-income or working-class whites. Moreover, these experiences could not erase the fact that I came from a social class different from that of the people on Clay Street and, though not an intellectual, had what one person described as "way, way too much schooling."

I am indebted to a number of persons who have been a tremendous help to me in this project. First comes my wife, Embry, who with our son, Andrew, shared the Clay Street experience with me. All my friends were her friends. Most of the things I did, she did. She recorded a good many observations herself and shared valuable insights with me during all phases of the project. She is in fact my best critic, whose opinions and ideas I respect most. As is discussed in more detail in the Appendix, without her help this particular study would have been extremely more difficult and perhaps impossible.

I am especially thankful to the project director, F. Stuart Chapin, Jr., for the freedom he allowed me, for the support—technical, professional, and moral—he gave me during the field experience, and for his suggestions concerning my analysis and presentation of the material. I am particularly grateful for his confidence in me, for his encouragement, and for his enthusiasm about the study, attitudes that were always present even when my own spirits were quite low. My colleague, Robert Zehner, also provided some very useful feedback regarding my transcripts and some important suggestions as to my general approach, direction, and data analysis.

Numerous others played very important roles in helping me produce this book. Fred Patten, a participant observer in a previous study undertaken by the Center for Urban and Regional Studies, gave me some important advice regarding my field methodology, as did Elliot Liebow, who spent an afternoon with me just before I moved into the neighborhood. Once I was in the community, Ruth Landman, chairman of the Department of Anthropology at American University, gave me needed perspective on my work when she and I got together for biweekly meetings to discuss my transcripts and problems I was having in the community. Also while I was in the field recording my observations on a tape recorder, I was most fortunate to have the help of Linda Killen in Chapel Hill whose skill as a typist borders on the miraculous. Linda not only typed two thousand pages of transcripts, but gave me some extremely good suggestions concerning the style and content of my earlier drafts, and she typed the final draft of the manuscript.

Back in Chapel Hill, I was very lucky to have an excellent typist in Miriam Winesette who typed two drafts of this book. I am grateful to her not only for her fine typing but for her enthusiasm and encouragement during some trying winter months. Sociologist Frank Mulvihill from the Center for Urban and Regional Studies provided much needed analytical help during conferences, coffee breaks, and bull sessions, and

Jim Causey contributed some very helpful suggestions for the
first draft; Kathy Vansant, also from the center, as my chief
editor and literary critic, was most responsible for making
the final draft coherent and readable. And Bev Mulvihill came
through in short notice to produce review copies of the first
draft, as did Greg McDonald, who helped with last-minute
typing.

I am also grateful to friends who took the time to read
early versions of this manuscript and to provide useful comments—Bill Goodykoontz, Charlie Hinkle, Mike Maloney,
Rosanne Coggeshall, and Sally Hunter—and to Ronnie Martin
for proofreading the final draft, a task totally beyond my
ability at that time.

Finally, I am most grateful to the people on Clay Street—
especially June and Sam and Barry and Bobbi—who with me
wrote this book about themselves. These people accepted me
and Embry and Andrew as members of their family. They
shared themselves and their lives with me in a way I still find
hard to understand. I will always feel close to them, respect
them, and consider myself fortunate to have known them.

Introduction

Recently there has been a great deal of interest in learning about the blue collar worker. Numerous books and articles have been written about how white, working-class people think, feel, and behave, and about their place in American society. Even films and television programs have focused on blue collar workers and working-class families. Consequently a portrait has emerged of "the typical blue collar family."

A typical portrait is one of a second-generation, thirty-nine-year-old Polish immigrant who is a factory worker and who owns a $17,000 home in an older subdivision of an eastern industrial city. His wife stays home, keeps house, and minds their three children, two of whom are being bussed away from their neighborhood school. On Wednesdays he bowls in an all-male league and most evenings stops by the local tavern on the way home for "drinks with the boys." On Tuesdays his wife occasionally plays bingo, and on Sundays she regularly attends the Roman Catholic Church. (He usually goes with her on special occasions.) Their life style is orderly and routine. Their best friends are their neighbors; and they maintain close relationships with both sets of parents, who live nearby, and with various brothers and sisters, nieces and nephews. They are family-centered and generally considered somewhat wary of outsiders.

Recently, the portrait has been altered to include a hard hat and an American flag. This blue collar family is, above all else, worried and confused. Its members are worried about their neighborhood becoming racially integrated, about the decline of their property values, about the safety of their neighborhood, about the bussing of their children, about inflation. They are confused by college students who demonstrate against America's oldest institutions, by the war their

oldest son is fighting in, by the demands for what they inter-
pret as more handouts for those who can't or won't work.
Moreover, they feel they are having to pay the costs for social
change advocated by college students and elitist politicians.
And so the portrait goes: The blue collar worker is per-
plexed, trapped, and tormented and represents a force in
American society ripe for political exploitation.

While there are doubtless many such families living in the
United States, not only in eastern industrial cities but throughout the country, this family is not the only type of working-
class family. Obviously, within a vast blue collar work force
and within a country as large and diverse as the United States,
there is considerable variation in regard to life styles and
values. The purpose of this book is to contribute to the understanding of the varieties of life styles within the working class.
Although the family portraits of the "hard living" families on
Clay Street are in some ways like the "typical" blue collar
family, what stands out is not the similarities but the differences.

In regard to background characteristics, the families presented in this book differ from the "typical" blue collar family
in three ways: they do a different kind of blue collar work,
they have a different ethnic identity, and perhaps most important they have unstable family situations. The men who
lived on Clay Street did not work in factories but were employed in service-oriented work. They were painters, plaster-
ers, auto mechanics, construction workers, plumbers, repair-
men, truck drivers, etc. Some were self-employed, and most
were nonunion. There was a contempt for factory work,
"having to take orders," working for a big corporation. To
the extent that these families had any ethnic identification,
it was having southern origins. Many of the people were
southern migrants who had moved to the city years before
but who maintained some nostalgia for the farms of North
Carolina or the mountains of West Virginia even though there
was really no "home" to return to. Finally, the hard living
families on Clay Street were not stable. Practically everyone
had been married at least once before; many had consensual
marriages or marital relationships that were tenuous. I suggest that this last characteristic—family instability—is most im-

portant because the life styles of the stable families in the
Clay Street neighborhood were in many respects much closer
to the stereotype of the typical working class family than they
were to the hard living families described here.

Who, then, are these particular working-class people? How
do they fit into the American social system? Since many have
ties to the South, they might be thought of as "southern
migrants," and since they have unstable family situations,
they might be labeled "the unstable working class," although
neither of these labels is quite appropriate. Before I undertook this study, I talked to numerous outsiders knowledgeable
of this community—planners, social workers, government
officials. Invariably these outsiders labeled the residents of
Clay Street as "rednecks." The people on Clay Street were
confused and dismayed by this label, preferring to call themselves "just plain folks."

This particular book is part of a larger study undertaken by
the Center for Urban and Regional Studies at the University of North Carolina at Chapel Hill on the values, activities,
and life ways of the people living in a working-class suburb of
Washington, D.C. My role as participant observer involved
my living in the community for one year and getting to know
as much about the people as possible. I lived on Clay Street
with my wife, Embry, and small son, Andrew, from August
1970 through August 1971. This book is about the families I
got to know best.

The material that follows is essentially the story of their
lives during the one year I knew them. All names of persons
and places have been changed. Most of the dialogue is not
verbatim but rather my recounting of what was said, observations that I tried to record as soon after the event as possible. Although some distortion is unavoidable, I think I have
been reasonably accurate and true to the people and to the
events. In any event, what doubt might occur in the reader's
mind was anticipated by one of my neighbors, who toward
the end of my stay on Clay Street made the following observation:

> You know, all this shit you're going to write in your
> book and all that you're going to put down, nobody's
> going to believe it. They're going to say you made it up.

They're going to call it fiction. They ain't going to believe the things that go on around this neighborhood. Course I know there are skeletons in everybody's closet. But you put the real stuff in your book and wait and see. They're going to say people don't live like that. But the people who're gonna read your book, they just don't know. They don't know what the world is like.

One of the most difficult tasks that confronted me in my work was explaining to the people what I was doing in the community. I would usually stutter and stumble around for words, mumbling something like, "Well, I am on a government research project. See, we feel that people in government don't have much understanding for the way real people live, people in neighborhoods like this. Often they are the ones who are making plans and decisions which affect your lives and yet they don't know who you are. They decide what happens to your neighborhood; yet they have no idea of what your neighborhood is like or what it is like to live here. My job is just to experience firsthand what it is like to live here, to get to know the people, and to understand your problems. I'll write it all up; and if anybody reads it, maybe they will be a little more sensitive to your problems and the way you see things. . . ."

"Wait a minute," often came the reply. "Hit me with that one again. You mean to tell me the federal government is paying you a salary just to live here, get to know folks and write it up, where it'll collect dust on some egghead's shelf?"

"Yep."

"You mean this is what you are getting *paid* to do?" There was usually a moment of puzzled silence, then a smile, and often a deep, almost delirious laugh: "Well, goddamn, ain't that just like the federal government!"

This is my "report." My one hope is that it won't collect dust on some "egghead's" shelf but will be read, and that it will make some readers more sensitive to the kinds of problems other human beings face and the values they hold.

The first part of the book is about the Shackelfords—Barry and Bobbi Jean, both in their early thirties, their four young children, and Walt Walters, Bobbi's aging stepfather. When we moved to Clay Street, the Shackelfords lived in a run-down, two-story house across the street from our duplex. When they were evicted from that house a few weeks later, they moved into a deteriorating three-room duplex apartment about a block away. The Shackelfords were probably the poorest family on Clay Street and among the poorest in the entire community. Their income for the year I knew them was well under $5,000. Although Barry was a self-employed house painter–subcontractor, he was an alcoholic and worked only sporadically.

The family of Part Two, the Mosebys, by comparison was different. Sam Moseby at age fifty-three was an experienced mechanic who worked for a Dodge dealer in Washington as a front-end specialist. Although his weekly pay check varied according to the work volume, the check was regular and occasionally was as high as $250 a week take-home. Their yearly income was close to $13,000. The Moseby family was older and smaller than the Shackelfords. Sam's wife, June, was forty-six; and their only child, Sammy, was five. (June and Sam each had three grown children by previous marriages.) Living with them was Barney, Sam's unemployed forty-two-year-old brother. Though small, their one-bedroom duplex apartment was in much better condition than the Shackelfords' apartment.

From one perspective, these two families were dramatically different. The Shackelfords were concerned with surviving from one day to the next—getting food on the table, paying the rent, getting bills paid, getting family members to the doctor. Their daily routine was chaotic and unpredictable. They had few close friends in the neighborhood. In contrast, the Mosebys had little difficulty paying the bills or purchasing what they wanted. Their daily routine was orderly and predictable. June Moseby, who had numerous friends on Clay Street, spent hours every day chatting with neighbors and listening to their problems. Dominating the Mosebys' concerns were the marital problems of June Moseby's three grown children as well as the occasional problems of neighbors and friends. The differences between the life styles of these two families will be apparent in the pages that follow.

From another perspective, however, there are some similarities in the life styles and values of these two families. These similarities come across in certain common themes that were present in the lives of many of the families on Clay Street. For instance, the Mosebys were heavy drinkers, as were most families on Clay Street, though not to the extent of Barry, who was drunk most of the time. June and Sam Moseby, like the Shackelfords, had been married before; and June's grown children were finding marriage difficult. Though not as shaky as the relationship between Barry and Bobbi Jean, June and Sam's relationship at times was quite tenuous. Both families were tough and outspoken. Neither participated in many formal community activities. Both were cynical about the political process. Both had done a lot of moving around and were hardly settled or rooted at their present location. Both had strong feelings of individualism. Depending on how one looks at these two families, then, they can be seen as being very different or as being in many respects the same.

The sameness of these two families and indeed of many of the families on Clay Street I have called hard living, a way of life explored in detail in Part Three. More than anything else, hard living refers to an approach to life that is intense, episodic, and uninhibited. There is a strong emphasis on individualism, on being true to oneself. Though it is an oversimplification to say that the hard living people have no concern for the future, it can be said that they are preoccupied with the problems and drama of day-to-day life, particularly personal relationships.

Hard living stood in direct contrast to a more conservative view toward life—what might be called settled living—which was characteristic of many other families on Clay Street and throughout the larger community and more similar to the portrait of the typical blue collar family. These families—usually church-going, teetotaling, politically and socially conservative—tended to look down on hard living families as "reckless," "irresponsible," and "lower class." In describing some extremely hard living families, these families would occasionally use the term "white trash." In contrast to the hard living families, their life styles were more cautious and refined. Their marriages were stable. They were more concerned about what others thought. Home-owning, they were rooted in the community and tended to belong to community groups. They were more protective of their children, often exercising strict discipline. In contrast to most of the children of hard living families, many of their children went to college. (None of June's or Sam's six grown children, for instance, had completed high school. Only June's son, Ted, had a high school equivalency, which he acquired in the Army.) These "respectable" members of the community represented the other extreme. The life history of Pete Dale is presented as an example of this life style.

These two opposing life styles—hard living and settled living—represent two ends of a continuum. They represent two opposing "pulls" or forces many people in this community felt throughout their lives. Caught between these two pulls, some people tended to shift dramatically from hard living to settled living and back again. At one point in a person's life he or she might be extremely hard living, at another a very settled person. For instance, it was usually acceptable for young people to run around and live hard before settling down to a settled life style. Those individuals who never settled down were the ones who remained hard living. The Shackelfords had never really settled down. Both June and Sam Moseby had been less settled at earlier points in their lives, and all of June's children were struggling with the conflicting desires of living hard or settling down. Often it was extremely hard for a person to reconcile these two opposing forces.

Within a given family some brothers or sisters pursued one course of life, some another. Both June and Sam had brothers and sisters who were stable, church-going, home-owning families. Both Barry and Bobbi Jean had relatives who were settled and "well-to-do." Similarly most of the settled families I knew admitted they had brothers or sisters who were "black sheep," "no-goods," "run-arounds." Thus hard living touched many of the families in the area, even those who were the most temperate, the most rigid, the most upright. To get a sense of the threat it presented, even to many of the most settled families, all one had to do was listen to a few Southern

Baptist or Independent Fundamentalist Sunday sermons. The ministers often preached against the powers of Satan and "the ways of the flesh." They had seen Satan steal members of their congregations, they said, leading them down the road to ruin: drinking, running around, living in sin. These ministers were talking about hard living. Few people in their congregations misunderstood them.

An older suburb of Washington, D.C., Clay Street itself was not a run-down neighborhood. Brick garden apartments occupied one side of the street; duplexes and single-family frame houses with asbestos siding occupied the other. The houses were for the most part two-story structures with small front porches and tiny patches of grass out front. About half were owner-occupied. Driveways separated each house from its neighbor. Built in the 1920s and 1930s, the houses were showing signs of age, though most were still in adequate condition, needing only a new coat of paint, a new window screen, a new gutter here and there. The average selling price for the houses was around $18,000, with rents for two-bedroom apartments and duplexes averaging around $120 per month.

In the summer Clay Street was shady and during most of the day active with children of all ages playing on the sidewalks and in the street and with women carrying laundry or going shopping. When the men came home in the evenings, activity increased. Families would sit out on their porches or stoops, drinking beer and puttering around in the yard, working on their houses or gardens or cars, or chatting with neighbors.

When I first moved to Clay Street, I was most impressed by the numbers of old cars jacked up on cinder blocks, by the American flags flying from some people's porches, by the number of dogs and "beware of dog" signs, by the chain link fences that protected some of the houses, by the trees and the shade and the small gardens, by the number of old folks rocking on their porches. I was also impressed by a few old, shabby houses, with excessive amounts of debris and junk out front—old toys, bedsprings, lumber, tires, and old cars. In one of these houses lived the Shackelfords. . . .

One

THE SHACKELFORDS:
A HARD LIVING FAMILY

1

One Day with Bobbi Jean

When we moved to Clay Street, Bobbi Jean and Barry Shackelford lived across the street three doors away. Their two-story single-family house had screens missing from the front door and the windows, shingles missing from the roof and walls, and there always seemed to be an unusual amount of junk on their front porch. I heard a neighborhood child refer to their house as "the dirty house," and one of our next-door neighbors called it the "roach house." "If there is one goddamned cockroach in that house," he said, "I swear to God there are four and a half million. . . ."

Barry Shackelford, a thirty-four-year-old house painter, was self-employed as a subcontractor when I met him in the fall. His wife of eight years, Bobbi Jean, was thirty-one; and they had three children—Cindy, seven, Billy, five, and Lyman (called Littlebit), three. Bobbi Jean's son by her first marriage, Walter (called Bubba), was thirteen and lived with them, as did Bobbi Jean's sixty-three-year-old stepfather, Walt Walters. When I first met them, they had been living on Clay Street for almost a year and a half.

The day I met Bobbi Jean, she described her husband as an alcoholic who worked only now and then, mainly when he felt like it. Barry was born on the outskirts of Washington, D.C., in what was then farm land (now a subdivision) and spent his childhood living in various houses in that general area. He quit school after the eighth grade, married when he was eighteen, and by that marriage had a fourteen-year-old son whom he rarely saw. Most of his life Barry had been a painter, carpenter, or plasterer. Bobbi Jean described him as "an interior decorator."

Bobbi Jean was born in Richmond, Virginia, where she

lived until she was eight. When her mother divorced Bobbi Jean's father and married Walt Walters, they moved to Washington where Walt was a house painter and subcontractor. Bobbi Jean grew up in the Near Northeast. She dropped out of school and married when she was sixteen and later moved a few miles out of Washington near her husband's army base. Her first marriage lasted almost five years.

Since Bobbi Jean and Barry were both only children, they had few close relatives. Bobbi Jean's cousins lived in Richmond. Though Barry's cousins lived farther out in the county, he saw them rarely. Barry's mother lived in the country near the Chesapeake Bay and was remarried for the third time. Barry's father lived only a few miles away and was not married at the time. Like Barry, he was an alcoholic, and the two could not get along. Barry occasionally saw his mother but rarely his father. Bobbi Jean's mother, who was also an alcoholic, died five years ago; but since her stepfather Walt lived with them, he was very much a part of their family.

The Shackelfords' income was unsteady. Bobbi Jean received $60 a month in public assistance (AFDC) for Bubba. (Her first husband had disappeared and could not be located to pay child support.) Walt received $110 a month in combined social security and old-age assistance benefits. Bobbi Jean also received food stamps. In filling out welfare forms, Bobbi Jean listed Barry's "average weekly earnings" at $60, though she said she was sure that they were actually much less.

For their eight-room Clay Street house they were paying $150 a month not counting utilities, which included an extremely high heating bill in the winter months. They were evicted from that house shortly after I arrived in the neighborhood and moved a few blocks away to a second-floor apartment that consisted of two rooms, a kitchen, and the use of an attic for which they paid $90 a month rent. Since the house they moved to was only two blocks from Clay Street, the neighborhoods were very similar, except that the newer one was located on a main thoroughfare and there were fewer children. Consequently, after they moved, while Bobbi Jean and Barry rarely returned to their old neighborhood, their *children came over practically every day to play with the other children on Clay Street.*

Bobbi Jean doesn't wake up at any special time. In fact she rarely even sets an alarm clock, for by the time the sun rises she usually has been awake for quite a while. Today is no exception. At four in the morning she is sitting in the kitchen, drinking coffee and smoking a cigarette. In the next room are Barry and her seven-year-old daughter, Cindy. Barry is snoring loudly. In the room next to them are her stepfather, Walt, who is moaning, and her two youngest boys, Billy and Littlebit, all sleeping on the same bed. Bubba is asleep in the attic. Though three rooms and an attic are hardly enough for a family of seven, Bobbi Jeans says it is better than the last place they lived, which although it had eight rooms, had holes in the walls, leaky plumbing, rats, and an incredible number of cockroaches.

Although Bobbi Jean would like to go back to sleep, in some ways she enjoys being up at this hour. It is the only quiet time of the day. Except for barks from Cleo, Barry's basset hound, or the occasional sound of a Mack truck passing along the highway in front of their apartment, it is peaceful, in fact one of the few peaceful times of the day.

Around five Bobbi Jean decides she will try going back to sleep again and goes into the bedroom. To get into the room she must step over Barry's paint cans and some of his tools, ease around the cot Barry is sleeping on, and step over Billy's hamsters. Bobbi flops down in the bed next to Cindy and tries to go back to sleep. It is beginning to get light and the birds are singing. Bobbi Jean lights another cigarette, turns on the radio to her favorite station, and listens to the early morning country music show. Everyone else goes on sleeping. Walt has been moaning all night, but since he is still asleep, Bobbi Jean decides not to give him any pain medicine. Ever since his eyes were operated on for cataracts about six weeks before, they have pained him and he has had trouble sleeping.

At six-thirty she gets up again, puts on her bathrobe, and goes outside to sit on the front porch. Bobbi Jean sits down on the porch steps, listening to the birds and watching the

early rush hour traffic begin to build up along the highway.
Just before seven, Harry, Bubba's friend from up the street,
tosses the paper up on the front porch.

"Hi, Bobbi Jean, how's Bubba?"

"Okay, I guess," Bobbi Jean replies.

"Tell him Patsy wants to see him."

Bobbi Jean laughs. The girls are after Bubba. He is good-
looking and big for his age. Too big, Bobbi Jean often says,
since he has been put back twice and is two years older than
most of the children in his sixth-grade class.

Bobbi Jean begins to look through the Washington *Post.*
She would prefer to read the *News,* but since up until a few
months before Bubba delivered the *Post,* she felt obligated to
take it. Bubba quit his route as a paper boy when his boss
failed to back him up on a difficult collection. A few weeks
later he got a job working on weekends at a car wash. But
the car wash hasn't worked out. Bubba was often the only
white boy working there; and since he had trouble getting to
work, he finally quit and now does not have a job.

By eight o'clock Bobbi Jean has finished browsing through
the paper and decides it is time she checked upstairs to see
who is up. As expected, everyone but Barry and Bubba is up
and hungry. Walt is sitting in his favorite spot beside the front
window overlooking the street and listening to the news on
the radio. Even though he can't see, he spends most of his
time in the chair beside the window.

Before she gets to the top of the stairs, Bobbi Jean is met
by cries of "Mamma, we want our bottles!"

"Well, just hold your asses, kids, I'm doing the best I goddamn well can," Bobbi Jean shouts as she goes to the
refrigerator, pours some milk into a pan, and heats it on the
stove. Since her three youngest still prefer bottles over solid
foods, Bobbi Jean has never tried to break them of the habit.
"I know they are a little old for bottles, especially Cindy,"
Bobbi Jean admits, "but eventually they'll get tired of them
and will drink out of a glass. Hell, Bubba was past the second
grade before he gave up his!" While the milk is warming,
Bobbi Jean goes into Walt's room. "How are you feeling this
morning, Daddy?" she asks softly.

"Pretty shitty," Walt replies. "My eyes, my goddamn eyes. Bobbi Jean, do you think I'll ever be able to see again? Do you think the doctors done right?"

"Sure, Daddy, sure they did. You just wait. In a few weeks you'll see just like you used to. And you'll be able to paint again, and hunt and fish."

"Goddamn, I'd like that. I sure would."

"Whatcha want to eat for breakfast, Daddy?"

"Ain't hungry, darling."

"Now, Daddy, you know you ought to eat. How 'bout some eggs and scrapple?"

"Okay," Walt replies, "I guess I'll try some."

After pouring the children their bottles, Bobbi Jean goes about scrambling some eggs and scrapple. The children are now restless, running about in their underpants, in and out of the kitchen, back into Walt's room, jumping on the bed and then running into the other bedroom. Barry sleeps through it all.

"All right," Bobbi Jean shouts, "I've had enough! If you kids want to play, get your asses outside! I'm fixing Daddy his breakfast." When the kids pay her no mind, Bobbi Jean raises her voice, "I said, *outside!*" Still no reaction from the children. Just at that time the youngest, Littlebit, comes racing into the kitchen, tripping on the cat who gives a loud squawk and jumps up on the table. Littlebit starts to cry.

"Okay," shouts Bobbi Jean, "what did I tell you?" She gives Littlebit three firm swats on the fanny and he starts to cry even louder. "I said get *outside,* and the next time this happens, I swear to God, somebody is really going to get their hind parts spanked." Cindy laughs. "And that goes for you, too, Miss Priss!"

The three children continue playing inside, not making quite so much noise, as Bobbi Jean finishes scrambling the eggs and scrapple. It is almost eight-thirty when Barry appears in the doorway. He is tall and thin, has buck teeth (actually they are an upper set of dentures; he lost his lower set years ago), and is wearing blue jeans, a red plaid shirt, and a red stocking cap. Barry has not taken these clothes off for over a week. He almost always sleeps in his clothes and is never

[handwritten margin note: never enough dough / drinks when he can]

without his red stocking cap, even in the summer. Barry stands in the doorway rubbing his eyes. He and Bobbi Jean briefly look at each other, but say nothing. Bobbi Jean frowns.

Barry chuckles and walks over to the refrigerator, opens the door, and pulls out a bottle of Old German beer. He opens the bottle, sprinkles a little salt in it, and takes a long swig. Then he disappears into the bedroom. Ignoring Barry, Bobbi takes the coffee off the stove.

Bobbi Jean has no idea what Barry will do today. She knows he has a job in Washington he hasn't finished yet; but today is Wednesday and Barry has not yet worked any this week. Monday the truck wouldn't start. And yesterday morning when Barry finally fixed the truck, he and Mack from downstairs had started drinking and Barry never got going. And last night! She could kill Barry for making so much noise. No one could go to sleep with Barry and Mack hollering and carrying on. Around midnight when he passed out, Bobbi Jean's nerves were so shaken she couldn't sleep herself. She got only two or three hours of sleep at the most.

[handwritten margin note: still not enough]

"Okay, Daddy, your breakfast is ready," Bobbi Jean calls to the front room. Then she goes and helps Walt into the kitchen. Walt sits down at the table and feels around for the plate, knife, and fork. Bobbi Jean slaps at a cockroach that scampers across the table.

"What was that?" asks Walt.

"Goddamn roaches are back, Daddy. I got to call the exterminator first thing."

As Walt starts eating, Barry appears in the doorway again, paint in hand. "Well, goddamn, shithead is gonna work today," Bobbi Jean mutters. Barry laughs sheepishly and goes downstairs, carrying the paint and a sackful of the remaining beer.

Hearing the truck door slam, Bobbi looks out and sees Barry in the front seat. The truck is a '53 Ford pickup with a '60 Ford motor, which Barry installed himself two years ago. He loves the truck, and Bobbi Jean is the only other person he lets drive it. Barry knows all its quirks, and when it breaks down, if he has the money to purchase the necessary part, he can usually get it going again very quickly. Last year when

Barry got ambitious, he built a camper which permanently sits on the back of the truck. In fact, when the truck is running, Barry affectionately refers to it as "the camper." When it is broken down, it is simply "the goddamned truck." Most of the time it is "the goddamned truck."

Two old cars rest in the Shackelford back yard beside the truck. A 1960 Ford station wagon, which is Bobbi Jean's, has a broken transmission, which went out about six months ago. The other is a 1954 Ford station wagon that Barry bought a few months ago as a source for parts for the truck.

Nothing happens when Barry tries to start the engine. After about thirty seconds, Barry jumps out of the cab, kicks the front fender of the truck, and hollers, "Stupid motherfucking truck!" He opens the other door, pulls out the battery, and brings it upstairs.

"What's the matter, B.?" Bobbi Jean asks. Her voice is more sympathetic.

"Oh shit," Barry replies, "it's the sonofabitch battery again. Motherfucker went out last night. But I outfoxed the bastard. Got me another battery and recharged the sonofabitch last night."

Barry exchanges the dead battery for the recharged one (this ritual occurs at least once a week) and takes the good battery outside. The truck starts up. After letting it idle for a few minutes, Barry pulls out into the back alley and then onto the main highway. Bobbi Jean is not sure where Barry is going—she hopes he is going into Washington to finish up the job he's been working on for three weeks—or when he will return.

After Walt finishes his breakfast, Bobbi Jean tries to do a little cleaning up in the kitchen. For Bobbi Jean house cleaning is a monumental task. Seven people packed into three rooms means there is not enough room to put things. The children never seem to pick up their toys or their clothes; and Barry insists on leaving his paint cans, battery recharger, fishing gear, and tools strewn about. Bobbi Jean says she could pick up after all of them, but she doesn't have the energy, and besides, there is no place to put things as it is.

Bobbi Jean looks over the three rooms. As for their belongings, they don't have a great deal: a kitchen table and three chairs, two double beds (one in each of the other rooms), a roll-away, one old easy chair with the stuffing coming out, three chests of drawers, and two end tables. Three old TV sets are stacked in one corner, with only the top one barely working. The walls are bare except for two mirrors and a beat-up photograph of a basset hound which looks just like Barry's dog. In one corner are several old cardboard boxes that contain the children's clothes and toys. In another corner are Barry's most prized possessions: three shotguns and a .22 rifle. Bobbi Jean looks around at toys, clothes, and Barry's junk on the floor. "It's just not worth it," she sighs as she scrapes the remains of Walt's food into the open garbage can in the kitchen. "I ain't going to try to clean this shit up today."

At nine o'clock it is time for Walt's first medicine routine. Bobbi Jean goes into the bathroom and returns with a bottle of eye medicine. As Walt tilts his head, she carefully puts three drops into each eye and then gives Walt two pain tablets. Walt then sits back in his chair beside the window and turns up his radio, which is playing country music.

Bobbi Jean decides to wash the breakfast dishes, but before she gets started she decides to call Carol, a friend from up the street, to see if Carol will be going to the supermarket. Since the children are getting restless and climbing all over Bobbi Jean, she can hardly hear Carol for all the noise. "Just a minute, Carol," she says, turning to her children. "Get out, goddammit, every one of you, *outside,* I can't hear myself think! If you are going to play, play *outside.*" Still wearing only their underpants, the children race down the stairway onto the front porch. It is finally quiet. Carol says that she isn't going to the store today, so Bobbi thanks her and hangs up.

Bobbi sits down, smokes another cigarette, and has another cup of coffee. She never eats breakfast and only nibbles here and there the rest of the day. What she can't understand is why her stomach seems to be getting fatter and fatter. She couldn't be pregnant, since she had her tubes tied when she had Littlebit. Barry doesn't like her stomach getting fat either. She knows it has something to do with problems in her uterus. The doctors told her she should have a hysterectomy six months ago, but when in the last six months has she had time? With Walt sick and Barry sick or drunk, who would mind the children? She figures the problem with her uterus and her excessive bleeding during menstruation are also why she has so little energy. Sometimes it is all she can do just to get up from finishing a cup of coffee, let alone tend to all the chores that need tending to. In the back of her mind she fears cancer, but she refuses to think about it. This morning, however, she manages to get up, as she always does, and finishes doing the dishes.

It is now already ten-thirty and time for Walt's insulin shot. When the public health nurse first showed Bobbi how to give the shot, she thought she could never be able to do it; but she knows her stepfather's life depends on it, since this year he had a severe diabetic attack and spent ten days in the hospital. First Bobbi tests Walt's urine to see how much insulin to give him. The paper she dips into the urine shows 2+. This means she will give Walt the full amount. She tests the needle, swabs Walt's thigh with some alcohol, and then, gritting her teeth, injects the fluid into his leg.

"Now, Daddy, how was that?"

"Didn't hurt much, honey," Walt replies. "You're getting much better."

Before Bobbi finishes giving Walt his shot, Billy is back inside crying with a bloody nose. He says Cindy threw a rock and hit him. Bobbi Jean is furious. "Cindy! Where is that Miss Priss, I'll whip her hind parts good!" she shouts. "Here," she says to Billy as she places a wet washcloth on his nose, "hold this on your nose, I'm going to get Cindy." Cindy bounds up the stairs, meeting her mother at the top.

"I didn't do it, Mamma. I didn't, I didn't, I didn't, I promise!" she screams.

"You know you are never supposed to throw a rock at anybody, you know that, Miss Cynthia! Now I'm gonna whip your hind parts good!"

When Cindy protests again, Bobbi Jean gives in. "Well, when your daddy gets home, you're going to have some explaining to do. Now get outside and don't throw any more rocks!" Cindy scampers down the stairs as Billy holds the washcloth over his nose, moaning in the bathroom.

About five minutes later, Billy has recovered and, still sobbing, goes out to play again. But Littlebit comes upstairs. Bobbi Jean greets him sharply, "Well, what's wrong with *you?*"

"Got a cold."

"Got a cold? You had a cold yesterday."

"Don't feel good," Littlebit whimpers.

"Well then, go to bed. If you got a cold, you ain't got no business running around outside. Get in bed and stay there."

"Want a bottle," Littlebit adds.

"Okay, if you want a bottle, I'll fix it. Now get your ass in bed. Right now!"

Littlebit perks up and runs and jumps in the bed beside Walt's chair. Bobbi Jean goes into the kitchen to heat some milk.

Since a pile of old clothes lies in the hallway, Bobbi realizes that unless she gets the laundry done today no one will have any clean clothes to wear. As she bundles the clothes up, Bubba charges down the attic stairs. "Boy," says Bobbi, "you sure slept late today. It's almost eleven o'clock!" Smiling, Bubba goes into the kitchen where he makes himself a peanut butter and jelly sandwich for breakfast. "By the way," says Bobbi Jean, "who is this Patsy girl anyway?"

Bubba smiles sheepishly. "Oh, just a girl, Mom."

"Well, Harry says she wants to see you." Bubba shrugs his shoulders and continues fixing his sandwich.

"Well, I'm going to the laundry, so watch out for the kids, okay?" Then Bobbi Jean looks at her watch. "Jesus Christ, it's almost lunch time. I'd better fix something for the kids first." She goes back to the kitchen, fries some scrapple, and puts out a loaf of bread on the table. "When the kids come up from playing, tell them their lunch is on the table, okay? But first help me carry some of this laundry."

Bubba carries one large bundle and Bobbi Jean another as they walk two blocks down the street to the laundromat. Bubba returns to finish his sandwich and watch the children. Bobbi Jean usually doesn't mind doing the laundry because it gets her out of the house to a place where there is almost always someone she knows who is also doing laundry. However, she has had a few unpleasant experiences with this laundromat. On two occasions drunks tried to pick her up. Both times she pulled out her switch blade, which she always carries, and flashed it in their faces, telling them to "get your fucking hands off me," and the men left her alone. Also blacks tend to use this laundromat. Bobbi says she doesn't have anything against blacks per se, though she adds, "Sometimes the niggers come in and take all the dryers and washers, and you can't get any laundry done." Today there is no one in the laundromat, white or black, and Bobbi is disappointed. She would rather have blacks there than nobody at all.

It is after twelve-thirty when Bobbi returns home, and the house is fairly quiet. Littlebit is asleep on the bed, Walt is beside his window listening to country music, and the others are gone. The cat is on the kitchen table finishing up the children's leftovers.

"Hungry, Daddy?" Bobbi asks as she gets to the top of the stairs. Before the old man answers, she remarks: "Where's Bubba? I left a whole load of laundry for him to bring back from the laundromat." Walt shakes his head, and Bobbi adds, "Well, somebody can just steal those clothes because I ain't gonna walk my ass down there. I'm too goddamned tired, and it's too goddamned hot out."

"Hot in here, too," Walt replies.

Bobbi goes into the kitchen and puts together an egg salad sandwich for Walt. She takes a few bites from the egg salad, which she made last week, but does not make herself a sandwich. She takes the sandwich to Walt, then spreads out the laundry on the bed and begins sorting it. When Bubba comes up the stairs a few minutes later, Bobbi hollers to him to get the rest of the laundry.

The afternoon is fairly quiet. After sorting the laundry and putting the things away, Bobbi decides to go down and sit on the front porch, since it is becoming extremely hot inside. (She does not put clean sheets on either bed. During the hot summer Bobbi finds it easier not to bother with sheets, and they sleep on the bare mattress.) Just as she gets to the head

Might be prejudiced but not a racist [handwritten marginal note]

of the stairs the phone rings. It is Irene, Big John Higgins's mother, who regularly calls Bobbi to chat. She and Barry used to live across the street from B.J. when they lived on Clay Street, and they both detest him. Christmas before last B.J.'s cousin Don was over at Bobbi's having a beer with Barry, and B.J. came in drunk and mad and smacked Don across the face several times in front of the kids. Bobbi still has a bitter taste regarding that incident and considers B.J. and most of his drunk relatives who live there "common trash." Bobbi asks Irene about the fight between B.J. and May Jones, B.J.'s girl friend.

"Hot damn," says Bobbi, gleaming, "so the old bitch is leaving again, going down country. Well, that shows her ass right. Any woman that would live with that man is crazy." Irene agrees.

It is cooler on the porch. The tiny front yard has two trees, which provide plenty of shade, and a hedge gives some privacy and protects the children from spilling out into the traffic. Still, Bobbi can sit on the porch steps and see everyone who passes by. This is where she likes to sit, and hardly an afternoon passes that someone doesn't stop for a few moments on the way to the laundromat, store, or bus station. This afternoon Mrs. Taylor, a lady Bobbi doesn't know too well, pauses to ask about Bobbi's children. Mrs. Taylor has a daughter Cindy's age, though Cindy has not been at her house lately. Bobbi explains that Cindy had her ear operated on several weeks ago; she has felt bad and has remained at home.

Just as Bobbi is beginning to wonder where the children are, they come running around the house and plop down beside their mother on the porch. They are out of breath and tell her they've been playing with a friend on Clay Street and have run all the way home from there. When Bobbi asks why they ran home, they say the superintendent of the apartments on Clay Street told them they didn't live on Clay Street any more and they had no business playing there. Bobbi frowns and reaches in her pockets for some change. Giving each of the children a dime, she mutters, "The super don't own the goddamn street. Now you kids go and get yourself something at the store." They squeal with delight and race to the store.

About two-thirty Alton Short wanders up, drunk as usual, asking if Barry has gone to work yet. Al and Barry were supposed to work together today, but Al overslept. Though he once was a friend, Bobbi now despises Al and at first refuses to answer him. She has known Al for years; he is almost her stepfather's age and has painted for Walt as long as she can remember. She never liked his drinking but could put up with it, since compared to Barry's it wasn't so bad. But when Al bought Bubba a half pint of vodka for Bubba to spike punch for the sixth-grade graduation party, this was too much. When the teachers found it was Bubba who did it, he got suspended from school. Bobbi was so proud of Bubba on that day, but the vodka episode ruined everything. As far as Bobbi is concerned, it was all Alton Short's fault. He is no longer welcome in her house.

"Didya hear what I said, Bobbi?" slurs Al. "I was gonna work with Barry. Is he upstairs?"

"He's already gone to work, goddammit, he left early this morning," Bobbi snarls back.

"Oh shit," says Al, belching, "that's what I figured." He then starts around toward the back of the building. "Well, if Barry ain't in, I guess I'll stop by and talk to old Mack."

"Haven't seen him or Kate all day," Bobbi remarks. "Think Kate's sick, and Mack, he said he was going down to the welfare." Al disappears around the back of the house.

For the next hour and a half Bobbi continues sitting on the steps, watching the children playing. At four o'clock she goes back upstairs to give Walt some more pain medicine. Walt says his left eye is really bothering him. "If it gets much worse, when Barry comes home, we'll go to the doctor's, or the emergency room," Bobbi says, trying to comfort him.

Just before four-thirty Kate calls from downstairs to borrow some sugar. Bobbi pours some sugar in a cup and gives it to Cindy to take downstairs. "Every goddamned day," Bobbi mutters, "she wants sugar, or butter, or an egg, or milk. I know she's sick, but don't she ever go to the store? Probably too drunk to go to the store."

At four-thirty Bobbi looks out the window and sees the

truck pulling up. Barry gets out and comes stomping up the stairs.

"Hi, punkin puss," he says to Bobbi, smiling. "Got to do me a favor. Could you drive me across town to pick up some tile? We need some tile to finish this job."

Bobbi smiles back. She never knows what to expect from Barry, since quite often by this hour he will be drunk. But not today, and she is relieved. "What's the matter, need me to drive you? Sure, B., sure I will."

One of Barry's idiosyncrasies concerns his driving. Since he has no driver's license, sometimes he will get nervous about driving the truck. (Barry has gone without a license for several years, ever since he had a bad wreck and was charged with drunken driving.) He could get a license now but can't afford the high-risk insurance. At times, almost always when he is stone sober, Barry will worry about getting stopped and will try to get someone else, usually Bobbi, to drive the truck. Ironically, when he is drunk, he refuses to let anyone else drive. Bobbi usually gives in and drives if Barry wants her to; and she does this afternoon, after announcing to Walt that she is leaving. All three children want to go, including Littlebit, who now feels better. Barry agrees if they will ride in the back of the truck. The children love to ride in the truck.

Since the trip across town in rush hour traffic takes over an hour, everyone is exhausted and hungry when the Shackelfords return home. Because Bobbi was without transportation to go shopping earlier in the day, there is nothing to eat. Barry and Bubba agree to walk down to the corner store. Bobbi gives them some money and then rummages around and finds a can of tomato soup to heat up for Walt. The three children are fussing and screaming, and Bobbi is losing patience herself. When she heats some milk and pours the children's bottles, they quiet down. Cindy turns on the TV and the three of them go in and lie on the bed, drinking their milk and watching the barely visible latest episode of "Superman." After she finishes heating Walt's soup, Bobbi helps him to the kitchen table.

A few minutes later Barry and Bubba return from the store with two sacks, one containing a loaf of bread, milk, and sandwich spread, the other containing eight bottles of Old German beer. "This is all we could buy with the money you gave us, Mom," Bubba says as he reaches the top of the stairs.

Barry smirks. "Yep, had to get me some brew, you know." He puts his bag in the refrigerator, opens a bottle, and takes a long swig.

Taking Bubba's sack, Bobbi puts the bread and sandwich spread on the table. "Well," she says, "I ain't all that goddamn hungry myself, but if anybody is, here's all we got to eat." Bubba fixes himself two sandwiches, pours a tall glass of milk, and then goes to his room in the attic to eat by himself.

Barry and Bobbi rarely eat anything; and for this reason, among others, there is no scheduled mealtime at the Shackelford household. Bobbi always prepares food for her father, and since he is diabetic, she does the best she can to give him the right kind of foods. She also tries to be sure the children get enough to eat. But as for set mealtimes, there are none. When enough people are hungry, Bobbi puts out on the table what food is available, and people eat when they feel like it.

Barry also has a quirk in regard to eating. Since he has only an upper set of dentures and since these dentures are glued together with airplane glue—Barry got mugged the past fall and his dentures broke in two when they fell out of his mouth and hit the sidewalk—it is very difficult for him to eat hard foods. So when Barry decides to try to eat hard foods, he always takes his food and goes into a room by himself and gums it. He is embarrassed for anyone, including members of his own family, to see him eat like this. When Barry is drinking, however, he rarely eats; and this evening he has eight Old German beers to keep him company.

"Hey, you know something?" Barry remarks to Bobbi. "I got a real good thing. Where's Bubba? I want him to go with me. I found a TV, and if I can fix the sonofabitch, maybe we'll have a good TV."

"Oh boy!" Cindy shouts. "A good TV."

Barry calls Bubba, who agrees to go with him to pick up the TV which is at a friend's house. Barry's painting partner, Tarby Jones, had found the TV in an old house and agreed to trade it for one of Barry's bows. Barry, Cindy, and Bubba get in the truck and head off to Tarby's.

Bobbi mutters, "All we need is another goddamned TV that don't work," and tells her stepfather she is going out to sit on the porch to watch Billy and Littlebit, who are playing in the yard with two children from up the street. A little after seven Mack wanders out of the downstairs apartment. Mack is big and has an immense potbelly and always wears his work clothes, although he has not worked for over a year.

"Hi," he mumbles. "Got a dollar and fifty-two cents?"

"Shit," says Bobbi, "if I had a dollar and fifty-two cents, do you think I would lend it to you so you could go and get yourself a pint of that fucking whiskey?"

"Now, Bobbi, is that any way to talk to a friend and a neighbor?" Mack says, laughing.

"Friend and neighbor, my ass." Bobbi frowns.

Mack's eyes twinkle. He enjoys seeing Bobbi angry. "What's wrong, your old man drunk?"

"Not yet, but that stupid bastard is gone after a TV. We already got three, none of 'em work worth shit, and now that sonofabitch thinks he can fix one Tarby Jones found on the job."

"Our TV ain't working so good either. Maybe Barry will give me a dollar fifty-two for it," laughs Mack.

"Pretty goddamned funny."

After a few moments of silence Mack sits down on the porch beside Bobbi. "Well, how you do at the welfare?" she asks.

"Welfare?"

"Yeah, that's where you went today, wasn't it?"

"Oh yeah. They're gonna give me eighty-nine dollars."

"Eighty-nine dollars! Now that's some shit. That's what it is. Some shit."

"Oh, come on, Bobbi," Mack whines. "You know I can't work because I have these convulsions."

"Convulsions, my ass. You got the DT's. You know damn well you could work if you'd stop drinking."

"Well, I got doctors' papers saying I can't work and I can't.

Believe me, I'd rather work than sit at home on my ass all day."

"Okay," says Bobbi, "you can't work, okay. I don't mind you getting eighty-nine dollars. Hell, God knows a body needs more than that to stay alive. I ain't against you getting eighty-nine dollars a month; maybe you'll quit borrowing from us. What I want to know is how come the goddamned welfare department won't give me but sixty dollars a month and a few measly food stamps?" Bobbi is practically shouting now. "My husband can't work either. At least he don't, and what the hell are we supposed to do? I got a friend, you know, Carol, whose husband was like Barry, worked sometimes, sometimes didn't. Well, she left his ass, and they gave her over two hundred fifty a month, and now she's doing a shack-up job with somebody else and she still gets welfare, and I don't. Now does that make sense?"

"Shit no," says Mack.

"Well, the whole welfare thing is one big fucked-up mess!"

Just about that time Freddy, a friend from up the street, walks by. Mack flags him down, persuades him to give him $1.52, waves a dollar bill to Bobbi, and heads off to the liquor store. Bobbi shakes her head.

The truck pulls up in back, and Bobbi hears Barry hollering at Bubba, "I said watch it, goddamm it, don't go so fast. We'll drop the set." Barry and Bubba inch their way around the house and struggle up the stairs with the old TV console. "Yes, sir," says Barry, "it ain't color; but, goddamn, we'll have us a real nice TV."

Cindy is jumping up and down hollering, "Oh boy, oh boy!"

"Okay, honey," says Barry, "you just wait. Go outside and play and I'll fix the TV for you." Barry and Bubba set the TV down in the bedroom. Barry opens another beer, then begins to unscrew the back of the set.

In the next room Walt calls to Barry, "I'd like to help you fix it, but my eyes . . ."

"Aw, don't worry," Barry replies. "You just stay where you are."

Complaining about welfare

"When they get well, maybe I can see the TV when you fix it."

"Sure, Granddaddy," says Bubba.

Bobbi remains on the porch until around eight o'clock. Returning with his pint, Mack goes upstairs to see what he can do to help Barry fix the TV. By eight-thirty Barry is beginning to feel the beer—he is now on the fifth bottle of the beer he bought an hour and a half ago—and is becoming impatient with Bubba. When Barry tells Bubba not to touch the TV any more, Bubba shrugs his shoulders and walks out, telling his mother he is going over to Patsy's.

Mack sits on the bed giving Barry suggestions as Barry takes out tubes, dusts them off, and then puts them back inside the set. Bobbi comes upstairs and sits beside Walt on the bed. About that time Kate, Mack's girl friend, slowly climbs the stairs. She appears to be quite a bit older than Mack. She is extremely thin and has tight-drawn lips, hollow cheeks, and bloodshot eyes.

"Is Mack up here?" she drawls. "Oh yeah, I hear his big mouth in there. I knew I could find him here. You know, if everybody had as big a mouth as fat ass's over there, we'd all be a bunch of goddamned giants!" Everybody laughs, except Mack.

"Now, what did I do to deserve all that?" Mack hollers back. "Here I am, helping Barry fix his TV and you are calling me a bunch of names."

Kate is drunk. "You know, if I had forty-two cents, forty-two cents' bus fare, I'd give it to that fat sonofabitch, put him on the bus, and say good-by." Only Barry laughs at this comment.

"Well," says Kate, "all I can say is I feel sorry for Mack. I'd feel sorry for any sonofabitch as dumb as he is." Then Kate turns around and starts down the stairs again. "Well, I just came up here to see where fat ass is. Now I know where he is, I guess I'll be on my way. . . ." Kate wobbles and almost trips but manages to make it to the bottom. Mack laughs uneasily as he and Barry continue dusting the tubes.

Bobbi walks into the bedroom and says firmly, "Okay, goddamn, you guys have played around enough. Now it's getting on nine o'clock and I got to give the kids a bath, and we all got to get some sleep. When are you gonna cut this shit out?"

"Oh, come on, Bobbi," pleads Barry.

"Come on, my ass! We didn't get no sleep last night because you were hollering and carrying on."

"Okay, honeybunch, time you're ready for bed, we'll be finished."

"Okay," says Bobbi indignantly and hollers out the window, "Littlebit, Billy, Cindy! Come get your bath!" Littlebit and Billy come racing up the stairs. Bobbi turns on the water and orders them into the tub. She can't find Cindy.

Bobbi dries off the children, who then flop down in the bed beside Walt, who is still sitting beside the window listening to the radio. After taking a shower herself, Bobbi comes out in her bathrobe to find Barry and Mack still working on the TV. Cindy is now upstairs, and when she says she doesn't want a bath, Bobbi doesn't object. "Okay, honey, just go to bed. It's late and we're all tired." She then turns to Barry, "B., you promised. . . ."

"Okay, goddammit, I said I'd move it and I will. Just give me time!" Reluctantly he and Mack shove the TV into the hallway and then into the kitchen.

As Bobbi collapses on the bed, Cindy runs and lies down beside her mother. Barry and Mack are discussing where they might get some money to buy some more beer. The last words Bobbi hears are Barry's: "Goddamn, this fucking TV! Tarby told me the only thing wrong with the sonofabitch was a dusty tube. . . ." Mack is laughing.

2

Fall

My opportunity to meet Bobbi came when one day an official county notice appeared, tacked to their front door on Clay Street: "Condemned. House Not Fit for Human Habitation." I introduced myself as an urban planner who was concerned with the problems people were having in this area, and I noticed their house had been condemned. Bobbi took it from there. She was a short woman with straight brown hair, dark brown eyes, and a dark complexion. She must have been a very pretty woman once, but standing on the front porch talking to me, she looked quite bedraggled.

"You're goddamned right this house is condemned," she snapped back. "They came by last week and condemned it. They say it's not fit to live in, it's not fit for human habitation, and I strongly agree. This place is not fit for a human being or even an animal to live in. It's horrible."

The old man who was sitting on the porch added, "Goddamn worst place I've ever seen. Goddamn."

"The problem is," she said, "we don't know where to go. Hell, we're a family. Got seven in the family. My stepfather and my husband and four kids. And the kids are in what they call the destructive age. Nobody will rent to us. And we had trouble finding this place. What do you do when you've got to rent a house, and you've got a family of seven? You know what we've got to do? We're going to have to split up, that's what we're going to have to do. Daddy's gonna have to take the oldest son and maybe the daughter, and me and my husband, we'll try to take the smaller ones. I don't know what we're going to do. We're supposed to be out in one month. October first, hell, that's two weeks away." The more she talked, the angrier Bobbi got.

"Hell, I don't mind leaving this place. It's lucky we've lived this long in it anyway. It caught on fire, has holes in the floor, holes in the walls, the plumbing don't work, we freeze in the winter. It's a wonder we've lived here this long. We've lived here for two years.

"The first year we lived here we shared this apartment with somebody else. There was another family upstairs. But the building inspector came and he said that this was a single-family house and that one of the families had to leave. So the family upstairs left. So we took over the house, both floors. And now we're paying a hundred fifty a month and we pay all our heat and utilities out of that. Well, the electrical system, first of all, hadn't been changed until the building inspector said it had to be. There already had been a couple of fires, shorts all the time. It's a wonder one of the kids hasn't been electrocuted. So they put in a new electrical system, but still it doesn't work and the utility bill is high. But that's not as bad as the heating problem. There are no panes in the windows in the back rooms and no radiator in the bathroom or the kitchen, so it's sort of cold in those rooms. But it's not much colder in there than it is in the rest of the house during the winter, 'cause the heat just goes out of the house. Just like trying to heat the great outdoors.

"It's damned horrible. We want to leave the place, but we don't know where to go. Now, we can't own, because to own a house you've got to put a hundred down or more, and we don't have it. We have enough trouble getting by, finding clothes for the children and food on the table. The refrigerator doesn't work, so we have to buy food almost every day. We can't stock up. And nobody will rent to us because the family is too big. Anyway, you don't find that many apartments with four bedrooms." Bobbi paused for a moment, then looked at me and sighed.

"Yeah, you might say we got problems in this house. And let me tell you one thing. You're interested in this urban renewal stuff and urban problems. We have never gotten help from anybody! It's the colored people who get all the help. Now, my husband is a plasterer, interior decorator is what I call him, but I guess other people would call him a plasterer. He subcontracts himself out to people fixing up old

[margin handwritten note: complaining about the house paying bills]

houses. And he's been in nigger town lots of times and fixed
up houses for niggers lots of times. And I've been in those
houses. And let me tell you, Jack, they live better than we
do! And there's lots of folks running around the streets saying, 'What can we do for the niggers?' Yeah, well, what can
you do for white folks is what I want to know. We've been
living worse in this shit than anybody I saw in them colored
sections."

This was my introduction to Bobbi. She invited me inside
to see for myself how bad the house was. She pointed out the
holes in the walls, the broken windowpanes, and the shaky
railings. Cockroaches were everywhere. Bobbi said the landlord refused to exterminate; and when she had called the exterminator herself, he had thrown up his hands and told her
it was no use. Bobbi said, "I'm ashamed to admit it, but
they've taken over our goddamned house. We had to get the
telephone man to come and put a new telephone upstairs.
He had to drill a hole in the wall, and he stuck his hand in
the wall and when he pulled his arm out it was covered with
roaches. It was so black you could hardly see his skin. He
hollered and ran out of the house. It was embarrassing, I tell
you, very embarrassing. . . ."

The next time I saw Bobbi was a week later when she was
down talking to our neighbor, June Moseby, in front of our
house. This time her problem was not with her house, though
things were still the same, but with Billy. Bobbi was telling
June: "Did you hear what happened last night? You didn't
hear us screaming? Well, Timmy Bryant, a kid from up the
street, crammed a spoon down my little boy Billy's throat and
it almost killed him. We rushed him to the hospital. The doctor said it came within a tissue of killing him, cutting off the
main artery which pumps the blood to his brain. They weren't
sure if he was going to come through it because it was a very
delicate situation, and still is. They can't sew it up. They have
to let it heal by itself. And if it don't heal by itself, they're going to have to try to sew it up and it might get infected. I was
so frightened, and I'm still so frightened I don't know what
to do."

The two children had been playing, and Timmy Bryant asked Billy if he could do a special trick, putting a spoon in his mouth and flipping the end of it, humming, pretending he was an airplane. When Billy tried it, Timmy slapped the spoon down Billy's throat, cutting a big hole, which Bobbi said was about an inch and a half in diameter.

June remarked to me after Bobbi left that that family seemed to have more than their share of problems. This turned out to be a classic understatement.

For several weeks it appeared that the Shackelfords were going to have to split up. In trying to help them find a new apartment I soon realized that what Bobbi had said was true. No apartment houses in the area rented to families with more than two children. (Even so, there were no vacancies of any kind in any of the apartment houses.) Since Barry was working at the time, the Shackelfords probably could not qualify for public housing; just in case, however, I checked with the County Housing Authority to find they already had a waiting list of some three hundred families and were not taking any more names. The Shackelfords had one more week they could remain on Clay Street and had no idea of where they were going to go next.

The next day I passed by the Shackelfords and saw Walt sitting on the front porch. He greeted me with the good news: "Have you heard? They got a house. Bobbi's got a house. Yeah, just up the street on the main highway. Yeah, I'm real glad, real glad. Maybe not so much for myself 'cause I'm getting old. I'm real glad for them, especially for the kids."

Walt said B. J. Higgins, a friend from across the street, had heard of a vacant apartment in an old house just two blocks away and had passed the word along. Bobbi came out of the house and was very enthusiastic about the apartment. "Oh yes, we're so proud," she said, "we're so lucky. Big John, the man across the street, found it for us. A friend of his is fixing it up, and it had been for rent for, oh, about a week. And I went over there and signed the papers. Of course, I had to lie. I had to lie because it says in the lease you can only have four people, and we have seven. So I had to tell a

[handwritten in left margin: Trying to find housing]

lie, but how else could I get a house? Nowhere, nowhere, can you get an apartment if you've got more than two children. So I told them that I had two children; and if they ever find out, then we'll face that bridge when we come to it. It's a nice apartment. Lots, lots nicer than this house. And the rent is only ninety dollars a month. It's the second and third story of an old house. Bubba can have his own room. Oh, we're just so proud to have it."

I met Barry while helping the Shackelfords move. He was sitting on B. J. Higgins's porch talking to B.J. and May Jones, B.J.'s girl friend, and had on painter's overalls and a painter's cap. In his hand was a gallon stoppered jug. "Hiya," he said to me, "glad to meetya. Want a snort? Well, I can't offer you no snort. We just finished this one up. Too bad."

B.J., a plump man in his fifties dressed in overalls, responded, "Yeah, it's a damn shame. I sure would like another snort of that stuff."

Bobbi turned to Barry. "Okay, Barry, it's about time you got going. We've got to move this afternoon, and you haven't done a goddamn thing. I've been over there working all day, and it's about time you gave me a hand."

"You're right, punkin. I'm getting ready to get started right now. I'll be right over there before you can bat an eye."

B.J. and May continued talking. We chatted for a few minutes about how fortunate it was that they'd been able to find a house. As Barry got up to go, May came out with a tray of three glasses of beer. Barry said, "Oh me, I sure can't pass that down. I'll just have me a little nip and then I'll get me to work." He sat down again and continued talking about the weather, the house across the street, the difficulty in finding houses nowadays, the job that he and B.J. would be working on the next day.

B.J. kept saying, "Okay, Barry. Don't you forget, goddammit. Eight o'clock tomorrow morning we've got to get over there and get this job done."

"Big John, seven-thirty. Would you believe, I'm going to be there at seven-thirty?"

A few minutes later Cindy came over and said, "Daddy,

I'm going to kick your hind parts if you don't get over there and help Mommy."

"Now, that's no way to talk to me, kiddo. I'm getting over there in just one minute, and I'm going to kick *your* hind parts."

Cindy laughed. "Well, anyway, Mommy says she's going to kick your ass if you don't get over there and start working."

"Okay, honeybunch, I'm on my way." He got up to go for a second time.

"Have just a little more," said May, pouring some more beer into Barry's glass.

"Well, just another sip." We talked for another thirty minutes, and finally, when there was no more beer, Barry said, "Okay, let's go to work."

We started loading his old Ford truck. Bobbi would bring out some boxes and then spray the boxes with roach killer. Barry and I brought out some heavier things, such as the bureaus. Each time we would bring out a drawer or box or piece of furniture, we would drop it on the ground or bang it against something to make the roaches fall off.

As we carried our first load to the new apartment, Barry said, "Well, it ain't much. Let me tell you something. I know it ain't much. If I had my way, I wouldn't live here. And I wouldn't live where we just lived before. But we're doing the best we can; and I tell you, all a man can do is do the best he can with what he's got. And this is the best we can do with what we've got. Ninety dollars a month. We can afford to pay that. I figure it will run us a hundred fifty when you pay all the utilities, and we can afford that. What I want to do, if I ever get my way, is to buy some land somewhere. If we start putting the money away now, we can get us a little land somewhere and then I'm going to build my own house. See, I can get the material for free, 'cause there'll be a little paper left over from this job, some bricks from that, and some boards from this job. Over the course of a year or two I can get all the material, so it wouldn't cost us nothing. The labor's going to be free. All I want to do is save that money and build us our own house out in the country where the dogs can run, and we don't have to put up with any goddamn neighbors. This is what we're going to do next year. Next year."

After carrying the furniture upstairs, Barry pointed toward the roof of the house. "Hey, look at that," he said, "that's a hornets' nest. That would be great for Cindy to take to school. It ain't a perfect hornets' nest, but you know something, them hornets, they've done the best they can with what they've got." Barry laughed.

When we returned to Clay Street, Barry invited me to sit on the porch and have one more beer. "You know, I'm an alcoholic," he said. "Now, I don't pull no bones. I tell the truth and that's what I am. You already know it anyway. I'm an alcoholic and that's why I drink so much, but it keeps me going. Now, you don't know alcoholics, so I probably ought to tell you about what sort of things we drink." Barry then went into elaborate detail describing the various drinks he started the day with—beer and tomato juice, coffee and Canadian Club, or beer and salt.

By that time Bobbi had come out on the porch and Barry turned to her and said, "But I tell you, I tell you one thing. I ain't never laid a hand on Bobbi. Oh no. I come home, I got my pay check, I give it to her, and I say, 'Bobbi, just give me a little bit for myself to keep me going this week.' And she does and I spend it on liquor. And she takes the rest of it and buys groceries and clothes for the kids. Course about Wednesday of the next week I've run out and have to go back and get a little bit more, but she gives it to me. Ain't that right, Bobbi?"

"That's right. That's what he does."

Bobbi then changed the subject and began talking about an experience she had had the past weekend when they were visiting Barry's mother near the coast. She began, "See, Barry and his stepdaddy were in the other room and I was left there with my mother-in-law. She said, 'Look at this.' And she showed me a picture, or at least she said it was a picture. I said, 'Well, I don't see nothing.' 'Well, you look at it and see if you don't see something. If you look at it long enough, you will see the face of God.' 'Oh no, I won't.' That's what I said, 'I won't either.'

"Well, anyway, I looked at that thing. I looked at it and didn't see nothing, and then, after twenty-five minutes, I saw it. I saw the face of God. And at that minute I said, 'Tomorrow we're going to find us a house.' That was on Saturday. Sunday we found the house and signed the lease. And I saw the face of God. You could see it—the eyebrows, the big white eyebrows, the eyes, and then you could see the beard and, oh, the mustache. Oh, it was the most beautiful thing I've ever seen. She said it was a photograph taken by a Chinaman in a snowstorm a long time ago. And sometimes it takes people hours, sometimes days, sometimes just a matter of seconds, to see the face of God. But when you see the face of God, then you know. You just know something special. It's kind of like, like I knew that I was going to rent that house the next day. And we did. We rented."

"That's right," said Barry. "That's absolutely right. That is right. Now, I'm an atheist myself. I don't believe in no God, but I believe she saw the face of God. And if you'll believe her, if you believe in God, then you can see the face of God. And what I'm going to do is buy me one of them things and put it up in our house and you can see it, too, when I get it. That's what I'm going to do." Barry paused a moment, then continued, "You know, as I said, I don't believe in no God. I'm an atheist. But sometimes I have those feelings, too. Like last week. I can look at the leaves on the trees across from our house. I knew it was going to get cold. And I told B.J., I told Big John, I says, 'B.J., it's going to be cold in about four days.' And sure enough, it got cold. Course it got cold the next day, but I had that feeling, you know, that mysterious feeling. You get those. And that's what the face of God was like. It gave you that mysterious feeling. Now, I didn't see it myself, but I believe Bobbi, and I believe my mother. That is enough if they said it was true. You've got to see that. The face of God."

It took the Shackelfords several days to move their belongings. The next day nothing got done because Barry had one of his spells. Bobbi was very upset about it. When I showed up to help them move, she said, "Yeah, it was one of them heart attacks. I know it was a heart attack because that's how my grandmother died. I know how she looked when she died, and I know how Barry looked. Believe me, he had a god-damned heart attack. And this ain't the first one of them spells neither. He's had four or five of them; and frankly, I'm real worried about him. But Barry see a doctor? Never. Sonofa-bitch is gonna die and leave me with four kids and not a cent. That's what's going to happen."

The next day Barry was feeling better, and with the help of Bubba and his friends we got a lot done. By the end of the following day, we were just about finished. On the last haul I was riding back with Bobbi when she remarked to me, "See that shack falling down?" and pointed to a house on the corner in about the same condition as their Clay Street house. "White trash lives in that house. Now, we may be poor, but, goddamm it, we ain't trash, and the folks who live in that house are. They are the Cobbs and that's where Shirley Baker is living. I used to know Shirley when she lived on Clay Street, and I swear to God, she would do a shack-up job with anybody who came along. She has one bastard al-ready and is pregnant with another. And I know for a fact that the Cobbs' fourteen-year-old daughter has been laying with guys on the Cobbs' front porch! That's what kind of girl *she* is."

When we got back to the Clay Street house, Bubba was standing on the front porch. He called to his mother, "Hey, Mom, remember tonight's the night for the PTA, and you said you would go, and it's gonna be starting in a few minutes."

"Okay, Bubba, I said I would go and I will." Bobbi said good-by and went inside to make one last check.

For three weeks after the Shackelfords got settled in their new apartment I rarely saw them. The children would still come down to play with the children on Clay Street, but Bobbi and Barry were never around. Since the people on Clay Street tended to associate primarily with neighbors and since the Shackelfords no longer lived on Clay Street, I concluded I would probably see very little of them again. Then about a month after they had moved, the old truck appeared in front of our house. Bobbi rolled down the window and called for Billy, who was playing with a friend. When I walked out,

Barry called me over and asked if I wanted to go hunting next weekend to celebrate Bubba's thirteenth birthday. Barry said Bubba and he both had been looking forward to this for a long time. I told him that if the trip came off I would like to go.

"What do you mean, come off?" he said. "Hell yes, it's gonna come off. It's Bubba's thirteenth birthday, and I'm gonna take him hunting."

The trip did not in fact come off that weekend because Barry had not finished his job and he lacked the finances. The next week the status of the trip changed daily. On Monday Barry was as excited as ever; on Tuesday the trip was off; on Wednesday Barry was sick; and on Thursday we were going again.

On Friday morning about ten o'clock, I assumed Barry should have a better idea about the trip, so I gave him a call. His answer was typical: "Oh, hi, Joe. Well, let me tell you. We got some problems about this trip. We've got some problems, but . . . well, if you can understand, if you'll go along with it . . . what I mean to say is . . . we're going to go on the trip. We're going to go on the trip! I don't care what. Are you with me? Are you with me, Joe?"

"I'm going if you're going."

"Okay, that's all I want to know. That's all I want to hear. Goddammit, we're going on the trip. Shit, I don't care. Just come over right now, and we'll get going. We'll leave before noon."

I gathered up my things, tossed them in the back of the car, and drove up the hill to their house. When I got to Bobbi and Barry's, it was almost noon, and things were as chaotic as ever. Littlebit and Billy were running about in their underpants screaming and hollering. Walt was sitting in his usual place by the front window rocking, with Cindy seated on his lap. Barry was in the kitchen sitting with Bobbi. A third person, a fat man with gray curly hair, who was introduced as Al, was also there. We shook hands and I sat down. They were looking at a map.

"Well, Joe, the problem is this. We aren't sure where we're going to go. See . . . I mean, well, we've got lots of problems, but that's one of them. I know about where this place is, but I'm not sure exactly where it is, and I don't know what we're going to do, but I'm looking over this map and trying to find it. I know there's a waterfall and an old Scout camp nearby, and I think it's near Hagerstown or Cumberland. I don't remember, but I'll know once I get there. Maybe, if we just set off in that direction, we'll run into it. 'Cause I've been there a couple of times before. But it was a year ago and, uh . . . I just wish I could think of the name of that goddamn place. Shit, Bobbi, what is it? Goddammit, Bobbi, you know what it is."

"Barry, I don't know what it is. I wasn't with you that time."

"But shit, Bobbi, I told you about it. I told you where that place was."

"Well, I don't know where it is, Barry. I don't know." Al sat there with a puzzled look on his face, scratching his head and muttering, "I've been on some goddamn camping trips before, but this is a goddamnedest, sonofabitch, motherfucking camping trip I've ever been on. Shit, we ain't ever going to get going. Shit, it's noon and we were supposed to get off by ten this morning. Goddamn."

"Shut up, Al," growled Barry. "I'm going to find out where this place is. You just leave it to me, okay?"

Al was about sixty years old, with an enormous potbelly, very thick glasses. He had a dazed look on his face, due, probably, to being in a continual state of semidrunkenness.

As we sat at the table I noticed several roaches crawling around the kitchen. "Oh shit," said Bobbi. "Goddammit, there's another roach. They're coming back, Barry, they're coming back. I tell you, they followed us." Barry just shook his head and walked in the other room.

Bubba then came back and started horsing around with his sister, Cindy. When Barry returned, Bubba accidentally bumped into Barry. "Goddammit, Bubba, watch what you're doing, okay?" snarled Barry, clenching his fist as if he were going to hit Bubba. Everyone was very tense and in a bad humor. We wanted to get the camping trip on the road, to get moving, to get out of the house, but we just couldn't get started. Barry blamed Bobbi, Bobbi blamed Barry, both blamed Walt, Walt blamed everybody else. The main problem had to do with money. At that moment no one had any money. Barry had counted on having money, but since he had not finished the job over the past week, he had only made $50—hardly enough to finance this camping trip. Walt, however, had been supervising a job for the last several weeks for a real estate man and was supposed to get his pay that day, also. He was due some $275. So after much thought and discussion, Walt agreed that when he got his money he would lend Barry what we needed.

So it was all decided. I would drive Bobbi out to Barry's boss's office to pick up Walt's pay check. When we returned at five, the car would be packed and ready to go. In the meantime Al and Barry would get all the gear together, get the hunting licenses, get their guns and ammunition.

About four we left for the office. Bobbi, Bubba, Cindy, and I set out in my car. On the way we went through some areas of the District where blacks lived. The houses were quite nice, much nicer than any of the houses on Clay Street. As we passed through these areas, Bobbi commented: "Joe, look here. See those houses. Colored folks live in those houses. Good colored. I mean good colored. They keep it up. Those are nice houses. They're expensive houses. They used to be all white. Just a few years ago, five or ten years ago. But now there's colored folks that live in there. But they aren't dirt like you find in most places in Washington. I mean, they're good colored."

About four-fifteen we got to the real estate office. Bobbi said: "Listen, we can't go in there before four-thirty because the man told me to come between four-thirty and five. And so I'm not going to get there until four-thirty. So let's wait in the car. You know, I look so bad I don't know whether I ought to go in there or not. I look so horrible." She was dressed in paint-stained blue jeans and had on an old ragged coat. "But we need the money so bad I'm going to go in there anyway. I don't care what that man thinks. You see, this ain't Barry's boss. I don't know this man. This is the guy Walt works for, and he don't know me, and I don't know him. I just want that money." She then looked across the street, saw a hot dog stand, and told Bubba to go and get us all a hot dog since she was hungry.

As we were sitting in the car eating hot dogs, Bobbi noticed a young man walking past. She raised her eyebrows and said, "Heyya, honey, howya doing?" Then she turned very red and said to me, with some embarrassment: "Oh, Joe, I'm sorry. You're going to get the wrong idea of me. I thought you were Barry there for a minute. I always holler at young guys when Barry's around because when I'm with him he always hollers and whistles at young girls. So it's sort of a joke we have between us."

Then she looked at her watch. "Oh my God, Jesus Christ, it's almost four-thirty! In one minute it will be four-thirty. Come on, Bubba, come on, Cindy, we've got to get up there. We've got to get there at four-thirty. That's what they said, between four-thirty and five and not a minute before. And it's almost four-thirty. Come on." She grabbed Cindy and jerked her out of the back seat. Bubba dropped his hot dog and squeezed out of the back, and all three of them raced up to the real estate building. About five minutes later I saw them come out of the door running even faster. As they came up to the car Bobbi said, panting, "You aren't going to believe this, that man left two minutes before we got there. He left with the money. I don't know what we're going to do."

"You mean he told you to get there between four-thirty and five, and then he left before four-thirty with the money?"

"That's exactly what I mean. Now we are really up shit's creek. Anyway, I'm going to call home right now and see what they want me to do." Bobbi went to make a telephone call while the kids stayed with me. A few minutes later she came back. "Come on, step on it! We got to get to another place fast. There's still a chance we can get the money."

We drove to Barry's boss's office. Bobbi and the two children raced upstairs to the office, and a few minutes later they returned, jubilant. Bobbi had the money. She kissed the check and showed it to me. "Oh, baby, you don't know how glad I am to see you," she said to the check. "Look at this. Two hundred and seventy-five dollars. We got it, we got it,

we got it! Hurrah, yippeee! Barry's going to be so happy.
There it was up there with the secretary. Hot damn almighty."

As we drove back through the black neighborhood, Bobbi
whistled very loudly and said, "Jesus Christ, look at that,"
pointing to a very attractive young black woman. "That's a
nigger, Joe! Can you believe that? Those nigger women, some
of them really do have it."

Bubba chimed in from the back seat, "Yeah, Mom, guys
tell me that it's better than white stuff."

Bobbi said, "Well, that girl was something. Sure glad that
Barry wasn't with us. No telling what he would have done."

By this time it was well after five-thirty, completely dark
outside, and I was beginning to wonder just when we were
going to get off on our camping trip. Bobbi exclaimed, "Hey,
we've got to get this check cashed. I just forgot. Come on,
we've got to get the check cashed."

"Which bank do you want to go to?" I asked.

"Bank, hell, we don't go to no goddamn bank. We get our
checks cashed at the liquor store. That's our bank."

Off we went to Tom's liquor store. "Yes, sir, this is where
we do all our banking business. They know us here. They
know that our checks are good. We don't go to no goddamn
bank. I never had no goddamn checking account. I don't
believe in those things." Bobbi went in to get the check cashed
and came out with an armful of sodas and a sackful of pop-
corn and candy, which she gave to the children. "Here, Joe,"
she said, handing me a Pepsi, "it's payday and we've got
something to celebrate. Now, let's get on home."

Since it was almost six when we got back, I expected to
find Barry and Al fuming, wanting to know where we had
been and why we had taken so long. Unfortunately, neither
Barry nor Al was there. They were still out doing their thing,
whatever their thing was. I never found out. At six-thirty
when they did show up, they weren't much further along in
preparing for the hunting trip than they were when we left.

"Well, what do we do next?" I asked Barry. "We've got
the money. When do we leave?"

"Well, now we've got to get our hunting licenses," he replied. "Now, there is a hunting place across the street, Bill's,

see, but I don't want to go there 'cause those people treated me like trash the last time I went in there when I hocked my gun and my bow and arrow. They think I'm just trash in there, and I'm not going back there. So we're going to go to Suitland's to get our hunting licenses, and I've got to buy some arrows for Bubba, and we've got to get ready to go. But Suitland's is a long way off. It's down in the southeast. Take us forty-five minutes to get there. So we better get moving now."

I groaned. "Well, Barry, why can't we just go and get the stuff one time across the street. It will save us an hour and a half or two hours."

"From those sons of bitches? No, goddammit, I'm not going over there. Treated me like trash the last time I was in there. We're going to Suitland's. Anyway, we still haven't got no food. Bobbi's got to go and get the food."

On the way to Suitland's we pulled into Tom's liquor store and Barry came out with a case of beer, four bottles of wine, and a bottle of whiskey. "Yes, sir, yes, sir, we're going on a trip after all. You know, I had some doubts up until today. In fact up until a few minutes ago. But now I think we are actually going to go on this hunting trip after all." Barry then opened a beer and began guzzling it down. "Hot damn, that tastes good."

Suitland seemed like a thousand miles away, but finally, after weaving through rush hour traffic and going on a few back roads, we arrived there ready to make our final purchases. I assumed we would go into the store, buy the licenses, pick up a few things, and leave; but it didn't work out that way. We stayed in the store a good hour, talking about hunting, the weather, the right kind of bow, the right kind of gun, the right kind of ammunition—all this as the clock ticked away toward nine o'clock. I realized that this was one of the main highlights of the trip, and it was not to be taken lightly or passed over quickly. Barry was enjoying every minute of it. He asked the man behind the counter to take out each kind of arrow, looked at each carefully, and told Bubba what he thought would be the best arrow to buy. He then looked at knives, at bowstrings, at arrow points. He meticulously exam-

[handwritten marginalia, rotated: "They went to Suitland? They went to pur to equipment — important part of the trip"]

ined every item and made come comments to the salesman, who would usually reply that Barry was right.

They ended up spending much more money than they had anticipated. Bubba spent seventeen dollars for his deer stamp and arrows; Barry spent thirty-seven dollars (six for his and Bubba's licenses, six for a deer stamp, and of course, the arrows, bowstring, knife, deer scent, gloves, arrow holder, and the booze). Caught up in the spirit of it all, I even ended up spending ten dollars buying a knife I knew I didn't need.

When the time came to get a string for Bubba's bow, the salesman looked at the bow and remarked, "I don't think I'd shoot this bow. I think it's an unsafe bow. I'll call the boss in." Barry's face dropped. When the boss came over, the salesman said, "Hey, boss, what do you think about this bow? Doesn't look any good to me. Do you think this bow is safe to shoot? See where there's a crack in it?"

The boss nervously looked at Barry, then at the bow, and replied, "Ain't nothing wrong with this goddamn bow."

Barry hollered, "Goddamn, there better not be anything wrong with that goddamn bow! You sure as hell sold it to me!"

"I know I did, I know I did," said the boss, who then turned his back and walked off.

"Why, that no-good sonofabitch! I just bought that bow in here a few weeks ago. What do you mean, it's no good to shoot?"

The salesman then said, "Oh, it's fine to shoot. I don't know what I was talking about. I mean, it's a good bow. I don't know, I don't know what I was thinking about."

"Goddamn," muttered Barry, "I've heard of being screwed before . . ."

Finally we were ready to leave Suitland's, with everything we needed plus things we did not need. Barry was searching through his pockets. "Goddammit, I can't figure out where all the money went to. Did I get robbed? Goddammit, I'm out thirty-seven dollars. What did I spend the money on? I've been robbed!"

Since it was now about nine-thirty, I suggested we stop on

the way back to pick up some dinner. Barry agreed that was a good idea, so we stopped at the Red Barn and bought a bucket of chicken and some cole slaw. When we returned, everything was quite chaotic with the kids screaming, Barry puttering about trying to get his guns together, the basset hound barking, the cats meowing.

Bobbi came up the stairs carrying a huge bag of groceries, saying, "Goddammit, I've got you all some good food! Some peanut butter, some bacon, some ham, eggs, oh, you're going to have a great time. Some hot dogs." Al was following her with another sack of groceries. They paused briefly to have a piece of chicken each.

At this point little Cindy, who was getting very interested in the hunting trip, announced that she wanted to go. "Okay, you can go hunting," said Barry. "I think we got room for you."

"Oh boy, oh boy, I'm going to go!" She scampered to the back room to get some of her things.

Al said that he was unable to locate another gun. I said that I didn't have a gun either, at which point Walt offered me the use of his twelve-gauge bolt-action shotgun. When Bubba picked up the old man's .22 automatic, Walt said, "Goddammit, Bubba, leave that gun here. If you take that gun, what am I going to protect the house with? Got to have me a gun here to protect the house. Okay?"

"Oh yeah, okay. I'm sorry. I forgot about that."

Barry said, "Yeah, goddammit, you think we're going to leave him without a gun? Shit, he's got to protect the house."

"I'm sorry," said Bubba.

"Well, you'd better be sorry, leaving a man without any guns to protect his house. We sure ain't going to do that."

"Yeah," said Walt, "you never can tell what will happen. Here I am with Bobbi and the children. Just never know what's going to happen. Got to have me a gun."

So we left Walt with his .22 and began to pack the rest of the things in the truck. As we were loading the truck, Barry decided it should be moved a little closer to the house, so he got in and started the motor. Just then there was a mild explosion. Barry stopped the truck and got out, exclaiming,

*ran over
some of his
beer*

"Jesus Christ, what was that?" He had stored the case of beer under the wheel of the truck. The truck had rolled over the case smashing several cans, causing some to explode. "Oh no," said Barry, "you don't know how I hate to see that happen. Anything but beer. Oh no, I hate to see wasted beer. That hurts me as much as anything." He then picked up some of the fizzing cans and desperately poured the liquor down his throat. "Oh boy, that tastes good. I don't believe in wasting none of this stuff."

By ten o'clock it looked as if we were almost ready to go. We were going to take my car and the truck. Since Barry did not have a license, Al would be driving the truck. The problem was that Al was under strict orders not to drive, especially at night, since he had had several heart attacks. But Al *did* have a license. By ten-thirty both the car and the truck were loaded, but we still did not know where we were going.

"Oh shit, goddamn," said Barry, "I think I'll recognize it once we get up in that area. Goddammit, let's go." As Bubba jumped in the front seat with me, I started the car and off we went. (Cindy changed her mind and decided not to go.) According to my calculations, our destination was about 120 miles away. A good 100 miles would be on interstate. I figured we should get to the general vicinity by one-thirty in the morning at the latest.

Before we left I mentioned to Barry the remote possibility that we might become separated. Though he didn't think that was likely, he agreed just in case, by some strange fluke, we did get separated to meet at a designated stop. I suggested the police station at Hancock, Maryland, and we agreed that this would be the location. Barry's last words were, "But don't worry, we won't get separated. You don't have to worry about that. Just don't drive too fast. The camper, she don't go more than fifty miles an hour."

We were off. However, we had gone only a few blocks when I noticed that the truck was not behind us. I turned to Bubba and asked, "How in the world could we have lost them? After only a few blocks?"

"Well, Al's driving and he's been drinking pretty much today. And when Al drinks, he drives slow, awful slow.

When he's sober, he really drives fast, but when he's got that much liquor in him, he drives like he does now, about thirty miles an hour." We pulled over to the side and waited; in a few minutes the old truck pulled up behind us. Barry poked his head out the window and shouted, "Hey, slow down. Don't drive so fast. Also, don't forget, we've got to get some gas. Stop on the road before we get up to the big highway." We set off again, driving a few miles and then pulling into a gas station just before we hit the interstate. Besides gas we also needed some ice and, as Barry noted, some more beer. Already, after only three hours, about a third of the beer was gone.

So we set off again. This time we planned not to stop before we got to Hancock. Things went pretty well for the first sixty miles. From the gas station to Hancock only two turns were necessary: we had to get on the beltway and we had to get from there to the interstate, which would take us to Hancock. As soon as we got on the beltway, I looked back and noticed that the truck was swerving from one side of the road to the other in zigzag fashion. Bubba remarked, "It will be easy to tell when they're behind us 'cause there aren't many cars that drive like that on the road. Also, look at the headlights. See the right headlight points down and off to the side of the road. When we see those lights behind us, we'll know that it's the truck."

The turnoff was the first difficulty. The old truck didn't make the turn. Since Bubba and I were anxious to see if they had made the turn, after driving a few miles past the turnoff we pulled over and waited fifteen minutes for the truck to catch up. When the truck didn't show, we decided to drive on to the police station at Hancock, arriving there around one in the morning.

Fortunately, Hancock did have a police station. When we pulled up to a dinky building with a police sign on it, there was no sign of the truck. After waiting about an hour, we decided to try to get some sleep, which I found difficult with big Mack trucks passing. But around three-thirty or four I must have drifted off. I remember looking at my watch at four-fifteen and noting that wherever Barry and Al were, they must have gotten lost, or been in a wreck or broken down. Anyway, something drastic must have happened. Bubba was huddled in the back, shivering and unable to sleep. The next thing I remember was feeling my car shake and hearing the loud sputtering of the truck. Then I heard Barry hollering outside the car. "Let's go hunting! Come on, here we are. Let's go, let's go!" He was standing on the bumper, frantically shaking the car.

"Where in the hell have you guys been?" I asked. "My God, it's five-fifteen in the morning."

"Yeah, well, when you let a wino drive, that's what happens. Old Al, I knew he couldn't drive, that old wino. I knew. He was so drunk he couldn't keep the camper on the road. He missed that second turn, and we got off on some road, and it took us another hour or two—I don't know how long—to get back. We couldn't ever find any exits, so we turned around and went the wrong way. Oh hell, I don't know where we've been, but let's go. I'm ready to go hunting. After old wino messed us up on that one, I told him I wanted to drive. Even though I don't have no license, I know I can drive that old truck better than he can. And once I took over we got going pretty well, except once we got up to Hancock we couldn't find the police station. Hell, we've been in this area two or three hours. I've had to fill up with gas twice since we left you. Two full tanks of gas."

"My God," I said, "you've been on the road straight since we left you, and that was about eleven-thirty. You've been driving for almost six straight hours!"

"Shit yes, we've been driving a long way. Two full tanks of gas, and I'm already out now. That means three tanks of gas. Goddamn, I don't know where we've been. I ended up at a town thirty miles west and a town thirty miles east, and they tell me to go back one way and then go another way, and I asked, each time I asked whether they'd seen your car, if they'd seen a VW with a luggage rack. Nobody's seen you. Hell, I ended up almost over in Cumberland once. Hell, I must have driven three or four hundred miles, just around here. But I found you now. Let's go hunting, let's go hunting."

"Yeah, let's go," I muttered, "let's go."

[left margin handwritten note: After driving hundreds of miles Bang finally found them at the police station.]

Barry said, "Anyway, I've got an idea. Let's go back down the road to a diner where there are a lot of hunters, and we can ask the hunters, all these people going hunting just like we are, we can ask them where this place is. I can describe it and we can find out directions how to get there."

Bubba was gradually waking up in the back seat, grunting, "Where are we, where are we?" Off we went down the road, stopping next at the gas station where Bubba and I had previously stopped to get directions. We went inside to find the place bustling with activity at five-thirty in the morning. Everyone was a hunter. We all ordered big breakfasts except for Al, who stayed out in the car and slept. Barry went over and asked a group getting ready to leave if they could help us with directions.

"Listen, let me tell you," he told them, "we're lost. We don't know what we're doing or where we're going. We're all confused. But we're looking for a place, it's somewhere near here. I think it's on Highway 40. All I know is that there's an old camp off to the left, an old Boy Scout camp, a waterfall, and a place where you can camp, and it's in the mountains. Have you ever heard of a place like that?"

One of the hunters scratched his head and said, "Hey, I think I know the place. It's up past Fifteen Mile Creek." Then he gave us directions how to get there.

"Great," I said. "Now if you could just write these down because we have had trouble following directions." So he wrote down the directions, which seemed easy enough to follow. We thanked the man, finished breakfast, and set out again.

When I asked Barry why he was so wide awake having driven so long without any sleep, he said that at one of the places they stopped a truck driver gave him one of his pep pills, which perked him up.

We drove for about fifteen minutes before we realized that we had somehow gotten off the track, so we stopped again and Barry went into a gas station, talked for a few moments with the attendant, and returned very enthusiastically. "I know the way," he shouted, "just follow me." We drove another fifteen miles before Barry stopped again and admitted

we were lost once more. The process repeated itself several
times: Barry racing into a gas station and racing out again
with a big grin on his face, hopping into the truck and
scratching off, with Bubba and me following. Al slept through
it all.

Two hours later and three more stops for directions, we
found a hunting area. It was not *the* hunting area Barry had
been pursuing, but it was a state hunting ground; and since
it was almost nine o'clock we were all ready to do some hunting. Even Al was awake and restless to hunt. At last we were
someplace we could stop, unpack, set up camp, and go
through the motions of hunting.

"This ain't the place I was looking for, but it looks a lot
like it," said Barry. "I think it will be a pretty good place.
Goddammit, I knew we shouldn't have let that wino drive.
That's what happens when you let a wino drive. Now, I'm an
alcoholic, and so I guess I shouldn't say nothing about a wino.
But at least I don't drink wine." He took another sip of beer,
then took a deep breath of fresh mountain air and shouted,
"Man, it's great to be here!"

I was unaware of it at the time, but the hunting trip was
Barry's high point for the year I lived on Clay Street. After
we finally arrived, Barry was at his best. He was in an en-
vironment he loved and was doing something he could do
well. For once Barry seemed to be in control.

Since the firearm season for deer was a week away and
since Barry was after deer, not squirrels or rabbit, he hunted
with his bow and arrow. The rest of us carried shotguns. However, none of us shot a single time, for those woods contained
few living animals of any variety. We saw no squirrels, rab-
bits, or game birds. Barry swore he saw a deer but not
within bow shot. He said he had never seen a forest so deso-
late, remarking: "I figure all them animals and squirrels done
been shot out of here. We come too late."

But the bad luck did not keep Barry from thoroughly enjoying himself. He seemed to love every minute of what he
was doing. Since he had been hunting every year since he
was ten or eleven, he was an expert. He stalked game like an

Indian. His eyes never stopped moving. He knew where the squirrels' nests were, where the squirrels had been feeding, where the deer had been feeding, how fresh a deer track was. He walked so lightly on leaves he could hardly be heard. He seemed to blend in with the woods and leaves, becoming a part of the surroundings.

Barry was also a good teacher. He had taught Bubba how to hunt, and he gave the three of us a lot of advice. "Hey, look," he would say, "see that hole up there in the tree? That's a squirrel's nest. Now, it's pretty used 'cause you can tell it's smooth. Now, squirrels have been there. And look down here. See these acorns? Squirrels have been feeding here. Now, this is an area where there are probably some squirrels. But you've got to look at the trees, too. There have got to be nut trees, hickory trees are the best. And if you look around, there are some hickories here. So this is a spot to hunt squirrel. If you want to go about this thing right, you sit down beside a tree all day starting about six in the morning, just before sunrise, and you'd get yourself your limit of squirrels. Unless they've all been shot out, which has probably happened here. You have to be patient. You have to look, be alert all the time. It's not easy if you want to get your limit of squirrels." Then he pointed to deer tracks—he guessed they were probably twenty-four hours old—and showed us a thicket where in all likelihood you would find a rabbit.

In camp there was time for talking and for drinking. In fact, except for Bubba, who did not drink, we consumed all the liquor the first day: a case of beer, four bottles of wine, and a bottle of whiskey. Bubba did a lot of practicing with his bow and arrow, setting up a target in front of a tree. Barry was very proud of Bubba's accuracy.

At one point Barry said, "You know, it's really great to be out here. I don't have no problems out here. This is just where I ought to be."

Al said, "You know, you should never have gotten married. That's your problem."

"Hell it is," said Barry, "I'm damn glad I got married. If I hadn't gotten married, I'd either be in jail or dead, you can bet your bottom dollar on that. It ain't marriage I'm

[margin handwritten note: Barry good teacher and hunter/their use of natural environment]

against. I don't know what it is. It's just so many problems, so many things that get you down back home. But out here in the fresh air, hunting the deer, camping. There's something about this that does a man's soul good."

"Yeah, I know what you mean," said Al. "I feel the same way. It's just different out here."

"I don't know," said Barry, "if I could just straighten myself out—if I could just pull myself together—I'd like to build a house in the country. I'd really like to live in the country and have a garden and raise some animals. Build a house myself and buy the right kind of clothes for my kids and for Bobbi. Eat the right kind of food and have a decent house. I'd like to do that. I'd really like to do that. Maybe if I joined the union I could still make eight dollars an hour or so— work a forty-hour week. I'd like to straighten myself out. I don't know. I just—I don't know."

We talked about past hunting trips, about how proud Barry was of Bubba, about how great it was to be outdoors here in this place at this time.

"You know, I'm sort of sorry that Cindy didn't come along. She would have enjoyed this. I think Bobbi would have, too. Yeah, next time I'll have to bring them along. They'd really have a good time."

The next day we ran out of both food and liquor; and since we weren't having any luck anyway, we decided to return home a day early. I left a few hours before the others, and when I got home, I called Bobbi to tell her Barry's plans.

"Well, I'm glad you had such a good time, but sorry you didn't get a deer," she said. "You know, I went to the doctor yesterday with all the trouble I've been having with my menstrual period, the bleeding and all. They said I got to go into the hospital tomorrow to have my ovaries removed. And I don't know how long I'll be in the hospital, maybe several weeks. Anyway, I hope Barry and Bubba get back before I go in tomorrow morning. If they don't get back, with Walt's eyes, I don't know who would watch the kids. . . ."

Bobbi's operation did not take place the following day as anticipated. When she went to the county hospital, she was informed that she could not be admitted unless she deposited $150 as a down payment. They told her since her husband was employed she probably could not qualify for Medicaid, though if she wanted she could talk with the medical social worker. On Wednesday Bobbi saw the medical social worker, who helped her fill out the forms for Medicaid. Her operation was rescheduled for the following week, November 18.

Up until the day before the operation, Bobbi was uncertain both as to how long she would be in the hospital and as to exactly what the operation would entail. The afternoon preceding the operation, however, the nurse called Bobbi and told her to be at the hospital by six-thirty in the morning since the operation would be on an "in and out" basis. Bobbi could return home that afternoon. Bobbi was still not sure exactly what they were going to do to her.

On the afternoon of the operation, I called to see if Bobbi had returned. She was already home and reported the experience had been terrible: "Well, I'm living, but I swear to God I hope I never have another one of them operations. They couldn't find my veins for a transfusion; and when the doctor finally got there, he was so goddamned pissed off it was awful. He was cussing left and right, 'cause the other medical people had screwed up somehow. Saying stuff like 'You lousy bastards, you're wasting my time! You idiots, how come you weren't ready?' Well, hearing him cuss them out I was getting real nervous. The doctor, he didn't say nothing to me. Hell, I still wasn't sure what the hell they were going to do to me!

"And after the goddamned operation I never saw the doctor! I'm hurting like hell and he never prescribed any pain medicine. I don't know what's going to happen. I guess I should have stayed in the hospital. They told me I could spend the night. But after hearing the doctor and all, I don't know, I just didn't want to stay there. I told them, 'No, I'd rather go home.' I know I shouldn't have said that. I know I shouldn't have come home. I shouldn't have. 'Cause I need the rest and I'm not going to get it around home. But they didn't really seem to care that much. If only the doctor had told me something, it would have made a difference."

Bobbi never talked to the doctor again. The only contact she had with him after the operation was a bill she received for $300. A note was attached to the bill explaining that the doctor did not participate in the Medicaid program. Just after Christmas she received another bill and a letter saying that if the bill was not paid by the first of February her account would be turned over to a collection agency. When Bobbi got this letter, she laughed, saying, "Let them come after us, Jack, what are they going to take? Our kitchen table, our three broken TV's?" This was Bobbi's last communication from the doctor; and for whatever the reason, she was not approached by a collection agency.

Bobbi's health problems continued. Since her bleeding was worse than ever, she concluded the operation had done her no good. But it was not Bobbi but Barry and Walt whose health problems began to get the best of them.

Just before Christmas Barry came down with pneumonia— at least that is what everyone said it was. He had high temperature for over a week and was unable to work, but he refused to see a doctor. This came at a very bad time, since the Shackelfords had done no Christmas shopping. Although for a while it looked as though there would be no Christmas at the Shackelford household this year, everyone pitched in and rallied to the cause. Bobbi not only drove Barry to his job but worked alongside him, scraping off old paint and painting the trim, her specialty. Walt came too and did what he could, which with his bad eyes turned out to be mostly giving moral support. Bubba did quite a lot, working alongside Barry and Bobbi, and on several days, the three smaller children were there as well. They mostly got in the way but tried to do what they could, carrying smaller items such as paint brushes, rags, and scrapers. The day before Christmas Eve they finished. Barry picked up his check that evening, and Bobbi went Christmas shopping that night. She bought each of the children a small transistor radio, and Bubba a cassette tape recorder. She bought a racing set and toy trucks for the two boys and a doll for Cindy. Bubba gave his mother a Teflon skillet and a punch bowl. Barry bought a Christmas tree on Christmas Eve—he had wanted to chop down a tree in the

country, but it was too late—and Cindy and Bobbi cut out
ornaments to hang on the tree. On Christmas Day they ate
turkey. Everyone agreed it was a great Christmas.

But after Christmas health problems began to converge.
Barry was still sick. He had never gotten over his fever and
chills; and working on the house, often painting out of doors
in the freezing cold, just made things worse. The day after
Christmas he was back in bed again.

Cindy was having her problems. Since she was doing very
poorly in the first grade, her teacher recommended she have
a hearing test. Just after Christmas Bobbi took her to the
county health clinic where an ear specialist told Bobbi her
child had severe hearing problems. She was almost deaf in one
ear and had lost 25 per cent of her hearing in the other. The
hearing loss was probably caused by an ear infection but
could be corrected by an operation. Bobbi was upset by the
diagnosis and made an appointment for Cindy to return to see
the doctor at the clinic as soon as possible—in the middle of
March.

Walt began feeling bad a few days after Christmas, too.
He started running a high fever, had chest pains, and was
having trouble breathing. Though Bobbi was convinced he
was having heart trouble, Walt insisted he was not sick enough
to call the doctor. If this weren't enough, Billy came down
with the chicken pox, which he naturally passed on to the
other children. So for the first two weeks of January just
about everyone was home sick.

3

Winter

I was visiting the various sick members of the Shackelford household one day the first week in January. Bobbi was most worried about Barry. "I don't know what to do with him," she said. "He won't go see a doctor. I finally got him to go to the emergency room yesterday. They say he ain't got pneumonia but an infection of the lymph glands. See," she said, pointing to Barry's arm, "under his arm it's all swollen. They gave Barry some drugs to take, but he's worse today."

"Well, I don't want to go to a goddamned doctor," said Barry, "because I don't want nobody cutting on my arm. I just don't have no use for doctors."

"You see," said Bobbi, "they said the swelling was due to blood poisoning. Before Christmas Barry's finger got infected, and the blood poisoning is what is making him sick. But frankly, I don't know whether to believe them doctors or not. What's really bothering us is that we're so behind in our bills and Barry don't know when he'll be able to work. We're flat broke and we got three hundred sixty-five dollars in bills: the rent, water, electricity, telephone, and some Christmas bills, too."

"I've just got to work," said Barry. "I've got to get started again."

Bobbi replied, "Well, you've got to go to a doctor first, so he can help you get well."

Just about that time there was a loud knocking on the door downstairs. "Can I come in? Can I come in?"

"Who's that?" asked Bobbi.

"I don't know," Barry said.

"Can I come in, it's Mr. Brant."

"Oh my God!" exclaimed Bobbi. "Jesus Christ, oh my God, it's the landlord. Oh God." She hopped up. "Get away, children. Run, hide under the bed. Get under the bed, Little-bit. Hide, hide, it's the landlord and you've got—"

"Mr. Brant," came a voice from downstairs, "and the building inspector."

"Jesus Christ, the building inspector! I haven't cleaned up. It's a mess. What am I going to do? It's a mess."

Barry shook his head. "The building inspector. Oh shit, what is he coming here for? What are they going to do when they see all the people here? All the children? Thank God Bubba's not here. But Walt, what's Walt doing? Is he asleep?" Walt was sitting at the window in the next room. "Oh well, well, here they come."

Just at that point they reached the top of the stairs—Mr. Brant, the landlord, and two building inspectors. They looked around in the kitchen and the bathroom before they came in the bedroom. "What about this bathroom?" asked one of the inspectors.

Bobbi said, "Well, he came to tile it. He came to tile it on Christmas Eve, but we were just too busy. There was so much for us to do so we told him not to do it that day and to come back some other day and they said they'd be back sometime after Christmas. But they haven't come to tile it yet. But we like this place. We like this place real good."

Mr. Brant never came into the room we were in, but one of the building inspectors did, walked to the center of the room, and looked around. Bobbi said, "Let me tell you, mister, we've lived in lots of places, but this is about the nicest place we've ever lived in. We really like it."

Barry then said, "Mr. Brant, I'm sorry about the basement —er, uh, I mean, I'm going to fix it up when I get time. I've been sick and I just haven't had a chance."

Mr. Brant didn't say anything. The men walked around through the two rooms, looking at the ceiling and checking the windows. One of the inspectors said, "Excuse me, ma'am, how many people live here?"

"Oh—uh—just me and my husband and my two children. I'm baby-sitting today. I just have two boys."

The building inspector wrote that down; then he asked, "How many adults live in this house?"

"Oh, just me and my husband. That's all. I'm baby-sitting today."

He looked at me and then he looked in the next room at Walt, who was sitting by the window, shook his head, and marked something else down on the pad. "Well, thank you, ma'am," he replied, and walked out the door. The three men mumbled something that couldn't be heard from our room and then walked down the stairs.

Bobbi said, "Oh my God, what do you think they're going to do? Do you think he suspected that any more than four people live in this apartment?"

Barry shook his head, saying, "I just hope he don't see the basement. My dog's down there and I ain't supposed to have a dog. Plus the fact the place looks like shit. I've got all my paint down there, and the dog's been shitting down there. If he goes down in the basement, we've had it."

The building inspector walked out the door, around the corner, and immediately went down to the basement. Bobbi and Barry both peered out the window, trying to see what was happening. The first thing they saw was the basset hound Cleo run out the door and down the street.

Barry exclaimed, "Goddamn, there goes Cleo! They let that dog out. What we going to do?" Cleo was free, barking and heading off down the alley. "Well, that's it. They saw that basement. We're finished, that's it, we're through."

After staying in the basement a few minutes, the men came out. Again, we all three listened at the window to see if we could hear what they were saying. I couldn't hear anything, but Bobbi said she heard them say that the house was not fit for a two-family dwelling and that one of the units would have to be eliminated. The three men then went into the apartment underneath and banged around for a few minutes as we all continued to sit there, not saying anything, waiting for them to leave. In about twenty minutes, after they departed, we went to look for Cleo. The dog hadn't gone too far, fortunately; and Bobbi, who had followed me out the door, had managed to find him about a hundred yards down the alley. She dragged him back and put him back down in the basement, which was, in fact, quite a mess.

"Goddamn," said Barry, "I just hope he didn't get pissed off about the basement. I'm afraid they're really going to get pissed off about that basement—it was in some mess."

"Well," said Bobbi, "I really love this apartment, and I hope we don't have to leave 'cause I don't know where we'd go. It sure is better than that last place we lived in. We don't have all the room we need, but it sure is a better place. I mean, the landlord sent the exterminator and got rid of some of the cockroaches, and they're going to tile the bathroom. I mean, it's just a nice place. And we know our neighbors, too, and they don't mind us living up here."

The Shackelfords never found out why the building inspectors were there; but since they were allowed to remain, they concluded they must have passed the inspection.

Over the next two weeks Barry's condition stayed the same. Walt, on the other hand, got much worse. On January 16 he finally agreed to see a doctor and the following day was admitted to Rogers Memorial Hospital in Washington. Bobbi took Walt there instead of the county hospital because she remembered that a very good doctor, who had helped her before, was associated with this hospital. The doctor told Bobbi that Walt's diabetes was very serious and that he would have to remain in the hospital for several days.

Before Walt went to the hospital, his spirits were very low. He told me that he was fed up with Barry and Bobbi, fed up with the way they had been acting and carrying on. He had lent them three hundred dollars a month for the last three months and had not gotten back a penny of it. "Oh," said Walt, "Barry came in one day and offered ten dollars as the first installment. But I ain't seen anything after that ten dollars. It would be okay if Barry cared. It would be okay if he really was trying. But he ain't. He don't give a damn. And now I'm going into the hospital. And I don't know how long I'll be in the hospital. And I don't know what the shit they're going to do without me. Who is going to look after the kids? The only time Barry ever goes to work, Bobbi goes with him. If it wasn't for Bobbi, Barry would never go to work. I guess they'll realize then how much I mean to them. But I don't know how they're going to get along. And I ain't got that much more money. I ain't been able to work. Hell, I worked more than Barry did last year. I earned about two thousand dollars. That's almost more than Barry made. That on top of getting a hundred ten a month social security and welfare, plus food stamps. How much did Barry earn last year? Not much, not much."

Things were beginning to get to Bobbi, too. "I'm real worried," she told me. "I'm worried about Daddy and I'm worried about Barry and I'm worried about me. Daddy's heart's real bad. I know it is, plus his diabetes. He's got some water or something in the main valve of his heart, and I mean it's really serious. And I'm worried about Barry because his arm is getting no better, no better at all. I don't know what the doctor's going to say about it. And I'm worried about me because I've had my third period since December. And I've lost so much blood I can hardly walk. I feel so weak. I'm much worse than I was before I had that operation. I went to another doctor yesterday, and he told me that I should have had only one period and there's something pretty wrong, and I'm going to have to go back in the hospital, too. I'm really worried. I hope it's nothing real serious, but the doctor seemed real worried about it. Who is going to watch over the children? Lord only knows."

Bobbi went to the doctor again the following day and returned even more depressed. She telephoned me as soon as she returned. "They said it's at the cancer stage. They said I might have cancer. They got to operate as soon as possible. A hysterectomy. They got to do a hysterectomy as soon as they can. They said they'd like to do it today or as soon as possible, but I told them about Barry and about Walt, and so I don't know when they're going to be able to do it. He said he couldn't believe those other doctors had done what they done. He said he didn't know who those doctors were, but they didn't do me right. That they should have known it was a serious problem. But they didn't, they sent me home without telling me nothing. What's more, they should have packed me. He asked me how long I was packed. I wasn't packed at all! He said that I could have died. I could have hemorrhaged and that if I had there was nothing they could have done to stop it.

"I'm sure glad I went to this doctor, though. He was one of the doctors I went to when I had Billy. I never went back to them, but they're top doctors, some of the tops in Washington. And they really care about you. He spent about forty minutes talking to me. They're good doctors. And they're going to fix me up, they're going to fix me up okay."

"Why didn't you go to them before?" I asked.

"Well, I just didn't think of it. I don't know. It had been a while since I had Billy. They wanted to tie my tubes after I had Billy, but I was too young, so then of course I had another baby, Littlebit. But the doctor I had, he referred me to another doctor, and I just didn't remember those two in the District. I wish I had, though, 'cause the other doctor, he sure didn't do me right. You know, the doctor wanted to put me on tranquilizers, what with all I've been through and all the weight on my shoulders. But I told him no, I don't take no tranquilizers, no aspirin, no nothing. All the talk about dope and all that, you know. I just don't want nothing to do with it. I don't even take an aspirin. I get petrified when I think about narcotics and dope and stuff like that. And I know I've got this headache. It's due to my uterus, the doctor said. But I want to fight it myself. I don't want any help from any medical prescriptions."

Bobbi paused for a moment, then continued: "I tell you, times ain't easy. I got up at six this morning. We're flat broke. Ain't got no money, no food. Al lent us ten dollars and bought us some eggs and milk and bread for the children so they could eat. But we ain't got nothing. Ain't paid no bills, haven't paid the rent. So I got up at six, got dressed, tried to feed the children, and went over to the welfare. I walked all the way down there, all the way down the road. Got there before seven and it was thirteen degrees. And you better believe it was cold! The wind was whistling. I was the sixth person in line. The first person in line said he got there at five in the morning.

"We waited and about eight-thirty they let us in the building. A long line then. And I saw a caseworker. After nine I saw a caseworker, and they told me that we qualified for emergency help—that is, if we could get proof that Barry was sick and couldn't work. So now I've got to get Barry's doctor's signature and get him to sign these papers so we can show that Barry's not working.

"I had to take Barry to the doctor this afternoon; and of course the kids didn't have no baby-sitter. Poor Billy with the chicken pox, he didn't have nobody to stay with him. We put Littlebit in the car with us, and I went downstairs and asked Kate and Mack if they'd look after Billy and they said they couldn't. They had originally said they would; but since they were down there, I asked if they'd just sort of look in and see how he was doing. And they said they would. So I asked Billy if Mack or Kate had been up to look in on him and he said no. About that time there was a knock on the door, and Mack, drunk, that sonofabitch, looked in the door and said, 'Hey, you okay, kid? How you kids doing?' The only reason he did that was 'cause he knew we were home. He heard us up here walking around. Lucky, Billy was okay, nothing had happened to him. Can you imagine what would have happened if the welfare people had come around and found that kid there by himself without anybody to look after him? They would have really gone after me. They might have taken him away from me.

"Then we took Barry to the doctors' and they said he was worse than ever so they gave him some more medicine and said that if he doesn't get better by Friday they'd have to operate. Don't know what's causing that lump under his arm, but it's worse and he can't work. But we're so out of money right now, so far behind on rent and bills—haven't paid an electric bill, or phone bill, or gas bill. Way behind on the rent. And we're paying two dollars a day for every day we don't pay the rent. We're going to have to pay double before the month is out. So far behind on that that Barry, hell, he got up today and drove a man to get his car. The man said he had to pick up a hundred dollars and if Barry would drive him out, he'd give Barry ten. So Barry, he's been out all day driving the man. He hasn't had his medicine. He hasn't had any heat on his bump. He's been out all day driving this man

to get his car and I hope he comes back with the ten dollars—
if it doesn't kill him. Well, what can we do? We don't have
any money for food. We've got to get that welfare!"

The next day I stopped by the Shackelfords' again to see
what happened regarding Bobbi's application for emergency
welfare. When I got there around ten o'clock, Barry was outside bent over Pop's (Kate's father's) Hess Oil truck. Kate
was in the cab of the truck. Apparently the gears were
jammed, and Barry was doing the best he could to unstick
them. It was freezing cold with the chill factor making the
temperature well below zero. Barry had on an unbuttoned
wool shirt and, of course, his red stocking cap.

After cursing the gears, Kate hollered, "Let's give it up,
Barry. We ain't going to fix it. Let's go inside and get a drink."
So we all went inside. Seated at the kitchen table was an old
man I'd never seen before, whom Kate introduced as Mack's
dad. He had long white hair and was unshaven. Beside him
was an empty bottle of whiskey and a half-full glass which
he was sipping from. Mack was still asleep in the bedroom.

After horsing around a bit, cursing the truck, and wondering what they were going to do with it, Barry and Kate asked
me to go across the street and buy a fifth of Bradley's blended
whiskey for them. I did this, returned, and then went upstairs
to see Bobbi.

Bobbi was steaming mad. "You know, Joe, I've had it. I
can't stand those sons of bitches down there. They're driving
me out of my mind. I've had it. I tell you I can't stand
it. They're a bad influence on Barry; they make noise; they
come up here at all hours of the day and night and want
whiskey, want money, want food. And we don't have it.
For God's sake. They make much more money than we do.
When Kate's daddy works, he makes two hundred fifty
a week. And then he comes up and wants to borrow whiskey
and money. Jesus, I've had it. They're a terrible influence
on Barry. He's down there day and night. They knock on
their ceiling and Barry hears it and runs down there. And
Barry, when he gets some beer, will knock on the floor, and
they'll hear it through their ceiling and come up. Oh, those
people are cheap. It's a sick situation. Kate and her alcoholic

father, Mack and his alcoholic father. The four of them drunk
almost all the time.

"And when we want to borrow something from them, they
hardly ever give it to us. We wanted to borrow some sugar
last week. I sent down one of the kids, Cindy, for some sugar,
and she came back with a teaspoonful. They said that was all
they had. I was down there the next day and saw they had a
great big canful of sugar. I tell you, I've had it. As long as
they are down there, Barry's going to keep on drinking, keep
on getting in trouble, keep on not working.

"The whole thing is just a mess, one big mess. And I'm
afraid, I'm afraid, Joe, they'll come up here some night when
Barry's not here. And I don't know what they'll do. And here
I am all by myself and I can't lock the door, and I don't have
anybody to protect me, and Walt's not here any more. I just
don't know what Mack will do. He's all the time making passes
at me and hitting me on my ass and stuff like that. I just don't
know. I'm afraid of that Mack. I don't know what he'll do
when he's drunk, and he's drunk about ninety per cent of the
time."

While Bobbi was talking, Barry came upstairs. He seemed
to be feeling pretty good, whistling and hollering and singing
a song to the tune of "Down by the Old Mill Stream," the
words to which went: "Down by the old mill stream, that's
where I first met Jean. It was hairy and black and she called
it her crack, but it looked like a manhole to me. . . ." He
went haw-haw-haw after each verse. Bobbi was not impressed;
nor was Al, who was seated at the table next to Bobbi. Al
had been sober for several weeks.

Barry said, "Where are the eggs? Where're the eggs,
honey? They want some eggs downstairs."

"Eggs, shit. Those bastards aren't getting any eggs."

"Ah, come on, Bobbi. Jesus Christ, goddamn, they need
some eggs. They ain't got nothing to eat down there."

"*They* ain't got nothing to eat!" Bobbi screamed. "What
do you think *we* have to eat? We don't have any money. Don't
you realize we haven't paid the rent, we haven't paid the bills,
and the only reason we've got any eggs and bacon in the icebox right now is because Alton gave us ten dollars. And now

you want to take a half-dozen eggs to give to those tramps down below?"

"Don't call them that, don't call them that. That's not right."

"I'm saying that when they come up here, they all the time want money. No telling how much money. And they always want food. And they don't ever pay any of it back. And when we want something from them, they never give it to us. It's as simple as that and I'm sick of it. They aren't getting any eggs."

By this time Barry had found the eggs and taken six out of the carton, placed the eggs in his pocket, and said, "Ah, come on, honey, they need something to eat."

"Oh hell," sighed Bobbi, "go ahead. Take the eggs. But remember, you've got a family up here, understand. Your family is up here and not down there, and I want you to come back up here and not spend all your time downstairs with those sots."

"Okay, I'll be up." He left and returned a few minutes later.

Al was shaking his head. "What Bobbi said is right. They're no good. They're no good for anybody. They're a bad influence on Barry."

When Barry returned he continued to sing the same song. "Hot damn," he chuckled, "I'm glad to get my ten dollars. Gave the guy a ride down to the coast yesterday, one hundred miles or whatever, and he gave me ten dollars plus two dollars for gas. That old bootlegger." Again Barry laughed.

I asked, "Who was he?"

"Oh, he's a bootlegger and a numbers man besides. He's B.J.'s cousin, Red. Used to live with B.J. but don't live there no more."

Bobbi then came back from the other room and said, "You know, I finally got through to the welfare people. Got the doctor to sign the papers last night and I went down to welfare first thing this morning and they let me have my check. And this month it's for a hundred eighty-nine dollars. Out of that I've got to pay ninety dollars for rent, then I've got my gas and electricity for ninety dollars. The way we figure it, if we pay all we have to pay on the bills—that means leaving some for the next time—that means we'll have eight dollars left this month. Now for forty-six dollars out of that one eighty-nine, I can get a hundred forty-four dollars' worth of food stamps. So that means we're going to be in pretty good shape. We're going to be able to pay the rent and eat and be able to pay off most of the bills, though not all, not all."

Barry said, "That's right, that's right. Like the insurance man. We're three weeks behind on our insurance. It's going to lapse if we don't pay pretty soon." There was a brief silence.

"But," said Bobbi, "the welfare people are real nice and they treated me nice. They offered me some coffee. I didn't have to wait that long, and I didn't have no trouble getting the check. Next month we'll get one, too. Including Bubba's sixty dollars, it will be two hundred and fifty. It ain't much, but it will get us through these two months. And I don't know, I don't know about Barry, I don't know how long it will be before he can work, but I've heard it might be as much as two or three months. I talked to one person, and he said he'd known a couple of guys who had what Barry has and they died with it. So I don't know. I'm real worried, myself. You just got to face it. It will be a while anyway before he can work. A good while.

"I'm real depressed and things get me down right now, but there's one thing I'm thankful for. It's Barry. You know, there haven't been many days that we've been married—I mean all these years and we've been married, Jesus, a long time—there ain't been many nights that passed when Barry hasn't told me that he loves me before he went to sleep. I mean to tell you, Barry will lean over and whisper in my ear, 'I love you, baby.' And he don't do me no wrong. He don't treat me wrong. He don't beat me. He's the most understanding, kindest husband . . ."

"Oh shit," said Barry, who blushed and shook his head, "I shouldn't be in the room when you say that sort of stuff."

"No, I don't want you to leave. I want you to hear this."

"Aw shucks." Barry reached over and put his arm around Bobbi, kissing her on the cheek.

"I mean to tell you that's right. I'm going in the hospital

next week and I'll be there two weeks, at least, the doctor said. When I'm gone I know Barry's not going to have no other women. I know if I was in the hospital longer than that, I know he wouldn't have no more women. I just know he wouldn't. Isn't that right, Barry, ain't that right?"

Barry laughed.

Al said, "If he says yes, he's a liar. A goddamn liar. You know damn well that ain't right, Barry."

Barry didn't say anything. "I'd like a little bit right now, baby. How about just a little bit."

"I can't, Barry, you know it. I just can't do it. You know why."

"Oh, come on, baby, just a little bit, just a little dibble, a little dibble."

"Now, Barry, that's nasty, that's nasty," said Al, chuckling.

For the next week things stayed about the same. Bobbi tried to visit Walt in the hospital at least once a day and to nurse Barry and Billy, Littlebit and Cindy, all of whom now had the chicken pox. On January 25 she received a call from one of the nurses at her doctor's office that she was scheduled to be operated on the next Thursday. Bobbi told the nurse that she could not have the operation, that her husband was due to go into the hospital soon, and that her children were sick with no one to care for them. "I know it's important," said Bobbi, "but what could I do? I told the nurse as soon as all this blows over, first thing, I'll call her up and have my operation. She said I was taking a risk, and I told her I would promise to call her back. What else could I do?"

Barry had not been soaking his arm as he was supposed to. On the contrary, he went on a drunk for the entire week, spending most of his time downstairs with Mack and Kate. He and Bobbi were angry with each other most of the time, Bobbi because Barry wasn't taking care of himself and was drinking, and Barry because Bobbi was giving him a hard time. On Friday evening, only a week after Bobbi had said Barry never beat her, things exploded.

Bobbi explained what happened: "Joe, me and Barry, we got in a fight Friday. It was pretty bad. He kicked me something awful. He was drunk, had been drinking liquor, was

down at Mack's. Mack has been beating on the floor all the
time with his broom and Barry's been going down there drinking liquor. He came back Friday night and he was roaring
drunk. Now, you've seen Barry drinking beer, but you ain't
never seen him drunk with liquor. 'Cause let me tell you, he's
nasty. He's mean and nasty. And Friday night he'd been drinking liquor.

"Well, Bubba came up to go on his paper route, and he
had some change. Bubba always has to have change when
he goes on his route—you know, to make change for people
when they hand him a ten-dollar bill or something like that.
Well, Barry wanted that change to go out and buy a bottle.
Bubba told him no, he couldn't have it. So Barry went after
Bubba. He tried to hit him and started kicking him. Well, I
didn't know what to do, so I got in front of Bubba and tried
to protect him. But Barry took a swing at me and told me I
was a bitch and to get out of his way, that he wanted
the money. Bubba had money and Barry wanted it. I mean,
he was really drunk. Now, this has happened before. It
hasn't happened in a long time, but it's happened before. I
remember one time it happened I took out a warrant on him.
Had him on parole. But this was something awful. Bubba got
away. He stumbled downstairs, and he was upset. He hates
Barry. I'm afraid he'll do something to Barry. You know, he's
big, he's stronger than Barry, and Barry is going to push him
too far one of these days. Friday evening he came pretty
close.

"Bubba got away, but that left me there by myself. Barry
went after me and started kicking me. Hurt me something awful. Well, I told him to get out. To go downstairs or to come
up here, but he couldn't do both. So he left. I mean to tell
you, when that man drinks he goes out of his mind. I mean,
when he drinks liquor. It's that Mack. That man is a bad influence. I told the doctor that I couldn't come over because
my husband and my father were in the hospital, but I tell you
something else. I wouldn't trust Barry to stay with the kids. He
wouldn't stay with them. Whenever Mack beats on the floor
down there with his broom, Barry will go down and start
drinking. I tell you we're all sick of that. Bubba hates Barry's

guts and so does Cindy. Cindy told Barry to his face this weekend. She said, 'I hate your guts, Barry.' She does. I mean, it ain't right. You know it ain't right and he knows it ain't right, but he keeps on going down there and drinking with that Mack. . . ."

Feelings between Barry and Bobbi had a chance to cool off, for on Monday Barry's doctor informed him he would be admitted to the hospital. Barry went into Rogers Memorial on January 27 and stayed in a room down the hall from Walt. Bobbi was able to combine visits, and Barry and Walt were able to keep each other company.

Rogers Memorial Hospital is located near the old neighborhood Bobbi grew up in. The area is now black and very rundown. As we would pass through the neighborhood on the way to the hospital, Bobbi would reminisce about the good old days. "Yes, sir, a few years back this was a real nice place to live. Streets were clean, folks were friendly, and you could walk anywhere you wanted without being afraid of getting raped, robbed, or murdered. Then the colored started moving in, and look at it. Niggers everywhere. Look at the trash and garbage on the sidewalks. Rape and murder and rioting. I wouldn't live here now if you paid me a million bucks!" (Al, however, still lived in the area.) I made the trip with Bobbi several times; and each time she made a similar comment, expressing her dismay at what had happened to her old neighborhood.

One evening when we were visiting Walt and Barry, just as Bubba, Bobbi, and I got in the elevator, five teen-age black girls came running down the hall toward the elevator; and Bobbi held the door open so they could get on. Once in the closed elevator, no one said a word. They stared at us and we stared at them. Before they got off on the third floor, one girl looked at Bobbi and with contempt in her voice said to the others, "Shit, man, look at that. White socks. White dirty socks." She pointed at Bobbi's feet and the blacks all snickered, "Dirty white socks, bullshit!" The black girls all had Afros and were nicely dressed. As they left the elevator, they started guffawing.

Bobbi turned very red. She did, in fact, have on dirty white socks. Not only that, her shoes had holes in them. Her hair was in curlers and she was wearing a ratty old coat—her only coat. For a moment she was silent. Then as we got off on the fourth floor, she whispered, "This is why I don't like to come here. Those nigger girls have some nerve. It's this way almost every time. Those goddamned jigs, all the time making fun of you."

Barry's operation kept being put off. Bobbi was not sure why, since the doctors never told her anything, but she thought they were trying to let his arm drain on its own. Bobbi's biggest problem was operating the truck, which was going through one of its temperamental periods. Three times the truck overheated on the way to the hospital, and each time Bobbi or Bubba had to walk several blocks to a gas station for water. By pouring in a mixture of water and antifreeze the truck started up again each time, but Bobbi did not know how long that would last. Of course, the battery went down every night. However, Bobbi would always have a recharged battery on hand and would exchange them every morning.

On the last day of January, when Walt was released from the hospital, Bobbi was very excited. But from this time on her life would be a little more difficult since, as the doctors informed her, she was now Walt's nurse. She would have to test his urine and give him insulin injections every day. The doctors stressed the importance of Walt's eating the right foods and especially staying away from fried or greasy foods. Bobbi practiced giving Walt his shot several times in the hospital and said she was going to try to keep Walt from cooking his fried chicken, fried pork chops, and fried herring. (Before he went into the hospital he enjoyed cooking these foods himself, which were practically all he ate.)

"I got one of my men home," Bobbi called to tell me. "Now there is one more to go."

When Barry was finally operated on February 2, two gallons of fluid were drained from the swelling under his arm. After it was all over, Barry said he was relieved and felt much better, though Bobbi remained skeptical. The doctors had told neither her nor Barry anything; and Bobbi by now had come to expect the worst. She was convinced that so much fluid meant Barry was sicker than the doctors were letting on.

Money was now completely out, but on February 4 the emergency welfare came through. Since the truck was finally out of commission, the next day Bobbi asked me to give her a ride to do some errands. We first drove to the liquor store where Bobbi cashed her welfare check of $250.

"Joe, I sure am glad the liquor store will cash this check, because the goddamn bank won't. The goddamn bank won't cash a check unless you have an account there. Now, what kind of person who gets a welfare check is going to have a goddamn checking account at a bank, just tell me that? Well, I know Tom will come through. He always does."

Next we headed to Brant Construction Company where Bobbi paid her rent. On the way there when I mentioned something about getting a parking ticket, Bobbi erupted. "Goddamn police officers. That goddamn motherfucking policewoman, shit. That woman ain't for shit. All she does is go around every day and give people parking tickets. Goddamn, that woman's bad news. Let me tell you, Jack, she's laying with all those policemen. That's why they keep her on the force. Let me tell you, that woman ain't worth shit." Bobbi was in a particularly angry mood that day.

We got to Brant's. Bobbi went in and came out a few minutes later, saying she'd really told off the secretary. "Mr. Brant wasn't there, but I told that goddamn secretary, I told her to tell Mr. Brant to keep his goddamn mouth shut about us not paying our rent. We pay our rent on time, we always pay our rent on time, we always have paid our rent on time, and he ain't got no goddamn business telling people otherwise. If I hear that he's done that again, I want to talk to him personally."

After paying the rent, we went back to the welfare department and waited in line almost an hour for Bobbi to purchase her food stamps. After getting them, she asked me to drive her to the supermarket where she used forty-seven dollars' worth of food stamps to purchase groceries. Leaving the groceries at her place, we then went across town to Silver Spring where we picked up a check for the thirty-five dollars

Barry's boss owed him; and finally, around three o'clock, we made a trip to the hospital to visit Barry. By this hour I was exhausted, but Bobbi was still going strong. She commented that I looked tired, and then added, "This is one of my running days, running everywhere and doing things. I'm just thankful we got some money to run with!"

Barry was depressed. He said he still did not know what was wrong with him or how long he would continue to be in the hospital. He said the doctor had not seen him after the operation, and the nurses said they weren't sure what the results of the operation were. Bobbi said she had tried to contact the doctor to find out about the results of the tests on the f'·iid but hadn't had any luck.

On the way home Bobbi said she thought the reason the doctors weren't talking was because they had found something very seriously wrong with Barry, and they didn't want to break the news to them. "You see," she said, "doctors don't like to tell you bad things. For instance, they never told me how serious my first little girl was when she died. They never told me that. They said they didn't want to break the news to me. But I wish they had, I wish they would tell me. It's better knowing where you stand than not knowing anything at all. And that's the way it is right now with Barry, and that's the way it's been with me so many times with my children. Doctors just don't like to tell you nothing. That's just the way they are."

Bobbi said she was very worried that the lymph gland was something serious such as cancer. Tom, the guy in the liquor store, had been a medic in the Navy and said he knew a lot about strange diseases. He told Bobbi that 90 per cent of the time when a person has a swelling under the lymph gland it is fatal; and nothing can be done about it. Bobbi thought he said it meant you had Parkinson's disease. "I don't know what I'd do if Barry died. I just don't know. I don't know how I'd get by. I just don't know what would happen." Bobbi paused and then said: "Of course, there is the insurance. I've got a lot of insurance on that man, got ten thousand dollars on him. Equitable Insurance policy. That would be something. But I just don't know, the money wouldn't make up for it. I don't know what I'd do with the money, either. What I'd like to do is invest it, you know, so that it would earn money for me. I'd have an income coming in each year and wouldn't have to worry about it.

"But what really bothers me," she said, "is that if Barry learned he was near death or had a real serious problem, he might go and kill himself so I would get the money faster since right now we are in such bad straits. So that's why I hope they don't tell him if there is anything real serious wrong with him. I hope they don't tell him, 'cause Barry, he's crazy enough to do something like that."

Barry remained in the hospital four more days and had no idea until the last minute when he would be getting out. In fact, the day of his discharge from the hospital, Bobbi and Barry were both resigned to a long stay for him. Since the doctors were inaccessible, Bobbi continued talking to Tom at the liquor store and Tom kept giving Bobbi gloomy analyses. The name of the disease was not Parkinson's, he told Bobbi, but Hodgkin's disease, which he thought was a type of cancer; and from all the symptoms, Tom was convinced that Barry had it. Bobbi told me that she believed Tom and was sure that Barry had Hodgkin's disease and would probably never come out of the hospital. She told me this on the morning of February 8. That afternoon, however, we brought Barry home. Bobbi still remained skeptical. "I tell you, I know he has it. The only reason they are letting him out is 'cause they can't do nothing for him any more."

Barry did not believe Tom, however, and was in a rare mood of exuberance when we got to the hospital to take him home. He had finally talked to the doctor, who told him he was okay, except he must remain in bed and soak his arm every day for one month. The moment we got outside the hospital Barry turned to Bobbi and said, "Hot damn. Where's the closest liquor store?"

Bobbi scowled. "Listen, goddammit, if you got money, you spend it. I ain't got any money myself. We're flat broke. If you can go round up some booze or a piece of ass, you go ahead. Let me know how you come out." Barry gave an

Out of hospital / gets drunk w/ Mack

embarrassed laugh and put on his red stocking cap. The three of us returned home.

Barry's release from the hospital was something of a mixed blessing. Bobbi was glad Barry was home and was relieved that he was getting better, though she was still convinced there was more to the problem than the doctors were telling. But while Barry was in the hospital, she could postpone facing some of the realities of having Barry at home. She could forget about his drinking and about the tension between Barry and Bubba. She could hope that when Barry got out of the hospital, somehow things might be different. Of course, things weren't different, and no sooner had Barry walked in the door did he leave to check on Mack. That evening he got drunk again.

The first task facing Barry was to get the truck running. So the next day in freezing cold Barry spent most of the time lying on the ground under the truck tinkering with the motor. He finally concluded he needed two new parts for the clutch; but since they had no money, there was little he could do to fix it. Reluctantly he decided to pawn two of his shotguns. With the pawn money, he purchased the parts and the following day spent several hours installing them.

Bobbi was glad to see the truck running again but was otherwise furious at Barry. That afternoon he was supposed to go to the doctor to have his arm checked. (The doctor in the hospital had turned both Barry and Walt over to a general practitioner who would follow their progress. The doctor, Dr. Di Banca, had agreed to see them both that afternoon.) Barry was finishing up his work on the truck when Bobbi came out and said, "Goddammit, Barry, it's time to go. I ain't going to put up with this shit any more. What you did last night, and you have been out all day working on that goddamn car. Shit, are you coming or not?"

"Oh shut up. I've got to finish this."

"Shut up hell. It's time to go to the doctor's. Let's go."

Barry reluctantly agreed to get moving. He went to shave and put on his clean shirt. Whenever Walt and Barry went to the doctor's office, they always put on a coat and tie. Walt had on a clean, but wrinkled, white shirt; and Barry went upstairs to put on his old coat and a clean white shirt.

While Barry was dressing, Bubba came to Bobbi and handed her a sealed note from his teacher. Bobbi exploded. "Goddammit, Bubba, you've done it again! You've gotten into trouble. Shit. I tell you, buddy, you've fucked up again. Listen, only one more time like this, and it's going to be all for you. I've warned you. I've told you to straighten up. I told you. And goddammit, you fucked up again. Listen, buddy, I don't know what I'm going to do with you; I just don't know what I'm going to do with you."

Bubba stood speechless and then managed to mutter something to the effect: "Momma, you haven't read the note yet. You don't know what it says."

"I don't have to read the note. Where are my glasses? I know what it says. I know it's going to be bad."

"But Momma, you don't know what it's going to be."

"Well, where are my glasses?" Bobbi furiously stomped out of the room to find her glasses. Then she opened the note and read it to herself. Everyone in the room watched Bobbi's expression as she read it. Her face tightened as she began to frown. "Goddamn, I knew it, I knew it." She slammed the note on the table. "You have *really* fucked up this time!"

"Well, what did I do, Mom? I've been pretty good. I haven't done nothing."

"It says here that you are not going to be transferred from the sixth grade into junior high. I'll read you the note. 'Dear Mrs. Shackelford: I have tried very hard as you know to get your son, Walter, transferred out of elementary school into the junior high school. As we have discussed, you know and I know that he will be much better off with children his own age. He is too old to be in the elementary school. However, I am very sorry to report to you today that I have failed. I have been unable to get Walter transferred. This is very unfortunate because he has a difficult time relating to children so much younger than he is. Walter is a good boy and he tries very hard. Sometimes he acts up, and lately he's been into a little trouble, but he tries very hard. I'm very sorry that the transfer will not be able to take place. Yours sincerely, Walter's teacher.' Well, shit, now you know, now you know. Your teacher was going to try to get you transferred, and it didn't work out. So there, there."

Bubba brushed a tear aside and choked on a few words, none of which were intelligible. Then he managed to say, "Momma, I didn't do nothing wrong. I didn't do nothing wrong."

Bobbi didn't say anything. She just stood there with her arms crossed. Walt sat at the kitchen table, staring at Bubba.

I managed to say, "Bobbi, I didn't think the letter said that Bubba did anything that bad. It's just that he couldn't be transferred."

"Well, it's going to be hard going for you, Bubba, that's all I've got to say. It's going to be hard going. And that's just tough shit."

Bubba walked out of the room and went upstairs.

Bobbi said, "Come on, Barry, let's get the hell out of here. We've got to go to the goddamned doctor's, and I'm tired of waiting around to put up with this shit. I'm really sick of it. I'm really goddamn sick of it."

Barry said, "Hold your tongue, nasty mouth. I'm coming as fast as I goddamn can. Where's my razor?"

Bobbi was getting more and more furious. Standing with her arms crossed, she was patting her foot nervously on the floor. "That Barry, I don't know what I'm going to do with him. Up late last night drinking down there with Mack, getting up early this morning, working on the car. Out in the cold, didn't have the proper clothes on, froze to death, using that bad arm. I just don't know what I'm going to do with him."

In about five minutes Barry was ready to go, and the four of us left. As we got on the road Bobbi seemed to perk up. In fact her temperament changed rather dramatically. She no longer seemed to be put out with Barry and started laughing and joking, telling a few jokes herself. She said nothing about Bubba.

After three hours of waiting in Dr. Di Banca's office, the doctor took a look at both Barry and Walt. Walt came out first saying that he was doing okay. Barry came out shaking his head. The doctor told him his veins had collapsed in his right arm, due to overexertion, and that he might have hurt his arm permanently. When we got in the car, Bobbi turned to Barry and remarked, "It serves you right. The doctor said to stay in bed!"

"But if I didn't fix the goddamn truck, how the hell are we gonna get around?"

Bobbi was silent. We rode for a while with no one saying anything. Then Bobbi changed the subject. "You know, if Barry's going to be another month before he can do any work at all, I just don't think I can go in the hospital. I think I'll have to wait until things get straightened out here before I go in the hospital."

During the winter and spring of this year, financial crises tended to occur on a regular basis several times each month. When bills were due on the first of the month, the Shackelfords were usually completely broke. They would borrow from Al, Mack and Kate, Barry's mother and stepfather (whom they rarely saw), or me, to get them through until the fourth when Bobbi's emergency welfare was supposed to be issued. Walt also received a social security check for $67 on or near the fourth of the month. Thus, on the fourth the crisis usually subsided temporarily. (Bobbi had to go down to the welfare department; Walt received his check in the mail.) With the $300 Bobbi would purchase food stamps ($144 for $46) and pay off some of the back bills. By the middle of the month, however, the money would run out, and the Shackelfords would be again without funds. Fortunately, Walt was due to receive his $50 in welfare to compensate his social security payments on the twelfth of the month; and this amount would usually get them through another two weeks—almost until the first of the month. If by some chance the checks did not arrive on time, an even more desperate situation would result.

Such was the situation on February 17 when Walt's welfare check was already five days late. When I got over to the Shackelfords that morning around ten, things were in chaos. As I came upstairs I could hear Bobbi screaming at Billy: "Get my robe, goddammit, get my robe."

Billy was enjoying the whole ordeal immensely because

only he knew where Bobbi's robe was, and he wasn't telling. He came back a few minutes later, "Is this it, Mom?"

Bobbi screamed from behind the door, "Hell no, that's not it, you little bastard! You know a napkin's not a robe. Go back and get my robe, for God's sake."

"Okay, Mom." He scampered upstairs and came back a few minutes later, this time with the top of his pajamas. "Mom, is this it?"

"Shit. Your daddy's going to beat your hind parts. I've had it with you, you little sonofabitch. You ain't ever staying home from school again."

About five minutes later, on Billy's third trip, he returned smiling sheepishly, this time carrying Bobbi's robe.

"It's about goddamn time. Your daddy is going to whack your hind parts good." Billy squealed and ran upstairs.

Walt was particularly depressed this morning, sitting looking out the window. He shook his head. "I can't see nothing. The cataracts are so bad I can't see nothing at all." The first thing he asked me was, "Did you check the mail? Do we have any mail downstairs? Has the mailman come yet?" Walt had asked me this question every day for the last week. I shook my head, saying that I didn't think there was anything in the mailbox but I didn't think the mailman had come yet. "Well, I don't know where it is. They probably sent it to the wrong address, 'cause they do almost every time. But it was supposed to be here on Friday, and today's Wednesday and there ain't no check. I don't know what we're going to do. We ain't hardly got no money left."

Bobbi said, "Oh, we got about two dollars and fifty cents, and there are only two more weeks left in the month. That is plenty of money." She laughed sarcastically. Barry came out of the bathroom clean-shaven and seemed to be feeling pretty good. He had a bright look about him. Bobbi whispered as we went in the other room, "Barry ain't been drinking for two or three days. Hasn't had a drop to drink. He's been doing real good."

Barry came in the kitchen as Bobbi poured me a cup of coffee. He asked, "No welfare check, huh, Walt?"

"No, I don't know where it is. It's supposed to be here today. I don't know what we're going to do. I guess we'll call up again." Bobbi went in the next room to call the welfare department. She had called them every day this week, several times each day.

Barry said to Walt: "Well, we done hocked my guns and my bow. We ain't got much left to hock. I sure would like to get those things out of hock, but we ain't got no money to do that. We got to pay that interest and all. I'm afraid we're going to lose the bow and the guns. Sure as hell hope your check comes in." Barry paused for a moment, then continued: "Well, it ain't the first time, and it ain't the second or the third. Hell, I can't count how many times I've hocked these things over the last couple of years. So far I've been able to get them back, though. But now, hell, without working and all, who knows?"

We chatted on for a while sitting around the table, drinking coffee. Bobbi had made two calls to the welfare department, not getting through either time, and came back cursing loudly. "Goddamn welfare department. Sonofabitch bastards" —a phrase she kept repeating, as if she were talking to herself.

About the middle of the morning it was time to give Walt his insulin shot. Since Bobbi had had a hard time giving Walt the needle yesterday, Barry volunteered today, and the three of them went into the bedroom where Barry poked the needle in Walt's leg. When they came back a few minutes later, Barry said: "I sure would like to get back to work. These bills, unpaid bills, are really getting me down. I just don't know what's going to happen. I sure as hell would like to get back to work. I got work waiting for me. If I stay out much longer, hell, I just don't know what's going to happen."

Since it was one of the few times I had heard Barry talk about work, I asked him how he felt about his work, if he liked his job. "Hell yes, I like what I do. You're goddamn right. I like working for myself. I like going into a house and having everything to do—the plastering, the painting, the carpentry, the woodwork. See, when I go into a house I do everything. I'm like an interior decorator. The only thing I don't do is electricity and plumbing. And I like to work for myself. I'm my own boss. Damn right, I like it. I'd like to get back to work right now. This goddamn arm, it's getting worse. The knot's bigger than it's ever been. I've been feeling bad and having chills and fever. I'm worn out. I don't know, I don't know. I'm just afraid I'm going to have to go back into the hospital."

When he left the room, Bobbi whispered to me, "It's much worse, Joe. Much worse than it's ever been. I know he's going to have to go back."

Then Barry went in the other room and came back with *The Popular Mechanics Encyclopedia* on "How to Do It," and opened it to a section on building your own boat. "Look at this. I'm going to build myself this new pontoon boat. It's going to be just great." He went over the diagram, showing me detail by detail what was necessary in order to build a pontoon boat, which would be ideal for fishing, frogging, turtling, and various other such sports.

I asked, "When are you going to start?"

"Any day now. Just got to get the materials. I don't think it will cost anything. Need some styrofoam to put in these pontoons and just need some plywood and some lumber. Going to start looking around. I think I can get it all scrap throwaway. Bubba will help us. It will be some boat. We can take it down to the river and I'll show you where I've been turtling and fishing and just about everything you can think of."

As Barry was talking about turtles and catfish and carp, Bobbi went in the other room to call the doctor about Barry's arm. She came back a few minutes later cursing more violently than she had cursed the welfare department. "Goddamn sonofabitch bastard. Goddammit." She went on like this for a few minutes, talking to herself in a monotone. "That goddamn doctor. I know he's there. What do you mean 'not there'? He was there five minutes ago when I called! He's just trying to avoid me. That's what he's trying to do. Sonofabitch. Doctors. Goddamn doctors."

Barry paid no attention to Bobbi and went on talking about all the turtles he was going to catch once he got his boat built. Talking about turtles and fish got Barry to thinking about how good it would be to eat some of the herring they had caught last spring. He opened the closet door and pulled out a barrel, which was full of salted herring. Picking at the salt, he uncovered three or four herring, pulled them out, and put them in a bowl of water on the sink. The smell of these salted herring was almost unbearable. "Yep, once I get talking about fish, just got to have me some fish. It will take a while to get these things ready to eat. Got to soak them, boil them, and soak them some more. And tomorrow evening they might be ready to eat."

Bobbi and Barry got to talking about a place called Lovers Lane near the river. Bobbi said that she wanted to take me there someday, and they both laughed about the good times they had had there. Bobbi remarked: "You know, me and Barry, we've really had some good times. Things have been bad sometimes, sometimes they've been real bad, but we've had some real good times."

Billy was playing around on the floor with a red carnation. Bobbi said, "Let me see that. You see this, Barry? See this flower? This is the prettiest flower in the whole world. And when I die, I want these all over me everywhere. Red ones."

Barry said, "Ah shit, don't talk like that. Don't talk about dying."

"Well, everybody's got to go," Bobbi replied.

"Hell, honey, if you died, what would I do?"

It seemed like most of the morning and part of the afternoon we talked about hunting and fishing and turtling. I asked Barry if he had ever thought about being a naturalist or forest ranger or something like that. He nodded his head but didn't say anything. Then Bobbi remarked, "Well, I think you'd be a good one. But it's paper work, reading, that's what's keeping him from doing something like that." Bobbi whispered to me when Barry was out of the room that Barry could barely read and write and that this had kept him from doing lots of things he would really have liked to do.

Later in the day I called the welfare department as I promised Bobbi I would. After several attempts I finally got through and talked to a caseworker, who said the check was there and could be picked up. "Thank God," said Walt when I told him the news.

That afternoon I spent some time with Barry recording his

life history. Because Bobbi was not there to keep the children
out of the way—we usually recorded in the truck in the back
yard—they were continually running in and out of the kitchen,
and it was almost impossible to get anything accomplished. In
the midst of all the confusion and interruptions Barry shook
his head, saying: "You know, it's hard for me to talk about
my life. I mean, it's real painful, because there are lots of
things I don't want to talk about. Lots of sad things. Sure,
I wish things had been different; and sure, I wish I was better. If any man tells you he doesn't wish he was better, he's
lying. Everybody wants to be better. I know lots of things
I did was real common and real bad and I'm sorry for lots of
it. And right now my life's really about the best it's ever been.
I mean, I feel better about my life than I've ever felt about
it. But it is still—well, look around you. Look at the house.
Lots of bad things. I mean, I'm not on my feet, and I'd like
for it to be different. If a man tells you anything different,
he's lying.

"I guess I missed a lot of opportunities, too, in my life. And
one thing Bobbi talked about, about me not being able to
read and write all that good—I mean, I can read okay, but I
have a hard time writing. I really don't have no education.
They just pushed me on through school, and I quit as soon as
I could. I guess that was a real problem for me, education.
I mean, if I'd had more education, I could have been a foreman on two or three jobs; but the paper work, I was scared
of it; I was scared I couldn't do it. Now, don't get me wrong.
I don't think I'm any worse than anybody. I don't think anybody's any better than me, and these college kids—hell, a lot
of them ain't got no common sense. There's lots of things I
can do better than any college kids. I mean, like doing up a
whole house, taking care of everything, and hunting and trap-
ping and fishing and getting by. Hell, I'm better than any college kid in stuff like that. But I tell you, when I think about it,
I realize that if I had more education, my life might be different."

Just about that time Bubba came upstairs, having gotten
off early from school. Drinking a Pepsi and eating a candy
bar, he sat down beside us and began talking. I noticed Barry

was very gentle with Bubba. Seeming to be interested in what Bubba was doing, he said, "Honey, we're trying to do some recording. Maybe you could go downstairs and watch the kids. We'd really appreciate it. That would be real nice." Bubba agreed, and when he came back about twenty minutes later, Barry still didn't get mad at him. He treated him in the same gentle manner.

Later that day, however, when we were down in the kitchen, Bubba came back, wearing his love and peace khaki shirt. (Bubba had been accused by his teacher of being a hippie!) When Bubba made a comment that Barry was wearing the shirt Barry had promised to give him, Barry erupted violently. "Goddammit, are you going to cut the sleeves off this shirt just like you cut the sleeves off that shirt? If you are, I'll be goddamned if I'm going to give it to you! Shit, I'm taking it back, you sonofabitch."

"But gee, you gave me that shirt," Bubba whined, "you gave me that shirt. I can do what I want with it."

"You damn well can't! You ain't going to cut the sleeves off this goddamn shirt. I'm taking it back."

"Ah, come on, you said I could have it."

"Shit, you can't have it. I'm taking it back, you sonofabitch." Barry stomped out of the room.

"Gee whiz," said Bubba as he charged downstairs, slamming the door behind him.

Bobbi, who had just come upstairs, shrugged her shoulders. "Well, it's Barry's shirt. He's got a right to take it back, especially if Bubba's just going to cut the sleeves off of it and put all those hippie slogans on it."

Barry stood at the top of the stairs. "You little punk," he shouted, "cut off any more sleeves off my shirt and your ass is getting thrown out of this house. Do you hear me?" Bubba did not answer. Bobbi and Barry went downstairs and got in the truck to go get Walt's check.

February might be described as "going fishing month" at the Shackelford household. February 18, the day after they picked up Walt's check, turned out to be a beautiful day and warm enough to fish, at least warm enough for Barry to fish.

Feb fish mo month He rounded up his fishing gear, which consisted of several old cane poles, some tangled fishing line and rusty hooks, and two old steel casting rods that didn't work. He had rigged a device for electrocuting worms, a gadget that worked exceptionally well in bringing the worms to the surface. Barry threw all the equipment and gear in the back of the truck and headed off to the river. Naturally I went with him.

Always caught fish Barry proceeded to go fishing every single day for the next two weeks. As Bobbi would say, "Once that Barry makes up his mind about something, he sticks to it. Wish the hell the sonofabitch would make up his mind to work for a change!" The fishing ritual was always the same. The first stop was Tom's liquor store where I usually ended up contributing $1.34 for an eight-pack of Old German beer, then we would drive to the river and park at the edge of the bridge. Very excited on the way to the river, Barry would sing country ballads as loud as he could. After parking the truck, he would race down the embankment and very carefully bait the hooks, setting out four or five poles at fifteen-foot intervals. Then he would sit down on a rock, open a beer, and carefully watch each of the poles. I would be assigned one pole to watch. And always, *always,* Barry caught fish. Usually they were small catfish, about six or eight inches long; and on a good day he would come back with a bucketful.

One evening the next week when I went up to see the Shackelfords, things seemed in more disarray than usual. When I hollered upstairs, "Is anybody home?" nobody answered.

When I hollered again, Walt replied weakly, "Yeah, Joe, come on up."

Once at the top of the stairs, I found out everyone was home. Bobbi was sprawled out on one bed, Barry on the rollaway, Littlebit was asleep beside Bobbi, and Walt was sprawled out on his bed. I asked, "Afternoon nap time?" Bobbi just moaned.

Barry sat up on the bed and said, "She's sick, real sick."

"What's wrong?"

Bobbi said, "I don't know. I got this horrible headache, and I've been puking." She looked horrible.

After sitting there a few minutes, I asked if there was anything I could do. She said no. Barry then asked me if I wanted
to go fishing. Bobbi turned to Barry and said, "Barry, I'm
tired of you drinking downstairs with Mack and Kate. And
you ain't nothing but an ass-licker, going down there and
spending time with Mack and all that. Going down there and
lending him cigarettes and coming up and getting eggs and
being nice to him. Nothing but a common ass-licker. That's
all you are."

"Well, fuck you," said Barry.

"I bet you wish you could," replied Bobbi, managing a
faint smile.

Barry laughed. "Yeah, I guess so."

"Well, if you did, it would be the best piece of ass you ever
got."

Barry laughed again. "You're right there. Not a bad piece
of ass."

Chuckling, Bobbi said, "You all have a good time fishing,
honey. Have a real good time. Enjoy yourself."

When we got to the river, there were twenty or so people
fishing. All were black. We got our stuff out of the back of
the truck and wandered down the embankment. Since a
group of black men were fishing at Barry's favorite spot, we
went upstream a bit. We hadn't been there more than a few
minutes when the black guy across the river hollered, "Hey,
Barry." He had on a big straw hat and was fishing with a
woman. He took off his hat and waved.

Barry looked up attentively. "It's Jackie. Well I'll be
damned. Hiya, Jackie, how are you doing?"

"Just fine, just fine. Whoopee, I got one!"

"Thataway," yelled Barry, "thataway." Jackie pulled in a
catfish as Barry yelled, "He's a whopper! Goddamn channel
cat." The fish was about six inches long.

"You said it, he's a big one, ain't he?" Jackie yelled. "Hey
fellers, Barry's here!"

"Hiya, Barry," some other black guys hollered from down
the river, "how you doing?"

Barry yelled, "Just fine. Good to see you guys."

I asked, "Who the hell are they?"

"Oh, those guys? Well, that's Jack and some of Jack's buddies. Used to work with them. Used to work for Walt. He's a painter, too, and does some plastering. Also a friend of Bobbi's. He's one of Bobbi's oldest friends. And a helluva great guy. I mean to tell you, one hell of a great guy."

The conversation back and forth across the river continued throughout the afternoon. I asked Barry, "Is that Jack's wife he's fishing with?"

"Oh hell no. He don't got no wife; and if he did, he wouldn't bring her out here. He's a great guy. I mean, he's been in jail and all. He's had a pretty hard life. Runs a whore house. Maybe it's one of the girls he's got working for him he is fishing with. But let me tell you, you won't find any man better than Jackie. He's the finest."

While we were fishing, some of Jack's friends brought Barry a couple of beers. He thanked them. They would yell words of encouragement to Barry, which he would return enthusiastically. They weren't fishing too far away from us and pulled in, among other things, one shoe, one shirt, and one pair of pants. Barry thought this was hilarious. "I'd like a fifteen-inch tire, please," he hollered.

"We'll see if we can't get it for you. What size shoe do you wear? Too bad, this is a ten." There was nothing like fishing in the rivers around Washington.

On March 1, after Barry had been pursuing fishing avidly for almost two weeks, I got a call from Bobbi and asked her how Barry was doing. "Ah, he caught a few fish, caught a few. How many do you think he caught?"

I guessed, "Twenty-five . . . sixteen . . . eight . . . five . . ."

"Nope. You know what bothers me is his arm, under his arm. It looks like—well, the only thing I can think to describe it, and I'm telling it like it is, it looks like a woman's titty. It's pointed and bulges out. I don't know, I don't know what he's going to do. I don't know if it's a bad thing or not, but it sure as hell looks different. It's all red, and swollen, and as I say, it looks just like a woman's titty."

"Have you tried to get the doctor?"

"Oh yes, I've tried and tried, but I can't reach him. I don't know what to do."

"Well, if it breaks, or gets worse, why don't you go to the emergency room of the hospital?"

"I guess that's what we'll have to do. Of course, Barry, he don't want to go nowhere. All he can think of is fishing. How many fish do you think he caught?"

"I don't know. I give up."

"Guess."

"Okay. Thirty fish." I could hear Barry in the background. "How many did he say?"

"He caught forty-six fish!"

"How long was he out there?"

"Oh, a couple hours."

"Let me talk to Barry." Barry got on the phone. "You caught forty-six fish?"

"Hell yes, but it wasn't nothing. I'll tell you what was something, though. I had six fish on three poles all at the same time!" Barry used two hooks on each line.

"What about your arm?"

"Just like Bobbi says, it looks like a woman's titty. That's exactly what it looks like."

"Well, what are you going to do about it? If it gets worse, maybe you ought to go to the emergency room."

"Oh hell, it ain't going to get no worse. Anyway, I'm glad to see it happen. I'm glad to see it come to a head. It's about time anyway. You want to go fishing tomorrow? Me and Walt are going to go."

After March 1, when the weather turned bad, Barry eased off fishing. It was financial crisis time again. But on March 4 Walt's social security check came through. The welfare check was due the next day. After Walt received his check, I went with Bobbi and Barry to get it cashed. They both were in good spirits, since among other things it was the first time in two weeks that they had any cash on hand.

I rode with them in the old truck. It was raining hard, a cold icy rain. First, we went to Tom's liquor store to get it cashed, where we bought beer and cigarettes. Just as Barry was purchasing his Valley Forge beer, he looked up and remarked that his boss had a liquor bottle a lot bigger than the one on display in the store. "I bet that liquor bottle is five gallons. And it's full of liquor never been drunk. Yes sir, my boss is really something."

Bobbi said, "My foot. The hell with you! I've seen that liquor bottle and it's no bigger than that one right up there."

"Shit, it is too bigger. It's a lot damn bigger. It's twice as big, maybe three times."

"My ass it is."

They went on like this for a few moments before Barry turned to the liquor store salesman and asked, "How much does that thing hold up there?"

"One gallon."

"Well, they make bigger ones than that, don't they?"

"Not that I know of."

"You mean that's the biggest liquor bottle they make?"

"It's the biggest one as far as I know."

Bobbi said, "I told you so. Hot damn, let me have the money."

Barry said, "We ain't bet no money yet, but we will bet some. How much do you want to put on it?"

"Twenty-five dollars."

"All right, goddammit, we'll bet."

We walked out of the liquor store, Barry looking at the liquor bottle, shaking his head and saying, "Shit, I tell you what we'll bet. We'll bet twenty-five pieces of ass without you saying 'ouch' once. Haw-haw-haw."

"My ass you will."

"Well, how about a motel? And whoever loses pays for the room and the booze. Like to get me some Seagram's 7 and a couple of six-packs? Then we can really do it up right, huh, baby?"

"Yeah," said Bobbi, laughing. Then she turned to me and said, "We really love each other, Joe."

When we got back, Al was there with his new car. He had just purchased a 1963 Ford for sixty-five dollars—another one of Al's "good deals." Since the last two of Al's good deals weren't running, maybe he would have better luck with this one. Al was talking to Walt. Cindy was screaming, almost deliriously. Bobbi was calmly sitting on the bed, not paying too much attention to Cindy as she casually remarked to me that Cindy was having another fit. "She has these pretty much," she said. "There's not much you can do about it but let her cry. The reason she's crying now is 'cause she's afraid to go to the ear doctor tomorrow."

Barry went over to Cindy trying to calm her. "Now, sweet baby doll, it's going to be all right, sweet baby. Now, come on, honey, talk to Daddy."

"I don't want to talk to you. I don't want to go. Will you go, Daddy?"

Barry thought for a moment. "Yeah, I'll go."

"Well, what about Joe? Will he go? Will he go with me, too?"

"She wants you to go with her." I said I would. "We'll all go, all three of us. We'll all go with you to the doctor," said Barry.

She stopped screaming and, still sobbing a little, went over to the bed to sit down beside her mother. Walt pulled some cash out of his pocket and handed Cindy ten dollars. "Here, sweetie, here, take this. This will make you feel better." Cindy looked at the ten-dollar bill, crumpled it up in her fingers, unfolded it, then put it in her lap and quit crying. Bubba had wandered up by that time. Walt pulled out another ten dollars and gave it to Bubba.

"Thanks a lot, thanks a lot," said Bubba.

When Barry saw this, he turned to Bubba. "Well, what you going to do with it, Bubba?" His voice was belligerent.

"I don't know."

"Well, what did you do with the nine dollars you earned at the car wash this weekend?" he snarled.

"I spent it."

"Goddamn!" Barry's voice was becoming angrier. "I knew it, I knew it. You don't give a damn about nothing, you little punk." Bubba didn't say anything. "What did you spend it on?"

"Well, I had to buy my school lunch and some other stuff at school."

"Shit. Your granddad lent you some money last week, and you didn't pay him back. And now you're taking another ten dollars. What you going to do with that?"

"I'm going to buy me some new shoes."

"Some new shoes, shit!" His voice was getting louder. "You don't need any goddamn new shoes!"

"But I do need some new shoes. These are the only pair I've got," Bubba said defensively. He was wearing a pair of old boots.

"Well, why didn't you pay your granddaddy back when you earned that nine dollars, or why didn't you ask your mother or me if we needed the money? We ain't got no goddamn money in this house at all and you earned nine dollars, kept it for yourself, and spent it all on that shit. Goddamn, you sonofabitch."

Bubba still didn't say anything. Walt muttered something under his breath about not needing any new shoes. But Bubba was determined to get some new shoes.

Bobbi said, "Well, it's his money, and he can do with it what he wants to."

Barry said, "I know he can do what he wants to, goddammit, but here we are sitting here in the house not having a damn cent and that sonofabitch goes out and spends it on something for himself without asking anybody else around here if they needed the money—nobody. That's how much he cares about us."

Since Cindy had it in her mind to buy some new shoes, too, Bobbi agreed that she could, that she would take the children to Jupiter Discount Store and buy them all new shoes, or whatever they wanted. Billy said he wanted a game and Littlebit said he wanted a truck. "Okay, I'll get everybody what they want. But we don't know how we're going to get there. Al?" Al agreed to give them a ride.

While we were waiting for Al, Bubba decided to occupy his time with his tape recorder. He brought it into the kitchen, where Barry and I were. Barry turned to Bubba: "Well, what are you going to do with that tape recorder?"

"The mike's busted and I got to get it fixed."

"Well, where are you going to get it fixed?"

"I don't know."

"You got any money to get it fixed?"

"Nope."

"Goddamn, you do. What about the money your grand-daddy just gave you?"

"I'm going to use that to buy me some shoes."

"Shit. You don't give a damn about that tape recorder. That's what we gave you for Christmas, and you don't give a damn about it."

"I do. That's why I want to get it fixed."

"Shit, if you wanted to get it fixed, you'd get it fixed right now."

"I could fix it if I had a soldering iron, but I don't have one."

I suggested we take it over to the TV repair shop across the street to see if they could fix it. With some reluctance, Barry agreed to go with us. Barry walked in and said, "You got a soldering iron? Want to get this mike fixed."

"I'm sorry, we don't fix tape recorders," the man said, "especially not the small Japanese ones." Barry then proceeded to argue with the man, who became very angry after a few of Barry's comments, saying, "I told you once, we don't fix these things." Then he called the owner of the store out, saying that Barry was trying to intimidate him into fixing the tape recorder. The man took a look at the recorder and said that it couldn't be fixed, that a new mike would have to be purchased, and that you could buy one for $1.50. Barry then said he knew where a new mike could be bought, naming the store where they had purchased the recorder. Bubba said, "We didn't purchase the tape recorder there."

Barry shook his head, thanked the man, and as soon as we got out the door, looked at Bubba and said, "Goddammit, don't you ever correct me again like that in front of somebody else. You made a fool of me. I don't want you to ever do that again."

"But we didn't buy the thing there."

"I don't give a damn. Don't you ever correct me in front of somebody else like that, okay?"

"Okay."

We went to the liquor store to get some beer, and it was about five when we returned. I went back in the kitchen and waited to see who was going to Jupiter. Barry finished off a beer, then turned to Bubba. "Goddammit, Bubba, what are you going to get when you get to Jupiter's?"

"I told you I'm going to get some new shoes."

"Shit, you don't need any goddamn new shoes." He was shouting this time. To protect himself, Bubba shrugged his shoulders and growled under his breath, mimicking Barry. Barry then screamed, "Don't you growl at me! Don't you try to make fun of me, you little punk. You no-good goddamn punk! You ain't worth shit." Barry's fists were clenched; his face was tight with rage. "I'm going to kill your ass!" He charged toward Bubba, who turned to his side and tightened his muscles, as if preparing himself for Barry's blow. Something held Barry back; he didn't hit him.

Bobbi entered the room and said, "Okay, Barry, it's Bubba's money. If you don't like the way he spends it, that's too bad. Maybe I don't like it either, but it's his money, he earned it."

"I know it's his goddamn money, but we've supported him. We buy his clothes, we buy his food, we buy his shoes, we buy everything for him. And he don't ever thank us. Shit, when he makes his money he just keeps it for himself and goes off and spends it for himself and doesn't think about us. I think that's some punk, some no-good goddamn punk. I'm really going to get that sonofabitch someday." Bubba still didn't say anything. With watery eyes he turned around and left the room.

Then Cindy came in skipping about and started talking to Barry. "You know where my teacher come from. Her come from Florida."

"Don't say that. Don't say *her* come from Florida; say *she* come from Florida."

"Well, my teacher, her come from—"

"Not that way. It's not *her* come, it's *she* come."

"My teacher . . ." Cindy became very self-conscious and started stuttering. "My teacher, er . . . er . . . my teacher . . ."

Bobbi said, "Look, Barry, let her talk the way she wants to."

"Goddammit, it's not *her* come, it's *she* come from Florida."

Bobbi sighed, rather disgustedly, and said, "Barry, let her talk the way she wants to."

"Shit," said Barry, taking another swig of his beer.

By that time Bobbi had been able to gather up the children, get them dressed and ready to go to Jupiter. Everyone was going but Billy, who had been sick now for over a week with a bad cold and a cough. It was very quiet after everyone had left. Walt came in, and he, Barry, and I chatted for a few minutes, then I departed.

The next day was Cindy's visit to the hearing specialist at the public health clinic. As we had promised, Barry and I accompanied Bobbi and Cindy to the county hospital. While we were sitting in the lobby, Barry did some girl-watching, making comments like, "Man, she's got some nice hind parts. . . . Baby, you wouldn't want to do nothing, would you?"

Bobbi tried to look disgusted whenever he would make a comment. Twice Cindy started talking back to Barry, saying, "You act so dumb, you act so silly, why did you come?" This really hurt Barry. He became quiet and sullen and had a very dejected look on his face.

Bobbi said, "You know, when we were being brought up, kids didn't treat their parents the way that these kids now do. It's terrible the way some show no respect for their elders. I know what my mother would have done if I'd talked back like Cindy is talking now. And I bet yours would have done the same thing, wouldn't she?"

I asked, "Why do you think it is?"

"It's these schools. Cindy was okay before she went to school. Now that she's been to school for a year, she just treats us like she didn't have no respect for us—I don't know. It's the lack of discipline for one thing, and I guess it's some of the other kids, too. They come from families that don't teach no respect, families where there is a bad home life—you know. She hears a lot of bad words. Yep, take Cindy's friend Billy-

John, you know how he is. He goes around saying those words all the time. He'd come up here and say them but Barry won't let him. Barry will slap him down if he comes. But he goes home and talks like that and his daddy, Big John, he don't do nothing. It's bad families, that's what it is, families that just don't bring their kids up right, don't show them discipline."

Barry then said, "Okay, Cindy, I don't want to hear nothing more, or I'm really going to get mad at you." When Cindy talked back to Barry twice more, he didn't say anything. He just sat there with a sick, sullen look on his face.

Bobbi said, "You know, I think there's another thing, too, about these schools. I think when they started taking prayers out of the schools—that was one of the first things that went wrong. I don't know, there's just something about it. When you don't have a prayer in the school, how can you expect your children to be brought up right, you know what I mean? It's taking the prayers out, that's one of the bad things about our schools."

Cindy was then called on to go into the doctor's office, and Barry and Bobbi went with her. I stayed out, thinking three would be too many. Half an hour later, when they returned, all three were very upset. The doctor told them that Cindy's ear problem was very serious and that she should be operated on as quickly as possible. She had lost 75 per cent of her hearing in one ear and 25 per cent in the other due to a very serious infection. The doctor said the infection was probably caused by allergy, perhaps asthma. He assured them that there was a high likelihood of success in such an ear operation, although it was extremely delicate and took highly skilled surgeons to do it. Consequently, she would have to go to Johns Hopkins in Baltimore; and it would probably not be until April before an opportunity for such an operation was available. Barry said the doctor tried to explain exactly what they would do. Such an operation might allow her to regain most of her hearing; but if she did not have the operation, she would surely go deaf within a few years.

On the way back Barry said that although all along he thought Cindy had been faking it, now he realized that she had a hearing problem after all. He didn't understand all the doctor had told Cindy, but he was convinced they were doing the right thing to have her operated on.

When we returned, we checked the mail to find no welfare check. This was not unusual since the check invariably was sent to the old address on Clay Street. At the time, therefore, Bobbi only sighed and commented, "Guess I'll be on the goddamned phone again all day tomorrow trying to get through to the welfare." She let it go at that.

The next day, however, Bobbi called and was very upset. I asked if she had received the welfare check.

"We received Bubba's check, for sixty dollars, but that was all. There wasn't no more check. I'm really upset. I'm really mad, too, Joe. I'm really, really mad."

"What happened?"

"Well, when there wasn't no check we called the welfare department. I called my case worker and asked her what happened. She said we weren't supposed to get no more check because there weren't any medical papers filled out for Barry. I told her that we had sent in medical papers. We sent them in last month. She said there weren't any in the file."

I told Bobbi I remembered her filling out the papers; in fact, I filled them out for her, and I mailed the letter myself.

"That's right," she said, "we sent it in a month ago, and it said Barry was going to be sick for at least another month. Well, they said they lost the papers, or they couldn't find them, and it wasn't the first time either. They have been known to lose medical papers before. Well, let me tell you, I'm up against something awful. We don't have no food stamps. I've got two hundred forty dollars' worth of bills to pay right away, and the rent's due, the insurance is due, electric bill, heat bill, God knows what else. I can't pay any of it, and I can't get any food stamps and we don't have any food."

I said, "Well, you do have some fish," trying to make a bad joke.

Bobbi laughed. "That's what everybody tells me. I got fish, but I can't stand fish!"

I asked, "What are you going to do?"

"I've been trying to get the welfare department all day, ever since I found out that we didn't get no check. I called

and called and called and the line was busy. Or I called and
nobody answered the phone. It must have rang fifty times, so
I got fed up and I went down there and that's when I found
out that Barry didn't have no check. So I talked to my caseworker. She went searching around, looked everywhere, and
couldn't find any medical records. So I said, 'Look, I can prove
to you that Barry is sick, has been sick, and can't work. All
you have to do is call Dr. Di Banca. He's the one that signed
the medical file; he's the one that sent it in. If you call him,
he'll tell you that my husband is sick and can't work.' " Bobbi
said the caseworker agreed; but when she called and asked to
speak to Dr. Di Banca, the receptionist said he wasn't there.
Then the caseworker asked if Barry Shackelford was capable
of working. The receptionist told her Barry Shackelford could
start to work Monday. "That's what she said, Joe, that Barry
can start to work on Monday! And it said right there on that
medical record that Barry was going to be out for one more
month." Bobbi was shouting. "One month, and that paper
was filed something like February fifteenth, right? So that
means Barry's not supposed to work until the middle of
March, right? Well, then, tell me this, goddammit, why in
heaven's name did that receptionist tell that caseworker that
Barry could start to work Monday? Why, tell me that, why?
What right did she have to do that? Why did she do it?"

I replied, "She had no right to diagnose what's wrong with
Barry. She's not the doctor."

"Goddamn sonofabitch, that's what I say! That bitch is
really screwing us to the wall. And I'll tell you something.
That Dr. Di Banca is going to hear about this. She can't say
something like that. She can't do that to us. I'm going to tell
Dr. Di Banca about her and put it to him just like it is, that's
what I'm going to do."

"In the meantime," I asked, "how are you going to get by?"

"Well, the caseworker, she must be thinking I was trying to
put something over on her. So she said that if Barry is going
to work, I don't receive any food stamps or any other assistance. I got real desperate then. I told her we had to have the
money, that my husband couldn't work, regardless of what
that goddamn receptionist said, and that we had to have some

kind of help. I then told her that there was another doctor,
Dr. Cantor, who had operated on Barry, and Barry was supposed to see him this week but hadn't because Dr. Cantor had
been busy both times we'd been there. The caseworker told
me that there was a chance of Barry still getting a check if I
could get Dr. Cantor to fill out a form and return it first thing
Monday morning. So I called up Dr. Cantor right away. He
said that he'd been wanting to see Barry anyway and that we
should come in tomorrow around noon. So Barry and I are
going to the hospital tomorrow to see Dr. Cantor. I'm hoping
he'll take a look at Barry and fill out the form and then I'll
go over to the welfare department first thing Monday, and
they may, or may not, be able to help me.

"It ain't right, it just ain't right. It ain't right to treat us this
way. Call up and they don't answer; call up and it's busy; go
down and talk to your caseworker—and I went back and got
another caseworker. I don't know what the hell happened to
my first caseworker. She told me she didn't know anything
about it. I mean, I'm just sick of it, it's driving me nuts. I don't
know what we're going to do. Shit, it just makes you want to
puke. Just today I heard on the radio they're trying to do away
with this, this help that Barry got. They're trying to do away
with the money you get when your husband's done left and
you've got a lot of kids to support. I heard that on the radio."

"Who is trying to do it?"

"Nixon, that sonofabitch. He's the one. He's trying to take
away everything. I tell you, it's some goddamn world we live
in, some goddamn world. Now they're trying to take away
everything and there ain't a hell of a lot to take away. Goddamn world we live in."

The next day Dr. Cantor examined Barry and signed the
necessary forms saying he would not be able to work until
April 1. Bobbi took the forms to the welfare department, and
the following Monday, March 8, she was able to pick up her
check. Dr. Cantor said Barry's arm seemed to be coming along
all right.

I went with Bobbi to pick up her check Monday. Standing
in line for food stamps, she expressed very strong negative
feelings about Barry. She started off by saying she was fed

up. "Joe, I've had it. I've really lost patience with Barry. He's really gone too far this time. He's been drunk since Friday. He's been picking on Bubba and all the kids. He's been picking on me. He's been pushing Bubba around and he's been drinking something awful. I'm really worn out. I've lost my patience, I've had it.

"It started Friday afternoon when he and Mack started drinking and haven't quit. In fact, he kept us up last night. Three in the morning. Drinking, hollering, pushing the kids around, looking at TV. Wouldn't let nobody go to sleep. When he's drunk, he's just a different person. He's the most horrible sonofabitch you'll ever want to see. And I tell you, I just can't stand it no more. I'm thinking about leaving. I'm sure enough thinking about leaving. Pack up the kids and taking off somewhere as far as hell so he can't find us. The only reason I stay around now is for the school for the kids and because of Daddy. And because I'm afraid Barry would find us. If that time comes when I can get out of here, leave, I'm going to do it. 'Cause I tell you, Joe, it's just not right. I just can't stand it any longer. He don't want to work. He's not going to work. And the way he treats Bubba, that's the worst. I'm afraid one day he'll push Bubba too far, and Bubba will kill him. I just dread the day when that happens, though I must admit that we'd probably all be better off if he was dead. I know it sounds like a horrible thing to say; but when he was there in the hospital, with the thing under his arm, if he'd gone on and died we'd probably all be better off than we are now. He's drinking away what little money we got. Bubba went out and earned twenty-five dollars this weekend at the car wash. And of course Barry wanted it. That's why he was pushing him around. He doesn't like it 'cause Bubba makes money and wants to go out and buy himself a new jacket and some new clothes. He doesn't think Bubba ought to do that.

"Oh, I tell you I'm just fed up. I'm worn out plumb through. I want to leave. If there was just somewhere to go. You ask me why I don't go on in the hospital and have my hysterectomy when my doctors tell me I should, when I'm feeling sicker and sicker every day, you ask me why I don't go in?" Bobbi stared at me in the eyes and said bitterly: "I'll tell you why I don't go in the hospital. I don't go because I don't trust Barry Shackelford, my husband, with my children. I do not trust him. I don't know what he would do with those children. I simply don't trust him. There's no love no more, there's no love and there's not even any respect. I don't respect him any more. I'm sick of him. I can't take him no more!

"There's a lot you don't know about. Like last summer. When Barry starts drinking, you just don't know what he'll do. He called Cindy into his room. She'd been lying there with her granddaddy, asleep. Barry had been asleep. He woke up, he'd been drinking, he was mad. He called Cindy into his room and then he beat her. Whacked her across the face and beat her up pretty bad, for no reason. He said she woke him up, pulled his hair. But that's not true. She'll tell you; Daddy will tell you; and I'll tell you. She was asleep there beside him. Beat her up for no reason. He hit Bubba in the stomach yesterday, pretty damn hard and for no reason. Bubba didn't hit back. One of these days he will.

"I tell you, if my mother was still alive, she would have killed Barry. That's why she died. I'm sure of it. The good Lord was keeping her from doing something she didn't have no business doing. But she wouldn't put up with that shit. The way he acts. He won't let me work. He don't want Bubba to work. I would go out and be making good money, but he doesn't want me to. He wants to be the one who supports the family, who makes all the money, and he'd rather us live in goddamn filth and the kids go without any clothes on their backs and we not eat, before I go out and work. He wants to be the big worker, but hell, look what he's doing. He ain't working. He don't want to work. I don't think he's capable of putting in a good day's work. I just don't think so.

"He's like Dr. Jekyll and Mr. Hyde. He's been drinking too much lately and I can't stand it. He needs to see a psychiatrist. I've been told that. I was told that this summer after he got beat up and they took him in the emergency ward in the hospital. But hell, he won't go. He's too damned stubborn. He wouldn't go to a psychiatrist. But he damn sure as hell needs to go to one. Let me tell you, the kids hate him, Joe. Cindy, she hates his guts. You heard her say it: 'Mommy, we need a new daddy. It's time to get us a new daddy.' Well, Barry laughs about it, but I know and he knows deep down inside that she's dead serious. She hates his guts, and Bubba hates his guts, and now Billy and Littlebit, they're beginning to hate his guts. But they're too small really to know what's happening. But they understand. They realize what kind of guy he is. Dr. Di Banca knows it, too, 'cause Dr. Di Banca had to see me just before I had Cindy. That was when Barry beat me up, beat me up real bad. And Dr. Di Banca knows it, he knows Barry beat me up like that. That's why I think he didn't go to the hospital to see Barry that much. I just don't think he cares that much about Barry since he knows what Barry's done to me."

We finally got up to the window and purchased Bobbi's stamps and went back to her house where we had the usual cup of coffee. Barry was still asleep. The night before he had threatened Bobbi that if she woke him up before he was ready to get up, he would beat her. So Bobbi was very careful to leave that morning without disturbing him. After we had been there about fifteen minutes, he began to stir. Bobbi made the comment, "The old sothead, the old devil, is getting up. It's about goddamned time." Barry got up slowly, came in the room, grunted a couple of times, then went in the bathroom. Bobbi sat there scowling. Barry came back a few minutes later, and grinning sheepishly, he opened the icebox and pulled out a beer.

Bobbi said angrily, "You aren't going to start it again this early, are you?"

"Just one, Bobbi, just going to have this one."

"You goddamn sot drunk! When are you going to sober up, Barry? When are you going to quit acting like such a goddamn shit?"

Barry laughed nervously and took a gulp of beer. He said, "Why don't you kiss my ass."

" 'Cause your ass is everywhere, and I'm sick of it!"

Walt came in about this time and started frying salted herring. Bobbi said, "I'm sick of you, Barry. I'm really sick.

When are you going to do something about yourself? Now
Joe's here, and I guess I've been running my big mouth, but
I told him what you've been up to, and he said he'd like to
go with you to the AA when you're ready to go."

Barry paused, then startled everyone by saying, "Okay,
Bobbi, I'll go to the next meeting they have."

"You will?" Bobbi rushed up and hugged Barry and kissed
him. Her face brightened for the first time in days.

"Yeah, I will. You just call up and find out when it is and
then we'll go."

Bobbi sighed and then looked at me and said, "Well, I'll
be, I can't believe it." She called and found out that the next
AA meeting was to be Wednesday evening, in two days.

Two days later, I called Bobbi early in the morning to see
how Barry was doing. She said that he had gone to work
yesterday for a few hours and had managed to finish painting
the woodwork, but he had about one full day's work left to do
before he would finish up the job he started before Christmas.
Instead of working today he went to help Al finish up a job
and was not back yet.

Around five in the afternoon, when Bobbi called back, she
was very discouraged. Barry had returned about two but was
already pretty drunk. He had started out drinking beer that
morning, but one of the guys who was working with Al had
some whiskey. "I don't think Barry's going to want to go tonight. He's really pretty drunk now. He's already picked on
Bubba, told him to get out of the house, yelled and screamed
at him. He's cussed at me, he's cussed at all the kids. He's
hollered and screamed and cussed some more. I tell you, I'm
so disgusted I don't know what I'm going to do. I mean, I'm
so disgusted. . . . If I thought rat poison would do any good,
I'd put some in his food right now, that no good lousy sonofabitch. You know," she said, "you can shit on me and rub it
in, that's all right. I'll stand up and take some more. I've been
shit on many a time in my life and I'll be shit on again. But
when you start giving my children a hard time, when you
start treating them like shit when they ain't done nothing and
it's not their fault, then that's another matter. And that's why
I'm mad at Barry right now. The way he's treating my chil-

dren, it just ain't right. They didn't ask to be brought into this world. They didn't ask for what they are getting, and look at what Barry is doing to them."

In the middle of the conversation Barry returned from downstairs and I heard him speak in a loud voice, "I want the keys to the truck."

"Well, you aren't going to have the keys to the truck."

"I ain't going to go nowhere. I'm just going to sit out in the cab of the truck and have a few beers with Mack." Barry's speech was slurred and he spoke with a stammer, as he always did when he was drunk.

"Well, you ain't going to have them, because the last time you said that you took the truck and left and went fishing, and I needed the truck that afternoon. I ain't going to let you have the keys."

Barry raised his voice. "I want the goddamn keys."

"Well, you can't have them. You just can't have them. I ain't letting you have them."

"Shit, Bobbi, goddammit, give me the keys!"

Barry was screaming now, and Bobbi screamed back, "No!"

Once more Barry screamed, louder than before, "I want the goddamn keys and I want them now or . . ." Bobbi gave him the keys. Not saying anything else, he went downstairs.

"You see, Joe, see what I'm putting up with? He's going to go down to the truck, drive it around, smashed, roaring drunk like he is, without a driver's license, probably will wreck the goddamn truck and where is that going to leave us? Or me? 'Cause the car is in my name, and it's my insurance he's driving under. Nobody will have a license if he has a wreck." At that point one of the children hollered, "Daddy's getting in the car and leaving." Bobbi didn't say anything.

Then she said, "I don't think he'll want to go to the AA meeting tonight, Joe. I could have told you this would happen. When the time comes to do something like this, he can never go through with it. I might have known, I might have known."

After Bobbi hung up, I recalled a comment she made earlier that day. "You know, Joe, there ought to be a law, there ought to be a law making people go to an alcoholic program, or the AA, or something like that. It just ain't right to let somebody do what Barry is doing to us. They ought to make them go to a program which will do something for them."

I gave up on the idea of going out that evening. However, about seven-fifteen Barry called to ask if I was still ready to go with him. I said yes, I was, but I wasn't sure he was going.

"You weren't sure I'm going? Hell, I said I was going, didn't I? Goddamn yes, I'm going! I'm going to pick you up at seven-thirty. You'd better be ready." Barry sounded very enthusiastic over the phone, though his speech was slurred.

About seven forty-five Barry and Bobbi arrived. The meeting we were to attend was described to me by Bobbi as an AA meeting. When we got there I realized it was not an AA meeting at all, but a part of the county parole program. All the people at the meeting had been arrested for alcohol-related offenses. All the men were on parole, and part of their parole required them to attend these meetings. This was how Barry got involved: When he was on parole several years before, he had to attend these meetings for eighteen months. That was how he knew Mr. Clark, the supervisor of the parole program in the county, who was speaking when we entered.

The meeting was held in a Methodist church. We got there a little late. Barry was very nervous. As we entered the building, he was muttering under his breath, "Goddamn, it's been a long time. Goddamn, it's been a hell of a long time. Shit, I don't know if I want to go in there or not."

Bobbi said, "Come on, Barry, let's go. You've got to do it sometime."

"I know, but before I was forced to do it. Now I'm doing it on my own free will." He turned to me and said, "You know, this ain't so much for me, Joe, as it is for you. I want you to see what it's like and maybe bring your tape recorder and record some. It's not so much for me. I don't think it's going to help me none. But it will be good for your study."

The church auditorium, medium-sized, was completely full. Since there were not enough chairs, a few people were standing in the back. About one hundred people were there, mostly young men Barry's age. Many had on work jackets or work clothes. Many had slicked-down hair and ducktails. Everyone was quiet as Mr. Clark talked. As the three of us entered the room, Mr. Clark looked at us and exclaimed, "Why, hello, Barry, welcome back. It's been a long time."

Barry stood in the back of the room and said, "Mr. Clark, thank you, Mr. Clark. I know it's been a long time, but it's good to be back."

"Have a seat, Barry. They're getting some more chairs out now."

Somebody brought out a few more chairs and the three of us sat down in the back row. Mr. Clark continued talking. He was a pudgy gentleman in his late forties, had a receding hairline, and was an articulate speaker. He used no notes and was talking about what it meant to be an alcoholic. "How many of you feel like I felt this afternoon?" he asked. "It had been a hard day at work, nothing had gone right; it got off to a bad start when my wife growled at me over the breakfast table. Got back home, the cat had had a litter of kittens, the kids had done badly in school, and my mother-in-law was giving me hell. I thought to myself, what a rotten day, nobody cares! How many of you felt this way?" He paused as various men nodded. "But there's one thing you need to know: Somebody cares."

Before Mr. Clark could go any further, Barry stood up and said, "Mr. Clark, I know, I know somebody cares. And I want you to meet two people here with me tonight. My wife, Bobbi, she came with me, she cares; and he's my friend, Joe. And he wants to say a few words. Stand up, Joe." Barry pulled me by the arm out of my chair and nudged me out in the aisle. "Now, Joe, say—tell them a few things, Joe, tell them." It was obvious to everyone in the room that Barry was very drunk and not in control of what he was doing. Everybody turned around and stared at us. Barry stood up and stammered, "I know—I know how much you care."

Mr. Clark responded firmly, "That's all right, Barry. I know you know, and it's good to have you back. But *I'm* talking tonight, so just sit down and let me talk. Tonight is my turn, you'll get your chance, and I'll meet your friend after the meeting."

Barry said, "But I want to talk! I want to talk. Let me have the microphone. I want to tell people what it's like to be an alcoholic."

"Not now, Barry. This is not the time nor the place. Later."

"But I want to talk!" Barry was shouting.

"Barry, sit down!" Bobbi whispered. "Sit down, Barry, sit down." Barry sat down.

There was some murmuring throughout the room as people stared at us, but Mr. Clark started going again, talking about what it meant to be in the particular program, what the state was trying to do for these people, who had committed various offenses that had to do with being drunk or being an alcoholic. "I want everyone in the room who is an alcoholic to stand up." Fifteen people, including Barry, stood. "Thank you. Now, there are fifteen people in this room who are being honest, but there are a lot more of you who aren't. You may not call yourself an alcoholic. You may call yourself a beer hog. Most of you drink beer. It doesn't make any difference. . . . I tell you right now, ninety per cent of you are here right now because you have an inferiority complex, because you're using alcohol to escape. That's why you are here, because you just can't stand the world unless you've got a crutch to help you through. But the crutch that you're using is destroying your life and making things worse than they were before."

Barry said, "That's right, that's right."

Bobbi whispered, "No, Barry, be quiet."

Louder, Barry said, "That's right, Mr. Clark. Let me get up there and talk. I want to tell it like it is."

Mr. Clark told Barry what he had said before: "Please, Barry, not here." Then he went on to outline the main elements of the state rehabilitation program for alcoholics.

Barry interrupted several times during the rest of Mr. Clark's speech. Each time Bobbi would say, "Quiet, quiet, please, Barry, please," trying to keep him from disrupting the meeting.

At one point Clark said, "You know, a lot of you guys,

especially the ones out there who hit your old lady, tell me
your wife is part of your problem, and I know it's true. In
fact, I told one lady, 'If I was married to you, I'd be an
alcoholic, too.' I know the old lady is very much involved in
all your problems, that's why we'd like to have your wives
come here this evening. We've straightened out many an
alcoholic only to see him start back again on the bottle when
he gets home."

Barry said, "Amen. That's the goddamned truth. My wife's
right here now, trying to tell me to shut up." Everyone looked
around and stared at Bobbi. "She's right here trying to tell
me to shut up. It's not right for her to tell me to shut up. I'm
going to talk and tell it like it is. I'm going to tell you what it's
like to be an alcoholic."

People continued staring at Barry as he stood there, sway-
ing back and forth. I stared at the floor, but managed to notice Bobbi, who was looking down in her lap with her fists
clinched and had a very tight expression on her lips. Mr.
Clark said, "For the last time, Barry. No, no more. This is the
time for me to talk, not you! No more!"

"Well, I was just trying, I was just trying. No offense, Mr.
Clark, sir. I'm sorry, no offense."

After the meeting broke up, Bobbi and Barry went forward
to talk to Mr. Clark. Barry stayed back and said, "You know,
maybe I shouldn't have said what I said at the meeting. In
fact, I'm sort of embarrassed to go up and talk to Mr. Clark
now. I don't know what he's going to think of me." Barry
went up anyway and I followed.

Clark extended a hand and said, "Hello, Barry, how are
you?"

"I'm not too good, Mr. Clark. I've slipped down again. I've
slipped downhill."

"I know, Barry, and you know you've broken one of the
big rules, don't you?"

"Yeah, yeah."

"That rule is, you are not supposed to drink before you
come here, Barry. It is not right for you to do this. And I want
you to promise me one thing. Don't ever come back to one of

these meetings if you are drunk. Don't ever do it again, Barry. Is that clear?"

"Er . . . yes, sir, Mr. Clark, yes, sir, yes, sir. I'm real sorry, Mr. Clark. I know I shouldn't of done it. I know I shouldn't of done it."

"That's right, Barry. You shouldn't have. If you want to help yourself and get help, you've got to follow the few basic rules. One of them is, don't come to one of these meetings drunk."

"Yes, sir, yes, sir."

Then he asked Barry, "How's your house? Have you worked out that problem you had a while back?"

"Oh, that problem, with the shingles? Yeah, we worked that out, but we lost our house."

Bobbi said, "That's right. We lost our house."

"I'm really sorry to hear that."

Bobbi said, "We live in an apartment now, but it's not like living in your own house."

We left the meeting and went out to the truck. On the way out, Barry said, "You know, I think I blew it. I don't think I should have talked out like I did in the meeting. I'm supposed to set an example for these guys, but that ain't much of an example, is it?"

Bobbi said, "It sure ain't."

"Oh God, oh God, I really blew it. Oh shit. I did the wrong thing. I went and done the wrong thing." Barry broke down and started crying. "I went and done the wrong thing," he muttered between sobs. "Oh God, oh God."

Bobbi and I went to the truck and got in, but Barry kept walking. Bobbi said sympathetically, "Hey, B., the truck's back here." Barry didn't seem to hear us. He just kept crying, walking forward. "Come on, B., the truck's back here." He paused in the middle of the road, then turned around and slowly walked back to the truck. On the way home, no one said anything.

Just as we got to my house, Barry said, "Joe, you going to come back with me next week?"

"I will if you want me to."

"I do. I want to go back."

I said, "But there's one thing—if you're going to go back to those meetings, Barry, I'm not going to go with you unless you are stone sober. I won't go if you're drunk."

"Well, goddamn, you sonofabitch. That ain't worth shit. You want to help me or not? You have just gone and blown it, buddy, you have just gone and blown it, 'cause I ain't going back."

I shrugged my shoulders as I got out and said, "Well, that's the way it is, Barry. You heard what Mr. Clark said."

"Well shit."

As they left I heard him mention to Bobbi, "You know, I know I done wrong. I know I shouldn't of opened my mouth like that; I probably shouldn't of come. And I know what he said was right. But what I got to do the first thing I get home, I'm going to open me a beer." They drove away.

Barry went to meeting and made a scene of himself then he felt guilty and cried.

4

Spring

The next week, on March 11, Barry got a call from his boss, Milton Goldstein, informing Barry that his vacation was over. Goldstein said he had something for Barry to do and that if he did not get started this week he need not ask for any more work to do. "In other words," said Barry, "if I don't get my ass in gear, I'm fired."

So Barry started back to work. Goldstein was in the business of buying old houses, usually in the ghetto, superficially fixing them up, and selling them to blacks. Barry not only painted but did papering, plastering, and some carpentry as well. I went to work with Barry several days the next few weeks and was quite impressed with his speed and efficiency. Bobbi told me before we left, "Barry is a damn good worker when he works. He is so good, in fact, that's why Milton puts up with his drinking. If Barry wasn't a good worker, he sure as hell couldn't get away with carrying on the way he does."

The problem was, there were too many things to keep Barry from getting started. Alcohol and bad health were, of course, the primary deterrents; but there was also the truck. Over the year Barry must have missed several weeks' work because of problems with the truck.

He worked hard for the first three days of the week; but on Thursday when I showed up at eight-thirty, he warned me we might have some truck problems. At this early hour Barry and Bubba were already going at each other. Bubba had borrowed a can of paint to paint the door to his room. Unfortunately, some clothes were hanging next to the door; and when the door was opened, it had brushed against the clothes. Barry was furious. He was shouting, "Goddammit, you sonofabitch bastard! Bubba, you dumb shit, you stupid motherfucker, I'm going to beat your ass."

"But Daddy, I couldn't help it. You said I could borrow the paint."

"Borrow the paint! Goddammit, you done got paint every-where. You got paint on your mother's coat, you got paint on my clothes. You stupid shit, you dumb, stupid shit."

When I got to the top of the stairs, Bubba had a bewildered look on his face and was standing in the hall. Barry was back in the bedroom stomping around. The argument was resolved only because Bubba left the house.

Bobbi was sitting on Walt's bed, and Walt was at his usual place by the window. Al was in the room sitting by the door. They continued discussing the catastrophe of Bubba and the paint. Bobbi was also put out at Bubba, but not as angry as Barry. I didn't say anything for a few minutes, trying not to get involved in a family argument. Bobbi said, "Poor Bubba, he just can't do anything right. I'm afraid he's going to get suspended from school for acting up in class; and when he does, Barry and I are going to have to appear before the Board of Education."

I asked, "Why is that?"

Walt responded, "Because he ain't been brought up right, that's why."

Bobbi said, "Well, that's the way it always is. When a per-son gets suspended, the parents have to appear before the Board of Education. And let me tell you, if that ain't going to be some shit. When I get there in front of the Board of Education, I tell you what I'm going to ask them. I'm going to ask them why they let girls and boys kiss and play games and make all kind of noise in the sixth grade. They can't con-trol those kids. I'm going to ask why they allow something like that to go on at the county schools. That's what I'm go-ing to ask. I tell you, it's not Bubba. It's everybody else just as much as Bubba that's raising hell in that classroom. That teacher can't control those kids. She's no good. You just have to go there to see it. It's lousy, it's no good, it's just not the way a school ought to be. There's no discipline in that school."

Al said, "That's right. There's no discipline any more in school. Now, when I was in school, let me tell you—the male teachers, they'd kick your ass, and the female teachers, they'd whop your knuckles with a ruler. They are too soft nowadays. They don't hit the kids any more. No wonder there ain't no discipline in those schools. . . ."

Barry, who wasn't paying much attention to the conversation in Walt's room, was busy collecting paint cans and other tools for painting. When I asked if I could help, he repeated, "We might have some trouble starting the truck, but other than that we'll be okay." All three of us went downstairs into the back yard and put the paint and tools into the truck. Barry got in and got ready to start the truck. He said, "Hold your breath," as he got in the cab and turned on the starter. Nothing happened.

"Goddammit, goddammit, sonofabitch, I'm goddamned sick of this shit! I just put in a new starter on the goddamn truck, and new generator on the goddamn truck, a new voltage relay on the goddamn truck. Shit, what could be wrong with it? I bought B.J.'s car for a goddamn thirty dollars and transferred all those other parts. And I know I got everything fixed all right. Why won't the sonofabitch start, for God's sake?"

He got out and looked at the motor. Al got out and looked at the motor. I got out and looked at the motor. Al suggested it might have something to do with the booster. Barry nodded, "That must be it." So he got down on the truck and began unscrewing a small part, which he called a booster. It took about an hour to transfer the booster from B.J.'s car. Finally it was completed and Barry was ready to start the truck again. Nothing happened.

"Goddammit, sonofabitch, shit! I can't understand this."

Al said, "Must be the starter."

"Starter, hell. I just put in a new starter in the goddamn truck."

"Maybe the one you put in ain't worth shit."

"Well, let me see the old starter." So Barry and Al pulled out the old starter that had just come out of the truck and tested it with a battery. It worked fine.

Al laughed, "See, the starter works okay. You took out a good starter and put in a bad one."

"That sonofabitch B.J.! But how did *he* start the damn car?"

"I don't know, but I remember he had to rock it back and forth."

"That's right. Well, let's try rocking the sonofabitch."

We rocked the truck and got a little action out of the starter. It turned over a couple of times but not enough to start. We rocked it a couple more times and got a little more action, but still not enough to start the truck. Barry said, "Well, I think I understand what's wrong with it now. Our starter works partaway and his starter works partaway. So if we take off the good part and put it with the good part of ours, we'll have a good starter."

"Right," said Al.

Barry took out the starter and put it beside the original one; then he took out the top part of the starter, the Bendix, which Barry was convinced was bad on his but good on B.J.'s, and put it with the good bottom part. This all took about an hour. Barry got in the cab and tried to start it up. Nothing happened.

"Well, ain't that some shit! Goddamn, sonofabitch, this pisses me off."

Al mumbled, "Me too."

By this time Mack had come out of the house and was curiously watching what was going on. "It seems like you got something wrong with your starter," he said.

"Got a new starter in there."

"Maybe it's the regulator."

"Got one of them in there, too."

"What about the booster?"

"Just put one in."

"What about the voltage relay?"

"Put that in yesterday."

"Well hell, there ain't nothing left to do to the goddamn thing!"

"You're goddamn right! I just put in every kind of part that has anything to do with starting the sonofabitch and it still won't start." Barry got out of the truck and walked around and stared at the engine. He looked at it for a good fifteen minutes trying to think what to do next.

Al said, "I don't know what else to do. Let me know when you fix it," and he went inside.

By this time everyone had already started drinking beer. Mack was trying to figure how he could bum some money from anyone to go and buy some whiskey. A guy walked by on the street and hollered hello. After he passed Mack said, "Goddammit, I should have asked him for some money. I know he's always good for a touch."

I asked who the guy was.

Barry said, "Ah hell, he's just another goddamn drunk who lives up the street. I sure as hell would like to get going." He looked at his watch and it was almost eleven-thirty. "Shit, you know what today is? It's Bobbi's birthday and I got to get her a present, and I ain't got any goddamn money at all. I thought that if we could get this job finished, I could go by and get some money and buy her a present. Goddamn, I got to get her a present. I just got to, got to get her a present. . . ."

Ordinarily the day would have been lost, for by this hour Barry had already consumed a six-pack and was beginning to care less and less about getting the job finished. But today was a special day. It was Bobbi's birthday; and if Barry worked hard and finished the job, he could get paid. So the three of us pushed the truck out in the alley, and Al pushed us with his car to get the engine going. Fortunately, the motor did not give out in the Washington traffic, and we were able to get to the job. Unfortunately, we didn't finish, and Barry was not able to buy Bobbi a pants suit as he had hoped.

Now that Barry was working again, his drinking altered slightly. When he was sick, Barry drank practically all the time—but with one or two exceptions, refrained from going on any of his notorious binges. Now, although he was sober more of the time, his binges increased. As Bobbi would hasten to point out, there was a big difference between his drinking and his binges.

One of Barry's binges unfortunately coincided with Cindy's seventh birthday party. Cindy was very excited about her seventh birthday. She had been talking about it for weeks, and

Bobbi had promised to give her a very special birthday party. Bobbi decorated the kitchen with crepe paper and got cake and ice cream and hung balloons from the ceiling. Eleven of Cindy's friends were invited. Everything was going to be just right, just as Cindy wanted it. It was going to be a perfect seventh birthday. Bobbi had purchased a new, very pretty, blue pants suit for Cindy, which Cindy proudly wore around the house. Things were going okay except for the fact that Barry was around, and Barry was drunk. Barry, in fact, had been drunk since the day before when he received sixty dollars for finishing up his last job. He kept all the money himself and spent some of it on booze. By this time, he had been on one of his wild drunks for about twelve hours. Bobbi told me that she was praying to herself that he would pass out before the party got started.

No such luck. Bobbi recounted what happened: "Everything was going okay, Joe, and then Barry, he come out and started cussing. He started cussing at Mack first. You never heard such language. Motherfucker this, motherfucker that. . . . Well, some of those kids I don't think are used to that kind of language. Anyway, motherfucker this, motherfucker that, goddamned shit, sonofabitch, motherfucker this, that, screaming hollering, saying he was going to beat Mack's ass."

"Why was he mad at Mack?" I asked.

"Oh hell, just drunk. You know how he gets when he's drunk. He's mad at everybody. Well, he comes in the kitchen and he sees those balloons. He sees the crepe paper and he sees all the kids there. He doesn't know what's happening. So he starts tearing up the place, ripping down the paper and popping the balloons and saying stuff like motherfucker and shit. Screaming and hollering. And I like to cried. Cindy like to cried. And all the kids, they just turned around and watched. There was nothing we could do 'cause he was mad drunk. After he finished tearing up the place, he stumbled back in, lay down on the bed, and passed out. But by that time it was too late. Cindy came to me crying, saying she never wanted to have no birthday party again."

My experience with Barry's binges occurred the first week in April during herring dipping season. Herring dipping, like hunting, was one of the events in the year that Barry did not miss. Just as he had gone hunting every year for as long as he could remember, every year Barry had gone herring dipping. The sport consisted of tying a special net to the end of a long pole, dipping the net into a creek, and pulling the net out of the water just as the herring swam past. Each spring the herring swam up the tributaries of the Chesapeake Bay to spawn. Each spring Barry was alongside one of those streams with his net.

One Saturday morning Barry called me and wanted to know if I would go herring dipping with him. He was obviously drunk, but said that since he had had a little to drink, I could drive.

He said, "I talked to B.J. and he's going herring dipping, too. I'm getting ready to go right now. Course Bobbi, the old lady, she don't know and she might not like it. But I'm going anyway. I say fuck her. Now, you want to go?"

"Yes, why not?"

"Okay, I'm trying to get my things together. I'll be down to pick you up soon."

After I talked to Barry I saw Carlyle James, another neighbor, who said that he, too, had talked to B.J. that morning and was also going fishing. We made plans to converge on B.J.'s house as close to one o'clock as possible. Naturally, Barry was late. So late, in fact, that B.J. gave up and left. When Barney Moseby showed up just as Barry arrived around one-fifteen, Barry invited him to go, too. Cindy was with Barry, sitting in the front seat shouting, "We're going herring dipping; we're going herring dipping!"

So Barry, Barney, Carlyle, Cindy, and I went in the old truck, which still didn't start by itself, which lacked a hand brake, and which had a very bad transmission and only one headlight. Barney and Cindy got in the back. I got in the driver's seat with Barry in the middle and Carlyle by the window. Barry was saying, "I think it's all going to work out; I think it's all going to work out." When I tried to put the truck in first, I ground the gears.

"Goddammit, don't you know how to drive this truck?" shouted Barry. "Don't grind the goddamn gear! Better let me drive. I'm the only one who knows how to drive this goddamn truck." I tried again, again grinding the gear into first. Barry snapped, "You stupid sonofabitch, get out of the driver's seat." Putting his foot on the clutch, he got the truck into first with only a slight grinding sound and off we went. But I was still in the driver's seat.

Barry said, "We got to stop at the liquor store." There was a six-pack of beer beside him on the seat, but it wasn't enough. "And we also got to get some gas," he added. As we were getting gas, all of a sudden Barry turned to me and said, "Look, it's my goddamned truck. You don't know how to drive."

"But Barry . . ."

"You think I'm drunk? You stupid sonofabitch. Goddammit, I can drive this car as well as anybody. Get out of my truck. It's my truck, and you get out of the truck, you stupid sonofabitch."

Carlyle pleaded, "Barry, you better let him drive. You've been drinking."

"Drinking? Hell, I ain't drunk, you goddamn bastard. I ain't drunk. Shut up."

"Well, let him drive."

"You shut up. I'll drive." Barry pushed me out of the cab. "You sonofabitch, it is my truck, and I'm the only one who knows how to drive it."

Carlyle moaned, "Oh my God."

We headed off. Barry got the gear into first without a single grinding sound. "It's my truck. I know every part of this truck. I know how to make it run and nobody else does and nobody else is going to drive it. Nobody."

"But how come you asked me on the phone if I could drive? I thought you wanted me to drive."

"Drive, shit. That was just to get me out of the house. My old lady don't like me driving. But I ain't drunk, goddammit. I ain't drunk. Now, to the liquor store."

We stopped at a discount liquor store. I went in and purchased two six-packs of Ballantine and a half pint of Seagram's 7 for Carlyle. When I got out, Barry demanded a beer. Neither Carlyle nor I wanted to give it to him, but when he began screaming and hollering and cussing, Carlyle consented to let him have a can. Barry took a gulp as the truck lurched and swerved from one lane to the other. Somebody's horn blew behind us and we heard brakes screeching.

Barry hollered out the window. "You goddamn sonofabitch bastard, whore, whoever the hell you are. Watch where you're going!" At this point Barry was straddling the white line, swerving from one side to the other. Carlyle said, "Oh my God" and quickly opened up his Seagram's 7, took a long gulp, then nudged me and whispered, "This is the only way I'm going to make it. Oh God."

We had about forty miles to go. Through town, then the beltway, and finally taking the old Indian Head Highway about ten miles to the Little Piscataway River. I took a deep breath and resigned myself to whatever was going to happen. Fortunately there were no major incidents. Actually, Barry did surprisingly well. I gave directions on which way to turn, and he managed to stay in his lane most of the way.

When Barry got drunk, he liked to play around with the truck, leaving it in second gear as long as possible. Today he got it up to fifty miles an hour in second, a feat that made the truck rattle from bumper to bumper and rattle so fiercely that I thought the whole thing was going to fall apart. He also liked to pretend he had four gears and to drive like a Nascar race driver. Today Barry said he was Richard Petty. Carlyle was frozen in the middle, taking long swigs from the Seagram's 7 bottle. I consoled myself by thinking it was no more dangerous being in a truck with a drunk driver than being the good driver whom the drunk driver hits.

Belligerent, Barry was cussing practically everybody. He had the most hostility and vehemence for Bubba. When I asked if Bubba had gone herring dipping with them yesterday, he said, "That sonofabitch? Thank God, no. That chicken-shit bastard." He looked at me and said, "You think Bubba's a good guy, don't you? I've heard you say it. You think he's a good guy. Well, let me tell you something. That no-good shit ain't worth a goddamn shit. He's a little whorehound is what he is—a goddamn, motherfucking bastard. I hate every gut he has in his body. He ain't worth shit, and

don't you ever forget it. He ain't worth nothing!" Bubba
wasn't the only one he had it in for. He was cussing his kids,
me, Carlyle, Bobbi, B.J., Al, Kate, and Mack. All the people
he knew were no-good, lousy bastards. At one point he said,
"You two chicken-shit bastards. You're giving me a hard time.
You're scared. You think I'm drunk, think I can't drive. Shit,
I can drive damn good. My old lady puts up with this shit
twenty-four hours a day, and here you guys have been with
me an hour and already talking like old ladies. You ain't
worth shit. You bastards."

Carlyle muttered, "I just want to get there, that's all I want
to do."

The Piscataway River was more like a small creek than a
river, being at most about thirty feet wide. We drove down
under the Indian Head bridge, where over one hundred herring dippers were already dipping away. The area underneath
the bridge resembled a garbage dump—with beer cans, trash,
soft drink cans, and dead fish everywhere. No grass, just dirt.
And every twenty feet along the bank there would be two or
three people with a long pole resting on a forked stick. At
the end of the pole was a four- or five-foot-square net which
every so often the person would pull out of the water. Usually
there would be one or two herring in it—sometimes as many
as a dozen.

We went under the bridge and parked alongside two trucks,
which had campers mounted on top of them. Barry said this
was the family that had been there last night, and he wanted
to dip beside them because they had brought him good luck.
Most of the cars were old trucks, and most of the people had
on work clothes. There were several campers. People sat
out along the banks and drank beer. There were lots of families—many fathers and sons working together, drinking beer
and laughing. Occasionally, when someone would get a good
catch, he would holler, "Herring, herring." And when everyone was having luck all along the river, you could hear people bellowing out, "Herring, herring, here they come." About
half the people were black. The blacks and whites mingled
and chatted, though generally the blacks were downstream
and the whites went upstream.

B.J., who was dipping across the creek, was doing better than we were. He hung his net from the bridge and pulled out over a bushel before the day was over. Barry lost interest after the first couple of hours. He said he wanted me to catch fish more than he wanted to catch fish himself. So he sat on the bank, drinking and chatting with the families dipping next to us. Carlyle and I manned the net for the last few hours. Carlyle had a good time, though he too became fairly drunk by the time he finished off his Seagram's. Cindy played with some of the children and was very enthusiastic about our catching some fish.

Before the afternoon was over, people were giving away buckets of herring. One fellow downstream said he already had thirty buckets; and since he didn't like herring himself, he wanted to give as much to us as we would take. The family next to us also gave us some, so finally we did end up with two buckets, though we caught few ourselves.

By six-thirty it was beginning to get dark, and I suggested we leave, since we had told Bobbi we would be home by six. When we finally got off at seven-thirty, fires were being built and people were singing and hollering and drinking. One guy next to us was burning old tires; he said he always brought along his old tires when he went herring dipping because they made a nice light when it got dark. Lanterns were being lit; and all along the river, as far up and as far down as you could see, you could hear the sounds of nets slipping in the water, people chatting and occasionally hollering, "Herring, herring."

The ride back can only be described as a horror show. That night I became convinced that Barry Shackelford, if he didn't straighten out soon, was going to die a violent death. The only questions remaining were how, when, and how many people he was going to take with him.

When Barry staggered to the truck about seven-thirty, he could hardly stand up. He was well drunk that morning; and since he had been with us, he had consumed all but three of the beers. I don't think he had any liquor, though there were lots of people drinking liquor and he could have taken a snort or two. He insisted on driving. There was nothing I could do to convince him to let me drive. Every time I suggested it he would say, "You think I'm goddamned drunk? You stupid sonofabitch. I'm not drunk. I'm sober as hell. I can drive. Anyway, my baby is with me and I wouldn't do nothing to hurt Cindy."

At one point in the afternoon, when a man had offered Cindy some herring, Barry had said, "Come over here, Cindy, and thank the man. Take off your hat and thank the man."

"I don't want to take off my hat. I've got an earache," Cindy complained.

"Goddammit, take off your hat. I said take off your hat!"

"Daddy, I got an *earache*."

"Oh yeah, ears, she got trouble with her ears. Honey, I'm sorry. That's all right."

When we got in the truck, Cindy sat on my lap. Barry tried to persuade her to get in the back, but she wouldn't do it. She said she didn't want to ride back there by herself. (Barney had gone home earlier with B.J.) Carlyle volunteered to ride back there with her, but Barry finally agreed that the four of us would ride in the front.

Of course, we had to jump-start the truck, but before long we were on the road. Barry was now cussing furiously. "Goddammit, motherfucking bastards, shit," he would shout as a car came up behind him or passed him.

Cindy responded several times by saying, "Daddy, you ought to have your mouth washed out with soap. That's a cuss word you're saying."

"Oh shit, I'm sorry. That's right, Cindy. You're right. I ain't going to use any more of that goddamn language."

"You ought to have your mouth washed out with soap! I'm going to tell Mommy."

"You're right, you're right. I should have my mouth washed out with soap. I'm sorry, honey. I'm sorry. I'm sorry."

Before we had driven more than a hundred yards, Barry had driven off onto the shoulder of the road for the first time. Unfortunately, it wasn't the last. It was quite difficult for him to stay in his lane. When we would hear honks or screeches, Barry would hang his head out the window and shake his fist.

"Goddammit, sonofabitch, whore-bastard. Watch where you're going, goddammit!"

I would shout, "Barry, stay in your lane!"

"Shut up, I can drive, goddammit."

After we had gone about three miles, Barry asked, "Where in the hell are we? Shit, I've never seen this place before. Shit, I don't know where we are. I'm lost." Since I did have a vague idea of where we were, I volunteered to give directions. "That's good," said Barry, " 'cause I've never been here before. Which lane do we get in here? Which lane?"

"Stay in your lane, Barry!" I would shout as he would swerve over to the left lane. "Barry, stay in your goddamn lane! You want us all to be killed?" There would be honks and screeches as the truck would lurch back into the right lane.

"Shit, I ain't drunk. I know how to drive. We ain't all going to get killed. It's the other people who don't know how to drive, goddammit."

Carlyle nudged me in the ribs and I could see that he was as scared as I was. He offered me one of the last remaining beers and I took it. It didn't do much good. When we managed to make it back to the interstate, Barry said, "I've never seen this place before. I'm completely lost. I think you've given me the wrong damn directions." At that point the Washington Monument was visible in the distance.

Carlyle groaned, "Brother, he is really gone."

When we got close to home, Barry began recognizing familiar places and got angry at me for continuing to give directions. "Goddammit, I know where we are. Shit, I've been here before. I know where we are. You don't have to tell me how to drive. I don't want you to tell me where to go. I know exactly where we are. You think I'm drunk or something?"

When we finally made it to Clay Street, around eight-thirty, Carlyle, Cindy, and I breathed a sigh of relief. As I got out of the car, Barry said, "Yeah, I guess we had a couple of close calls. But shit, you don't have to worry. Shouldn't get worried. I know how to drive. I'm a good driver."

After that experience my relationship with Barry was never the same.

March had been less difficult financially than the preceding months. The welfare had come through on March 8, and Barry got paid for the job he was working on. For the first time since before Thanksgiving, the Shackelfords weren't desperate for money, though they were still averaging about two months behind on most of their bills.

April, however, was another difficult month. Emergency aid had been terminated, and Barry went for most of the month without work. Before the end of the month, the Shackelfords were desperate again.

Bobbi, however, still received the AFDC check for Bubba and still qualified for food stamps. On the morning of April 7 I accompanied her to the welfare department to be recertified. When I picked her up at six-thirty in the morning, Bobbi was waiting for me and said that she had been up since five. When we arrived at seven, a half-dozen people were ahead of us. By seven-thirty there were sixteen; by eight there were thirty; and by eight-thirty, when the receptionist arrived, there were well over fifty people, mostly white, mostly women, with a scattering of blacks and a scattering of older males. Also there were at least a half-dozen long-haired young people.

While we were waiting, Bobbi and the black woman sitting next to her agreed that they knew exactly what was going to happen. Bobbi said: "Listen, I can tell you. I've been here enough times, I know exactly what the routine is going to be. About eight-thirty, when they are supposed to open up, the caseworkers will come wandering in. Some of them will have coffee, some of them won't. They won't say a word; they'll just breeze past the line of people, sort of turn their noses up, and go into the back room. Then a little after eight-thirty the receptionist will sort of mosey on out. She might look around and then go back in and get a cup of coffee. Take her first coffee break for about fifteen minutes. Then about eight forty-five they will be ready to start the line. They'll call out the names of the people who were there yesterday but who weren't seen. Then everybody will rush to the front and sort of jam around and try to get in front of the line. Then they'll take names of people today who are supposed to get certified. She'll see a few people, then take another coffee break, smoke a cigarette, sort of take it easy. By nine-fifteen or nine-thirty, if we're lucky and in the first of the line, we'll get seen. That's what will happen. You mark my words."

Bobbi was exactly right. The receptionist came out about eight forty-five with a cup of coffee. She said, "Two lines will be formed. One for food stamps and one for public assistance."

"Which line is which?" someone asked.

"I don't know," said Bobbi.

"Well, which line am I in?" asked the person next to us.

"I guess you're in the food stamp line," said Bobbi.

People shifted lines. Two crude lines were formed. Though there was some shoving and pushing, most of the people were content to keep their original place in line. We should have been third, but some people hung around the reception desk and managed to get ahead of us.

The receptionist said, "I'm sorry, but only four people will be seen today for food stamps." The person who was fifth in line said, "Only four people? I've been here since six in the morning. The person who is first, he didn't get here until much later."

"I'm sorry. I wasn't here. I don't know," replied the receptionist condescendingly.

"But other people know. . . ." Several people voiced agreement.

"I'm sorry. I wasn't here, and I don't know who was first."

"But I came over here from way over the other side of the county. I can prove it. You can call my house. I can prove it. I can't come back tomorrow."

"I'm sorry."

"But that's not fair. There are two people who got ahead of me who weren't here . . ."

Bobbi said, "Ain't that some shit. We ain't going to get seen today. I knew it. I always have to come back."

There were several women standing in line with small children, who were crying. By this time the hallway was filled with smoke, and everyone seemed as discomforted as I felt. Bobbi commented to the receptionist, "Look, I was here before he was," pointing to the person ahead of us.

"I'm sorry. You'll have to wait your place in line."

"Listen, we were here at seven and he didn't come in until later." The receptionist took the gentleman's name anyway and said that he should go into room number three. When our turn came, being so far down the list, Bobbi was told to come back tomorrow. She later commented that it would take probably at least until eleven or eleven-thirty tomorrow to get re-certified for food stamps.

Bobbi went through this every single month. Every month she arrived between the hours of five and seven in the morning and stood in line for two or three hours. As we left the building, she said: "This is some shit, ain't it? This is some shit. What a fucking lousy place! The goddamn caseworkers get here late, gab around, take their coffee break, while we stand up waiting around, shoving and pushing. Treated like animals, just so that we can get some food to eat. It's some goddamn shit, that's all I've got to say.

"And you know what pisses me off most? These goddamn college students that come here. Look at them." She pointed to some of the people who had books under their arms and long hair. One of them was talking about a history exam that he had just taken. "These college kids, they got money. They got parents who got money or they wouldn't be in college. And they come here to get food stamps and push us around and make a big joke about it. I've heard them talk about all the fun they're going to have, about these love-ins and live-ins and all that kind of shit. That's what pisses me off, these college students who come here and joke about it when all the rest of us standing here don't know if we're going to eat or not the next day. Really pisses me off. I don't know what's worse. College students or these goddamn workers who come in late and take their coffee break and joke and laugh and all that sort of shit. I don't know. But I do know something. The whole thing is full of shit."

On April 20 Bobbi had her first visit from the caseworker. When she had been notified that the caseworker was going to visit, she became very excited. She spent the preceding day cleaning and straightening the house, and when the caseworker arrived, Bobbi was ready. Everything was picked up, and the house was very clean.

I happened to be there that day. The caseworker was a young woman in her early twenties who seemed very efficient. After the interview, which took place in the kitchen, Bobbi told the social worker good-by and came in Walt's room, where Walt, Al, and I were seated.

"Well," said Bobbi, "I think we've got a good social worker. She seems real nice. I told her my husband is an alcoholic, that he didn't work, and when he did, he didn't give his family enough money. She said she understood. In fact, she said the reason she was there was because someone had reported Barry. She told me there was a new program in the county for alcoholics that might be able to help Barry. Not only that, she told me they could get us a house and give us some welfare money to get by if things got worse. They'd find a house for us and pay the rent."

Walt asked, "What's going to happen to me? What's going to happen to me if they take you and the kids and put you in another place?"

"Well, you'll go with us. Don't worry about it."

"Well, I'd like to get out of here anyway. If my eyes would let me, I'd leave. My nerves are something awful. I just can't stand it any more. I can't stand to hear Barry carry on like he does late at night. I can't sleep. I can't stand to see him kicking the children around and cussing you out, cussing the kids out, cussing me out. If it keeps getting worse, I hope they'll put me in an old age home or something. I just can't stand it any more. I got to get away from it."

The caseworker's visit was part of a new county welfare program, which separated income maintenance from the provision of social services. The social service caseworkers were to check on all the cases to establish which were in need of further help. Two days later, Walt's caseworker made her visit. I was not there that day, but Bobbi described what happened:

"Daddy's caseworker was real nice, too. She was as nice as my caseworker. She helped Daddy out, and she told him that because he's so sick and all that they ought to get more money, and he's going to get sixty dollars more or something like that, I think.

"But it was sort of funny, Joe, you'd just die laughing. The caseworker came up and she was all nice and proper and all that. But Al, see, he'd been drinking and he was there, too. Drinking home-brew. Yeah, Al and Barry got their own thing working in the basement, and they've been putting it down. Well, you know, you bottle the beer. And sometimes it don't work too well, and it blows the top off the bottle. Well, goddammit, wouldn't you know, just before the caseworker gets there, Al is sitting there at the table and all of a sudden, *blam!* Goddamn, there was beer splattered everywhere, all over the kitchen! I said, 'Well shit, Daddy's caseworker is going to be here, we got to get all this shit cleaned up.' So I went to work cleaning beer up, and Al rinsed out the glass and everything. It looked pretty good.

"Well, Daddy's caseworker came up, and she was all nice and all and so proper. We were sitting there at the table talking, and all of a sudden—Al, see, he'd taken the beer, and he was in Daddy's room, drinking. He'd closed the door, and he wasn't going to let on that he was there. Well, all of a sudden, we were sitting there, and we heard *blam!* You could hear the beer splatter against the wall. *Blam!* two times more, all three bottles! I mean to tell you, goddamn, it was funny. I like to died laughing when all three bottles exploded. And God knows you could smell the beer. It even started trickling under the door. And we just sat there talking. She looked at Daddy, and she said, 'Mr. Walters, are you sure you don't drink?' Goddamn, I like to died laughing. Daddy, he says, 'Ah . . . no, no, I don't drink. Don't drink at all.' I'm sure the caseworker wonders what on earth caused them explosions and what on earth was making that smell that smelled so much like beer." (Walt was telling the truth. Two years before, when he discovered he had diabetes, he stopped drinking.)

Each caseworker informed Bobbi and Walt that she would return soon for another visit. Bobbi and Walt both were pleased.

Barry finished his job on April 16. On April 19 Goldstein called to tell Barry he had another job for him, and on April

21 Barry started to work repairing another old house. This time he and his friend Wade were going to work together on a job that would pay a total of $800 (out of which they would have to buy materials). But since Barry would not get paid until the last of the month, finances were still low.

On April 30, when Barry received $180 as a first installment on his new job, he got drunk. The next morning when he woke up, the $180 was gone. This was the last straw for Bobbi, who was beginning to lose patience with Barry. She called me the next morning and in desperation related the incident:

"It started several days ago, on Monday. Barry calls his boss about getting paid for his last job. Barry asked Milt to mail him the check. He owed him a hundred twenty-five. I said, 'Jesus Christ, goddamn, Barry, hell. You can't do that. We've got to pay the rent; we've got to buy groceries. You go and get the money.'

"Well, Barry, you know how he is. He finally agreed to go and get the money. Milt left early. Before Barry got there. He left a note and put the check in an envelope. Barry gets the note and the check, and he and Wade take off to go fishing. Just before they go, Barry's mother and stepfather, Blackie, come up. And Barry, he treats them like dirt. He don't say nothing to them. He just leaves and takes off to go fishing. Barry's mother, she says, 'Bobbi, are you having troubles?' 'Yes, I am.' They tell me they understand. They tell me they would have helped many times before, given me money and helped the children; but the reason they hadn't done it was because they thought that Barry would have gotten the benefit from it. He would have just used the money and bought whiskey or beer.

"Well, that night late Barry gets back from going fishing and he gives me fifty dollars. 'Barry, I thought you got a hundred twenty-five,' I say. He gives Daddy five dollars that he owed him. Barry says he only got seventy-five dollars. Well, he was owed one twenty-five! Why, praise you God Almighty, why did he only get seventy-five. Well, I don't know.

"'Okay,' I said, 'well, I would like some more money, Barry, because I have to pay the rent.' And Barry, he don't say nothing. Then he says, 'Hold on to what you've got for the rent.'

"Well, Jesus Christ, goddamn. I've got all this rent to pay, and we ain't got no food in the house. And I say, how am I going to save money for rent? Sure. So I say, 'You kiss my ass, Barry Shackelford.' That's what I said.

"Well, Barry, he called me every name in the book, from a common whore to a bitch to a goddamn motherfucker. That's what he calls me. That was Monday.

"Tuesday Barry comes home. He and Wade went out to work on the job. Now, Kate called up here to borrow some butter just as he was coming in. So Barry comes in and I lay down the phone to see if I have any butter. Hell, I don't have much, and I don't have any money left to buy food with either. Barry says, 'If you don't like Kate calling up all the goddamn time,' and he knows I don't 'cause I tell him I don't, 'why don't you just tell her?'

"Well, I go and tell Kate I ain't got any butter and hang up the phone. And then Barry says the same thing again. And I look at Barry and I say, 'Goddammit, Barry, maybe I would if you wouldn't spend so much goddamn time down there.'

"Well, he gets mad. He was drunk anyway and he gets roaring mad. I tell him that it's his damn fault that we don't have any food around the house and he ought to start doing something about it. So he grabs my arm and starts hitting me, then he tries to throw me down the stairs. Well, hell, I get away from him 'cause he's so damn drunk, and I get a broom, and I whacked the goddamned broom three times over his head and break the broom. Praise you Jesus Christ, God Almighty, I break the broom on Barry's head into three pieces! Three pieces!

"That was Tuesday. On Wednesday, Daddy comments to me, he says, 'You know, Wade and Barry did a whole lot of work on that new house they're working on and they ought to draw a pretty big check.' I knew this was the truth, 'cause I knew they'd been working awfully hard, so I call up and talk to his boss. Now, I know the secretary real well and we sit and gossip about things and I tell her, 'You know, Barry and Wade have been working pretty hard.' 'Oh yeah, the boss is real pleased with the work they've been doing,' she says.

"And then I sort of asked her how much they were going to draw this week and that secretary tells me that they've got, waiting up there in the office right now, for Barry, a four-hundred-dollar check. Well, I got real excited about that. Four hundred dollars! I could pay the rent, buy groceries. You know, that's a nice chunk of money.

"Well, that night I called again. Barry hadn't gotten home so I called over there and talked to the secretary and she tells me that Barry has picked up his four-hundred-dollar check and has gone to get it cashed. Said he'd gone to the liquor store that Milton's father owns. So Barry gets home a little later, and so help me God he don't say nothing about it. I just wanted to see what he was going to do and he didn't say he had one goddamn penny.

"Then he goes out fishing. Just before he went out, he talked to Daddy for a little bit and didn't say nothing about four hundred dollars. And then Jerry comes up, the guy down the street, the guy who used to live above us on Clay Street. And Barry owes Jerry a couple of dollars, he says, so Barry offers him some home-brew. So they start to drink a beer, and before they'd gotten a couple of sips of that beer, Barry asks him if he wants to go fishing. He says yes, so they leave.

"They come back later, not too long after they leave, and park in the back of the house. Now I know, 'cause I heard Jerry say, that Jerry has a case of beer in the back of his truck. So, praise you God Almighty, they stay out there and drink beer in Jerry's truck until eleven at night. At eleven Barry comes in, soused. Mack comes up to borrow some milk about that time. Mack tells me, 'You know, Bobbi, Barry is really messed up. I had to leave, it got so bad down there. He's just sitting in the truck drinking, and he's really messed up.'

"Jesus Christ, don't I know it!

"Anyway, Barry comes up and he and Mack have another beer. It's getting late. Now Barry finally passes out. I knew he was going to have to pass out, I guess it was a little before midnight. So I go on and go to bed. Of course, when Barry's drinking nobody can go to sleep. That's why the kids don't go

to school! They've missed two or three days this week. 'Cause
Barry keeps them up so late they don't get any sleep. And
we can't get up in the morning.

"Well, thank God, Barry finally passed out. But about one-
thirty in the morning something happened to the window. It
fell shut; it was open. The window don't work too good anyway. Well, that woke Barry up. He jumps out of bed, runs
over, pulls the chest of drawers out, and sets it in the middle
of the floor. Then he jumps up again and sets off for the bathroom. He comes back a minute later and starts hollering and
jumping up and down. Barry, he's acting like a crazy man! He
said he wanted beer, he had to have a beer. He remembered
that he had some National beer hid under his bed. I knew they
were there, but I thought he had forgotten. He gets the beer,
starts drinking, starts jumping up and down, wakes all the
children. God knows, he probably woke the neighbors up.
And he starts to drink three beers. Runs in there and jumps
on Daddy's bed, starts talking to him. It's getting on to be
three in the morning and none of us have gone to sleep.

"Around five Barry comes back and says, 'Hey, baby, you
want to do it?' 'Goddammit, no, Barry, we've been up all
night!' He doesn't want me to get to sleep. He starts shaking
me and nudging me every time I start to doze off. 'Do you
want to, baby?' 'No!' I said. Goddamn, I didn't get any sleep
at all. The children didn't get any sleep, and it was getting on
to six in the morning. Finally, when the sun comes up, Barry
passes out again.

"Let me tell you, I know there is a God in heaven and a
God who cares. I know this to be true. And I prayed to God,
I prayed, 'Dear God, let him pass out.' And at daylight, thank
God, Barry passed out.

"Well, the next day Barry woke up after a couple hours'
sleep. We all woke up, but it was too late for the kids to go to
school. They hadn't gotten any sleep. And all he can think
about is the registration for the car. Now, that's why I think
Barry had some money. Because he wanted to go and get
some new tags for the truck because they expire tomorrow.
But I had the registration and I had it hid under my mattress,
see, so he couldn't find it.

"Well, he went rummaging around, looking for it, asking Daddy where it was. Daddy said he didn't know. Then he starts to get real mad because he can't find it. He starts a-ripping, roaring, snorting, hollering, screaming, and cussing. He said he wanted the registration. I said, 'Okay, goddammit, Barry. You can have it, but it's got my name on it. And if you want to get the tags, you're going to have to go down there with me 'cause I got to sign it.' 'Fuck you.' That's what he says to me. 'All right, get the tags. Fuck yourself, you sonofabitch.'

"So he takes the registration and heads off. That was today. He leaves and when he comes home this evening, that sonofabitch says he ain't got no money. He says he lost it all and don't know what happened to it. Says it was about a hundred eighty. Now, I know that they paid him all the four hundred. I know Barry got it. I know he gave some of it to Wade, don't know how much. And now he says he's lost all the rest of it. Now, ain't that some shit? And not only that, when Barry came home this evening he asked me for a dollar thirty-four—that's to buy eight beers. Goddamn, have you ever seen such nerve . . . ?"

Although two days later Barry found the money where he had hidden it, his relationship with Bobbi continued to deteriorate; and Bobbi continued thinking of leaving Barry. The social worker was the first person to encourage her to consider this option. When she made her second visit to see Bobbi on April 29, she told Bobbi that it seemed to her that Barry was the cause of most of Bobbi's problems and that Bobbi should talk with some counselors at the alcoholic rehabilitation center. Bobbi agreed to talk with the counselors and was most enthusiastic about leaving Barry and getting a new home. "Joe," she told me, "the welfare is going to help me find a new house where we'll have lots of room; and they say if I leave Barry, with Daddy's welfare and mine, we'll have over three hundred dollars a month coming in. That is sure more than Barry is bringing in now. The only thing is, I got to leave Barry; and if Barry gets wind that I'm gonna leave, God knows what he would d to me. . . . But I tell you I have had it. I just can't stand Barry any more. I haven't got any friends because of him. Nobody ever invites me over to their house because they're afraid he might come along. So I don't care what he says he's gonna do. I'm gonna leave that bastard!"

The next week on May 3 Bobbi went with her caseworker to see a counselor at the county alcoholic rehabilitation center. Bobbi was very excited before she left. Although she had been talking about how she was going to leave Barry, she really hoped there was something they could do to help Barry. When she returned home from the session, she was very depressed. "They said *I* was the one with a problem, not Barry. Now, ain't that some shit! They told me *I* was the one who needed help! What the hell am I going to do?" Bobbi paused, then in a soft voice answered her own question. "Well, they say I got three options. One—put his ass in jail for assault. Hell, as many times as that bastard has threatened me and pushed me around. The social worker says I could get him put in jail for sure. Two—have his ass committed to the nut house. Hell, he's crazy enough. Anybody can tell that. They also have a wing for drunks and they can put you away even if you don't want to go. God knows, Barry would never *agree* to go to a place like that. And three—they told me I could leave Barry and find a new place to live. They said I should join Al-anon, a group for husbands and wives of alcoholics. And this is what they recommended. They said Barry was too far gone. The AA or the alcoholic rehabilitation program wouldn't do him no good. Anyway, he would have to want to join them of his own free will, and you know Barry. So, now they say I'm the one who's got to make the decision."

The next day Bobbi called up to tell me she had made her decision. She was definitely going to leave Barry. That afternoon Bobbi called the caseworker to tell her the news and asked her when she would be able to move to a new place. The caseworker told Bobbi there had been some misunderstanding. She had never told Bobbi that the social services department would find her an apartment. Bobbi had to do this on her own. And as far as financial help was concerned, it would come only *after* Bobbi had left Barry.

Bobbi was distraught. "You know what she told me? She

said they couldn't get me a house because they didn't want to contribute to family breakup. They also said there was a housing shortage. Jesus Christ, don't I know it! We were lucky to find the dump we live in now, and it took us six months to find the rat hole on Clay Street." Bobbi laughed sarcastically. "You know something, Jack, I'm right back where I started from. There ain't a goddamned thing I can do!"

In many respects May was the worst month of the entire year for the Shackelfords. First, when Bobbi made her usual trip to the welfare department for certification for food stamps, she was informed that the department had new procedures for certification and that the information Bobbi had regarding Barry's income was insufficient. Consequently she could receive no more food stamps. The second week in May, when they had no food and no money, in desperation Bobbi called her caseworker, who arranged for Bobbi to receive fifty dollars' worth of emergency food. Still, this was hardly enough for them to eat well, and they had to limit themselves to one meal a day for the rest of the month.

Barry received a check for one hundred dollars for completing a job with Wade. When Barry went down to pick up the check, he told Goldstein he was expecting two hundred. Goldstein called him a "no-good sot and a bum" to his face and told him not to call him any more about work. This was the last check Barry ever received from Goldstein.

On top of that, since Walt did not receive his welfare check when he was supposed to, Bobbi had to spend several days calling the welfare department and talking with welfare caseworkers about it. On May 22, ten days late, he was reissued a new check for fifty-two dollars.

Two of the Shackelfords' friends died about that time. B.J.'s cousin, Don, died toward the end of April. According to Bobbi, Don was "another one of them neighborhood drunks," but also he was a nice guy whom both Barry and Bobbi liked. He did not hold a steady job, but lived with B.J., helping take care of Billy-John and occasionally working with B.J. cleaning bricks. About a week before he died, one morning when I was at the Shackelfords, he wandered upstairs and passed out on Walt's bed. The next week he died suddenly of a heart attack, at the age of sixty. Barry was a pallbearer at the funeral.

A few weeks later, on May 5, Kate's father died. Since he lived with Mack and Kate most of the time, Barry and Bobbi saw a lot of him and were upset about his death, too. Though he was an alcoholic, he worked as an oil burner repairman and made good money. He, too, was around sixty and died from carbon monoxide poisoning. Apparently he was drinking in the front seat of his parked car and passed out with the motor running. No one, neither Barry nor Bobbi nor Mack nor Kate, attended his funeral.

The big event of the month, however, was Cindy's ear operation. Several weeks before, the public health nurse called Bobbi to tell her the operation had been scheduled for May 13 at Johns Hopkins Hospital in Baltimore and that they should have Cindy there the preceding evening. Up until the last minute it was uncertain as to how they would get there. As usual, the truck was broken down and Barry was drunk. However, Barry rallied. He went out and hocked Bubba's gun and an old pair of binoculars and with the money bought the part to get the truck going. (Bobbi had thought for a while she would have to take the bus.) Al agreed to help Walt baby-sit while Bobbi and Barry were gone. They got Cindy to the hospital on time; and that evening and the evening following, they spent the night sleeping in the cab of the truck. Bobbi was very enthusiastic about the hospital and about how nice they were treated. "You just can't believe it," she said, "they actually told us what they were going to do to Cindy. They explained everything to us. It was really something. They treated us so nice." The operation was successful, and on May 15 Cindy returned home after two days in the hospital, with strict orders to remain in bed for two weeks.

Bobbi, Barry, and Cindy returned to an apartment that was literally devastated. I had been there the day before to see what I could do to help out. At that time Al had passed out on the bed, lying in his own vomit. Garbage and cockroaches were everywhere. No one had made any effort to pick up anything, Al being too drunk and Walt too blind. Billy

was home with a bad cold and Littlebit said he had an earache. No one had seen Bubba. Walt was very depressed by
the situation and put out with Al, who he said had made
things worse by drinking so much and getting sick.

Nevertheless, when they returned, Bobbi straightened
things up and made a place for Cindy to rest in their bed.
Before they went to the hospital, Bobbi had bought Cindy a
new nightgown, which Cindy was very proud of. When Cindy
first returned, she seemed to be enjoying her status as a
special person. She stayed in bed very patiently for the first
two days; but after her brothers started teasing her for "being lazy," when her mother was gone Cindy slipped outside
and started playing. Bobbi was furious at Cindy, but she just
refused to stay in bed. Reluctantly Bobbi gave in, and after
the first week Cindy was going her own way. I shuddered to
think what might happen to her ear, but at her two-week
checkup the doctors told Bobbi that Cindy's ears were doing
all right and that the operation had been successful.

Toward the end of May, since Barry still had not been
called by Goldstein about working, he was getting nervous.
He refused to talk about it except when he was drunk and he
would call Goldstein every name he could think of. The
Shackelfords borrowed money from everyone to get them
through—Barry's stepfather, Blackie, Al, Wade, and me.

Near the end of the month Barry finally got a call from
Goldstein, telling him he had a door for Barry to hang. This
was hardly what Barry would call a job since at best it would
bring only twenty-five dollars; but since Barry was desperate,
he said he would do it. He went to the house to hang the door
three times, but each time the people were gone and the house
was locked. The next day he got another call from the boss,
asking if he had fixed the door. Bobbi answered the phone
and said, "No."

Goldstein responded, "Should have known. The lousy
drunk. You tell your husband to get over there and fix that
door this afternoon. If by tomorrow morning the door is not
fixed, tell him we don't want him. He needn't *ever* call us
again about a job."

When Bobbi gave Barry the message, he had but one comment, "Fuck Goldstein." With that, a somewhat tenuous working relationship of three years was terminated. Bobbi stuck up for her husband. "I'm proud of Barry," she said, "I say, 'Fuck him,' too. He's got a lot of nerve. He's been screwing us all the time, that bastard. When we were down and out, he wouldn't even pay us the money he owed us. I say, 'Screw him,' and I'm proud of Barry."

5

Summer

On June 1 I stopped by the Shackelfords' to see how things were going. When I knocked on the door, Walt moaned feebly, "Come on up." He was by himself except for Littlebit, who was drinking a bottle and lying on the bed. Walt was in particularly low spirits.

"You know," he said, "I just don't understand nothing around this place. It's getting on my nerves so bad I can't even sleep. Now, take Bobbi. My forms had to go in last week —form for the welfare, about my diabetes diet. She didn't send them in. I told her to fill them out, but she just didn't do it. And so today she took off fixing to mail them when she took Cindy to the doctor. But why did she wait so long? And Barry, he's been on a drunk something awful. All weekend. Staying up late, hollering.

"Hell, a guy got shot last night. Barry and Mack and this drunk guy from up the street, Harry, a great big old guy. They were drinking around all day, hollering, cutting up, whatnot. And Mack found a gun, but it was broken. So they played around with the gun and finally got it fixed. And this big guy, Harry, he shot himself through the hand. Don't think he meant to. It just went off. They took him to the hospital.

"I can't get no sleep, can't even do no thinking around here. Don't know what this world is coming to. Barry, he made eight dollars this weekend, did some kind of work. Gave Bobbi four. And Bobbi, she sold her sewing machine to Daisey, Al's girl, and got twenty dollars for that. Just enough to get us through the weekend. But the rest of the money, Barry drunk it up. Oh man, did they holler and scream this weekend! I mean, it was something.

"You know, I don't know if Barry's going to get another

job any more. I don't think Goldstein's going to take him back.
Can't say I blame him. But that means Barry ain't going to
be able to find no work. Least it ain't going to be as easy."
Walt shook his head, looked out the window, took a deep
sigh, and settled back in his chair. "I just don't know. . . ."

About that time Mack came upstairs. When I asked him
about the shooting incident the night before, he confirmed
what Walt had told me. "Yeah, that guy Harry up the street.
He was playing around with the gun, pointing it all around,
and the damn thing went off in his hand. Lucky he didn't
kill nobody. I don't even think he did much to his hand. Anyway, he's in the hospital. We took him there last night. The
cops wanted to know what happened, who shot who. Hell,
Barry said tell them the niggers did it. They'll be looking for
niggers all night. That dumb Barry. He thought it was a big
joke, but it wasn't no big joke. You don't go around and tell
stuff like that unless it really happened."

Then Mack pulled out the gun, a small .22 revolver. "See
this. I found it last night in the garage. Barry hid it. That
stupid bastard. He was playing around with it yesterday when
the damn thing was loaded. I found it twice where he'd hid
it. But this last time I found it I unloaded the damn thing,
and I ain't going to tell Barry where it is. If he wants to know
what happened to it, I'll tell him I found it. Last time I found
it he said somebody stole it. I finally told him that I had it,
and he got real mad. But the way he's playing around with
that gun, loaded and all that, I tell you, you just got to be
careful."

Bobbi returned while I was talking to Mack and expressed
her disgust with the shooting incident. "Well, I knew something like this was going to happen. All I can say, you all are
lucky somebody didn't get killed. Like a bunch of children.
That's how you carry on."

While we were talking, Al, Daisey, and Barry stomped up
the stairs. Each one had a beer. Barry said, "Hold it, now
hold it. Don't nobody say nothing. Get out a pencil and paper
and write this down." I immediately got a pencil and paper.
"Harry Barnes, County Hospital, third floor. Goddamn,
Harry Barnes." He said it again very slowly. I wrote it down,

tore out the sheet, and gave it to Barry. "Okay, I want to go and see him. I want to go and see him right now."

"Who is that?" asked Bobbi.

"He's the guy who done blowed his hand off last night. But that ain't all he blowed off. Blowed off his goddamn leg, too. The bullet went through his hand and into his goddamn leg. Shit, I didn't realize that last night. But it did. And it ricocheted around the car and it's lucky it didn't kill one of us. I was sitting next to him not two inches away."

Barry took a gulp of his beer. Then Al joined in. "Well, you have no business playing with a loaded gun anyway. No damn business at all. What do you expect, playing with a loaded gun?"

"Well, I hid the goddamn gun."

"Hid it, hell," said Mack, "you put it right beside the seat. You didn't have any business playing with it. It's lucky none of you was killed. None of us, I should say—I was there, too."

Barry said, "Well, I want to go and see him. I want to go to the hospital. I just saw his wife out there, and she said he's in the hospital, and I want to go and see him. Shit, she looked at me like I'd done it or something. It wasn't my fault. He shot hisself."

Bobbi said, "Well, you better not go to the hospital. You want to get arrested?"

"Arrested? What did I do?"

"It was your gun, wasn't it? And you loaded the gun."

"It wasn't my goddamn gun. It was Mack's."

"Hell no," said Mack, "it was Ted's and he gave it to me. It wasn't my gun."

Bobbi asked, "But it was your bullet, wasn't it, Barry?"

"Shit yes, it was my bullet."

"Well, all I'm saying is, you handed him a gun with a bullet in it, and you better watch it, 'cause that's going to get you involved."

"Well shit, it wasn't my fault."

Walt said, "Anyway, they have to make an investigation. The police always make an investigation. And you just better stay away from there until the investigation is over with."

"Well, goddammit, it wasn't my fault, and I want to go and see him."

Daisey said, "Serves you all right. That's what you get for playing with loaded guns like little boys play with toys. It's damn stupid, that's what it is."

Bobbi said, "Well, it's a damn shame. After all, Harry's wife is pregnant, and that's all she needs. She's had a hard time anyway. That's all she needs, is for her husband to get shot."

Al changed the subject. "Well, I'm going to be an ordained minister. In two weeks I'll be an ordained minister. I've sent off for the papers, and I'll bless you all." He made the sign of the cross.

Barry said, "Ah shit." There were guffaws around the room.

Daisey said, "Now cut out that talk. That's the worst kind of sin you can do is to make fun of God. And that's all you're doing, making fun of God. It says so in the Bible. It is a sin to blaspheme, ain't that right? Blaspheming is a sin."

"It ain't no sin. I'm dead serious. I'm going to be an ordained minister. I've sent off for the papers. I can preach, I can bury, I can marry. If you got any problems, just come to me and I'll fix you up."

There were more laughs, but Bobbi shook her head in disgust and muttered, "I'm so sick of this shit."

Al said, "Well, I've been living in sin too long, and now I'm going to live right and be a minister of God."

Daisey said, "You're going to burn in hell, that's what you're going to do," and Barry added, "Yep, as I always say, better bury him in a chestnut coffin so you can hear him a-popping."

"I may burn in hell, but this ain't the worst thing I've done. Shit, I've broken every commandment there is. Says you can't commit adultry. Goddamn, no telling how many times I've committed adultry. Says you shouldn't rob. Goddamn, I've robbed, I've stolen, I've coveted. I've coveted my neighbor's wife many a time. I mean there ain't much I haven't done. Why not add one more?"

Daisey said, "Well, as I said before, what you're doing now is the worst kind of sin, making fun of God."

Barry said, "Well, you better make fun of Him now 'cause when you die, you and me is going to burn in hell."

Daisey said, "Yeah, and what's more, you got to go in the hospital June eighth. You better watch it. You might not come out."

"Well, if I don't come out, I don't come out. I guess that's the way it is. Anyway, I'll probably be an ordained minister by then, and I can bury myself if I don't come out." Daisey shook her head in disgust, as did Bobbi. Walt and Barry chuckled.

"Well," said Barry, "you might call me an atheist. I don't believe in no God. I don't believe in no heaven and no hell. I believe there's heaven and hell right here on this earth, that's what I believe. And you make it yourself. And I'll tell you something else. Right now I'm in hell. But I could get out of it. I've got to get myself straight. Got to get a job. Got to get out of this hell that I'm in right now."

Al remarked, "I'll tell you, when I die I want to be cremated first, because I know the devil's going to burn me, and I want to beat him to it. I want to get burned up here first before that sonofabitch devil gets his hands on me. What I want to know is, how's my wife doing down there with her boy friends?" He mentioned several by name. "I bet they're having one hell of a good time."

Bobbi said in a more serious tone, "You know, when Barry dies he wants to be cremated. I don't believe in that. I just don't believe in cremation, and I'm not going to cremate him."

"Goddammit, Bobbi, I want to be cremated."

"Well, I just don't believe in cremation. I tell you, I don't believe in it."

Barry replied, "I'll tell you something else. When I die, you may think this is funny, but when I die I want to be like this." He folded his hands over his chest, put his head back, and closed his eyes, looking very much like a corpse. "And between my hands, folded like they are right here, I want to have a rose. You might think it's funny, but I want to have a red rose in my hand."

Al muttered, "You sure you don't mean *Four Roses?*" Everybody laughed again.

Bobbi said, "Well, when I die I want to be buried in a red dress. I mean, I want to have the reddest dress you could ever find. That's what I want to have on. Red's my favorite color. Red is me. And I want to have a rich red dress on when I die."

"Well," said Al, standing up, "I've got to be moving on. Got some sermons to preach."

"Bullshit," said Daisey, as she followed him down the stairs. Al was singing "Onward Christian Soldiers."

After Al and Daisey left, the jovial mood changed very dramatically. Barry got one of his real somber expressions on his face, looking pained about something, and said to me, "I want to do three things right now. I want to go to my grand-mother's grave, to my daddy's house, and to the hospital to see Harry. I want to take the truck and I want you to go with me 'cause I ain't supposed to drive the truck by myself." I copped out. Barry was drunk, and I just couldn't stand an-other harrowing experience.

Barry said, "I've got to go." He then turned to Bobbi and said, "I want the keys to the truck!"

"You ain't going to have them," she replied firmly.

"I want them."

"You can't have them. If you want to go to the hospital, I'll take you after dinner, but I got work to do, and you don't have any business going to the hospital. You're drunk for one thing, and for another thing, Harry's wife is there."

"Well, I want to go, goddammit. I want to go to the cemetery."

"Well, the cemetery closes at five and it's five now."

Barry was becoming morose. "I want to go, I want to go. Give me the keys."

"No, you can't have them."

"I want them now, goddammit. I want them."

"No!"

Barry got up, looked Bobbi in the eye, and in an extremely gruff voice growled, "Give me the goddamn keys."

Taking a deep breath, Bobbi said, "All right, take the fucking keys and cram them up your ass. I'll be goddamn glad when Friday gets here, and I won't have to put up with this shit any more."

I asked, "What happens on Friday?"

"That's when the insurance runs out on the truck, and then nobody can drive that sonofabitch. Not me, not Barry, not anybody else." Bobbi reached in her pocketbook, pulling out the keys and dangling them in front of Barry's nose.

"Here, take them and cram them up your ass."

Barry took the keys, looked at them, and handed them back to Bobbi. She took the keys, shrugging her shoulders.

Barry said, "Now, nasty mouth, smart aleck, you have them back. All I said was I wanted the keys. I got them, felt them, and gave them back to you. So there."

Bobbi shook her head, "I am so sick and tired of this shit."

Barry said, "What, you think I'm some kind of a nut or something? You think I'm some kind of a nut? I ain't no nut!" He stomped out of the room saying, "You treat me like a little kid, that's what you treat me like, think I'm a damn nut."

Bobbi and I sat there with Walt. No one said anything. About a minute later Barry stomped back in. "All I wanted to do was go to see my grandmother's grave, go to my daddy's house, and go to see Harry. Now, what's wrong with that?"

In a softer tone Bobbi said, "There's nothing wrong with that. If you want to go to the hospital, we'll go after dinner. I'll take you."

Barry said, "And you know something else. . . ." Suddenly he changed into one of his sentimental moods. "You go outside in the alley, and there you'll see it. You all are going to think I'm crazy, every one of you in the room will think I'm crazy, but I don't care. You'll see the biggest, most beautiful yellow rose you've ever seen. I mean, it's opened up all pretty like, and it's going to be dead in a couple of days. But now it's just . . . oh, it's just so pretty, so pretty. And I mean, I wanted to cut that rose and put it on my grandmother's grave. That's what I wanted to do." Barry sniffed one of his drunken sobs. "Now, what's wrong with that? What's wrong with that?"

After a long moment of silence, Barry perked up and said, "Okay, I won't go now. We'll go after dinner." Bobbi shook her head and went back into the kitchen to start getting dinner ready. I got up and announced that I had to leave. Not only the Shackelford kids were present at that time but numerous other kids from the neighborhood. Somebody had hit Littlebit making a big red mark on the back of his neck and the children were asking help from anybody to go and find the big guys who beat him up. All this passed Barry by, who was sitting on the bed thinking about that yellow rose and his grandmother's grave. As I walked out the door, Barry turned to me and said, "You know, Joe, you should see that rose. I mean, it is really beautiful."

With Barry no longer working for Goldstein and with no prospects for welfare or food stamps, June got off to a gloomy start. Bobbi did not seem particularly concerned or upset, however, because she had more important things to think about—Bubba's graduation from the sixth grade. Bobbi had been looking forward to that day for some time and had put aside money to buy Bubba some new clothes and to get her hair done. She had gone shopping with Bubba a few days before and purchased a vest suit and a purple body shirt for him. The afternoon of his graduation she went to the beauty parlor to have her hair done in a beehive style. That evening when I gave her and Bubba a ride up to the school, she was effervescent. "Praise you God Almighty, the day has finally come! My boy is graduating from the sixth grade. I'm so proud of Bubba I just don't know what to say! I wouldn't miss this day for the world." Bubba was about a foot taller than any of his friends; and dressed in his purple shirt and striped vest, he looked more like a high school senior than a sixth-grader. He was almost as excited about his graduation as his mother.

Since I had to leave before the ceremony in order to take a local woman back to her relatives in West Virginia, I was gone for a few days and missed seeing Bubba receive his diploma. When I returned, I called Bobbi first thing to check on how the graduation had gone.

"The graduation? Oh," said Bobbi, "let me tell you. The graduation was okay. The kids were so cute, all dressed up and all, and Bubba was so handsome, but praise you God Almighty, you haven't heard the worst of it. Bubba, he got suspended from school!"

"Suspended from school?" I asked. "I thought he graduated."

"Yep, but they had a week left, and he's suspended from school. He's going to be taken to juvenile court, and they might even lock him up. That's what the principal said. Oh, she's mad, really mad. A half pint of vodka. He got caught with a half pint of vodka that Thursday night of graduation. Took it to the dance. Alton Short bought it for him. Al denies it, but I can prove it sure as hell. He calls me and Bubba both goddamn liars, but I can prove it, I can prove he bought it. . . . Now, eighteen of them took a drink. I know it was a half-pint, and eighteen of them took a drink. One girl squealed. The principal says the custodian has the bottle and is going to use it as evidence. But goddamn, that's a lie because *I* have the bottle! Bubba gave it to Daddy and Daddy gave it to me, so I don't care what that teacher says, she ain't got the bottle. But she says that unless Bubba tells her who gave him the bottle, she's going to take him to juvenile court. And Bubba ain't telling her.

"See, this was the way it was. I went over there to the liquor store to buy Kate a half pint of whiskey and I talked to Woody. Now, I don't know Woody, so I told him, 'I guess you know my husband, the one with the red hat.' 'You mean Barry?' 'Yeah. Well, I'm here to ask you about my son, Bubba. Was he in here last Thursday?' 'Yep.' I asked him if Bubba's friend Bobbi Higgins was there and he said yes. Anybody else? He said there was a fat, chunky man in his fifties with glasses. And that's who bought the bottle.

"Now who, praise you God Almighty, was that guy Al? And Al's calling everybody a liar. And now the teacher is so mad she wants to know who bought it, and Bubba, he didn't tell right off. And now Al, he swears he didn't do it.

Oh, I tell you, it's some shit. It really is some shit. I tell you, with friends like Alton Short who needs enemies?

"And old Barry, he ain't done nothing. He ain't got involved. See, he was drinking Thursday night, and he come home and Bubba come home and he and Bubba they really had it out. They started shoving each other around. And Barry was calling Bubba a sonofabitch and bastard and all that. Hell, I didn't know Bubba'd been drinking. If he had, Lord knows why he didn't hit Barry. But Barry ain't had a drink since then. He's been stone sober since Thursday. He told Bubba, 'You're lucky I wasn't up there at the school that night. I would have beaten your ass good.' And I told Barry, 'You're lucky you weren't up there or your ass would have been thrown in jail for being so drunk!'

"But you know, the whole thing is right comical, right comical, I say. 'Cause you know, all those kids that drank out of that bottle? Bubba's the only one that got suspended. And that's what they all wanted to do. Hell, they didn't want to go to school. But Bubba, he's the only one, and let me tell you, Jack, they're envious as hell of that boy. They wish they'd been suspended along with him."

Al became Bobbi's number one enemy. Since he had been a friend for years and considered himself a second father to Bobbi, I was sure that her hostile feelings would subside and she would change her mind about him. Al assured me Bobbi would forgive him in a few days and that before long it would be like old times. But not so. Bobbi never changed her mind. She said Al was not to enter her house ever again; and when I left the neighborhood the last of August, he had not done so.

Al's relationship to the Shackelfords was further complicated by a confrontation between him and Barry. Al told Barry about a new job, and they both started working for the subcontractor the next week. Barry was making four dollars an hour as a carpenter, and Al was hanging paper. Of course, Barry would rather be in business for himself, but that was no longer possible since a state law had gone into effect June 1 requiring all subcontractors to be licensed, have adequate insurance, and prove they paid taxes. Barry could not afford a license or insurance and had not paid any taxes for three years. His days as a subcontractor were over.

But four dollars an hour was not bad if Barry could work a forty-hour week. When he got his first check at the end of the second week in June, he was in good spirits. That afternoon, Barry drove down to repay me what he had borrowed. (Barry repaid every penny he borrowed from me over the year.) Al, who was in the truck with Barry, shouted, "We got a walking bar over here. Come on over." There was a case of beer between Al and Barry plus some bottles of whiskey, all of which were Al's.

Barry was exceptionally alert and appeared to be sober. He said, "You know, I ain't had anything to drink all week, not a drop."

I said, "You really look good."

"Well, I feel good. I feel real good. But I guess we're just like a bunch of niggers. Look at all this goddamn booze. We're gonna get drunk tonight."

After a brief pause, he said, "You know, Bobbi's got it in her mind that she's going to leave and the welfare is going to take care of her. Well, I think she's crazy as shit. But I'll tell you right now I've taken more off that woman than I should ever have to take off any woman. She's called me every name in the book. She's really run me in the ground. And if it wasn't for the kids, I would have busted out last week. I would have gotten on the bus and headed off. But it's the kids. Because of them, I'm staying. I've got the responsibility for my children and I know it. But Bobbi, she has really been giving me lots of shit, and I shouldn't have to take that off nobody. Don't get me wrong, don't get me wrong. I love Bobbi. I love her more than I can ever say, but it's just that I don't have to take that kind of shit off nobody."

Barry handed me ten dollars and said, "Here, this is what I owe you. Now we're all even. You know, if I'd had it, I would have paid you sooner. But I just didn't have it. But you know, whenever I borrow something, I'll always pay it back as soon as I have it. Sometimes it just takes a while."

Barry then reached in his pocket and pulled out a wrinkled rent receipt. "See this. Just paid for the month of May. I know

I'm still behind. Got to pay for June. Also got a lot of other bills to pay. And let me tell you, I'm going to work my ass. I'm going to work my ass off until I get paid up on all these back bills. I've been fucking off too long and it's time to get with it. Get off my ass and pay up these goddamn back bills. After all, I got a goddamn responsibility to the kids."

Al chuckled and said, "You know, Bobbi is sort of mad at my ass, too. And I'll tell you, I bought that bottle for Bubba. I bought it, but I didn't think that little sonafabitch would tell. He shouldn't of told. That just wasn't right. He shouldn't of told who bought it for him."

It was the next week that Barry and Al had their falling out. One morning Bobbi called me and with great enthusiasm gave me the news. "Well, it has done happened! Let me tell you, Jack, the shit is gonna hit the fan. Barry, he swears he is gonna kill Al!" Bobbi said this with great delight.

When I asked her why, she said she wasn't sure exactly but thought it had something to do with Al saying he was the father of her children. Last week Al had told the guys at work that he was Bubba's father. This made Bobbi angry when she heard about it; but Barry thought it was a funny joke and told Bobbi not to let it bother her. Then yesterday Barry came home and told Bobbi that Al had told the guys at work that *he* rather than Barry was the father of Cindy, Billy, and Littlebit. This was not funny. Alton Short had gone too far. With the money Barry had left over from last week, he got one of his shotguns out of hock and swore to Bobbi that he was going to kill Al.

That evening Bobbi called me back and was panicked. "It's gonna happen!" she exclaimed. "Al called and says he's coming over, and Barry's waiting for him in the alley. Barry's got his shotgun and it's loaded. He says he's going to kill Al and he means it. Believe me, he means it!" She said she had to hang up, but would call me back later.

Bobbi did not call back that night, but I heard from her the first thing the next morning. She started off talking about something else. "Well, it's happened," she said. "We got moving orders. The landlord done come by and given us moving orders. We got to move out. It happened just a few minutes ago. I was downstairs talking to Mack and Kate, but Daddy was here; and Mr. Brant, he come up to inspect our apartment. He says the house ain't fit for pigs, that we've done loused it up, and that we ain't got a right to tear up his house. I tell you, I ain't gonna worry about it because there's not a goddamn thing I can do. It might even be a blessing. Maybe it's my chance to break away."

I told Bobbi I was very sorry to hear the news. "But what about last night? What happened in the duel between Barry and Al?"

"Oh, that," she said nonchalantly. "Chicken shit Al didn't show up."

"You mean Al just didn't come over?"

"Hell no," said Bobbi in a disappointed voice, and then changed the subject back to the problem of finding another apartment.

The next day Al came by to repay some money he owed me. I told him I had heard of the misunderstanding between him and Barry and was very sorry to hear about it. Scratching his head, he said, "You know, it's a damn shame, a goddamn shame. Here we are; been friends for forty-two years. That's how long I've known Walt and been a friend of the family. And now it's all over; it's finished. I'll never set foot in that house again. I'll never speak to Bobbi or Barry again. It's all over."

"Well, what happened?" I asked.

"I'll tell you what happened. This guy, Lou, has been staying at my place. I don't see him that much, but he's a drunk, a no-good drunk. And he goes around telling all these dumb things. Like he told our boss that I had been screwing Bobbi for the last ten years. That I have been screwing Bobbi and that those kids, Cindy, Billy, and Littlebit, were all mine, not Barry's. That's what he told him.

"Well, Barry heard this and thought that I said it. So Barry calls me up last night. He calls me a motherfucker, he calls me a no-good motherfucker. Well, nobody calls me that. You can call me a lot of things. You can call me a sonofabitch, a bastard, but don't you call me a motherfucker. So I told Barry, 'Barry, you really mean that?' 'You're goddamn right I do.' So I told him, 'Put your money where your mouth is, you bastard. If that's the way you feel, you're nothing but a no-good sonofabitch, and I'm going to do to you what Bobbi's been wanting to do to you for the last three years. I'm going to blow your no-good goddamn brains out.' So Barry, he says, 'Oh yeah?' So I tell him, 'If you still think I'm a motherfucker, you meet me in the alley in one hour's time.' That was last night. Well, I was going to kill Barry. I'd had enough of that bastard anyway. I went and got my .44 Magnum from Ted. He's a colored guy, who keeps it for me. He knows I got a quick temper, and I like to use my hands rather than my gun if I can. But I went and got it from him. He pleaded with me not to take it 'cause he knew I'd use it. But I took it anyway, and he came along with me just to watch. He was going to try to persuade me to use my hands. You see, I know karate. But I took my gun, and I drove up to the alley, and I was there, and I was going to blow Barry's brains out. But Barry, he didn't show up, that chicken-shit bastard. He never came out of the house. I waited there for a good hour, hour and a half, but Barry never came out in the alley. He's a no-good chicken shit. Doesn't have the guts to come out."

Barry and Al no longer had to face each other at work because Barry got fired. On June 23 Bobbi called to tell me that Barry's boss had sworn out a warrant for Barry's arrest. Someone had broken into the office and stolen paint and building materials. His boss claimed it was Barry. "Of course, it ain't true," said Bobbi, " 'cause Barry, he was home all day drinking. I know he didn't do it. And besides, Barry steal paint?" Bobbi laughed. "Let me tell you, Jack, that is the last thing he would steal!"

Barry was unemployed only a week before he found another subcontractor willing to take him on. This fellow was an old friend, who operated out of his house just a few blocks away. The problem was that he, too, was an alcoholic and was as irregular as Barry in his work habits. Barry went to work just about every day; but more times than not he and his boss, Arnie Suggs, spent the day drinking and never left Suggs's house. Suggs also had a girl friend, who lived in Frederick; and once or twice a week he and Barry would go down to Frederick and spend the day. Sometimes they would spend the night as well, and Barry would be gone for days at a time. During the months of July and August, Bobbi and Barry saw very little of each other. Since Barry was bringing home some money on a regular basis, however, the financial squeeze eased up a bit.

Most of the immediate crises that arose during the last of June were averted. For whatever reasons, there was no follow-up on the warrant for Barry's arrest. Nor did the landlord, who had threatened to evict them, follow up his threats. Al and Barry made up, and Al joined Barry and started working for Arnie Suggs. Finally, with the help of Bobbi's social worker, she was able to be recertified for food stamps, though she had to pay twice as much for them. And best of all, the discovery of a past welfare department error increased Walt's welfare check from $52 to $110 a month.

Bobbi's social worker brought her a list of possible houses and apartment houses, which Bobbi spent some time calling, but none of them had vacancies. She was very enthusiastic about getting in a public housing project farther out in the country, one Bobbi described as "for white folks, not niggers." But since that project was still under construction, it would be months before anyone could move in. Bobbi's social worker continued to visit and encouraged Bobbi to make her move. But since there was nowhere for Bobbi to go, she stayed put.

Bobbi had been worried about her children failing their schoolwork. She was particularly worried about Cindy, who, according to her teacher, had a severe learning problem. Bobbi told me she was going to fight to be sure Cindy was promoted. "Listen here," she said, "if those bastards try to keep her back, you ain't never seen nothing like the shit that's going to hit the fan in that school. I mean, it's going to be like the goddamn *Titanic* sinking. I mean, goddamn, I'm going over there and raise some holy hell. God Almighty, if they try to fail that girl, if they even so much as *try* to fail her, I'm going up there and say, 'Listen here, Mrs. Lott, goddammit, you better let her go on, or you're going to mess up her like you messed up Bubba, keeping him back.'" Much to Bobbi's satisfaction, however, all her children, even Cindy, were promoted. (Cindy's teacher did say Cindy would be put in a special education class the next year.)

The Shackelfords' health problems continued. Walt finally had his cataracts operation on June 22 and was in the hospital for ten days. Bobbi visited him every day. Just as when Barry and Walt were in the hospital before, however, the doctor told them little; neither Bobbi nor Walt was sure how he was doing. When Walt returned home, the caseworker arranged to have a housekeeper come one day each week to help with cleaning the house. The housekeeper was black and Bobbi said she liked her fine, although the woman did considerably more chatting than house cleaning. Bobbi turned down having a public health nurse come a few hours each day to care for Walt, thinking that if she nursed Walt, she would be paid the amount that would go to the nurse. Bobbi never got paid, however.

Before Walt went to the hospital, he was very depressed about the home situation to which he would return. He told me, "You know, when the doctors told me that I got to stay in bed for six weeks after this operation, you know what I said? I said I'd rather die than come back here for six weeks without being able to leave. And I mean that. I mean, it's getting on my nerves, Joe. It's really bothering me. Staying up all night hollering. I can't sleep no more. I feel like I'm going to suffocate. I mean, I really would rather die than have to come back here and stay here for six weeks. I just don't want to come back."

Nevertheless, Walt did return to a home that was just as chaotic as before; and once home, his eyes continued to give him trouble. Although Bobbi gave him pain medicine and made numerous calls to his doctor, nothing seemed to do much good. One weekend when things got particularly bad, Bobbi pleaded with the doctors to take a look at Walt's eyes. They told her that she had been overreacting, that Walt's eyes were doing as well as could be expected, and that they must be patient. On Monday, when Bobbi brought Walt to the doctor's office—she had given up trying to call—they informed her that one of his eyes had hemorrhaged and that he would probably lose that eye permanently. Bobbi was furious, but she felt there was nothing she could do. When I left seven weeks after the operation, Walt's eyes were still paining him and he still could not see. Though the doctors assured Walt that one eye was coming along very well, Bobbi confessed that she never expected her stepfather to see again.

Bobbi's health had not gotten much better either. Her periods were still irregular, and she continued to lose excessive amounts of blood. Midway through the summer, she told me that on August 15 she would have her long-awaited operation. August 15 came and passed, however, without Bobbi's further mentioning the operation.

Bobbi's most pressing health problems were her severe headaches and chest pains, which had started the first of June. She finally went to a doctor, who told her the problems had to do with nervous tension. As a matter of principle, Bobbi refused to take tranquilizers. Nevertheless, the doctor prescribed some pills for Bobbi which he did not identify. One day she called me and said, "Hey, Joe, I want you to do me a big favor. I got me a medical book from Kate—she used to work in a doctor's office—but I can't read all the big words. I want to come over and let you read it."

So Bobbi came over and we plodded through the book together. We figured out that the pills prescribed were in fact tranquilizers. They were supposed to be for a person with cholic spasms, anxiety, and so on. Bobbi listened attentively and nodded her head, saying, "Uh-huh . . . oh . . . I see . . . well, goddamn, tranquilizers . . . that sonofabitch, the damnedest thing I've ever heard. He never told me he was prescribing tranquilizers." Reluctantly Bobbi continued taking the pills, admitting that they probably were doing her some good.

Things seemed to ease up a bit in August. Though Barry was not around much, he was working; and for the two weeks preceding our departure, he was sober. Bobbi talked less and less about leaving him, and the two of them seemed to be getting along much better. Although they were three months behind in their rent, it did not appear that Brant was going to evict them as long as they were making an effort to pay. With Bobbi's persuasion, Barry finally agreed to get a new set of dentures—it had been years since he lost his lower set and the airplane glue was not working well on his upper set—and the Medicaid card paid for them. With his new set of teeth he looked like a different person.

When our departure day of August 18 finally came around, Barry came down with the kids to help me load a U-Haul truck. He was more alert and talkative than I had seen him for some time. He said that he hadn't touched a drop of liquor for over two weeks. When I asked him if this was something permanent, he responded, "Ah shit, hell, I'll have me something to drink. It's just a matter of time. I've just been too busy to drink anything the last couple of weeks. Got too many bills to pay. Ah hell, no, you know better than to ask a dumb question like that. It ain't permanent."

Bobbi and the children helped us as well as Barry. We talked and joked around while we worked, without any mention of our leaving. We finished packing around six in the evening and sat on the porch talking. Barry commented that it wouldn't be long until hunting season came in and this year he was going to get the big buck.

Around seven-thirty Bobbi said, "Come on, kids, it's time to go. Walt's sick. His eyes are hurting him something awful and he needs somebody there." Barry, Bobbi, and Cindy got in the truck. The rest of the kids hopped in back. I waved good-by as the truck chugged up the hill.

Two

THE MOSEBYS:
A FAMILY CAUGHT BETWEEN

6

One Day with June

June and Sam Moseby were our neighbors on Clay Street. In his early fifties, Sam was a front-end mechanic for a large Dodge dealership in Washington. He and his forty-six-year-old wife, June, had been living together for six years and had a five-year-old son, Sammy. Sam had three grown children by a previous marriage, all of whom lived nearby but whom he saw only occasionally. June had been married twice before and had three children in their twenties. Between them, June and Sam had ten grandchildren. All of June's children were by her first husband, who was an alcoholic and whom she left after five years of marriage. Her second husband, twenty-seven years her elder, died of cancer eight years ago. In contrast to Sam's children, two of June's children were regular visitors on Clay Street; the third, who rarely kept in touch with her mother, lived in the country near the Chesapeake Bay.

June was born in Richmond where she spent the early years of her life. When she was seven, her family moved to the Washington area where June lived for eight years on the far outskirts of the city in a predominantly rural area. Sam was born in Washington, and all of his seven brothers and sisters still lived in the D.C. area (none lived in the city). Sam's bachelor brother, Barney, lived with Sam and June on Clay Street.

June had reddish brown hair, which was in curlers about half the time. The wrinkles around her eyes and her tightly drawn lips hinted she had had her share of troubles. June's face usually expressed exactly how she felt. While at times she would appear extremely glum and sorrowful, more often her eyes twinkled and her face beamed.

Sam wore horn-rimmed glasses and had thinning hair,

which was usually watered down and slicked back. He also had long sideburns and except for a "beer belly" appeared to be in very good physical condition, looking somewhat younger than his fifty-three years.

June had a high school diploma; Sam dropped out of Catholic parochial school after the eighth grade, as did his brother Barney. Before Barney lived with the Mosebys, he spent thirteen years in the State Institute for the Criminally Insane. Diagnosed as a "paranoid schizophrenic," Barney was unable to work and received $89 a month in welfare (Aid for the Permanently and Totally Disabled).

June and Sam lived on the ground floor of a one-bedroom duplex, for which they paid $110 a month, all utilities included. The duplex had a front porch and a patch of grass for a yard, large enough for a garden. While their house had once been a single-family house, it was then part of a large apartment house complex on the block. Having lived in the duplex for four years, June and Sam were almost the senior residents of the apartment houses, which occupied one entire side of Clay Street.

Every weekday at six in the morning, the alarm goes off at the Moseby household. This morning June is asleep on the couch in the living room, where she often sleeps when she and her husband are having an argument. Last night when Sam came home hot and dirty from working on cars all day, he was in an unusually grouchy mood. When their five-year-old son, Sammy, chased a ball into Sam's garden, tripped, and squashed a geranium, Sam hollered at Sammy more fiercely than usual; June hollered back at Sam, telling him to lay off. Since that time, about eight-thirty last evening, no one has said much to anyone else; and Sammy is sleeping on the bed beside Sam instead of his usual place on the roll-away.

Regardless of how mad June is at Sam, or Sam at June, however, she fixes his breakfast, prepares his lunch for him to take to the shop, and fixes his dinner when he comes home. On more than one occasion Sam has remarked, "A roof over your head, a job, good food, goddamn, what the hell does a sonofabitch want? This is living." The emphasis is more often than not on "food" and usually said when June can hear it. During the course of their six years together, June has faithfully and carefully paid attention to these duties; and so today, even though she is still mad at him, the first thing she does is go into the kitchen and begin to get Sam's lunch together—two pieces of fried chicken, a bacon-lettuce-and-tomato sandwich, and some potato chips, neatly wrapped in stay-fresh sandwich bags. Once, instead of the potato chips, she neatly wrapped a half-dozen condoms in a stay-fresh bag, but not today. Since she didn't sleep well on the couch last night, she is tired and doesn't feel like playing jokes. Finally, June fixes a thermos of iced tea. Sam says he couldn't work on cars all day unless he had the thermos of tea.

Sleeping in the storeroom adjacent to their small kitchen and snoring loudly as usual is Sam's hulk of a brother, Barney. June bangs around in the kitchen, though she knows the house could cave in and Barney would go on sleeping. He will wake up at his own good time, probably around ten, and then lumber into the kitchen, wearing the same clothes he slept in and has been wearing for over a week, and expecting breakfast. And begrudgingly, June will fix him his usual two eggs, six slices of bacon, four pieces of toast, juice and milk. It wouldn't be so bad if Barney were not in the kitchen where he's literally the first thing she lays eyes on each morning; but since they have only a one-bedroom apartment, where else is he going to sleep?

When I first met the Mosebys, June was quick to point out that Barney had mental problems. "He's—what do you call it? Mentally retarded or something like that. Anyway, he ain't all there, he don't work, and we're stuck with him. Sam has a brother with a big house, who says he makes lots of money. But not *him*. He wouldn't have Barney. We're the ones who got him."

By seven o'clock, when Sam's lunch and breakfast are fixed, June wanders back to the bedroom and gives him a firm nudge. "Okay, big Daddy, it's that time." Sam turns over, gets up, and staggers into the bathroom.

He gulps down a large bowl of cereal, juice, and coffee without saying much. He loves a big breakfast though he doesn't have the time to eat one except on weekends when he will have several eggs, a half pound of bacon or sausage, and grits, and will take an hour to linger at the kitchen table. By seven-thirty he is finished and drives away in his '59 Chrysler New Yorker. Although its blue color is fading and it is rusting around the fenders and full of dents, Sam loves that car. Roomy and powerful, it rides smoothly and everything is push-button. He bought it four years ago for three hundred dollars; and when it finally gives out, he says he'll get another one just like it. Although Sam could afford to get a new car with the wages he makes, he doesn't like to buy on time; and he likes the feel of a big, old New Yorker.

It takes Sam about thirty minutes to get to his job, which is located in the heart of the black ghetto in D.C. He doesn't like the location much, though he personally has had only one bad experience: during the riots of 1968, someone shot through his windshield when he was driving home. Since that time he has warned June never, *never*, to go into D.C. alone; and except for trips to work, he avoids going into Washington himself.

Sam has been a mechanic practically all his life. After dropping out of school in the eighth grade, he has worked on cars —mainly Chrysler products and mainly on front ends. Although he used to switch employers often, he has been with this dealer for almost ten years. More important, because of his reputation he doesn't feel he has to put up with unfair working conditions. "If those sons of bitches don't like what I do," he says, "I tell 'em to cram it up their ass, and I'll get me another job. I tell 'em I don't have to take no shit off them or nobody else. If that don't ride right, tough titty!" Sam refuses to work overtime or on weekends and has done so in only a few "emergency" cases.

Every Friday when he gets paid, Sam will hand his check, usually for over two hundred dollars, to June, who will deposit it and keep track of the finances. While June lends a lot of money to her children—most of it without Sam's knowledge—she tries to put as much as she can into savings. Since Sam does not have a retirement plan at work, June once remarked: "If there is anything I don't want to be, it's miserable poor in my old age. I was miserable poor when I was young and that's enough."

When Sam leaves, June sighs. It isn't so much that he got mad at Sammy unnecessarily last night that bothers her, but rather that Sam seems to be insensitive to most of her problems. She feels he just does not understand her. He does not understand how difficult it is for a woman to go through menopause, which at age forty-six is what is happening to June. He doesn't understand that June's three grown children need her help and draw on her feelings and emotions. He doesn't understand that Barney's being home all day and just sitting there watching TV is enough to drive anyone crazy. He doesn't understand and is often rude to some of her friends who stop by the house to chat and share their problems with her. There seems to be so much on her shoulders, so many people with problems and so few people around whom she can share *her* problems with. (June once remarked, however: "As mad as we might be at each other, that Sam, he ain't never laid a hand on me. So things could be worse.") This is why, after Sam leaves, the first thing June does is open the refrigerator door and take her first swig of the day from a half pint of Canadian Club whiskey. She's been doing this for years, and it helps her get through the day.

Closing the refrigerator door, June opens the freezer. The first big decision of the day is what to have for dinner. Before she has time to decide what to take out, the phone rings; it is Arlene, the youngest of her three children. Arlene, who turned twenty-one several months ago, has been married for five years, though she and her husband, Lester (called Les), a truck driver for REA, are now having their problems. He is from West Virginia; and although June and Sam thought he was too "country" at first, they have come to love him as one of the family. Somewhat disturbed by the situation, June still looks forward to the daily call from Arlene and has agreed that she won't lecture her if Arlene will just keep in touch.

After talking to Arlene, June lights a cigarette and turns on the color TV. This is the Mosebys' most prized possession, and it is left on from this hour until the last person is in bed, whether or not anyone happens to be looking at it. Usually

June isn't aware of what is on, and the color is rarely adjusted. Sam bought the set two years ago when he was in one of his grouchy moods. When he couldn't get the old black and white set to work properly, he stormed out, walked in the first TV store he came to, and purchased the biggest, most elaborate set in the store. The set cost over six hundred dollars, and he *is* still paying for it.

June sits on the couch smoking a cigarette, staring blindly at the set. (Both June and Sam smoke over two packs a day.) Since the next hour or so, when Barney and Sammy are asleep, is the only time she will have to herself the whole day, she likes to savor it. Though June thinks she probably should do some straightening, she decides not to, since she did some house cleaning yesterday and since she is not one for spick-and-span houses. Their furniture is old and worn, but the house as a whole looks cozy. With their limited space, they must use the dining room for storage space as well as for eating; and Sammy's toys are always strewn out on the floor. June says she would go crazy if she were too concerned with neatness. They also keep Sammy's bicycle in the dining room so it won't get stolen; and against the wall they keep a small electric organ and electric guitar, which Sam insisted they give Sammy for Christmas. June warned Sam that Sammy was too young for those presents, but Sam insisted, buying them on a whim just like he bought the TV. June is extremely proud of the fact that Sammy has never been without toys. Since neither she nor Sam could afford fancy presents for their other children, who are now grown, they consciously indulge themselves a little with Sammy. "After all," says June, "I'm like a grandmother to the boy, a grandmother with no in-between generation, and grandmothers have the right to spoil!"

Besides Sammy's toys, the dining room is also where Sam keeps most of his gadgets: his portable stereo and country music albums, a Polaroid camera, cassette recorder, two movie cameras, and three movie projectors—super 8 (for home movies), 8 mm. (for dirty movies), and a new one he got last Christmas that will show both types of film. As for the other items, some of them he got hot from Les, who has friends at

REA who get various items at reduced rates; and Sam hates to turn down a good deal.

Unlike many of the families on Clay Street, Sam and June do not own a single gun. Not being a hunter, Sam sees no need for a gun in his house. He occasionally remarks how stupid he thinks one of his friends is for having six guns in his house. "One of these days he's going to kill somebody with one of them guns, and it'll probably be a goddamn accident. Then he'll be sorry."

While Sam is proud of his cameras and stereo, June has collected numerous ornaments, which she has placed around the living room: a large ash tray with "Sammy" inscribed on it, a pottery statue of a pregnant grandmother (which Les and Arlene gave her when she was pregnant with Sammy), a colorful "Home, Sweet Home" wall hanging, and a dozen or so other china trinkets she and Sam have picked up at roadside stands.

June hardly has time to finish her cigarette when Dora knocks on the door and deposits her five-year-old son, Ray. Dora works as a secretary in Washington and leaves her son for June to baby-sit all day. Being the same age, Sammy and Ray usually keep each other entertained. Two other women often leave their children (two each) with June, and those times it can become very hectic in the one-bedroom house. June doesn't like to talk about charging anybody for anything and takes what the parents can afford to pay. Sam insists June should be firmer, since too many times the parents fail to pay anything at all. June snaps back that she doesn't do it for the money but to help people out.

After chatting briefly with June, Dora rushes off. Since, as usual, she failed to give Ray any breakfast, June starts scrambling some eggs. When Sammy hears Ray, he bounds into the kitchen, and June orders the two of them to clear out until breakfast is ready. While they are eating, two women from down the street knock on the door to see if June has any change for laundry money. (Since the laundromat is directly behind their house, June always keeps a jar of change.) June invites them in for coffee, but they can't stay.

When Barney arises at nine-thirty, June fixes him his breakfast, after which she is faced with washing the breakfast dishes and cleaning up the kitchen. Very often this must wait until the afternoon, depending on who stops in to leave their kids or get change. Today there are the usual interruptions: a next-door neighbor comes over to borrow sugar and ends up staying an hour, talking mainly about her four children and their respective problems in school; another woman from up the street calls to report that things aren't going well between her and her husband (he is drinking again and last night got a little rough); an old lady known to June only as Grammaw stops by for laundry change, has a beer, and catches the last half of a soap opera.

And so the morning passes. I lived next door to the Mosebys for one year on Clay Street, and at some point almost every day either I or my wife stopped by, like others, to catch up on the day's happenings. Rarely was June without someone sitting on the couch smoking a cigarette, sipping coffee or beer, and chatting. The person most frequently present, however, was Phyllis, a twenty-nine-year-old woman from two doors down, who moved to Clay Street in the mid-fall and gradually came to monopolize June's time. Phyllis had more than her share of personal problems. She had a severe case of emphysema, was convicted of shoplifting and given a suspended sentence early in the fall, and was on the verge of becoming an alcoholic as well as being a lesbian. She had been a local mail carrier until she was fired in the late spring. Although Phyllis lived on Clay Street with her grandmother ("Granny" as distinguished from "Grammaw"), she informed June and Sam that she had "adopted" them as parents. Although Phyllis's mother lived a few blocks away, she was a severe alcoholic, and the two despised each other. Sam, however, has little use for Phyllis, who quite frequently was the cause of family turmoil between him and June.

It is now almost noon, and Phyllis is still sitting on June's couch. June has gotten very little housework done. While she was talking with Phyllis, Ray and Sammy were playing tag in the dining room. Around eleven, Barney agreed to stop watching TV and play hide-and-seek with them outside, a gesture that helped quiet things down. Even so, the morning remained hectic with Sammy, Ray, and various other neighborhood children running into the house, at which times June and Phyllis would holler, "Outside, dammit!" and the kids would scamper out again.

June has often remarked that one of the problems with their house is that it is just too small. Although it is a duplex, it is like their own house, since the upstairs unit opens onto another street. Since it has a front porch and a small yard where Sam can do his gardening, Sam has stated emphatically that he will never move. June agrees that their apartment is much nicer than any of the other apartments on the block, though she admits she wouldn't mind owning a single-family house like the ones across the street. However, Sam refuses to consider buying; and besides, June tells everyone, they are too old to buy a house. Anyway, they both like this neighborhood where the people are friendly and not snooty like people you find in some newer areas.

June puts together some peanut butter and jelly sandwiches, pours some Coke for Sammy, Ray, and Barney, nibbles on a half a sandwich herself, and looks in the cupboard to see what she needs at the store. Barney will watch the children while June goes shopping. She is not sure whether or not she can trust Barney, since there is just no telling when he might go "bizerk" again as he used to do a few years back; but as long as he keeps taking the tranquilizers the doctor prescribed, she figures he will be okay. She knows Barney loves the kids and they love him; but if something went wrong, she could never forgive herself. Sammy is her reason for living, she tells people; and there is nothing that is going to keep her from living until the day he graduates from high school. After that day, she can die. Since so far none of her or Sam's children has fulfilled her expectations in this regard, June is already a little worried about Sammy.

June enjoys going to the store because it enables her to get out of the house and more important, she can drive her car. June says she loves her car even more than Sam loves his; and next to Sammy it is the thing she says she prizes most. Until three years ago, June did not know how to drive. One day Sam said he was fed up with giving June rides to shop and run errands and remarked: "Why don't you drive your own goddamn self?" June lit up and the next week took driving lessons. Two days after she got her permit, she backed Sam's car into a mailbox, putting another dent in the fender. Of course, if she had not told Sam, he probably would not have noticed it. But she did, and he was furious. "You're never, *never,* going to put your ass in the driver's seat of my car again!" he said. The next day Sam drove home a battered 1955 Plymouth he paid two hundred dollars for and said it was hers. A few months ago when the Plymouth quit, Sam got her a 1963 Dodge which is, as far as June is concerned, the most beautiful, the most elegant, the most luxurious car in the world and much nicer than that blue junk heap of her husband's.

Today June does not have much shopping to do. Since she decided to fix beef stew, she must buy some carrots and potatoes as well as some other items. They have a freezer, and June can take advantage of things such as meat sales, though generally she will go shopping two or three times a week, buying smaller quantities of food. (Sam often shops on the weekends, and together they often go to the Farmer's Market to buy large quantities of fresh vegetables in season, freezing what they don't eat.) Unlike most of her neighbors, who shop at the bigger stores in the shopping center ten minutes away, June shops at the smaller and older Safeway, which is only a few minutes away. It doesn't have as good a selection as the larger stores in the newer shopping centers, but June likes it and is in the habit of going there.

June quite often gives Granny or Grammaw or other women in the neighborhood who don't have cars rides to go grocery shopping. Today she gives Linda a ride. Linda is a twenty-three-year-old woman who lives in the apartments with her three small children. Since Barney agrees to watch her three- and five-year-olds, she brings only the baby with her. Of the twenty or so families who live in apartment units on Clay Street, six households are divorced or separated women with small children. Linda is the only who doesn't work and the only one who receives AFDC. Although Linda would like to work, so far she has not been able to work out the baby-sitting as have the others, who leave their children with relatives or neighbors. (She hired a baby-sitter for a few months, but the girl neglected the children and Linda had to quit her job as a secretary.)

June and Linda spend about forty-five minutes browsing through the store, with Linda doing considerably more shopping than June. June is particularly fond of Linda because June was about Linda's age when her first husband left her with her three small children the ages of Linda's children. June recalls many times when she did not know where the next meal was coming from and times when she received emergency help from church charities. Because Linda is in similar circumstances, June tries to do little things like watch her kids and give Linda rides to the store or to the welfare. Last Easter June took up a neighborhood collection, which amounted to over twelve dollars, so Linda could give her children their Easter outfits. Ironically, June's older daughter, who is Linda's age, with five children, finds herself in pretty much the same situation. But June has more or less given up on Ruby. She can't understand Ruby's apparent willingness to accept welfare and feels less sorry for her, especially since for over two years Ruby has been living with a man who June feels should work and support the children.

On the way home June makes her only brief excursion into Washington. She goes approximately two blocks into the District to the Stop and Shop Liquor Store where she buys a half pint of Canadian Club. Having known the guy behind the counter for years, June considers him a friend of the family's. When she and Sam set up housekeeping six years ago, he gave them a free bottle. Since John also is a dealer in dirty movies, Sam takes some delight in trading with or buying movies from him. Though June would like to stay and swap jokes, she declines, since Linda's baby is fussing and she is worried about Barney and the children.

The afternoon for June is much like the morning, except she will not let interruptions keep her from fixing the beef stew. The house chores can wait, but June knows how much dinner means to Sam and takes real pride in her cooking. Even though there are the usual phone calls and neighbors who stop by for change, June manages to get the stew done fairly easily. She even has time to go outside, sit on the porch, and watch the children playing in the street. Two or three of the children are black. While some of her neighbors have expressed concern about the blacks moving into the next block, June's response has been only, "Hell, folks got to live somewhere."

After distributing cookies to the children at the usual four o'clock "cookie time," June gets a glimpse of a couple of TV programs and is able to finish washing the breakfast dishes. At four forty-five the insurance man comes by, but since June doesn't have the $52 on hand to pay him—she has a $750 burial policy on Sam and $1,500 on Barney—he says he'll be back tomorrow. At five she breaks up a fight between Ray and another child. Dora comes back at five-fifteen for Ray, and around five-thirty June goes back into the kitchen to prepare for the homecoming of whom June sarcastically refers to as "The Great White Master."

Sam's return home from work is a ritual. During the year I was there, the event seldom varied and was rarely ever off more than five minutes from five-thirty. The car will stop, then back into the parking place on Clay Street, which in deference to Sam nobody ever parks in, even when people know he will not be using it. In the winter he will have on his work jacket and a baseball-type hat. In the summer his blue work shirt will be grease-stained and often wringing wet. He will carry his empty lunch pail in one hand, his thermos under one arm, and always, *always*, in his other hand he will carry a brown bag that contains a six-pack of Carling's Black Label and a half pint of Canadian Club whiskey, which he has purchased at the same Stop and Shop June visited earlier. (Over the year I often wondered why Sam didn't buy a *case* of beer and a case of *fifths* of Canadian Club at a time. Were he to purchase the whiskey in this fashion, he probably could save half his money. But few people on Clay Street purchased whiskey like this. The severe alcoholics tended to buy fifths instead of pints if they had the money. Perhaps this was Sam's way of disassociating himself from people he looked down on. Perhaps it was his way of rationing the amount he drank, for occasionally he would send Barney up to Frank's Corner Market for more beer if their children or neighbors happened to drop in, but rarely for more whiskey. When I asked Sam about it once, he mumbled something like, "Well bullshit, I don't know. I just do, that's all.")

When Sammy sees his father, he will run out and hug him around the knees; and Sam will smile, move the brown bag from his hand to under his arm, and rustle Sammy's hair. "Hiya, kid," he will say and then speak to Barney and nod to any of the neighbors who might be outdoors. If Sam's next-door neighbor is out working, Sam will chat with him before going in. The conversation will start with, "Goddamn, it's been a hot day; I'd like to have died in that sonofabitch shop," or "Goddamn, it was cold in there today," or "Goddamn, I'm tired of taking shit off that stupid-assed boss, who don't know a goddamned thing about cars," and then will quickly change to the ball game that evening or the bowling last Sunday, or whatever problems the neighbor has had at work that day.

Sam excuses himself, disappears inside, and returns with an opened can of Black Label. He usually offers a can to whoever happens to be around. In the summer the next thing he always does is examine his flower garden and do what's necessary to keep it in shape.

Invariably if there is a tricycle or wagon on the sidewalk in front of the house, Sam will holler, "Whose goddamn piece of shit is this? I've told these kids to keep their goddamn toys in their own goddamned yard. I'm going to throw this shit in the garbage where it belongs. . . ." He will then sit down beside Barney, who has been rocking on the porch most of the afternoon, and intersperse long gulps from the Black Label with a few grimacing swigs from the Canadian Club. Just as he finishes off the first beer, there is a call from indoors: "Well, big Daddy"—said with sarcasm—"come and get it."

Before this time, June and Sam have avoided having to speak to one another, partly because of the argument last night and partly because Sam can't stand hearing about neighborhood intrigue. He is tired, dirty, and doesn't want to be bothered with other people's problems. He assumes some calamity has occurred to someone—his kids, June's kids, the neighbors—so why talk about it. He would rather not talk at all than hear about Phyllis or her bitchy mother or somebody else. So quite often neither he nor June has much to say to one another, and the evening gets off to a shaky start. This evening is no exception. Everyone squeezes into the kitchen and gulps down the food, not saying very much. Sammy finishes first and runs outdoors to join one of his buddies. June busies herself serving the food and cleaning up. Barney stretches, belches, and goes back into the living room to watch "Batman and Robin"; and Sam has a third helping. It is a good meal.

By seven o'clock everyone except June, who is washing dishes, is on the front porch, enjoying the evening street activity. Sam is inspecting his garden a few more times and feeling a little guilty about last night, muttering, "The goddamn kid ought to know better than to tramp in the garden after a goddamn ball, what the shit. . . ." A young man from across the street, who is out washing his car, hollers over asking if the bowling team is doing any better. "Shit no," Sam hollers back, "but we're trying. Can't do too much goddamn worse, goddamn!"

As Sam begins watering his flowers, a 1960 battered red Dodge convertible pulls up and parks. Ted and his girl friend, Anita, get out and stroll toward Sam's front porch. Ted is June's twenty-five-year-old son, who works in the parts warehouse of a plumbing supply wholesaler and has been sleeping on June and Sam's couch off and on for the past five months. He and Anita are engaged and are planning to have a big Catholic church wedding. While June and Sam approve of Anita, they aren't very excited about the idea of a big church wedding. Since Ted has had some hard times lately, however— Anita will be his third wife—June says she will do anything she can to help him get himself together. Ted and Anita announce that they are going to the drive-in and can't stay long. Anita helps June finish in the kitchen while Ted drinks a beer on the front porch with Sam, who is listening to country music on the radio.

After finishing cleaning up, June and Anita come out on the front porch. Around eight, when Sam switches the radio to the ball game, Ted and Anita leave for the drive-in. By this hour many families are sitting on their stoops and more children are playing in the street. Some men are tinkering with their cars; but most folks are just sitting on their porches or stoops, drinking beer and watching the kids. In the wintertime it is completely different. Hardly anyone is on the street. Most everyone, like June and Sam, is inside watching TV.

Littleboy is barking unusually loudly tonight. Littleboy is one of the many neighborhood mutts who bark at everything that moves. Barney and Littleboy have an intimate relationship, although everyone else, especially June and Sam, despise the dog. Though Littleboy belongs to a neighbor up the street, he spends most of his time with Barney.

It is very interesting to watch what happens in the course of a normal evening. When Barney will be sitting on the porch petting Littleboy, June will come out and kick the dog, grumbling, "You goddamn cur, get off this porch! If I ever see you around this porch, I'll call the pound." Littleboy will then scamper home, usually hiding under a car up the street. As soon as June goes indoors, however, Littleboy will creep back down, cautiously looking out of the corner of his eye to see if June or Sam is around, sneak up around the side of the porch, and lie down beside Barney. Barney will begin petting Littleboy. A few minutes later another neighbor will stroll by and holler, "Goddamn sonofabitch, get out of here! No dogs allowed in these apartments. Get out of here, you damn dog." And the process will repeat itself. Sam and June have both talked about calling the pound. The super of their apartment has sworn he's going to call the pound; but so far, Littleboy has remained.

This evening after Harry Cheek, a neighbor from a few doors down, finishes washing his car, he wanders over and sits down on our front porch. We begin to chat about how hot it is, at which point June wanders over and makes a comment: "You got any spare beds in your house tonight? That sonofabitch kicked me out of bed again, he told me to get the hell out. So I'm coming over to spend the night with you."

We say, "Sure, sure," but find it hard to say anything more.

"You know, that character over there, he's really been giving me a hard time, and I just don't know what I'm going to do with him." June goes on to say how she is ready to leave if Sam doesn't begin to show he appreciates her.

Harry, who is a government clerk and a devout Baptist, seems very interested and in typical fashion brings up the subject of religion. He asks, "June, I've been wondering, what is your philosophy of life anyway?"

June gives Harry a funny look, replying, "Are you kidding?" Then after a pause, she becomes serious. "To me, love is important. Now, I don't go to church. . . ."

"Don't go to church?" Harry says. "How can you believe in God and love and not go to church?"

"I believe in love and God, and I was brought up a Baptist, but I'm sick of those hypocrites. Those no-good bastards. You know what they did to me? After my second husband died—and that was a hard time for me, let me tell you—I went out with another man, just for a ride, and to get some help and consolation. It's for damned sure those sons of bitches weren't giving me help. They ignored me; my husband was the backbone of the church, but they knew my background and past, and they didn't give a damn about me. Well, I have one word for those hypocrites. Those people aren't Christians. Most of the people who go to church are the same way. And since then I've had no use for the church."

Sam, who is watching from his porch, makes some comments, which everyone can hear. "There goes bigmouth again. Preaching as usual. Yak, yak, yak. Hey, Joe, when she gets on your nerves, send her somewhere else."

June talks on without paying him any mind. As we talk on more about religion, Harry becomes more abstract and June gets more annoyed, finally saying, "Listen, goddammit, I don't want to talk no more about religion, and I don't want to talk anything about politics either. You're a goddamn religious fanatic and what's more, you're a Republican, and I can't stand either one of those two animals. So forget it. I'm finished with this. Is that clear?" Harry laughs nervously.

By this time Sam, who has been making loud comments, can't contain himself any longer. He comes over very slowly, remarking, "What's all this bullshit about this bullshit religion? Now, I'm a Catholic, born and raised, but I'm a half-assed Catholic. I don't really give a goddamn about the Catholic Church. I used to go to it, but hell, the Catholic Church . . . well . . ." Sam talks on about his upbringing as a Catholic and the times he got in trouble with the nuns and kicked out of the Catholic school.

When June then brings up a point about baptism—the fact that she wasn't baptized until she was twenty-eight—Sam says: "How did they baptize you? By emersion? Did they stick your head in the water?" When June nods her head, Sam laughs. "Well, they should have drowned your goddamn ass! That's what they should have done. Drowned your goddamned ass then and there, and I would never had to put up with your loud yakkety-yak." Everyone laughs.

June and Sam are now talking to each other. Harry leaves, saying he has given up trying to get us to talk more about religion. After he has departed, June says, "Well, he's a damn religious fanatic. I tell you, if he was really religious, he wouldn't beat his wife; and I know for a fact that he beats his wife."

"Yeah," says Sam. "Goddamn sonofabitch, he's as much of a hypocrite as anybody else." June and Sam agree for the first time in twenty-four hours.

June continues on about how you have to live love rather than talk about it, and how a neighbor who came to her house three weeks ago in desperation now has found something new to live for and is displaying a new engagement ring. While the banter between Sam and June continues, it is much more lighthearted and jovial. When Littleboy wanders by, Sam and June both scowl. He tucks his tail and runs up the hill.

"By-by, Littleboy," Barney hollers from the front porch.

June then says, "Hey, you know what time it is? It's time for our TV show."

"That's right, goddamn. Tonight is Wednesday night."

Sam follows June as they go inside, and after a few minutes Sam hollers for Sammy to come and get his bath. Sam always gives Sammy his bath. Barney sits on the front porch talking to a guy from up the street; and sure enough, Littleboy, who is hiding under his favorite automobile, perks up his eyes, begins to wag his tail, and trots down very cautiously.

It is now about ten-thirty. Laughter still continues; occasional shouts come from up the street; lights are beginning to be turned off.

7

Fall

When we first moved into our duplex next to June and Sam, Ted, June's twenty-five-year-old son, was June's main concern.

Although Ted had gone against his mother's wishes by dropping out of high school, until recently June had been pleased with the way things had turned out. He had joined the Army where he learned electronics and was able to get his high school equivalency. During his two-year assignment in Germany, he fell in love and married a German girl, Helga, whom he proudly brought home with him when he got transferred back to the States.

After Ted got discharged, he and Helga moved into an apartment on Clay Street; and because of his army experience with electronics, Ted got a good-paying job with the telephone company as a special technician in a satellite communications center. Since Helga worked as a cashier at a supermarket, between them they had a good income. They bought a new Cougar, a color TV as big as Sam's, a walnut stereo console, and new furniture for their apartment.

Then about ten months before we moved to Clay Street, Helga ran off with the meat cutter where she worked. Before it was all over and Ted was able to get a divorce, he had taken an overdose of sleeping pills, spent a week on the mental ward of the county hospital, and lost his job.

In the spring of the year when he was at his lowest, he met Peg, who, Ted said, helped him get himself together. June and Sam despised Peg, however, claiming she was the person holding Ted down. Peg was six years older than Ted, had five children by a previous marriage, and was already a grandmother. (June said she found the grandmother thing particularly hard to take, since somehow that would make June an instant "step-great-grandmother.")

When we arrived on Clay Street, Ted and Peg had been married for one week; and Peg was five months' pregnant with Ted's child. (Sam, June, and Ted's sister Arlene all disputed that Peg was pregnant with *Ted's* child.) Ted was working temporarily at a nearby auto paint shop, scraping the paint off cars, and was planning to re-enlist in the Army.

Ted also was doing his best to avoid finance people. When he and Helga broke up, he stopped paying on all the bills. One by one, the color TV, the stereo, the new furniture, and the Cougar were repossessed; and various finance people were harassing June for her to tell them Ted's whereabouts. (June held firm, saying, "Just 'cause he's my son don't mean I know where he is.") The loan companies had not been able to find Ted, however, because he and Peg were temporarily staying with Hal, Peg's ex-husband, on his farm in the country. The living arrangements there were somewhat crowded, since four of Peg's five children were there as well as Hal's girl friend and her five children. Peg's fifteen-year-old was in West Virginia where she and her baby were visiting Peg's mother.

Ted insisted everybody got along fine and that he and Hal were best friends. Nevertheless, no one was surprised when Peg left to go down to West Virginia saying her mother was sick, and Ted quit his job at the paint shop to follow her the next week. In West Virginia Ted was able to get a job loading trucks and found a house. However, things did not work out. Ted returned to Clay Street after three weeks, saying that because Peg had taken to her old ways of drinking and running around, they had busted up for good. June and Sam were unimpressed. They said they knew Ted would be back.

"I've just got to pull myself together," Ted told me. "I just don't know what's happening to me. I've got to settle all these loans. I've got to declare bankruptcy. I've just got to start again. But I'll tell you one thing. I'm about as low as a person can get. So I've got to get better. I sure as hell can't get no worse off." Ted was able to get his old job back and started sleeping again on June and Sam's couch.

Three days after Ted's return I wandered over to June's to find him very upset. When I asked him if he was ready to go

bowling tonight as we had planned, he said no, that he was
going back to West Virginia.

"Back to West Virginia!" I exclaimed.

"Yeah, Peg is real sick. Had a gallstone attack. And I've
got to go home to be with her." When he asked me if I would
take him to the train that afternoon, I agreed, saying I
couldn't believe that his plans had changed so fast, since yesterday evening he had stated that he was going to make a new
start.

"Well, things happen like that," he said. "Peg is real sick.
Her mother called me last night pleading for me to come
home. Said that Peg had been delirious, calling for me. How
could I do anything else but go home to West Virginia?"
That day Ted had started back to work for Bob's Auto Repair.
He left that afternoon without giving any notice.

Later in the day I drove Ted down to Union Station. He
talked little about going to West Virginia, saying only that he
was more or less resigned to do what he had to do. "The thing
is," he said, "she needs me and wants me. She wants to
change. . . ." Ted paused, then added, "Anyway, I ain't got
no other place to go."

A little over a week later, in the first week of November,
Ted called June to say that everything was working out okay
but that Peg had lost the baby. Sam's comment was, "Bullshit,
that bitch never was pregnant. She just told Ted that to get him
to marry her."

After Ted's second departure to West Virginia, there was not
much talk about him. Whenever I would bring up the subject of Ted and Peg, June would just shake her head and Sam
would grumble something like: "That no-good bitch. I've told
that boy to stay away from that crazy woman. She ain't worth
shit. . . ."

June said she had enough to keep her busy anyway besides
worrying about Ted. Since Sammy was now in kindergarten,
June drove him and several neighborhood children to and
from school every day. She was particularly excited about
Sammy's being in school. She described Sammy's first day as
"one of the biggest days in my whole life. I know you'll think
I'm crazy for saying this, but to see my little boy go to school

for the first time . . . I don't know. Maybe I'm just one of them sentimental slobs. But it sorta shakes me up inside."

However, after a few weeks of Sammy's school, June remarked that school was making him somewhat harder to handle. She said she was worried about how to discipline him: "That goddamn little . . . well . . . he came home this afternoon—he's been getting on my nerves all week. He came home and started throwing rocks. Now, you know and I know that throwing rocks can hurt people. I've seen it happen before. I said this has got to come to a screeching halt. 'Okay, Sammy, no more rock throwing.' And before I turned around he had picked up another rock, thrown it, and hit his poor little friend on the head. Well, it didn't hurt him that much, but I got mad. I took out my belt and whipped him. Told him to sit down on the chair and if he so much as moved his ass I would whip him some more. Now, I know the little boy is spoiled. I know I've spoiled him. But he needs this. Well, Sam came home not too much later and saw Sammy in the chair, and Sammy said, 'Daddy, can I get up and go?' And Sammy . . . well, you know how he is . . . when he says, 'Daddy,' well, I don't get no help from Sam. He gave in right away. And when I told him what I'd done, he didn't understand at all, and when Sammy asked if he could sit in Barney's lap, his daddy said, 'Just go right on.' Now, the question I have is, how am I going to discipline that boy? How am I going to do anything when his daddy just don't co-operate? We've just got to work together, the way I see it. But, well—there's no understanding. I got mad at Sam, and he got mad at me, and now he's in the bedroom on the bed just to spite me, and well, I got all upset and bawled and Arlene called and she got all upset and nobody's speaking to nobody else. . . ."

Also about the same time, Barney's welfare check failed to arrive; and when June called to find out why, a social worker told her Barney was no longer eligible. When I asked June why, she growled: "Well, I'm furious. I don't know why. It took me three hours to finally talk to one of them caseworkers, and she just told me he was off the welfare and that was that. Course eighty-nine dollars ain't a lot, but it is something, and makes it easier for Sam and me to keep him. God knows, it ain't easy anyway. It don't cover what he eats, much less his clothes and all. I don't know what we're gonna do now. We sure can't afford to buy all Barney's medicine. . . ."

After June received the same response on two more calls to the social services bureau, I suggested she go down to the welfare agency herself and volunteered to go with her. The next Monday we went together. (It was one of the few times I put on a suit.) After waiting in the crowded lobby for over an hour, we finally got to see a social worker, who informed us that since Barney Moseby's file was missing, the social services department had assumed he was no longer eligible for public assistance. When we explained that his situation was the same as it was before, the worker apologetically agreed to have him reinstated, admitting that it was not the first time a file had been lost. June was convinced that had I not been along, dressed in my respectable gray suit and carrying an empty brief case, nothing would have happened. "It was because somebody was there who looked like somebody, that's why they treated us like people," she said. "If you come in looking stupid like you don't know anything, then they don't pay you no mind." The next month Barney's check came on time.

The big event of the fall, however, was Arlene's twenty-first birthday party. To celebrate, June and Sam took Arlene and Les to a country music dance put on by the local volunteer fire department. Sam's daughter, Barbara, and her husband joined them as well as June's daughter Ruby and Randy, the man she lived with, who came up from the country. In describing the event, June said, "Oh, it was wonderful, just plain wonderful. There was a real good country band and all, and everybody had such a good time. We even had a birthday cake for Arlene. We made it out of pretzels and lit a candle on it and we all sung happy birthday. Arlene, she was so tickled. . . ."

When I first met Arlene, the first thing she said to me was, "Listen, don't listen to what Mama says about me. Next to Sammy, I guess I'm the apple of Mom's eye. She brags on me, brags on me an awful lot, but I really don't deserve it. You see, I'm the only one of her kids to sort of come out okay, you know what I mean? I'm the only one—well, I haven't really made it, but I'm the best off of all the others."

Next to Sammy, Arlene was, in fact, June's baby and her favorite. Though she had had some problems when she was younger—skipping school and running around with a motorcycle gang—June told me on several occasions that Arlene had turned out the best of her three grown children. When Arlene had refused to go to school, June had her placed in a special Catholic school, a reform school, according to Arlene, where Arlene stayed for almost two years. Arlene said the school probably helped her "straighten up," but what really changed her life was Les Simkins, a lanky, shy fellow with thinning hair, glasses, and a strong West Virginia accent. Arlene was still sixteen when she met Les, who was thirty-one. They had known each other for about five months when Les called her on the phone one afternoon, saying, "Hey, baby, what'ya doing?" When Arlene replied "Not much," Les drawled, "Okay, baby, go and get a preacher. We're gonna get married!" That evening Arlene got a preacher and they got married with no one present from either family, since Les's family was back in West Virginia and June and Sam did not want Arlene to get married so young.

Les turned out to be a loyal husband, however, and their marriage had lasted for almost five years—much longer than Ted's first marriage (three years) or Ruby's first marriage (just over two years). They started their marriage living in Les's apartment in Washington, then moved after a few months to a small mobile home in a trailer park in the country where they lived for over two years. They also had lived in an apartment on Clay Street briefly before moving to their present location, an $18,000 three-bedroom, brick house in a new subdivision just off the beltway, a house that they were currently renting with an option to buy.

Arlene loved their house. The yard was much bigger than the yards on Clay Street; and they had a color TV, new furniture, a stereo, and practically an arsenal of guns, Les being an avid hunter and gun collector. They had two cars: a 1965 Squareback VW for Arlene, which she said was her "dream car," and a 1970 Camaro for Les. Although from Les's friends they had been able to get many of these items hot and at good prices, the Simkinses were up to their limit in credit buying. They had a fixed cash outlay of $480 in monthly payments; and since Les brought home only $103 a week from REA and Arlene $50 from her job as a cashier at a supermarket, paying all the bills was not easy. Only $120 a month remained for food, clothing, gas, fuel oil in the winter, etc. Arlene and Les often found themselves having to sell or trade some of their possessions to keep up their various credit payments. Les once told me, "You know, I'll always be in debt. I know that. I'll never be out of debt. So I might as well afford to get a little further in debt. That's the only way a person can afford to buy anything, if you don't have but so much money, and getting a little further in debt won't hurt you none. That is, if you can meet the payments."

Finances were one problem. Another problem had to do with the fact that they had not been able to have any children, and Arlene, like most young married women in the community, was desperate to have children. She had been going to a special clinic in Baltimore, which she said was dirty and not doing her any good. Consequently, when we first met them, they had just about given up trying to have a child and were going to start adoption procedures.

Though June was aware that Arlene and Les, like most married people, were having some marital problems, she was not prepared when Arlene told her on the day following her twenty-first birthday celebration that she was thinking seriously of leaving Les. June was distressed. She tried to talk about the problem to Sam, who only made things worse by telling June that Arlene was crazy to talk like that, since Les had given her everything a woman could want.

For the next few weeks, June kept in close contact with Arlene, urging her to try to talk things out before doing anything drastic. Arlene told her mother that Les was not aware of how much she wanted to have a child and that he was unwilling to start adoption procedures. (This would mean two hundred a month less income if Arlene quit her job.) She also felt Les had been too strict with her in regard to finances, forbidding her to spend money on clothes and getting mad at her for not balancing the checkbook. She didn't feel she was really appreciated or loved any more, and leaving Les would cause him to realize how much he needed her.

On November 15 a crisis occurred that accomplished Arlene's objective. On that day Arlene had to be rushed to the hospital in an ambulance after passing out in June's bathroom. The collapse was due to the excessive loss of blood Arlene had been experiencing during menstruation. Although the doctors informed her that her condition was not serious, it had been a scare for the entire family. After calling an ambulance, June notified Les, who left work immediately and went directly to the hospital where he stayed the entire night. The next day when Arlene was released, she returned to June's, where her mother could keep an eye on her; and Les came over every day after work and spent the night sleeping in the easy chair beside Arlene, who slept on the couch. At the end of the week Arlene informed me, "Everything is okay now between me and Les. After my accident and all—we ain't never been so close." June was beaming.

The reconciliation did not last. A month later, on December 12, Arlene called June to tell her that the same old problems were there and that things weren't going to work out after all. Making her mother promise not to tell Les anything, Arlene told June she was going to the country to stay with Ruby until she got things straight in her own mind. She was quitting her job at the supermarket and would send Les her ring, checkbook, and credit cards in the mail.

June was distressed enough by Arlene's leaving Les; that she was going to Ruby and Randy's made matters even worse. June and Ruby had never gotten along well, with Ruby more or less going her own way from an early age. When she was seventeen, she became pregnant by a man June considered undesirable. June pleaded for Ruby not to marry him, offering to keep the child so that Ruby could finish high school. "It happens to the best of us," she told Ruby. "Now, you just let me keep the little one till you finish school, and we'll make it through." But Ruby insisted on marrying the fellow, who confirmed all of June's worst fears by joining the D.C. Outlaws motorcycle gang. He grew shoulder-length hair and a beard, wore earrings, and did little to support Ruby, who, before they were divorced two years later, had given birth to another child. Ruby had no more luck with her second husband, who left her two weeks before her third child was born. And now there was Randy, with whom Ruby had been living for almost three years, had had one child by, but whom she had not married. (He had not gotten a divorce from his previous wife.) Though June liked Randy as a person, she resented him for working only sporadically and for making her daughter accept welfare and live in what June considered a "run-down, miserable shack." Yet what disturbed June most was that none of this seemed to bother Ruby. "She is one of them—what do you call it—'free spirits,' that's what she is. She goes her own way and does what she damn well pleases, and of all people, she's not the one to influence my baby. God only knows what she'll tell Arlene to do."

Arlene spent the next two weeks staying in the country with Randy and Ruby. Though the first night she had a change of heart and returned home with Les when he drove down to get her (June had hinted that she might be down there), she stayed only two days before the urge hit her to leave again. Since Ruby was pregnant again with her fifth child due around Christmas, Arlene said she wanted to be there to help out. Although Les was very upset by it, he said he was sure Arlene would soon realize she had a good thing going for her with him and would return. "Come Christmas," said Les, "you wait and see, Arlene will be back."

June said she felt caught in the middle. She had come to think a lot of Les, who she felt had been a pretty good husband, giving her daughter almost everything she wanted—except a child. Yet, since having a baby was very important to Arlene, June felt Les should co-operate in trying to adopt a child. The only thing June could do at the time, however, was let Arlene work things out for herself.

Ironically, it was neither Ted nor Arlene who occupied most of June's attention during the fall, but rather Phyllis, a new neighbor from down the street. Sometime during the middle of November, Phyllis arrived from California to share an efficiency apartment with her mother, Bertie, and her mother's boy friend, Zeek Grizzard. Phyllis was twenty-nine and stocky, with very short, bleached hair. Since she wore blue jeans and T-shirts practically all the time, at first she was quite frequently mistaken for a boy. Though there was some murmuring among neighbors as to exactly who or what she was, all doubts were cleared up when one afternoon Phyllis announced to June on June's front porch, "Okay, goddammit, let's get things straight. I'm a butch. Queer. Fairy. Whatever the hell you want to call it! I like girls better than boys, so what the shit?" June, who seemed somewhat amused by Phyllis's honesty, later asked me what I thought about Phyllis. When I replied that the fact she was a lesbian didn't make any difference to me, June remarked, "Well, it don't to me either. God knows, the poor child has her share of problems. Her mother's drinking and Zeek's drinking and her emphysema and all. What she needs is some love and understanding." Sam simply remarked, "What the shit? What's one more nut in the neighborhood?"

Phyllis had had a rather tumultuous childhood, living in a series of apartments, all located very near Clay Street. Her mother was married to three different men while Phyllis was growing up, only one of whom, according to Phyllis, was much good. She said that because her mother was drinking and running around with men, she was responsible for raising her five younger brothers and sisters. Phyllis became pregnant herself when she was fifteen, putting the baby boy up for adoption. Nevertheless, she finished high school, after which she decided to join the Marines. After serving three years as a woman Marine, she returned to the Clay Street neighborhood where she was able to get a job as a postal carrier. It was then that she developed emphysema, which caused her to resign from her job and move to Los Angeles where she had lived for five years before returning to Clay Street. (Her stepfather and two brothers lived in Los Angeles.) Now, since her emphysema was better, she had been able to get her old job back as a postal carrier. When she started work the first of December, she said she was determined to be "the goddamnedest best postal carrier in the city!" June admired Phyllis's spirit.

Phyllis soon began to take advantage of June's sympathy,

however, spending most of her nonworking hours sitting in the Mosebys' living room, consuming beer after beer. (She was rarely without a beer in her hand and often carried a six-pack with her as she walked from her apartment to the Mosebys'.) Sam's tolerance for Phyllis and her various problems soon began to fade when every evening when he returned home after a hard day working on cars, he found her sitting in his chair, guzzling his beer, half drunk, and usually shouting at someone. When he began to complain to June, she agreed that Phyllis was becoming a nuisance but refused to ask her to leave. Phyllis needed her, June said, and there was no one else to help.

Around the first week of December, Phyllis was arrested outside a large Washington department store carrying a $150 suede coat she had not paid for. By pleading guilty, she was given a suspended sentence; nevertheless, the experience was an ordeal for her and for June, who feared that if convicted Phyllis would lose her job as a postal carrier. This incident, plus the fact that Phyllis was in the process of breaking up with her girl friend, plus the fact that Phyllis and her mother, Bertie, were not getting along, occupied most of June's time during December—when she wasn't consoling Les or Arlene or trying to figure out how to save their marriage.

Sam, coming home at the regular time, drinking his beer, and watching TV, did his best to remain uninvolved. Whenever June would bring up the problem of what to do about Ted or Arlene or Phyllis, Sam would shake his head, saying, "I don't want to hear about it. I've been working hard all day. I'm tired and hungry. Goddammit, let me have my beer, a good meal, and some peace and quiet for a change. . . . I don't want nothing to do with the goddamn, crazy, mixed-up kids!" June would remind Sam that last year it was *his* daughter Barbara and her four children who ended up spending almost a month sleeping in the Mosebys' living room because Barbara's husband had left her. Sam would mutter that that wasn't his fault and turn up the television.

This was the way things stood at the middle of December when Ted returned from West Virginia. Everything was fine between him and Peg, he assured everyone. He had gotten back his job loading trucks and was making about ninety dollars a week, though he was employed on a temporary basis filling in for men on sick leave or vacation. Peg had straightened up and was being a good wife. He had come back to pick up Christmas presents for him, Peg, and the children, an action that infuriated Sam, who thought Ted had a lot of nerve to come back just to pick up Christmas presents.

When Ted heard about Arlene, he was shocked. He and Les were good friends, and Ted couldn't believe what had happened to him was now happening to his kid sister, the only one who in his opinion really had things going for her. He said it was his duty as big brother and as a guy who had been through it himself to set her straight. Since Ted and Arlene had always been close, he thought perhaps he could talk some sense into her where June and Sam had failed. Two days after his return he called me on a Sunday afternoon to tell me the good news. He had it all worked out. Arlene and Les were to be reunited that evening at the bowling alley. Ted explained how he had managed to do it:

"See, Arlene was down at Ruby's. So when we went down to bring Ruby and the kids some presents, there was Arlene. She didn't know I was here, and she got all shook up and broke down into tears and all that. See, Arlene and me, we got a thing. See, we understand each other. And I sat down and talked to her and tried to talk some sense into her. I tried to tell her. I said, 'Arlene, look, you're the only one of the kids who hasn't really fucked up yet, and now you're going to fuck up, too. You've got to *think!* Got to talk it out. If me and Helga had sat down and talked, we probably would never of gotten divorced. She'd of given me a second chance. But she walked away, and now look at my life and look at her life. Both ruined.'

"Well, she got all shook up and started crying and all, but she listened to what I said. She thought about it and she agreed. Now she's going to bowl, and she's going to be at the alley tonight. But the thing is, if you see Phyllis, if you see Phyllis, please tell her not to come. She's going to fuck it up. Phyllis keeps saying that it's not going to work out, that Arlene and Les aren't going to get back together. And she's going to fuck up the whole thing. So if you see Phyllis, tell her that she's not wanted tonight, okay?

"Well, I think it's going to work out. Of course, Arlene has to swallow her pride, and that's a hard thing to do. But what's more important than saving a marriage? And Les is so happy. He knows about it all. He's so happy he could almost cry. He says he's going to take a vacation the first of the year and take Arlene down to Florida, and Arlene's not going to have to work, and they're going to start adoption procedures. Well, as I say, I can't do nothing to help myself, but I'm pretty good at helping other people."

I was not sure why Ted had arranged for them to reunite at the duckpins bowling alley. Perhaps it was because, as a member of our team, Arlene would naturally be at the alley when Les got off work at nine-thirty. Duckpins bowling this fall had been a family activity for the Mosebys with Arlene bowling and Les and Ted—when he wasn't in West Virginia —there to share our beer, help with score-keeping, and give us moral support, which we needed since we were losing an average of five out of every six games. Phyllis was also usually there to participate in the fun and bowled occasionally as a substitute when she was needed. That was the problem. That afternoon Phyllis had left the neighborhood thinking she was going to bowl in Arlene's place. What happened that evening was hardly what Ted had in mind.

When we went over to the Mosebys to get Sam, June, and Ted to go to the bowling alley, June was in particularly high spirits. She was very nervous and very excited. "Oh boy, oh boy!" she kept saying. "I'm going to get my Christmas present tonight. I'm so happy I don't know what to say. My kids, my kids, they're coming home. They're coming home. You just don't know how much this means to me."

When we arrived at the bowling alley, Arlene was waiting for us at the door. No one said very much. Everyone acted as if things were normal. Ted assured Arlene that Les was coming as soon as he got off work, which would be at nine-thirty, an hour and a half away. Sam said, "Just think about bowling, everybody. We've got to win a game for a change." It seemed very difficult for us to get organized to bowl. After our opponents asked us to start several times, finally, without even rolling practice balls, we agreed to begin.

It was in the middle of that first game when it all happened. I was stepping up to roll my fourth frame when I overheard Ted mention to my wife, Embry, "Guess who walked in? Stoned." I heard a very loud voice behind me yell, "Goddammit, shit, fuck you! *I'm* bowling, goddammit! I came all the way over here to bowl, and I don't care what bitch is bowling, it's going to be *me* who bowls. You asked me to bowl. . . ."

It was Phyllis with a long-haired, teen-age boy I had never seen before. I rolled two balls down the gutter. After my final ball knocked over one pin, I walked back behind the bowling area to see what was going on.

Phyllis had grabbed Arlene by the collar and was screaming at her, "Look, you bitch, after what I've put up with, after how I've listened to you, *you* sit down and *I'll* bowl! I came all the way out here, missing a goddamn good party. You're not going to ruin my night. I'm bowling and you're sitting down. Is that clear?"

Arlene started to cry.

As I turned away, June groaned, "Oh God, she's going to ruin everything. Poor Arlene. Arlene's been so upset about this. I knew if Phyllis showed up, this would happen."

Arlene then broke away from Phyllis, going off to another table to sit by herself. By this time she was crying very loudly, in full view of a half-dozen other teams, all of whom were watching her with intense curiosity. To see Arlene break down after everything Ted had done to try to bring Arlene and Les back together was too much for Ted. Walking up to Phyllis, he said, "Look, Phyllis, we've had enough of this shit, okay? *Arlene's* bowling. We don't want you. We don't need you. Get lost, and take that boy friend or whatever you call him with you." Phyllis started to cry. It was my turn to bowl. I bowled three more balls—two of them down the gutter—and when I returned, Phyllis was gone. June came up to me and said, "Well, I'm sorry that Phyllis was so upset, but tonight is Arlene and Les's night. They are the ones that are important. Arlene and Les, my babies. Nothing—bowling, people, Phyllis—is going to interfere with Arlene and Les getting back together!"

What finally caused Phyllis to leave was Sam, who said, "You got carfare, kid? If you ain't got it, here it is. You're drunk. Get the hell out." Although Sam didn't say anything different from Ted, he said it with authority.

Just as I was mentioning to June how fortunate it was that Phyllis was gone, I looked around to see she had returned, angrier than before. She went up to Ted as if she were going to slug him. "Nobody cares about me," she screamed. "I'm the scapegoat. I'm always the scapegoat. You bastards, you lousy straight bastards! Nobody cares about me, nobody."

Nothing anyone said did any good. Phyllis was beyond any sort of reasoning at this point. Standing behind her was her friend, who had a pair of bowling shoes slung over his shoulder and a puzzled expression on his face, not saying a word.

Sam, returning from the beer counter, muttered, "Goddammit, I've had enough of this shit. This has got to come to a halt," and walked over to Phyllis and said, "Look, Phyllis, goddammit, cut this shit out!"

Phyllis sobbed, "Nobody cares about me, nobody. I'm always the scapegoat. . . ."

Sam's tone changed. "Well, shit, Phyllis, I mean, well, goddamn, shit. Don't you understand?" he stuttered.

"I understand. I understand that you don't love me. That's what I understand."

"Well, if it will help you any," said Sam, "I liked the spaghetti sauce you made for us last night." Phyllis threw herself into Sam's arms and started crying on his shoulder. He patted her on the back, saying, "Look, kid, just go home and sleep it off. Okay? Everything will be okay. Just go home and sleep it off."

"You won't believe this, you'll think it's funny," said Phyllis, sobbing, "but you're the only dad I got. You're the only people I got."

When I returned from my turn at bowling, Phyllis was gone for good. When I asked Sam what happened, he said,

"That guy, I'd like to kill him, that sonofabitch. I'd like to kill that bastard!"

"Which guy?"

"That guy that was with Phyllis. If he ever comes to my house I'm going to punch my fist down his mouth. He came up to me and said, 'Look, man, look, man.' I said, 'Look, man, shit,' and all he could say was 'Look, man, look, man.' Shit. 'Get the hell out of here!' I said. 'Just get this shit out, is that clear? Get it out!' I'd like to punch that little punk. A little punk, that's all he was."

Arlene was still sitting by herself at a table about fifteen feet away. June, Embry, and I were wandering around in circles. Sam was rubbing his hands together, looking rather pleased that at last he had managed to get rid of Phyllis. We were on the ninth frame of the first game, and strangely enough we weren't doing too much worse than we usually did.

Les came in the eighth frame of the second game, about nine forty-five. Just as I was stepping up to roll a ball down the alley, I looked over my shoulder to see him coming in the front door. Arlene saw him, too, and rushed toward him, throwing herself in his arms in a mad embrace almost exactly between the cash register and the beer counter. They both were weeping. This was too much for the rest of us, who for the rest of the evening tried to bowl as seriously as we could. Sam was having an exceptionally good game the third game, though no one was able to appreciate it.

Arlene and Les spent most of the time with their arms around each other, with the rest of us trying to leave them alone as much as possible. All I remember is Sam saying several times, "Goddammit, here I am bowling the best game of the goddamn year, and nobody's paying any attention to me. Shit, ain't that just like a young couple?" Then he smiled and nudged me in the ribs.

On the way home June was radiant. "You know, the good Lord has a plan. He has a plan. And I believe that this is one of his plans. Like He had it all figured out what was going to happen. I didn't know Ted was coming up here. On Friday Ted appeared at our steps without any hint that he was coming. And Ted was the one. He got Les and Arlene back to-

gether. Nobody else could have done it but Ted. He and
Arlene really have a thing between them. See, they really understand each other without having to say a word. It's all part
of the good Lord in heaven's plan. And now at last we can
enjoy Christmas! Two Christmases ago Ruby's kids were in a
foster home. Last Christmas, it was Ted and Helga. At last
we're going to have a good Christmas. This is the best Christmas present I've ever had! Now I think I can begin to sleep
—that is, if that sonofabitch Sam will just give me a chance,
and quit elbowing and snoring and nudging me out of the
bed." They both laughed.

Although bowling was not usually the stage for such drama
as occurred that evening, the Sunday following was quite similar. That night things got off to an unusually good start. Since
Ted had brought Peg up from West Virginia, they both
were there to cheer us on. I was quite impressed by their concern for June. They were seated at a table and had their arms
around each other's waist. When Ted said, "You know, we're
really worried about June," Peg nodded her head.

Arlene joined in. "Yes, we're really worried about Mom.
She has cirrhosis of the liver, we think."

"In fact, I'm pretty sure she's got it," added Ted. "She has
a pain in her side and a swelling sort of in her upper stomach.
And her legs are thin. She's been losing weight."

"That's right," said Peg, "my mom had it. She had a bad
case. But six years ago she stopped drinking and managed to
live."

Ted said, "You can't cure it. Unless you stop drinking, it
kills you. And we can't get June to go to a doctor. She just
refuses to go."

I asked, "How long has she been drinking like this?"

Ted said, "Oh, as long as I can remember. She's always
drank like this. Almost constantly every day. But you never
see her drinking. She usually takes a nip here and there. You
just know she's doing it, but she rarely ever shows it. Anyway, I'm afraid it's getting to her, and if she has cirrhosis of
the liver, it's going to kill her. And probably kill her soon.
We've got to get her to a doctor."

"Once my mom went to a doctor she was okay," said Peg.

"She made up her mind to stop drinking. I know that June could do the same thing. But we've got to do something fast."

Arlene then added, "You know, it's not just drinking. It's a lot of things."

"That's right," said Ted, "it's us. It's me and Peg. It's you and Les. It's Ruby, it's everything. She worries too much about us. It's not her fault. It's our fault. We've just caused her too much worry."

"That's right," said Arlene, "we've made her worry too much. We've put all our problems on her, and now it's beginning to get to her. We've got to help her."

Although Les wasn't in that conversation, I gather they all had been talking about June, because he mentioned the same thing to me later in the evening. "You know," he said, "we're really worried about June. We're afraid she's sick. And it's so many things. It's not just the drinking, but it's the way we've treated her. I don't care how bad my problems are, I'm not going to put them off on June any more. I'm keeping them to myself."

This all occurred during the first game. In the second game Ted came over to me, saying, "Hey, guess what, we've worked a miracle! Peg went over to Mom and told her she thought Mom ought to see a doctor and said that she would go with her. And Mom agreed to go to a doctor. Isn't that something! Mom agreed to go to a doctor this week and get a checkup. Maybe we can do something now. Maybe it's not too late."

The first few frames in this game went fairly well. When Sam got up and rolled his first ball down the side of the lane, knocking down only one pin, June hollered from the back, "What a shot! You're on your onezies. Come on, big Daddy, you can do better than that. You can knock over *two* next time." Sam then rolled the next ball down the middle, knocking over all the pins, making a spare. He raised his arm into the air as if he were going to wave, but instead, smiling, gave June the finger. She shouted, "Keep the faith, big Daddy. Thataway, Daddy. That's my big Daddy. Keep the faith, baby."

As the game continued, June began to look more sullen and stone-faced, as she would get when she was depressed for bowling poorly. She said to me, "They don't believe me. Nobody believes me, but it's true. I'm in labor. My daughter, Ruby, is in labor at this moment down there, and I feel the labor pains up here. Nobody believes me, but it's true. I'm in labor along with Ruby."

It was toward the end of that night that everything exploded. Just as I was getting ready to bowl, I noticed that Phyllis and Arlene were having a few harsh words. Since I was a good distance away, I couldn't hear what they were saying until all of a sudden Phyllis let out with, "You little bitch! You goddamn, cheap bitch! One more comment like that and I'm going to beat your ass right here in the bowling alley, goddammit." Everyone looked around to see Phyllis going after Arlene.

"You aren't going to hit me here, you bitch," shouted Arlene. "You shit, you can't talk to me like that."

Whatever it was that was bothering them, I figured it was their problem which they had to work out. I just hoped it would not come to blows. It turned out that Arlene and Phyllis were not the center of attention after all. Blows had already been exchanged in the back, and this was the focus of everyone's attention. Ted had smacked Peg. He had hit her, apparently fairly hard, and she was bawling loudly. Ted was cursing, Sam was cursing, and June was staring stone-faced into the air.

"What happened?" I asked Les, who seemed to be the least involved of anyone.

"It happened again. I told you Peg was no good. I told you she was a little tramp. I knew this would happen. I knew it would."

"What happened? What happened?"

"The same old thing, Joe. Just like it always happens. The same old thing."

"What?"

"Oh, I don't know, but Ted and Peg got into a fight."

Peg was accusing Ted of beating her, with Ted arguing, "I don't beat you, Peg, it's not true, I don't beat you." Like the preceding Sunday, all this was happening in the middle of four or five other teams, who were now more concerned with the show going on at the back table than with anything that was going on on the lanes.

Later, when Peg walked out, Ted followed her, not to return that evening. June never said a word about the incident. She didn't talk to anyone except to congratulate the members of the other team—including a seventy-three-year-old lady who was bowling well over one hundred each game. Sam, however, had had it. "That no-good bitch! She ought to go back to West Virginia where she belongs. If she ever puts her ass back in my house, I'm going to kick it out. That no-good lousy bitch! That's what she is, and I've had it with that bitch. I can't stand this shit no more. Ought to get on back to the mountains of West Virginia where she came from."

Three members of the other team seated at the table beside Sam all nodded and agreed. "Yes," said one lady, "that girl did seem sort of nasty." The elderly lady nodded, "Yes, she should go back to West Virginia." Sam said, "Goddamn right, the little bitch. She ought to get her ass back there and never show her ass up here again." The third lady at the table stared down at the floor and giggled.

The third game was a little quieter, except for the fact that Phyllis and Arlene had it out a few more times. On two occasions Arlene broke into tears, crying very loudly, wandering around the lanes and back to the table, sobbing, "I can't take any more. I just can't. I can't stand it. The bitch is driving me crazy."

Toward the end of the last game, when I went back to the beer counter, I noticed that a fight had broken out at the other end of the alley, apparently between two teams in another league. The guy next to me commented, "You know, it's been some night, hasn't it? Those people are fighting; and earlier down at the other end, a man smacked a woman. Smacked her hard. I saw it. Some night. Fights at both ends of the bowling alley. What do you think about that?"

"Some night."

June and Sam had little relief from June's children's problems that winter. If it wasn't Ted, it was Arlene; and when things looked up for them, Ruby was having her problems.

There was one respite, however—Christmas. Christmas was a special occasion, which everyone made a determined effort to make a pleasant event.

Little by little, June had been doing her Christmas shopping throughout the fall. She liked to give expensive presents to all her children and to Sam—especially, she liked to give gadgets like electric carving sets, electric can openers, transistor radios, etc. Fortunately, since Sam made good money and received a Christmas bonus, she usually was able to buy what she wanted. There was, however, one person who was extra special: Sammy. This year June and Sam got him a fancy five-speed chopper bike (one that listed for seventy-five dollars but that they were able to purchase for thirty-five dollars from Les's friends at REA). They also bought him two racing car sets, a walkie-talkie set, an outdoor bowling set, and numerous other small toys—trucks, soldiers, cars, etc.

Christmas Day was everything June had hoped for. Except for Ruby, who was due any minute with her fifth child, all June's children were there for the turkey dinner, with Sam's daughter Barbara and his son Olin and their families stopping by. Naturally Phyllis was there all day. She gave the Mosebys a new toaster, addressed "to my adopted parents." As usual there was plenty of drinking, joking, and horseplay. June later remarked, "It's too bad Christmas don't come more often. Everybody was so happy. . . ."

8

Winter

The Christmas calm did not last. June had been concerned
about Ruby for the past few weeks since Ruby's baby was
due anytime and she had already started having labor pains.
But now Ruby had been told by the welfare department that
since Randy was legally responsible for supporting the children, she would receive no more AFDC. Also, the county
hospital informed her that until she paid her previous bill of
$250 and put down a deposit of $100, she could not be admitted. Ruby then applied for Medicaid but was turned down.
If this wasn't enough, Ruby and Randy were being evicted
from their home and had no prospects of anywhere to go.

Long since having resigned herself to Ruby's stubbornness,
June knew there was little anyone could do. Ruby told her
mother, "Don't worry, Mom, things will take care of themselves. I'm not worrying about it, so why should you?" She
planned to have her baby at home, then call the ambulance
to take her and the baby to the emergency room for a
checkup. And Randy was out looking for a new place and a
job. (His employment problem stemmed from the fact he had
no car or driver's license and had difficulty getting to work.)

While June said there had always been some tension between her and Ruby, she admired Ruby's independence.
Though Ruby had more than her share of problems, she was
June's only child who seemed to get along without June's
help. "I guess she's just one of them lucky types," June said.
"You don't know how she's gonna come through it all; but
by God, she comes through it. Sure, I'm concerned. But I've
given up really worrying about her long ago."

June had not given up worry about Ted, however. In June's
words: "Peg ain't nothing more than a rebound for Teddy.
He was down and out after Helga left him and needed some-

body. I guess more than anything he needed to be needed. He always has. Peg helped him after he took the pills, so Ted feels obligated. Also, Peg needs somebody. That's why Ted puts up with her. But in heaven's name, Ted sure picked one hell of a messed-up woman to need him."

Whenever I brought up the subject of Peg with Ted, he would usually change the conversation to Helga, his first wife. He had really loved Helga and still did. He was trying to build a decent home for her when all of a sudden everything changed. He said he could not face the fact that she left him for another man. Were it not for Peg, he was convinced he would have died. She was the person who found him asleep and called the ambulance. Yes, he had trouble understanding Peg's strange ways. He knew she was "sorta messed up," yet after what she did for him, he felt he could not let her down.

Peg came from a large family and had several brothers living in the Washington area, though her parents and some of her family remained in Beckley, West Virginia. Ted said that as far as he could tell no one got along too well with Peg and that most of her family members he had met were as crazy as she. "When she is nice, she is wonderful," Ted said. "God knows, she loves her kids and wants to be a good mother. And a good wife. It's just that she kinda goes off the deep end every now and then. If I can stick by her and help her, then I think she'll come out okay. Anyway, if we was to split up for good, I swear I don't know what she would do."

After the bowling alley fight, Ted moved in with Les and Arlene, and Peg went back to her former husband's farm. It was to be only a temporary arrangement, however, since Peg's mother and stepfather were visiting for the week and were staying on the farm. Peg and Ted planned to leave with them at the end of the week to return to West Virginia. Les and Arlene told me they would be glad when Ted and Peg finally left, since Ted was eating their food and driving their cars but not helping out financially.

June made up her mind that as long as Ted was intent on staying with Peg, she would try to do her part. Sam grimaced when June informed him that she would not turn a daughter-in-law away from her house, and she agreed "to try to be nice to the poor child." The second week in January, June and Sam were put to the test when Peg was told to leave the farm by her ex-husband. She said she had nowhere else to go, so June took her in. Ted left Arlene and Les and joined Peg at the Mosebys'.

The Saturday evening Peg arrived, everyone was in good spirits. Late that afternoon Peg was burying Phyllis's beer in the snow, giggling, "Phyllis says she likes her beer cold, don't she?" June, who was watching with some amusement, shoveled some snow on the beer herself. I wandered inside with Peg and June, who were both laughing, as Sam brought out a six-pack of Black Label. (Ted had not yet arrived from Arlene's.) Peg opened a can, lit a cigarette, and motioned me over to sit beside her on the sofa. "You know," she whispered, "I'm so embarrassed about what happened last Sunday at the bowling alley. It wasn't right. I know that. Especially after what we were saying about Mom and all. You know, if me and Teddy can get back up to Beckley and he can get his old job back, then maybe we can fix our house up and all and the kids can join us. . . ."

June returned from the kitchen where she was preparing dinner and turned up the TV. When Peg said one of her favorite programs was on, I departed to have dinner. When I returned about an hour later, I thought I was in a different house. June was sullen-faced, sitting alone on the couch; and except for Barney, who was finishing his meal, no one else was present.

"Well, she's done left, walked out," June said. "Said, 'Ted don't love me no more,' called her uncle, and left. I swear to God, that woman's crazy. One minute she's fine, the next . . . I don't know. And when she started crying and all, Sam got up and went out to the store. But I wouldn't be a bit surprised if he don't come back tonight. You know how he can't stand that woman."

Two hours later, at nine o'clock, I noticed that Les and Arlene had arrived and that Sam had come back. When I went outside to empty the garbage, Arlene opened the door and rushed out. She was in tears, crying very loudly, "Oh, it's just terrible, terrible, terrible." Les then opened the door and

followed her out. "Get Ted out of there!" she screamed at
Les.

"Well, I can't, honey. I can't just drag him out. I'll do the
best I can."

"What's happened?" I asked.

Arlene sobbed, "Ted's driving Mother crazy. Mother's crying. Oh, it's just terrible, just terrible!"

"Well, what happened?"

"Peg cut her wrists. She tried to commit suicide. She called
up on the phone and told Ted she'd cut her wrists. Ted got
all upset. Sam said something like, 'Good riddance to that
bitch,' and Ted got real mad. Got real mad at Sam and they
began to have a fight. Then Ted got mad at Mom and said,
'Mom, if you cared you could stop all this. If you just cared.'
And Mom got all upset. That's what's happening now. Everybody's mad at everybody else. It's just one big fight. I don't
know what's going to happen. It's just terrible. I mean, it's just
terrible. And just think, Ted accused Mom of not helping,
after all that she'd done. It's just terrible."

I said, "Well, I tell you, I'm not sure what's going on. It's
too much for me to follow."

Then Les replied, "You remember what happened at the
bowling alley last week?"

"Yeah, what *did* happen at the bowling alley? I never really
found out."

"Well, the same thing's happening tonight. I mean, Peg
is no good. She's just no good. See, at the bowling alley Peg
got drunk and said something nasty, and Ted slapped her.
When she gets drunk, she all the time says something nasty.
Then Peg got mad and started crying. I tried to take them
home down country. I straightened things out okay then. I've
had to straighten them out so much. But it just keeps happening again and again. I tell you, Peg, she's no good. They were
supposed to go to West Virginia last week. I took a vacation
—a vacation I wanted to use to go hunting—I took off so I
could take them down to West Virginia. Then they decided
they didn't want to go. 'Cause Peg had gotten in a fight with
her mother and stepfather, and they were in a fight, and I just
wasted a whole vacation. I'm just sick of this. I'm fed up."

About that time Ted came out of the door. He had a sour expression on his face and was clenching his fists and grumbling under his breath. Les said, "Okay, Ted, let's go." Ted and Les then got in Les's car and started off.

"Where are they going?" I asked Arlene.

"Les's taking Ted over to Peg's."

"Where's Peg?"

"I don't know. Les said she might be at the Dixie Club. I don't know where she is. Maybe in Bladensburg or something like that."

Later that evening things got even more heated. Sam left to pick up Sammy, who had been spending the day with his cousin. Then Ted and Les arrived with Peg, whose wrists were bleeding very badly. They had tried to get her to go to the hospital, but she had refused, saying that they would put her in the mental institution since she had tried several times before to commit suicide. So they brought her to the Mosebys. June poured peroxide on the wounds and bandaged Peg's wrists with old rags. After June called Sam to come home, Sam returned with Sammy and took Ted and Peg to the farm in the country where Peg's mother and stepfather were visiting. June said that on the way Peg began to act up again. Sam stopped the car and cussed her out. Ted slapped her. When they got to her ex-husband's farm, they took Peg to her mother. Peg showed her mother her wrists and cried, "Look, Mom, look what Ted did! Look what Ted did to me."

Ted walked out, swearing he would never see Peg again. June said that she was glad; maybe at last, at long last, his relationship with Peg was finished.

The suicide episode was on Saturday. Sunday we had a relatively quiet, uneventful night bowling, losing three more games. Ted came to the alley to cheer us on and keep score, mentioning nothing about Peg.

Monday it was Les and Arlene.

About nine o'clock Monday evening, Les called the store where Arlene worked to ask her about something. (After she quit working at the supermarket, she got a job at an all-night drugstore.) She was due to get there slightly before nine, since her job started at nine. When the people at the store told him that she wasn't due until eleven, Les argued, "But she goes to work at nine every night."

The person on the other end of the line said, "You are misinformed, she doesn't get here until eleven every night."

Les immediately drove out to the drugstore where he found Arlene's car but no Arlene. He sat in the car and waited. Shortly before eleven Arlene drove up in someone else's car. The person driving was Lonnie, a man Les knew who lived near Ruby. When they saw Les standing there by the car, Lonnie put the car in reverse and screeched off. Les panicked. After calling Ted, he arrived around midnight at the Mosebys', and Ted and Les were up all night. Ted said Les was in a fit of rage. "He wanted to kill Lonnie," Ted said. "He wanted to go and get his gun." But Ted said he convinced Les not to do that and spent the rest of the evening trying to get him to talk things out.

That evening Les made several telephone calls to friends and to people who knew Arlene. From all the phone calls, he was able to put together the following facts: Arlene had been going with Lonnie for most of the last month. Between nine and eleven every evening, she had been with him. Apparently some of the time had been spent at a motel. When she was supposedly staying with Ruby, she was actually living with Lonnie. She had told several of her friends that she was leaving with Lonnie for good. The date was not supposed to be last night, but in a week or two when they were to go to Florida.

Lonnie was separated from his wife but not divorced. He had two children; and according to Ted, who knew him fairly well, he was a playboy and a run-around. "No one likes him," said Ted. "He is not even good looking, though he does drive a fancy new Mustang Mach I." Ted said he had almost gotten in fights with him upon occasion. Les, who also knew Lonnie, had never liked him.

Les made a call to Lonnie's apartment and told Lonnie's roommate that if he didn't hear from Lonnie within twenty-four hours, he was going to kill him. Ted said both he and Les agreed that it wouldn't have been so bad if Arlene really loved Lonnie and if Lonnie was really in love with Arlene. But they

knew that the situation was not that. Lonnie would take
Arlene for a while and then drop her as he always did. And
then where would Arlene be? "It wouldn't be so bad if he
was honest. It wouldn't be so bad if there was any future in
their relationship," Ted said, "but there ain't."

The next morning at eleven-thirty Les knocked on my door.
He looked horrible. He had rings under his eyes and was
trembling.

I said, "Les, I'm really sorry. I heard. Ted told me." Les
didn't take off his coat; he just stood in the door shaking. Then
he reached in his pocket and pulled out a gun.

"I'm going to kill that sonofabitch. Just let me at him. I'm
going to kill him, and there's nobody, nobody, in this world
who can stop me. What would you do, Joe? Tell me this, what
would you do if you were in my position?"

"Sit down, Les. Take your coat off. Let's talk this thing
out."

"Tell me, Joe, what would you do? I'm going to kill him."

"Well, that's one thing I wouldn't do. I wouldn't do anything stupid like that."

"It's not stupid, Joe. A man's got to get his revenge. What
would you do if your wife loved another man? And that man
was no good, didn't love her, was just using her. What would
you do?"

"I've never been in too many things like this, Les, so it's
difficult to say I understand. But we don't want to see you do
anything that will hurt yourself."

"It will make me feel better, to get it off my chest. I can't
take it any more—I'm going to kill him."

There was a knock at the door and Ted came in. Les
agreed to take off his coat and sit down.

"I'm going down there this afternoon. The only thing I'm
asking is for you two to go with me."

Ted said, "We'll go, you know we'll go. We'll stick by you."
"Okay."

Then Ted looked at Les and said, "Remember, Les, when
Helga left me. Remember what I did?" Sobbing, Les nodded.
"I had a gun, didn't I? And you kept me from using it.
I wanted to use it. I wanted to kill that sonofabitch who Helga

was running away with. But you took it away from me.
Why?"

Les said, "Because I didn't want you to do nothing rash.
Because I knew you were out of your head and couldn't think
straight. I didn't want you to do nothing you'd be sorry for
later."

"Well, that's the way it is now, Les. It's exactly that way
now. We don't want you to do nothing rash, nothing because
you're out of your head."

Les nodded and handed Ted the gun. "Okay, Ted, you guys
have convinced me. I won't use the gun. At least not now.
You can hold the gun."

Ted took it and opened the chamber. It was fully loaded.
Ted emptied the gun, putting the bullets in one pocket and the
gun in the other.

I sighed, "I feel better now. Using your gun on this guy
Lonnie is not going to solve anything."

"But it's *right*, Joe. There's a law on the books saying
adultery is not right. It's against the law. And I know it's right
for me to kill him. That's okay, if a man runs off with your
wife, you can do it. I know you can. I know it's not the way
to solve problems, but I've just got to get it off my chest. I've
got to get him."

Ted and I spent the rest of the day with Les, talking with
him, trying to keep his mind occupied. We left my house
around noon. The plan was to go to the country where Les
would confront Lonnie without a gun. If Lonnie had a gun,
that would be something else again, but Les promised that if
Lonnie was unarmed, he would not use his gun. He would
confront Lonnie and try to solve the problem in a quiet manner. If that didn't work, he would have it out with his fists.
Les said since he could kill a man with his fists, that was just
like having a gun. Ted convinced him that it was different.
At least they would be on something of an equal footing.

Before we left, we went over to June's to tell her we were
leaving; and as we opened the door, the phone rang. It was
Arlene. June picked up the phone and said, almost in a whisper, "Yes, yes, you did what? You left your VW keys with

David. . . . Oh, well, he's here. Yes, Les is here. Why don't you talk to him?"

Les said, "Let me talk to her, let me talk to her."

Ted, June, Barney, and I waited nervously in the living room while Les talked quietly on the phone. I tried not to listen; in fact, I turned up the TV and tried to watch a quiz show. It seemed as if he talked on the phone for an hour. At one point he turned to us and said, "She's in an airport. I can hear planes flying." At another point, "I don't know, maybe it's buses, maybe it's downtown. I don't know where she is. I don't know if it's long distance or not. She says she's leaving. She says she's gone for good." After talking a while longer, he hung up. "She says she's in love with Lonnie. I'll kill him! I'll kill him, so help me, I'll kill him. She said she's leaving, and it's for good. But then she started crying so maybe there's hope. She said she would call back in a few minutes."

In a few minutes the phone rang. Les walked over very calmly, let the phone ring three times, then picked it up, and again spoke in a soft voice. This time the conversation seemed to last even longer. After it was over, he walked back into the kitchen. Ted and I followed, and we all sat down at the kitchen table. Putting his head in his hands, Les stared at the floor. Ted and I didn't say anything. Les spoke very slowly, "Well, she asked me to meet her after work tomorrow morning at six-thirty. She wants me to meet her there. She says she's making up her mind once and for all, and she'll let me know at six-thirty this morning what she's going to do." Les began to sob. "What am I going to do? What am I going to do? She asked me to promise that I wouldn't do nothing to hurt her or Lonnie. But I couldn't do it. I just couldn't do it. I love her, I love her. I'll forgive her. It's human to forgive and forget. I can't never forget, ever, but I can forgive. And I love Arlene. I don't want to see her do this to herself or to me. Lonnie's no good for her. He's no good. He don't love her. He don't. I know him. He don't love her. Why won't she come back to me? I've given her everything I can. I love her, I love her." He began to weep even more.

June was pacing back and forth in the dining room, saying, "So help me God, if it's not one thing, it's another." Les, by this time, was on his way to being drunk. He had been drinking all night. He had had some breakfast, but he was taking gulps out of June's Canadian Club bottle in the refrigerator. He would talk for a while, then get up and take a swig from the bottle of whiskey, chasing the whiskey with Pepsi Cola or beer. June would come by and say halfheartedly, "Are you in my whiskey again? That's *my* whiskey, Les." She would manage a faint smile and then go about her business, trying to do the laundry.

Once, when she was back in the kitchen, June remarked, "The way I see it is she's my daughter, but she's done wrong. If I could sit down and talk to her, I'd shake her like nobody's ever shaken her before. She's done wrong. It's not right. She's ruining her life and your life and everybody else's. And I tell you, Les, I'd have one thing to say to her if I were you. 'Shit or get off the pot,' and I mean it, goddammit. 'Shit or get off the pot. No more of this shit. For God's sake, cut it out. Quit running around, quit behaving like a no-good you-know-what.' That's what you've got to say, Les."

Les replied, "I just can't be harsh. I love her too much. I can't hurt her. I just can't be harsh."

June said, "But you've got to. You can't let her do this to you."

"I just can't; that's being too harsh. I could kill Lonnie, but I love Arlene too much."

About that time, around one-thirty, Phyllis came in, sat down, and began to talk. Phyllis hadn't been there for more than five minutes when Les looked at her and said, "Don't take this personal, but how come you're a lesbian? How come —how did you get started?"

Phyllis, not the slightest bit embarrassed, replied, "Well, I guess I was about sixteen when I realized I liked girls more than boys and that I was more like a boy than a girl. Just like that."

Ted asked, "Well, didn't it have something to do with your experiences with men? I mean, didn't somebody get you pregnant when you were fifteen?"

Phyllis said, "Yeah, but that didn't have anything to do with it, believe me. I just was a tomboy when I was growing up and I always was and I always liked doing things that guys liked to do, and it's as simple as that. I'm very domineering and aggressive and I couldn't be married to a husband who would let me do that to him, and yet I couldn't be anything different. So it's just the way I am, that's all."

Les nodded.

Then the issue of religion came up when Les made a comment about how what Arlene was doing was just like what Lot's wife in the Bible did. He couldn't remember the story too well, but he thought it had something to do with her turning into a pillar of salt.

Phyllis remarked, "Well, shit, that was because she wasn't a Christian. That's why she turned into a pillar of salt. The good guys, they are the Christians in the Bible. And the bad guys, they were against the Christians."

I reminded Phyllis that as I recalled that story was in the Old Testament and happened a good many years before the birth of Christ.

"That doesn't make a goddamn bit of difference," she said. "I know the Bible backwards and forwards. My grandmother used to recite it to me all the time. She was a die-hard Baptist. Although I never read too much of it myself, I know it backwards and forwards."

Les said, "The New Testament. That ain't nothing. I know. The New Testament is just a revision of the Old Testament. It don't do you no good at all to read that. You ought to read the real thing, read the Old Testament. I know that 'cause I went to the Smithsonian and saw it on display."

Phyllis said, "Well, I tell you, I don't believe in God anyway. If there was a God, how come he don't show himself?"

Les said, "Phyllis, that's not right. There is a God. If there wasn't a God, how'd the Bible get written?"

"Men wrote the Bible," said Phyllis. "Men did, not God."

"No, that ain't right. It was written on scrolls. I saw the scrolls at the Smithsonian, that's what it was, scrolls. That's where the Old Testament came from."

"Shit yes, that might have been where it came from, but men wrote those scrolls."

"I don't know—"

June interrupted, "You've just got to have faith. You can't see God, you can't hear Him, you can't smell Him, you don't know where He is, you don't know what He's doing. You wonder how in the world things could be so screwed up. But you just got to have faith."

Phyllis remarked, "Well, I think all the people who go to church are a bunch of hypocrites anyway, and that's why I don't go to church. I used to go to a church out there on Fox Road, a Methodist church. When I was fifteen years old, I realized that they cared more about what you wore to church than anything else. They really didn't give a damn about you. They got mad at my little brothers and sisters for not being dressed properly and that was the last time I've ever been in a church. And, believe me, I'm not ever going in again, and I don't have any use for them. A bunch of hypocrites."

Les said, "Well, I feel the same way about that. I don't have no need for church either. But I believe in God. People who go to church are hypocrites. But I believe in God."

June said, "Well, I used to go to church all the time, taught Sunday school. And I enjoyed it, and I think one of the best things about it was when you went in there and you were feeling good, the minister would let you have it. Every time. You could always count on that. He'd preach a sermon that would make you feel about so high." She held her two fingers about two inches apart. "Now, I tell you, when you can go to church and the preacher can make you feel about so high, that means something's happening, right? Knock you down off your high horse. Takes the wind out of your sail. Now everybody's got a little bit of conceit, a little bit of uppitiness in them. And the preacher, he'll knock it out of you. That's what the preachers do that's good. I think that's good. So you can't say churches are all bad."

Les said, "Well, most ministers are phonies. Why don't they get out and work like everybody else? Hell, Jesus was a carpenter. If Jesus was a carpenter, shit, there's no reason why people who preach, ministers, can't get out and be carpenters or plumbers or mechanics or something like that. Shit, just sitting back and taking people's money. I know a church—and this is the honest to God's truth—I know a church where if you don't pay the ten per cent that you pledged at the first of the year, they will send a collection agency around to get it from you. I know this is true, and that's the way most churches are. If you don't give them ten per cent to support a minister, who don't do a goddamn thing, if you don't pay your ten per cent, a collection agency comes around. They finally get that money out of you. Bunch of hypocrites, that's what they are, a bunch of hypocrites."

I then asked June if she regretted not going to church.

"No," she said, "I don't regret it one bit."

Ted came back in the room. He was shaving and didn't have a shirt on. Phyllis said, "Shit, that really pisses me off. I wish to hell I could walk around without a shirt. Guys can do it, but I can't. Really pisses me off. At home I do it, but when you're at somebody's house, well, it's just not the proper thing."

June rolled her eyes in customary fashion and nodded, "No, Phyllis, it's *not* the proper thing."

Les seemed to be feeling a little better. He'd gotten his mind off his problem and had had quite a bit to drink. When Barney walked in, Les asked, "Don't take this personal, Barney, but weren't you arrested for manslaughter once? I mean, how come you killed a man, Barney?"

"Well, I never really killed a guy. I was arrested for robbery."

"Well, what was it like being there in the penitentiary those thirteen years? How did you get along there? Was it hard?"

"Yeah, it's pretty hard," Barney drawled, "but you've just got to adjust to it 'cause it's different from the outside world. You've just got to learn to live with it, with the people around you."

"Was it pretty hard?" Les asked again.

"Yeah, no fun. Pretty hard."

Later in the afternoon I looked out and saw a Thunderbird in front of the Mosebys' with Peg in the front seat. She looked terrible. She had a scarf around her head and was bundled up in a big coat. There was a man driving and two men in the back seat. When they stopped in front of the house, Phyllis went out and talked with them for about five minutes. Then they screeched off.

June later told me what had happened. "Well, they called here to get the keys to the West Virginia house. Ted talked to them on the phone this morning. Ted had the keys. I should have never let Ted talk to them." She reported the telephone conversation went like this:

Peg's brother told Ted, "Listen, nobody kicks my sister around. We're going to kill you. Get this straight. You aren't going to know when or where, but me and Peg's ex-husband, we don't like her to get kicked around like you've been kicking her around, and we're going to kill you."

Ted responded, "I don't like nobody kicking my mother around either. What would you do if a crazy woman went after your mother? That's what Peg did, and I don't like it. Besides, I didn't cut her wrists, I just slapped her a few times."

"It don't make no difference, we're going to kill you. You won't know when or where, but we're going to get you."

When Peg then screamed to get on the phone, she and Ted talked for a few minutes. June didn't repeat their conversation, but Ted was upset by it. After the telephone conversation was over, he left and went down to see Linda, a girl down the street.

When Peg and her friends pulled up later on, they wanted to see Ted.

"Where is that sonofabitch? We're going to kill his ass," they said.

"He's not here," said Phyllis, who had volunteered to go out and talk to them.

"Where is he?" Phyllis then made the mistake of saying he was down at Linda's. After she handed them the West Virginia keys, they screeched off, paused in front of Linda's apartment, and then left.

June said, "I'm worried. I think those folks are just bluffing. Actually, I think they are on dope. Ted said they are on dope, all of them. I don't know. I think they're just a lot of hot air. I don't know. But I was so proud of Ted. He stood up to Peg and said, 'Peg, you drug me down too long. You treated me like dirt too long. You never loved me, you know that. You don't love me now. And I'm not putting up with this shit any more. I'm through with it, Peg. I'm through with you, and I don't want to see you any more. No more. I don't want to see you. Get out of my life.' I was so proud of him. He really stood up like a man. But Peg's brother and ex-husband, I don't know. I don't think they'd kill Ted. Ted told them that he wasn't scared. Said he'd face them anytime. He wasn't scared of them. And I know he's not. I know Ted's not scared."

June paused a moment and then continued, "All my kids have to learn the hard way. Marriage ain't what these young folks think it is. It ain't no bed of roses."

When Les met Arlene at six-thirty the next morning, she agreed to return. The next day was June and Sam's sixth wedding anniversary. (Though they never went through any formal marriage procedures, they set aside January 16 to celebrate.) So she and Sam, Les and Arlene and Ted went to the Dixie Club, a night club with a live country music band. Everybody had a good time. Ted even met a couple of cute girls, one of them being Anita, his future fiancée.

The wedding anniversary was another brief interlude for June, because the next week Arlene and Les agreed to separate. This time, however, they mutually agreed on it. Two days before the agreement, Arlene and Les were at June's when Arlene got a call from Randy that Ruby was in labor. When Les saw Arlene packing her bags, he passed out from what everyone thought was a heart attack. The doctors said it wasn't a heart attack but "a case of the nerves." It turned out that Ruby's labor pains were a false alarm, too, but Les had had enough. He agreed to let Arlene go back down to Ruby's. To help make the monthly house payments, he decided to take in roomers.

The next week Ted went back to Peg. June refused to talk about it. Sam was unusually angry. He grumbled, "I told him, 'Teddy, I'm tired of this shit. You know I don't want that bitch in my house. Nothing against you, but if you come in here with that piece of shit, I'm going to kick her ass *and* your ass out. As long as you're with that bitch, I don't want to see you or her!" June basically agreed with Sam. They had warned

Ted; but when Peg called him up and pleaded with him, as before, he gave in. June said that if Ted wanted to ruin his life and go back with Peg, he could; but he shouldn't expect them to stand by him. Ted and Peg moved in with her uncle.

Things were quiet for about a week, but on the last day of January, June called up and was in low spirits. After forcing a laugh, she said, "Aw, it's the same old circus around here. Ah, Les's gone down to Ruby's. Says he's after that guy down there, he's going to kill him. His brother went with him, and we couldn't stop him. Then on top of that, Ted and Peg just showed up. They have been kicked out of every place they could find to stay, and they don't have any place to sleep tonight. And I don't know what Sam's going to do when he comes home and finds them here.

"Then, on top of that, I got a telephone call from Barbara, Sam's daughter. She's being evicted from her place. She's found a place for her oldest two kids to stay with neighbors so they can stay in school. But she and the twins don't have any place to stay. And what can you do? I told her if she couldn't find any place she could come here, but Sam just can't take that. She said she was going to call her mother and see if she could sleep there with her. She thinks she'll let her. I've just had enough. I'm just fed up. I just don't know what . . . and me and Sam, we're—you know, I don't know what he's going to say when he gets home tonight." She paused and then added, "Sam don't love me. The only love in my house is between me and Sammy. And if it wasn't for Barney, I'd pick up and take Sammy with me and we'd be gone. There's nobody else in the world to take care of Barney."

Les returned from the country the next day, saying that he had beaten up Lonnie, and adding that Lonnie had not really tried to fight back. Furthermore, Lonnie had told him that if he were Les he would have done the same thing. Lonnie denied he had been sleeping with Arlene. That had been just talk on Arlene's part. He said he had just talked to her and tried to help her out because he realized that she was in a bad way. When Les talked to Arlene, she admitted that she had been lying to him. Then Les said, "Well, you know, I feel a lot better about it. I've got it out of my system. I really pounded that guy. He wasn't the one to blame. It wasn't his fault. He said that Arlene's crazy, and I think she is crazy. I think she's going through a real hard time. But I feel better about it. I'm going to move back in my house now. I missed work today, but I ain't going to miss no more work. I'm not going to let it destroy me. I'm just going to be patient, just like June and Sam said, and just wait and see what happens. Maybe she'll come back and maybe she won't. Hell, I know one thing, that girl is having real mental problems. What I mean, she's on the verge of a breakdown or something, you know what I mean?"

Since Barbara was not able to find any other place for her four-year-old twins, she deposited them with June and Sam. Sammy slept with Sam. One of the twins slept on the roll-away, another on the couch; and June tried to sleep in the chair or on the couch with the twin. These sleeping arrangements continued for two weeks. On top of all this, Phyllis, who was sick with an attack of emphysema, was spending most of her time at June's.

All this was too much for Sam. He tolerated the twins for almost a week, until one evening when he returned home to find the house in disarray. Sam shouted, "Goddamn kids," sat down to eat, looked at his food, pushed his plate aside, said "Shit," and walked out the door. When he returned a few hours later, he said nothing to June. For the next week June and Sam said very little to each other. June was particularly put out with Sam. "The thing that makes me sick," she said, "that just eats my heart out, is that I have to put up with all of this, and Sam don't give a damn. Not about his own family. The twins are his grandchildren, not mine. But Sam gives me hell. He gives me hell for taking in *his* family. But how could I have turned them away?" At that point June started talking about leaving Sam.

Ted was finally able to get a new job. He had been out of work since coming down from the mountains in mid-December and was tired of staying with Arlene and Les or June and Sam. He didn't dare ask his old boss at the paint shop for a third chance, since he heard that the boss was furious. He happened to see a "help wanted" sign on the door of an old warehouse only a couple of blocks away, checked it out, and got the job working in the parts department of a plumbing wholesale supply company. Although the pay was low, only about eighty-five dollars a week, Ted said his boss told him that if he worked hard he could soon become a supervisor. Ted moved back in with Les when Peg went back to West Virginia to visit her sick grandmother. When she returned on February 7, she and Ted moved back to her uncle's house. She had twelve stitches on her throat when she returned. She said she was jumped one evening at a truck stop, robbed and beaten, and spent a day in the hospital—a story only Ted believed.

Ted stayed with Peg at her uncle's off and on for one week. (They spent two nights with Phyllis.) At the end of that week, on Friday, February 12, Peg played her last trick. No one was too clear as to exactly what happened that night; but according to Ted and to June, who got the details both from Ted and from Peg's uncle, this is the story:

Ted came home after cashing his first pay check, which amounted to $179 for over two weeks' work plus overtime. Peg was drinking when Ted got there. Since he had warned her several times that once she started drinking he was leaving for good, he reminded Peg, "You stop drinking, Peg, or I leave." At that point Peg picked up a butcher knife and jabbed it in Ted's ribs, just enough to prick the skin, warning him, "If you leave this house I'm going to cut your guts out." Ted struck Peg and took the knife. She screamed. Her uncle came rushing in, saw Ted with the knife standing over Peg, and knocked Ted unconscious.

When Ted came to the next morning, Peg was gone; and so was all the money in his wallet. Peg's uncle apologized for hitting him so hard and told him that Peg said her granddaughter was sick and needed her. She said she was going down country to her ex-husband Hal's place and for Ted not to worry. So Ted borrowed her uncle's car and drove down there to see what was going on. When he arrived, there was no Peg. Hal told him that Peg had been there, but she left early that morning with her second husband to go back to West Virginia. They had been planning the trip for about a week. Peg's second husband! Ted did not even know she had a second husband!

"Yeah," said Hal, "I thought you knew. Course, I didn't want to be the one to tell you, since she had never divorced the guy anyway."

Ted said he stood silently for a few minutes, then shook his head and laughed. "I may learn the hard way and the slow way, but by God, once I learn something, I learn it. I'm finished. Never again with that bitch."

In a few days Peg called Ted, apologizing for such a hasty departure and adding that her granddaughter was sick, that she needed the money to put her in a hospital, and that she had a ride down there with her second husband—that's why she left so quick. She promised to pay back all the money if Ted would just take her back. But Ted stood firm. Peg had played her last trick.

9

Spring

With the final departure of Peg and the twins, who left on the same day, life at the Mosebys' took on an unusual calm. Ted moved back in and started sleeping on the couch, and June moved back into the bedroom. June and Sam started speaking again. Peg had not been gone a week when Ted started seeing Anita, the girl he met at the Dixie Club, and began spending more time at her house than at June's. Anita worked as a waitress at a drive-in restaurant just a block away from Ted's work, and she bowled on a league the same time our league bowled. (After Arlene's departure for the country Ted had taken over her spot on our team.) Two weeks later he told June that he and Anita were going to run off and get married. June succeeded in convincing him to hold off a bit. "After all," she told Ted, "you *are* still married to Peg." Since Peg committed bigamy when she married him, he figured their marriage wasn't any good anyway. Nevertheless, he gave in and did not elope.

On March 5 Ruby's baby finally came—her fifth boy. It was around Christmas that she started having labor pains; and from that time on, every day June expected to hear something. It turned out the labor pains were actually due to a problem with her kidneys and the March 5 birth was more or less on time. Since Ruby was able to secure a Medicaid card, she was allowed in the hospital after all. In the meantime, Randy had found a cottage right on the Chesapeake Bay. In the summer they would have to move out; but for the next four months, it was theirs. Arlene was staying temporarily with Ruby, watching the children while Ruby was in the hospital. Randy, however, was still out of work. ("See, Mama," Ruby told June, "things did work out. . . .")

June's children's problems all at once seemed to be resolved, at least temporarily. Her biggest headache now was
Phyllis, who besides coming home from the post office with
large quantities of questionable merchandise, was getting
sicker and drinking more. One evening she started pounding
the plaster off her bathroom wall with her fists. She said that
because she had missed so much work, she was afraid she
would lose her job. She finally did, around the first of April,
but according to her supervisor's report not because of bad
health but rather "incompetence on the job."

This year spring came early to Clay Street. The first warm
day in March Sam was out digging up his garden. The next
several weekends he made excursions to the country, returning with buckets of good soil as well as several small trees and
bushes he decided would look good beside their house. As the
days grew longer and warmer and more people were puttering
around out of doors, some neighbors saw each other for the
first time in months. Windows opened letting in the fresh
spring air, and again you could hear sounds of country music,
laughter, and parents hollering at their children.

During the month of March we didn't see much of June's
kids; and June wasn't talking about them. Although Ted was
supposedly sleeping on the Mosebys' couch, he was rarely
there; and toward the end of the month, he and Anita offi-
cially got engaged, setting July 22 for a date. Anita's father
was a strict Catholic. (He was an Italian from New Jersey;
her mother, a Baptist from West Virginia.) Since he had
brought Anita up in the Catholic Church, Anita dreamed of a
big church wedding. Her father told her she could have her
choice of a big wedding or a houseful of furniture. Though
Ted wanted the furniture, Anita chose the wedding.

There were some problems, of course, since Ted had been
divorced. He and Anita enrolled in a special Catholic class for
engaged couples and filed the necessary papers for the church
to give approval. To make things simpler, Ted never told the
clergy or Anita's parents about Peg. "I thought I had best
let that one slide," he said. After talking to a lawyer, he
concluded it would take too long, cost too much, and be too

complicated to try to get a divorce from Peg. Since he had a chance to pull himself back up by marrying Anita, "a wonderful girl from a nice family," he said he wasn't going to blow it all because of some legal technicalities.

Les would drop by occasionally to get the latest word about Arlene. Since he had missed so much work, he was afraid of being fired. His two roomers had thrown several wild parties, made a mess of his house, and, worst of all, had paid him nothing; consequently, his financial worries increased. If things did not look up soon, Les said he was going to cut loose and drift. He had done this twice before, once when he dropped out of high school and drifted for about a year before getting drafted, and once when he got out of the Army. He even got married in Chicago, although that lasted only about six months. Les would show up every Sunday and watch us bowl, spending about half his time watching us and the other half watching some friends who bowled at the same time in another league.

As for Arlene, she and Lonnie were living together, though both June and Les were reluctant to talk about it. On the morning of April 9, however, almost two and one half months since Arlene's last departure, June came over to our house very excited. "I got a problem. Come here quick, I got a problem. Arlene's on the phone and she wants to come home. I can't talk to her. I'm all mixed up. There's been so much going on—last night with the fight up at the Grizzards and all." (Last night Zeek and Bertie were at each other again. Sam and June were called to help, but before they got there the police had been called in and the apartment was in shambles.) June paused a moment, then continued exuberantly, "Arlene is in tears and broken down, and I don't know what to do. She wants somebody to pick her up, but Sam has my car at the shop, and he won't let me drive his."

I told June I would do what I could and picked up the phone. Arlene was crying on the other end. "I've had enough of this shit," she said. "I'm coming home to Les." She said she was about forty miles out of town at the Virginia Motel and wanted to be picked up right away. June interrupted at this point, saying, "Look, tell Arlene to call back in twenty minutes, we'll go get Les. He's the one should pick her up."

Just as I was getting in my car to go find Les, he came driving up in his car, which was packed with Bertie Grizzard's belongings. Phyllis's half-sister, Becky, was in the front seat with him. When I told him the news, he stood there with a disbelieving look on his face.

"I can't believe it, I just can't," he said over and over. "My wife. She's coming home."

After unloading Bertie's stuff at Phyllis's, Les took off to go get Arlene. Later in the afternoon when he and Arlene returned, no one knew exactly what to say. Arlene didn't give anyone a chance.

"Don't touch me," she was saying to Les when they got out of the car. "Leave me alone. Who do you think you are, my husband?" Arlene was giggling and Les tried very hard to force a laugh.

"Now, honey," she said, "I want you to go out and buy me a whole bunch of new clothes, slacks, blouses, and some hotpants, okay?" Later, as they got in the car to go to the shopping center, June stood silently on the front porch with her arms crossed and a frown on her face.

That evening Arlene and Les joined Ted and Anita, my wife, Embry, and me at the Black Jack Club, a night club at the naval base. Everybody seemed to have a good time dancing and drinking, though it was obvious some tension still existed between Arlene and Les. Early the next morning I looked out my window to see Les walking around outside by himself. I opened the door and hollered, "How you doing, Les? That was lots of fun last night."

Les shrugged his shoulders and shook his head. "She's gone," he shouted back. "She took all her new clothes, hotpants, and all that stuff, and went back down to see Lonnie."

"When?"

"Last night when we got back. Arlene told me that things weren't right. She said she had tried it with me and it wasn't going to work out."

I exclaimed, *"Tried* it with you? She'd only been with you a few hours."

"I know," said Les. "But she doesn't think that it's going to

work out. So she took everything. All her clothes and stuff
and got a friend to drive her back down there." Les paused
for a moment and then added, "But she'll come back. She'll
come back again, and I'll take her in like a goddamned fool.
And June will and we all will. Just like a bunch of fools. But
what are you going to do? She's my wife and I love her."

Les was right. This time it was sooner than anyone expected and not by Arlene's own choosing. Lonnie dropped her
off for her to visit June the next week and did not return to
pick her up. Because Ted was sleeping on June's couch, Arlene stayed up the street with Tammy and Fred, a couple who
used to own a mobile home next to their mobile home when
they were first married.

Arlene said that at times things had been pretty rough. She
and Lonnie had been living at the Virginia Motel where Arlene worked as a cleaning lady so they could stay rent-free in
one of the units. Lonnie worked days in Alexandria as an
electrician and on some nights did not even make it back to
the motel. Though Arlene did not have a car, she could walk
or hitch a ride to some of the bars on the highway; but even
so, she said she often felt lonely and isolated. After Lonnie
got things straight, Arlene said, she was sure he would come
back and get her and they would get an apartment in Alexandria near his job. She was right. Three days later Lonnie
returned in his Mustang Mach I and off they went to Alexandria.

After Arlene's departure, I dropped by to chat. June was
very depressed. She sighed, "I wouldn't mind her doing this
so much if Lonnie was any good. And the way she is doing it.
It just ain't right. My baby. What did I do wrong?" June went
back to the kitchen and brought me a cup of coffee. She sat
down on the stuffed living room couch and sighed again.
"See that picture on top the TV?" she said. "That's a picture
of me and my younguns when I was married to Brownie."
The person in the photograph had short hair, wore granny
glasses, and looked much older than June looked, sitting on
the couch. "It don't look like me, does it? Well, it's not me. I
mean it is, but I was different then. Brownie was a deacon in

the Baptist Church, and we went to church every Sunday and prayer meetings on Wednesday. Lived out in the country; but it wasn't much of a life. He lived his life. I lived mine.

"I guess I got off to a bad start. You see, my first husband, Steve, he was good for nothing. I'll tell you about my husband, and so help me God if I'm telling one word that's not true, God strike me down this instant. You wouldn't believe how poor we were. Steve drank a lot and wouldn't do nothing to support our family. But I didn't work 'cause of the kids, and one winter things got pretty bad. I had all three then, little Arlene—not even a year old—the two others just toddlers, and we'd gone several weeks without having anything to eat. Hardly anything, just handouts at the church, the mission. It was just pitiful. I had to go to the mission for handouts almost every day for hot soup. We got Christmas baskets practically every Christmas for a number of years. We got clothes from churches just about every Christmas.

"This year we didn't have nothing at that time. To keep warm, I was cutting up the linoleum on the floor of this one-room shack. There was a potbellied stove in this shack. This one old shack had rats running under your bed at night and roaches, and we burned linoleum to keep warm.

"Well, in this shack, the linoleum went up several inches off the floor. There were several layers. I don't know who lived there before, but whoever it was had seen fit to put one layer of linoleum on top of another. Well, by the time I had gone through four layers of linoleum—I was down to the fourth level—I was cutting it up and I found a five-dollar bill which was broken in four pieces. I pasted the bill together with Scotch tape. I went down—it was snowing, I remember the night—to the grocer's and said, 'What can you give me for this bill? Will you take it, is it any good?' 'Yes, I'll take it,' he said. He gave me soup, bread, some food, and some coal.

"We came back, put the coal in the fire, ate a good dinner —the first one in God knows how long—and about that time my husband came in. He looked at the food on the table, he looked at the fire, and said, 'June, where'd you get the money?' I told him. Without saying anything else he hit me in the eye, gave me a black eye, jumped on me and tried to strangle me. Swearing at me, cussing at me, said I should have given half the money to him to buy himself a drink. I ran out of the house. By that time I'd had enough. He busted my tooth out—I had false teeth 'cause he'd knocked my other teeth out before, knocked them clear across the room. I ran to the grocer's, came back, and he was gone. I said, 'This is enough.' Picked up the kids. I didn't have anything else. Wrapped blankets around them and put on what little clothing we had. Took them to the store. I told the guy, 'John, I'm leaving. I've had enough. Do you know anywhere I can go?' He said, 'Yes, June, I know a place.' He took me out in the country to a room in a house owned by an old woman. Gave me a house full of groceries and paid the first month's rent. And I said, 'John, you're my benefactor. You've saved my life.' And I married that man. He became my next husband. He was twenty-seven years my elder. It was a marriage of convenience, that's all it was, a marriage of convenience."

June had married her first husband when she was sixteen. She dropped out of high school but was finally able to get a diploma going to school part-time after Ruby was born. When Steve worked, he was a Jack-of-all-trades, specializing in plumbing. The day she walked out on him they had been married almost six years.

John Brown was a grocer and a butcher; but after he married June, he gave that up and started working as a salesman for a janitor supply company in the Washington area. They moved out in the country and bought a house. June got a job working on the production line at Binders Straw Company, making $.86 an hour. When she finally quit fifteen years later, she was an inspector, making $1.96 an hour.

"As far as material things, I was much better off married to Brownie," she continued, "but it was not really a marriage. It was really like a father and four children. He never treated me like an equal or like a wife. I was always just another one of his children. He handled all the finances. I turned over my salary I was making at the straw company to him and got an allowance. God, I'll never do that again! He made most of the decisions; it was almost like I was a prisoner. But he was better than I had had, and I was too young to know no better.

"I was like my momma. My momma worshiped the ground my daddy walked on. She bent over backwards for him. Everything he said was right; everything he did was right. He could do no wrong, and she could do no right. It was terrible. That's not the way it should be, but that's the way it was for me then. It ain't going to be that way no more."

John died of cancer in 1962. June said he had gone crazy just before and had torn up all his papers, except his discharge from the Army—his honorable discharge, which June later found out was a dishonorable discharge that had been forged.

"I found out a lot of dirt about that man after they put him under, a lot of dirt. He had lived a hell of a life, but I never knew about it. He'd been married a couple times before, and I'm sure he must have been betting because his employer, who was really a nice man, told me he had lent him over ten thousand dollars during the time that Brownie had been working for him. I never knew about that. But he said that Brownie had paid him back every cent. I know he was betting or something."

Many problems arose when Brownie died. Since they had no savings, June had to give up the house. Perhaps worst of all, social security would not pay June anything because they had no marriage papers, and her three children had not been legally adopted by Brownie.

"Oh, they did pay two hundred fifty for the burial. But hell, that cost me eight hundred. There I was, left without a husband and without hardly a dime, and with three kids. It wasn't easy."

June's fellow workers at Binders Straw took up a collection amounting to $250. The Veterans Administration came through with another $250. And an insurance policy of $1,000 finally agreed to pay June the full amount, though she had to get a lawyer to get this out of the insurance people, who said they did not have to pay because John had cancer. June said that after John's death she got all his possessions —an American flag given to him for his service in France in World War I, a plaque signed by John Kennedy personally, and all his other things—and sent them to John's sister. She said she didn't want any of his personal items around. After the burial June never returned to his grave.

Right after John's death, Ruby got married. Ted dropped out of high school to go into the Army. June left the house and moved with Arlene into an apartment nearer the city. In 1962, while June and Arlene were living there, June met Sandy. She was out one night with some friends; he was out with some friends, and everybody seemed to know each other. They went out that night and played slot machines down on Route 301 and ended up at four in the morning in an all-night restaurant. From that night on, Sandy and June started seeing a lot of each other.

The years 1962 to 1964 were good years as June looked back on them. She had her first freedom. She was able to do what she wanted to do. She and Sandy would do something together practically every weekend. Sandy worked for Baker's Chevrolet and also worked part-time as a janitor for a church. June was still working at Binders Straw.

During the winter they went skiing, an experience June said was the highlight of her life. Often they would leave Arlene with Alva, Sandy's ex-wife; and when Alva would take off to do something, she would leave her children with June.

Besides skiing they went to auto races, drive-in movies, and camping in the summer. Ruby had married by that time; and when June didn't leave Arlene with Alva, she would leave her with Ruby. It was in 1964 that June met Sam. Arlene had gotten to be good friends with some of Sam's nieces and nephews. When Arlene called over there, occasionally she would talk to Sam. He started asking Arlene how old she was and what she looked like. Arlene said, "I'm too young for you, but I got a mother who is just about right."

"So that's how I met Sam. I don't know what it is," said June. "I love all my kids. But Arlene has always been something special. And just think, if it wasn't for her, I wouldn't have met Sam." She laughed when she said that; then her voice became quiet and she almost whispered as if she were talking to herself. "To see her mess her life up, when my own life has been so . . . well . . . you wish something better for your kids. Yet you see the same thing happening, and it seems like there is nothing you can do to stop it."

June's mother had been dead for several years; but her father was still alive, in fair health, and in his eighties. For the past few years he had been living with June's sister, Doris, and her husband on their farm in the country, about one hundred miles away. Though June would call occasionally and send him cards on his birthday and Father's Day, she and Sam were reluctant to go down and visit him, mainly because they felt uncomfortable around June's sister and brother-in-law. In Sam's words, they were just "too goddamn good—no drinking, smoking, or cussing and made you feel like shit. And all this religion stuff, religion, yak, yak, yak."

Toward the end of April, June's father went down to Raleigh to visit June's other sister and brother-in-law. He had been in Raleigh only two weeks when he suffered a severe heart attack. When June got word, she packed her bags and she and Sammy flew down to Raleigh the next morning. If things got better, Sam would drive down on the weekend and bring them home.

In the middle of the week June reported that her father was much better and that Sam should come on down as soon as he could get off on Friday. On Friday, the day Sam was supposed to leave, Arlene reappeared in the neighborhood. This time she was with Larry.

Larry was a mysterious character. First of all, he had been living with Phyllis for about a week. A huge guy in his mid-twenties, he was six-foot-four, weighed 234 pounds (information he readily volunteered), and had greasy blond hair with long sideburns. When I had asked who this character was and where he had come from, Phyllis had said, "Oh, Larry—I don't know where he's from, don't know where he's going. He's just staying here awhile."

"For how long?"

"Shit, I don't know."

"Well, who the hell is he?"

"Beats me."

Sam had said the same thing except that he remarked that Larry was married and had a wife who was in the hospital with some female disorders. Arlene had said that she liked Larry, that he was a nice guy, but she didn't know anything else about him.

On the Friday when Sam was to leave, Arlene showed up at our house about ten in the morning, obviously upset. The first thing she said was, "Did you hear the news? Well, me and Lonnie, we've busted up. Yep, we've busted up. I just left him. I left him this morning. Took all my clothes, and I doubt if I'll ever see him any more." Though she started off as if everything were fine, the more she got into it, the more upset she became and she started crying.

As far as I could piece things together, this is what happened: For the last two weeks, Lonnie had been running around with other women. He had been going out practically every evening and not taking Arlene with him. Arlene, on the other hand, had been keeping house, cooking breakfast, making lunch, cooking dinner for Lonnie and his five buddies, and living there with these guys, but apparently not getting in on any of the fun—bar-hopping, going to country and western music clubs, whoring around. So she was beginning to get a little upset and fed up with it all. The previous day Phyllis and her friend Larry arrived to "rescue" Arlene from the "trash" (Phyllis's term) she was running around with. I did not know who put Phyllis up to it, though I presumed it was her own idea without June's knowledge. She and Larry persuaded Arlene to leave Lonnie and come home.

Arlene put it this way: "Well, see, things weren't going too good. I mean, jeez, you know, Lonnie running around. So I was kinda upset. Well Phyllis, she kinda threatened me. I mean, it was like I was kidnapped! I mean, I didn't want to leave. I didn't want to leave Lonnie. I love Lonnie. I want to go back. I want to go back. I didn't really want to leave. . . ." The one thing she said she wanted to do was to get in touch with Lonnie to tell him that it was a mistake and ask if he would take her back. The problem was that she didn't know how to get in touch with Lonnie since she didn't know his job phone number and he didn't have a phone in the apartment. Only one of the six guys could be reached at work. Arlene finally called him only to find that he had been fired that day for missing too much work.

To complicate matters more, somehow Larry had the idea that Arlene was going to be his girl. He had agreed to pay for Arlene's divorce and separation if she would move in with him. Phyllis and Larry apparently had worked this out, but it didn't go over with Arlene, who said, "He wants to buy me, that's all he wants, just like to buy me. But I'm not going to be his whore. I'm just not going to do it. He wants me to move in and live with him, but it ain't right, and I don't want to do it."

Arlene spent the morning wondering what to do. She went up the street and talked with her friend Tammy, then came back and talked to us. Later in the morning we had to leave; and when we got back around four, Sam was pulling up to pick up his things before leaving for Raleigh. I was talking with him on his front porch just as Arlene and Phyllis drove up. Arlene got out, ran up to us, kissed Sam on the side of the cheek, and said, "I'm going to straighten up. I've decided not to go back to Lonnie. I've decided to get an apartment, to start dating, and to straighten up. I'm going to be a good girl and not give you any more trouble."

Before she arrived Sam was expressing his dissatisfaction with the whole thing. "Goddammit, I'm so sick of that shit. Here she's running around over there with trash and now she's running around here with this guy, Larry, a married man. He's got a wife and a kid. Shit, it's just jumping out of one frying pan into another. Fooling around with trash. When is that goddamn bitch going to straighten up?" When Arlene kissed him on the cheek and told him that she was going to change, he muttered, "I've heard that before."

Arlene left, went back to the car, and came back a few minutes later. Then things happened fast. First, Arlene had it out with Larry, who still thought she was going to move in with him. Apparently he was a little angry; but when he realized that she just didn't want to be his girl, he accepted it. Larry was a sweet, understanding guy—so everybody said. Then Sam took Arlene inside and cussed her out. I could hear him hollering at her from where I was in my front yard.

"Goddammit, you bitch. You've got to straighten up, Arlene. You can't do this. . . ." I didn't hear Arlene say anything, but about ten minutes later she ran out of the house crying and cussing Sam. "He don't understand, he don't understand, he don't understand." About fifteen minutes after that, Arlene was unloading all her clothes from Phyllis's trunk and moving them next door into the Mosebys' apartment. "I'm going down to North Carolina with Sam," she told me. "I've decided I'm going down there with Sam." Tears were still streaming down her cheeks. About thirty minutes after that, she and Sam got in the car and headed off to North Carolina.

Phyllis was standing on her front porch; and when I asked her what had happened, she replied, "Ah shit, I don't know. Trying to do the girl a favor, get her away from that trash she was running around with over there in Alexandria. I'm so tired of all this shit I don't know what I'm going to do. I'm just sick of it. I'm finished. I just am. Me and my girl, that's finished. My job, that's finished. All this shit going on over at our place. Arlene and this shit she's into. I'm just finished."

When the Mosebys returned home on Sunday, June was beaming. Her father was improving; she had enjoyed being at her sister's, who, according to June, was as crazy as she was; Arlene was going back to Les; and most important, Sam had come down to get her a day before she expected he would. Not only that, over the past week *he* had called *her* every evening to check on them. (Before she left, Sam's last words were, "Goddammit, I don't want a big telephone bill from any calls from down Raleigh.") June was going around laughing and telling everyone about how Sam called *her*.

Arlene unenthusiastically returned to Les after three days of sleeping on June's couch. She was there long enough to celebrate their fifth wedding anniversary on May 27 and then was off again. By this point no one was taking the matter too seriously. It had become obvious that she was out to do her thing in her own way, and there was nothing anyone could do to change her. Everyone by now had tried. (Arlene's latest reason for returning to Lonnie was that when she was seeing Ruby, Lonnie's two small children, who lived down there with Lonnie's wife, greeted Arlene, hugged her, and said, "Hi,

Momma, where's Daddy?") Also, by this time everyone was beginning to think something was wrong with Les for letting Arlene push him around. Sam had said several times, "Arlene's crazy to be running off from a hard-working guy who loves her, but Les is crazier for putting up with that shit." Over the summer Arlene proceeded to run up a six-hundred-dollar bill on Les's credit cards.

The person who apparently did change over the spring was Ruby. Although before the late spring I had met Ruby only twice and then only briefly, I felt I knew her since I had heard so much about her. I knew that June could not understand her and had a personality conflict with her. Arlene and Les had both talked about how horrible Ruby's house was and how they didn't approve of Ruby's receiving welfare. (Les also had an unmarried sister who with several children was in a similar situation.) Yet they enjoyed the company of both Ruby and Randy and regularly would go down to visit them and go drinking at the Legion Hut. And, of course, during the winter Arlene had more or less moved in with Ruby.

Toward the end of May while Arlene was still with Les, she asked us if we could give her a ride down to Ruby's so that she could pick up her income tax refund. We left around one-thirty in the afternoon and drove the eighty miles in a little over one and a half hours. It was a sunny, warm spring day. The rolling countryside was prettier than I had imagined. When we got down to the tiny bayside community where Ruby lived, we were even more impressed. The Chesapeake Bay was extremely blue that day. Ruby lived in a small cottage located in the center of a cluster of small cottages all surrounded by huge shrubs and big oak trees. Though old, her cottage was in fairly good condition. It had three bedrooms, a big, screened-in front porch, and was built of lumber, painted white with a white picket fence outside. From all we had heard, I assumed everything would be in complete chaos. This was not the case. Of course, Ruby's furniture was old and well used. Two TV sets were stacked in the corner, and there was not a lot on the walls—two old mirrors and a Woolworth painting. However, the house was as neat as June's.

Though a few toys were strewn about, the place was comfortable, orderly, and had personality and charm.

Ruby was home. Two of her children were playing along the beach. One was still at school, and her two youngest were home with her—the baby being only two months old. She greeted us warmly, as if she had been expecting us. In fact, we found out later that she had. The Spirit had told her that she was going to have visitors.

We sat down and began to chat. Arlene told Ruby that she had left Lonnie and gone back to Les, but she didn't really know what she wanted to do. Ruby seemed relatively unconcerned. She replied, "Oh, I see . . . well . . ." and then went on to talk about herself. During the course of the day, whenever Arlene brought up her problems Ruby seemed to be unconcerned. Similarly, when Ruby was talking about her recent experience in the Pentacostal Church, Arlene seemed bored. Each seemed to be oblivious to what the other was saying.

We had been talking only a few minutes when Ruby mentioned that she had just been to Washington for a revival. Arlene said, "You've been to Washington without calling us?"

"Well, it was Tuesday night. I just went up there and came back. But it was a great revival! I mean, it was really, really great." Such enthusiasm was rare on Clay Street. "I want to tell you, it was the best thing I've ever been to! The preacher, oh, he was great. And the music, oh, it was great." She showed me a picture of the man who preached—a young man who looked more like a country music singer than an evangelist. Then she showed me an album she had purchased entitled "Prophetic Music" put out by A. A. Allen of the Pentacostal Movement. "Oh yes, it was really something. I mean, there were people screaming and hollering; there were people speaking in tongues; there were people prophesizing; there were people rolling. I mean, it wasn't a Holy-rolly church or anything like that, but they were passing out in the aisles, and when you pass out, you know, they come and put a sheet over you. There were lots of folks passed out with sheets over them. And my friend, Gay, she has the gift of speaking in tongues and of prophesizing both. And that night she did both. Oh, it was wonderful, it was just wonderful. I'd hoped I could speak in tongues or have the gift of prophecy bestowed on me and I was kind of disappointed when it didn't come. I hoped it would, but it didn't."

When I asked her how long she had been involved with the Pentacostal Church, she replied, "Oh, I want to tell you, first of all, it's changed my whole life. I mean, I am a different person, I am competely different. And I can't explain exactly how, but I am. I've been involved in it three weeks. Three weeks ago I was saved. Three weeks ago last Sunday I was saved."

"How did it happen?"

"Oh, you are interested?" She perked up. "Not many folks are interested. I can't get Randy to listen to me at all. Most of the guys, they don't want anything to do with it. But if you're interested, I'll tell you. You see, this year's been kind of a hard year for me. We've been having lots of problems, me and Randy. In fact, I had made up my mind to leave him. I was going to leave him on a Thursday. I had it all worked out, 'cause we'd been fighting and all and just weren't getting along. I was going to move in with a girl friend not too far away in another small town—keep the kids until I could find a place, maybe move back up near where Mom is. We hadn't been able to pay the bills. Randy hadn't had any work for five months. He'd been trying, but couldn't get a job. We were going to have the heat turned off and had already lost the telephone. We didn't have enough money to buy groceries. I get some food stamps, but we used all those up. Oh, it was something awful.

"Anyway, Gay, my friend, she's been involved in this for two or three years. She has the gift of speaking in tongues and of prophesizing. She got me to come to her church. Told her, 'I don't believe in church. I mean, I believe in God and all that, but I think people who go to church are a bunch of hypocrites.' Course, I had been to church when I was little, with Mom, but I haven't been lately. When you go to church, even the Baptist Church, people just sit there and they wear their new clothes, and they try to show off, and they talk about what's happening. I mean, it's just socializing, that's all it is.

Trying to show off. And you go there and it just turns you
off, you know. You don't get anything out of it. It's dull. The
minister gets up there and hollers but it don't mean nothing.
So I didn't have no use for church and I told Gay that.
   "She said, 'I know how you feel. I felt the same way. I felt
exactly the same way. But this church is different.' I said,
'No, they're all the same.' Gay said, 'Trust me.' Gay is a friend
of mine, and I think a lot of her, so I said, 'Well, why not?
What do I have to lose?' So I went with Gay to church. This
was three weeks ago.
   "Well, something happened to me that day, something happened to me. I got cold chills and it was hot, it was hot in that
church, real hot. But I got cold chills running up and down
my spine, and my hands turned icy. And I got to trembling.
I used to think all this stuff was put on, but this was happening to *me!* And Gay, she'd told me, 'I have prayed for you,
and God is going to talk to you tomorrow.' She told me that
the day before. I said, 'Come on, Gay, I don't believe in that
stuff.' Well, that's what she said. She said that God had talked
to her and told her. Well, it happened. I went forward, I went
up toward the altar rail, and I was trembling and shaking
and scared. I didn't know what was going to happen. Gay
comes up and there I am, kneeling at the rail, and she starts
speaking in tongues and starts prophesizing and puts her hand
on my shoulder and I feel this trembling going through me
and I feel this spirit. I just feel it. And there's music and
there's singing and everybody's there and I feel this spirit coming on. Then Gay says, 'He's here, he's here! Jesus is here.'
'Oh, oh!' I said, 'he's here!' And I was afraid to look up 'cause
I knew I would see him. I knew he was there, there at the
altar, but I was afraid to look up. I knew I had to do it. But
I'd read in the Bible that he who sees the face of God will die,
so I was afraid I'd die. But I knew I just couldn't stand it if
I didn't look and see him. And when I looked up, it was glowing, the whole altar, with light. I didn't see Jesus or God, they
weren't there personally. But I mean, they were there, too.
You couldn't see them exactly, but I mean the whole altar
glowed. I mean, I can't explain it to you too well, but all I

know is that this light and this glowing and I knew that the presence of Jesus and God was there.

"And that's when I was saved, that day. And my life ain't been the same since. It's difficult to explain, as I say, but all I know is it's true. It happened to me, and now I can go on living. For three days I had the Spirit. I mean, I was radiating. People who have the Spirit radiate. You can see it; you can almost touch it; you can feel it. They're different. You can tell—the spark in their eyes, the way they talk, the love. They just radiate love. Well, I had it for two or three days. Randy, he realized it. He didn't know what had happened. He knew I was different, and he couldn't understand it. He still can't. He won't have anything to do with it. Most of the guys won't have anything to do with it. They just like to drink and go out and have a good time. And when their wives and girl friends get religion and get saved, they don't care that much about going out any more. So I can understand why the guys don't like it.

"Anyway, everybody will tell you I was different. Then I went to prayer meeting the next Wednesday, and the same thing happened again. We all got down and prayed and Jesus came. Everybody felt him, and I felt him. I felt his presence. And the next day, when I was going to leave Randy on that Thursday, I didn't leave him. I just knew that Jesus didn't want me to leave him. And the next week Randy, he got a job. And now he's going to work as an electrician's assistant. He was unemployed for five months, and then he got a job. It's Jesus that got him that job, I'm convinced.

"Well, everything has sort of been better since. I mean, we've gotten along much better. I've started reading these books. Gay's checked them out at the library. You know, I used to yell at my kids and all. I don't do that no more, 'cause it says in the Bible not to. It says use a stick. And so I use a stick now. But me and my kids, we seem to get along better. You know, I had these problems, and I get uptight and I just say, 'Oh, thank you, Jesus,' and somehow, it's like a burden is taken off my shoulders. 'Cause I know that Jesus does care, that Jesus loves me. He can take the burden. I don't have to carry it any more. Jesus carries it. He helps me carry the load. It's really funny, but I'll be in the kitchen doing work and just all of a sudden I'll say, 'Thank you, Jesus, O sweet Jesus.' And Randy, if he's there, he'll look at me sort of funny. And the kids—they look at me a little funny sometimes. But that's just the way it is. When you've got the Spirit, when you've got religion and you've been saved, you've got to talk like that. You know, it just comes natural. I mean, Jesus is with me all the time now. Like I say, my life has changed."

Ruby went on to say that she had been to two revivals since: one in a small town not too far away and the other last week in Washington, D.C. She was very enthusiastic about both. The revival in Washington was in the downtown area. When I asked her if there were black people there as well as white, she said, "Oh yes, yes, quite a few. In fact, I'd say about ninety-five per cent were colored. There were lots of folks there and, oh . . . only twenty or thirty white folks. It was really funny, the minister who was colored—there was one colored and one white—he was a good singer. He went around singing, and he came to a white person, a woman, who was a good singer, too, and they went around singing together. He asked her, 'Are you prejudiced?' 'No.' 'Do you believe Jesus is here today?' 'Hallelujah brother, I do!' He took her hand and they walked together around the church and he said, 'You know, I feel sorry for people who are prejudiced. I feel real sorry.' And everybody said hallelujah and hollered, screamed and sang. Oh, it was wonderful; it was just too wonderful to describe.

"But I was a little disappointed in myself because I'd kind of hoped I could speak in tongues myself. I mean, like Gay, and have the gift of prophecy. And I tried real hard, but, well, Jesus didn't give it to me. But he will, he will, in due time. . . ."

Ruby had held prayer meetings at her house the past three Wednesdays. Eight people attended, all women. She said there were quite a few, though, who belonged to the church. Some men belonged, but there were more women than men involved in the movement.

"You know, it's happening everywhere. Everywhere. Even hippies are going to Jesus. I've been reading about it, and I've seen them. It's everywhere, it's all over, it's just taking over. And it's the most wonderful thing. It gives you peace of mind. It gives you a different feeling about life, about everything. I'm working on Randy. He puts up with me. He hasn't come yet, but I'm working on it. Maybe he'll come along."

Ruby was particularly complimentary of her friend Gay. "You know, when we were down and out—don't ever tell Randy this, he don't know—but we had a eighty-eight-dollar electric bill and were a couple months behind on rent. Gay came over to me and said, 'You know, I prayed to Jesus last night about you, and Jesus talked to me. He told me that he wanted to give you some money, through me!' " Gay handed her an envelope with $165 in it to pay the rent and the bills and to buy the children some clothes. "But Gay told me that it was Jesus that gave her the money, that it was Jesus's money and Jesus wanted me to have it. Now that's what I call a real Christian."

While she was talking, her oldest child came home from the first grade and then all of us—Arlene, Embry, me, Ruby and her five children, and our son, Andrew—went out to the beach and went for a short walk. Two of the children went in swimming with all their clothes on.

Ruby said, "I really love it out here. It's so peaceful and quiet. It's too bad we're going to have to move. Come June twenty-third they start renting it out a week at a time at one hundred a week, and we're going to have to move on. I don't know what we're going to do or where we're going to go. I sure would like to stay here."

Later, after we departed, I asked Arlene what she thought about Ruby's religion. "Well," she said, "everybody has got a right to believe what they want to. But Ruby, she's all the time going on these weird kicks."

10

Summer

Compared to the early months of the year, summer at the Mosebys was quiet. Sam had his garden, which occupied most of his attention after work. Sammy, who was now home all day, occupied much of June's attention. And, of course, there was always Phyllis, who ever since she had lost her job in April had been spending most of her time at June's. Numerous other folks were always dropping in to borrow laundry money or to chat on June's front porch or living room.

In June the bowling season finally came to an end after thirty-six weeks of continuous play. Our team finished in last place with a won 12, lost 96 record—to the best of anyone's memory, the worst record in the history of the league. Besides the two evenings around Christmas, Phyllis's and Edith's (one of Phyllis's girl friends) confrontation with the manager in the women's john (where they were found doing some "heavy petting"), and Phyllis's numerous run-ins with members of other teams, the season was relaxing and enjoyable, even if we did keep on losing.

The bowling league offered an occasion every week for people to socialize and meet other people casually and informally. For many people in the league, bowling was their main social activity, some people bowling in as many as three or four leagues. It was also a family affair. Of the five member teams, most, like ours, were comprised of husband and wife couples plus a friend or relative, and some were one-family teams, often including three generations. Since younger couples usually brought their children, the lounge behind the bowling area resembled a kiddieland every Sunday evening with infants crying, preschoolers crawling under the seats, and numerous games of tag and chase going on everywhere.

While some people took their bowling very seriously, most people said they were there to meet people and have a good time. They did. Beer and pizza were everywhere. The sounds of children hollering, people laughing, endless chatter, and pin balls drowned out one's thoughts, and it was difficult not to get caught up in the spirit of the Sunday night league.

The big event of the bowling season was the final bowling banquet, which was included in the cost of $3.25 per person per set. (Poor people could not afford to bowl!) During the year everyone talked about the great banquet, when trophies were awarded and great food was served, followed by dancing. We were not disappointed. The banquet was held in the auditorium of a Catholic high school in the area. The food was good, and the rock band lively. Just as everyone bowled, at the banquet everyone danced—grandmas and grandpas, mothers and fathers, young couples. In typical fashion June and Sam let themselves go. "That's my big Daddy," June would say returning from the dance floor. "Can't he dance! He's the man I fell in love with." The highlight of the evening for us came when our team was awarded a beautiful gold trophy—a horse's ass for finishing in last place.

At several points in the year, usually following a particularly bad evening at the alley, June and Sam both remarked that they were going to quit the league after the season finished. June remarked that since some of the people were a little snooty, she and Sam didn't feel all that comfortable with them. At the bowling banquet, however, several people came up to June and told her how much they had enjoyed knowing her and Sam and how they hoped they would be in the league next year. On the way home, June and Sam for the first time were talking about who would replace Embry and me on the team next year. "Yes, sir," said June, "there are some real nice folks in that league, just good old, ordinary people. I think we'll do better next year, don't you, big Daddy?"

After the bowling league recessed for the summer, June and Sam had no formal social activities. (Most of the people in the league were playing in summer leagues, however.) Occasionally, on Friday evenings Sam would take June to Tom's Drive-in for a hot dog or fried fish. And for a special occasion they might go dancing with their kids at the Dixie Club; but since things remained up in the air between Arlene and Les, there were few special occasions. Mainly, they would sit out on their front porch, drink beer, chat with passing neighbors, or watch TV.

Sam's son, Olin, who was a motorcycle mechanic for the D.C. Police Department, came over with his wife and child several evenings over the summer—they lived in a new house about five miles away which Sam had never seen—as did Sam's daughter, Barbara, and her husband, Larry, who usually brought with him a new dirty movie to show on Sam's projector. For the most part, however, things were quiet.

The big event of the summer for the Mosebys was a trip to Florida. Like most things that happened in the Moseby household, it came about without a great deal of planning or forethought. Sam and June had never gone anywhere on Sam's vacation. The past summer when they failed to leave home, June got so upset with Sam she said that before his vacation was up she was ready to shoot him. Consequently, this year, with all the turmoil, June was dreading Sam's vacation.

Then on the Wednesday before the Friday Sam's vacation started, Sam casually mentioned to June, "Hey, you ain't never been to Florida, have you?" June perked up. Neither she nor Sam had ever seen Florida. In fact, June had been south of Raleigh only twice, when she and Sam went to the Darlington 500 auto race. "Shit," said Sam, "I got this vacation and all, so . . ." June hugged Sam and scooted back in the bedroom to start packing her bags.

They set off on Saturday morning with the goal of getting to Florida, if only to say they had been there. They left Barney with Sam's sister and took June's car, with Sammy riding in the back seat hollering, "Florida, Florida, we are going to Florida!"

They had decided to drive to Raleigh where they would spend the night with June's sister, then drive down to Myrtle Beach where they might spend a few days and then drive to Jacksonville for a day. On the way to Raleigh, however, it was getting late and they saw some signs advertising the Darlington 500 auto race. They both became nostalgic; and Sam remembered a motel where they had stayed for the races. Since they had not called June's sister, they decided to head for the motel and spend the night there. They could have made it to Myrtle Beach the next day, but Sam remembered he had a nephew who lived somewhere in Florida, he thought in Tampa. "Why not?" June explained later. "If we didn't make the move then, I'd probably die without ever seeing Florida." So they made the move, reached Tampa late the next night, looked up Sam's nephew, and ended up spending over a week with him, his wife and small child. When they returned ten days later, June was glowing. "Well," she said, "we couldn't go swimming in the Gulf 'cause of this red tide thing they got down there, but Florida is beyootiful, I mean really beyootiful." She was most enthusiastic about the Busch Beer Gardens and a place they stopped at on the way back on the border of North and South Carolina called South of the Border. Sam was almost as enthusiastic as June. He brought back several small palm trees, which he planted in his garden, and was exuberant about the grapefruit and orange trees that he reluctantly left behind. They both said they wanted to go back next year. "South of the Border" and "Busch Garden" bumper stickers remained on June's bumper the rest of the summer.

All June's children continued having their problems. Since Arlene continued leaving and returning, no one was ever sure exactly what her status was with Les. I was probably the only one who kept count. Toward the end of August, when Arlene was with Lonnie again, she had left Les eleven times in the past eight months.

Nothing went right for Les. One weekend when Arlene was home they went to the beach with Ted and Anita; and when they returned, his stereo, color TV, and all of Les's guns had been stolen. Worst of all, since all of these items were hot in the first place, Les had no insurance and could not even report the loss to the police. Although he suspected that one of his friends, who had been staying there, did it, he had no proof. Les also had been arrested for speeding—he was doing over 100 m.p.h. in a fifty-mile zone—and was afraid of losing his license, in which case he would have to quit his job as a truck driver.

Ted and Anita were having problems and postponed their wedding indefinitely. Ted assured June that they were still going to get married. The main problem was that the Catholic Church was giving them a hard time about his marriage to Helga.

The last of June, as expected, Ruby and Randy were forced to move, though fortunately they were able to find another house. This house was also on the Chesapeake Bay but was very old, in extremely poor condition, and was without water or electricity for the first few weeks. In his effort to find the house Randy missed so much work he got fired; so they were back where they started.

Life for Ruby continued to be difficult. Her family had been in their new place only a few weeks when Arlene and Lonnie and others visited one evening and caused such a disturbance drinking and hollering that the landlord gave them an eviction notice. This time, since they were unable to find a house, Ruby and Randy split up. Randy moved in with one of his friends, and Ruby took the children and moved in with Herb.

I'm not sure how Ruby met Herb. Herb was Dora's boy friend, Dora being the woman who left her son with June. Toward the middle of the summer it became obvious to everyone that Dora and Phyllis had something going. This was something of a surprise to most people because Dora had six children of her own, was in her late thirties, and gave the appearance of being very respectable—that is, not cursing, drinking heavily, or otherwise carrying on as did Phyllis and most of her friends. She also had a respectable job as a secretary working for the government. Dora was separated from her husband, who had custody of all her children except the youngest, Ray.

After her separation Dora had taken up with Herb, who was a plumber, made pretty good money, and had a nice brick home out in the country. He was separated from his wife and, according to June, worshiped the ground Dora walked on. They had been living together for almost a year before she became more interested in Phyllis.

When Dora and Phyllis's romance came out in the open and Dora moved in with Phyllis, Herb was left alone again. Since he had a big house and since Ruby was desperate for a place to live, it seemed to work out that Ruby would stay at Herb's temporarily. It also worked out for Arlene and Lonnie to stay there, too, since they had gotten evicted from Lonnie's apartment in Alexandria and were looking for a new place. This living arrangement continued through the remaining weeks of the summer. Ruby wanted out since she and Randy wanted to get back together, but they could find no housing. Arlene, who rarely visited her mother now that she was with Lonnie, said she and Lonnie had no idea how long they would remain with Herb or where they would move next. When we left Clay Street, nothing was settled with any of June's children except Ted, who still planned to marry Anita.

Phyllis, Dora, Granny, and Ray meanwhile got evicted from Phyllis's apartment on Clay Street. Phyllis had an argument with the landlord, Mr. Bactor, demanding that he repaint her apartment. If he refused, she said she would leave. At one time the landlord may have considered repainting her kitchen, but with this possibility he wasn't about to repaint anything. (There had been numerous complaints about the loud noises and fights, in Phyllis's apartment.) Phyllis later changed her mind about leaving. She loved Clay Street, she said, where the people, especially June and Sam, were not only like a family, they *were* her family. So instead of leaving, she withheld her rent and reported the landlord to the County Health Department. (At this point Phyllis's unemployment insurance had run out and they were living on Granny's social security. They did not have the money to pay the rent, even if they had wanted to.)

Nothing ever came of the inspection. Phyllis was too busy trying to go to school. She was taking a course in psychology in the County Community College which she was hoping to attend full-time next year; and she was too busy with Dora and Herb. The result was that Mr. Bactor padlocked her apartment and the four of them had no place to live. Around the first of August they disappeared from the neighborhood for good. Phyllis came back once or twice, but no one—not even June—was sure where she was or what had happened to her.

With Phyllis gone from the neighborhood, things became easier for June. Actually she had seen much less of Phyllis ever since Phyllis met Dora; and some of June's old friends, who had avoided her when Phyllis was around, were now stopping by again.

One of June's favorite people, Grammaw, left Clay Street to return to West Virginia. June did not even know Grammaw's real name—in fact she knew few people's last names on Clay Street. Grammaw was one of those ageless mountain women, who could have been sixty or one hundred. She could neither read nor write and had a wit and twinkle in her eye that June loved. She had been living with her daughter down the street for several years and had stopped by at least twice a week to chat about things, usually not saying much, just chuckling about what was going on at June's. (Grammaw was one of the few people who listened to June rather than talked.)

June and Sam saw a lot of their next-door neighbors, the Barrys, too; hardly a day passed without a casual chat from one front porch to the other. The Barrys had persuaded the Mosebys to join their bowling league and Sam and Fred Barry shared gardening ideas. The Barrys were the senior residents on the block. Fred had been superintendent of these apartments for twenty-nine years; and of all the people on the block, he was the most respected. When the Barrys' children gave Jane Barry a surprise party one evening in August, June and Sam were asked to come. June and Sam were amazed that they had been invited. "I just can't understand it," she said, "I mean *us*. I never thought we would ever get invited to a party for the Barrys. You know, they are kind of a closed group, and it is hard to break into a group like that. I guess we must be coming up in the world."

"Yeah," said Sam. "And this year Wally and Sarah"—a couple across the street whom I never met—"invited us to their twenty-fifth wedding anniversary. But we were in

Florida and couldn't go. Like you say, maybe we are getting up in the world." Then Sam took a swig of beer, threw back his head, and laughed.

June was silent for a moment. Then she replied with a twinkle in her eye, "Oh, what the shit. Mr. Bactor came by the other day and said, 'Lady, you know what you are?' 'What?' I said. 'You're a good-natured slob. That's what you are, a good-natured slob.' " June laughed. "And he is right. What we are are a couple of good-natured slobs." Sam took another swig of beer and laughed again.

Throughout the winter and spring when her children's problems seemed extremely bad, June was telling everyone she was leaving Sam on the first of September and had a plan all worked out. Everyone I talked to who was aware of June's intent was extremely critical. "She is out of her goddamned head if she leaves a hard-working man like Sam," Grammaw said. Others agreed. Throughout the summer, however, June talked less and less of leaving; and after the Florida trip there was no mention of it at all. In the middle of August, June and Sam signed up again for another try at the bowling league, and Ted and Anita agreed to take our place on the team.

We left Clay Street in August, 1971, exactly one year after we arrived. It was threatening rain and I was out stuffing the remaining baggage in the truck. A fellow from West Virginia who lived up the street—I never knew his name—came by. He got laid off that day because it looked like it was going to rain and construction work halted for the day. He was griping about the neighborhood, how there wasn't enough room, how it was too close to D.C., and how he would like to move farther out, how he really wanted to go back to West Virginia but there were just no jobs there.

After we chatted for a few minutes, he shrugged his shoulders and said, "Well, you're the lucky ones, the ones that get to leave to go back home. I guess I'll stay here a while longer. Can't go nowhere else."

Just before we had finished putting the final items in the truck, it started to rain. And just as it started to rain, Arlene and Lonnie drove up. They ran into the house.

After we finally got the car loaded up, I went in to say good-by to June. Embry had already said good-by in tears. June gave me a big hug and wished me luck. Arlene came running up the back of the house and said, "Joe, I want you to come to our wedding. Me and Lonnie, we're getting married!"

I said, "That's good. Congratulations. The best of luck. I hope it works out."

"Well, we'll let you know when the date is. It won't be too long. I'm so happy." She was smiling and giggling.

I said good-by to June again, got in the truck, and started off in the rain.

Three

HARD LIVING IN PERSPECTIVE

11

Pete Dale: Rejecting Hard Living

A few blocks from the Mosebys and the Shackelfords lived
Pete and Sally Dale and their twelve-year-old daughter,
Delores. At the age of sixty, Pete was a retired police officer,
employed part-time as a building inspector for the county
housing department. With his police pension and part-time
job, his income was about $12,000. He lived in a three-
bedroom, brick, ranch-style house—one of the few such
houses in the area. Their house was usually quite clean and
orderly. They had traditional furniture which, though purchased several years ago, still looked new.

Pete and Sally had lived in their house since the early
1950s. Because Pete had made the basement into a recreation
room and tried to keep the house in good condition, he
thought it would sell now for $17,000. Like many of their
neighbors, some of whom had lived in the neighborhood even
longer than the Dales, the Dales were active in the community. Sally was a member of several clubs at the Methodist
Church and bowled in a league, and Pete used to be a
volunteer fireman.

I first met Pete when I was visiting his next-door neighbors,
Tony and Maria DeAngelo, an Italian family who moved into
their two-story frame house at almost the same time Pete
and Sally Dale moved into theirs. He came over to the
DeAngelos' to try to persuade Tony to vote for a particular
candidate for county commissioner in the Democratic primary. Pete was a tall, pudgy man with gray, thinning hair,
who spoke in a low monotone with a southern accent.

After I was introduced by Tony as someone studying
community problems, Pete drawled, "Well, we got some here.
'Course it is still a nice place to live. But it's changing and

there are lots of folks worried. It's terrible the way the colored
are moving out from D.C. Once they move into the neighborhood, then it's too late for you to do anything about it. Whatever your study is, you better get on with it now, because next
year . . . Anyway, it's not only the colored. It's some of these
white families, too. Some of them are worse than the colored.
Drinking, carrying on. Lower class. White trash—that's what
folks around here call them. As I say, this neighborhood used
to be okay, and I suppose right now it still is, though I just
don't know how long it will stay that way."

Tony and Maria agreed with Pete that "colored" and
"lower-class whites" who have been moving into the area
were generally bringing the neighborhood down. Before leaving, Pete added, "Well, you know my children are different.
They bring coloreds to my house upon occasion. I don't like
it, but they invite them over when they have a party. I don't
like it one bit. But I'll accept it. I'll tolerate it. I know
the younger generation is different, and I know there is a difference between a nigger and a colored man. I know this.
But I'm prejudiced. I was born that way, and I'll always be
that way. I think the niggers ought to go back to Africa. . . ."

Because Pete Dale seemed to me to be an unusually
articulate person, I asked him if he would agree to recording
his life history for me. What follows is his own account of his
life:

> I was born in 1911 in a little town down in the moun-
> tains at the extreme southwest tip of the state of Virginia,
> directly in the mountains between Kentucky and Tennes-
> see. You cross one mountain and you went into Tennes-
> see; cross the other mountain and you went into Ken-
> tucky. We lived in a little world of our own. People were
> hard workers as a rule. There were very few bums or
> hookers. There wasn't much industry, but everyone
> worked who could find a job.
>
> I was out of school just after the Depression. The De-
> pression really came in '29 and reached its crux about
> '33, I suppose, but during that period I was fortunate
> enough to have a job on a railroad construction gang. I

was sixteen when I started—two dollars and twenty-four cents a day and after six months it got to two dollars and twenty-eight cents a day and then after six months or a year it ended up at two dollars and forty cents a day. Six days a week. The average salary was sixty-five dollars a month and we lived on it.

My father had left my mother with several children and then gone off. I was the oldest boy. I had a sister that was older, but she died when she was twenty-one. There were nine in our family, one girl and eight boys. At the present time there are five surviving boys. Maybe five. I have one brother that we haven't heard from since the late forties. There is a good possibility that he is dead.

He got into trouble in his late teens. He was working in Norfolk, Virginia, and the girl became pregnant. He took her to an abortionist and she died. He was an accessory to an abortion so he ran, he fled the scene. Meantime the war came along and he hadn't registered 'cause he knew if he did register they would get him—that's what he thought. So they finally arrested him in Florida for draft evasion and for the abortion deal. And they gave him one to three years in the penitentiary and he served his year or so at Petersburg Penitentiary. When he got out of the penitentiary, we never had any further contact with him. In later years I did attempt to trace him; I knew a man in the FBI and he searched the records and gave me all they had and said that the last report they had was when he was released. He had a probation officer in Norfolk, but the man is dead now. I rather think he went to Florida or Texas. He was quite good in the management field. At one time I understand he had operated a trucking business. So he may have become successful and gotten married and decided to sever the connections, or ties, with the old way of life, family and all. But I would rather believe he passed on.

My father was a fairly well educated man. He had been to college. He attended college at Bristol, Virginia for at least a portion of his college term, a couple of years or so. And then he went West as a young man. My father was twenty years older than my mother, and he went out West around the turn of the century, and he was out there twenty years. Then he came back and got a job with the post office, then he was town treasurer in our small town, and then he married my mother. Probably his best ability was in the restaurant field. He always operated a small restaurant. He was an excellent cook. And he made a passable living. He had a big family and kept them fed and clothed.

My mother came from a family that started off well-to-do. Her father had been in the state senate from Virginia on two different terms, and he was the Republican leader from that district. A lot of history connected with him. And he was wealthy at one time. But in later years he wasn't involved in any businesses and his estate ran down. So upon his death it wasn't worth near as much as it had been in previous years. There was a division among the heirs; there were four. My mother received a portion of that, one fourth of it being a small amount. That bought our home and that was probably the best thing that ever happened to us because without a home you have very little to start with.

Well, I worked on it after my father died. I was about fourteen or fifteen. But my mother had inherited money to hold for the next couple of years, so I went off to school. To Berea College, in Kentucky, although it was high school I was attending. I was down there a year and then I came back and my mother had spent everything she had. Then we lost the house we had. I don't remember just how this came about, whether she had borrowed on it or taken out the value of the house in cash from the estate. Anyway, I was able to get a railroad job. The railroad built houses out of boxcars. They put two boxcars together and made small houses. At this one location there were two of them. So I got one of these houses. It had a nice garden with it and we raised vegetables and kept chickens, even had a cow and a hog. So with me working on the railroad we lived nicely. But I would come in at night all pooped out and lay down on the couch until dinner was ready and then I'd eat and then chase around town until midnight, come in and get up and go to work the next day. This went on for several years. I walked down on the right of way of the railroad many a day with the actual perspiration, sweat, squashing in my shoes making much the same sound as if I had waded in a creek. Just that much perspiration. And then come home at night with an old blue denim shirt lined with seams of salt. In the summertime that railway was the hottest place and in the winter it was the coldest place. Well, that was the beginning experience.

Then I went to work on the railroad gang. And we traveled by rail and lived in freight cars. I did this for a couple of years, getting to and from home by hog-wagon train, back and forth. Then about the time I was twenty they organized the three C's, the CCC. At that time I was just out of work for the railroads. I had also been working for the State Highway Department, working with their right-of-way gang. I signed up for it and they took us by car to Bristol, Virginia, and from there we went by train to Fort Monroe, Virginia. They had a little indoctrination course there for a week or two and then they took us out to our camp, a place near Frederick, Virginia.

We were out in a field and we built tents. Gradually they built a wooden mess hall and made some improvements. I worked on the landscaping. It was a battlefield park, was what it was, Civil War.

I worked there a year and then we were discharged. I started to go back home, and I enlisted in the Army in Richmond, Virginia. They gave us an I.Q. test—I really didn't have much of an education, the equivalent of second-year high school, but I'd done a lot of reading and had an inquiring mind. And on this I.Q. test it seemed that every question they asked me, I had some knowledge of it. It was a multiple choice, and for some reason I was able to read through this thing and pick out the right answers, and they were amazed. I was permitted to join the Army then and they sent me to Fort Monmouth, New York. I stayed there for a couple of weeks and then I went to Hawaii. I stayed there six years.

Meantime, when I was home on furlough in '37 I had met my wife, and while I was away those last three years in Hawaii, we corresponded. I more or less committed myself to marry her and asked her to be my wife in my letters. So when I got back I stayed at home in Virginia for a few weeks. She was from Norton, Virginia, a small town twelve miles away and had been reared in a farming valley not too far from my home.

I went to work in Kingsport, Tennessee, a town about

forty miles away. I knew there wasn't any place nearby,
so I was looking around for a job, and I took an examina-
tion for clerk-typist in the government and I got a call to
go to Portsmouth, Virginia. I went down there and it
turned out it was a job in the payroll clerk's office. Twelve
hundred sixty dollars a year. Pretty good money in those
days—'41—although the wages were starting to move up
then. From there I got another call to come to Washington at a clerk-typist job which paid fourteen hundred
forty dollars. So I came on to Washington.

Meantime I had given my wife an engagement ring
when I was in Portsmouth, and then we made plans for
marriage and I borrowed fifty dollars from a lending
company and went down to my home and we were married in the home of the people she lived with. She had
lived with them for many years and they thought the
world of her. After she came out of the orphanage, she
got a job with them, and they were more or less parents
to her.

Then we came on to Washington, and we walked from
Union Station to a boardinghouse where I had made arrangements for us to stay, and we carried our suitcases,
'cause we only had about two dollars. And all we had in
the world was what was in those suitcases. We didn't
know anybody in town or anything, except I did have a
job. This was Saturday and I was going to work Monday.
We went to the boardinghouse and we squared away
there. Thirty dollars a month and it included two meals a
day.

My wife, Sally, she wanted to go to work but didn't
think this was feasible. So I worked and would bring
home something like fifty-five dollars every two weeks
and we were quite happy with it. For the two of us our
board was seventy dollars a month, which left us with
something like thirty dollars a month. And thirty dollars
was a lot of money in those days. Then I started looking
around for a better job and I saw the police department
job. It started at nineteen hundred dollars. So I took the
exam and I got called up for that and went to work for
the police department. Then I began to bring home
checks for seventy-five dollars. Well, it was a different
world, you know. So we moved into a better apartment.

When we first came to Washington we lived on Thir-

teenth Street, N.W., just north of Massachusetts Avenue.
Washington was a beautiful city in those days—this was
in the early forties. It was a better kept city than it has
been lately. The blight hadn't killed a lot of the trees as
it has in recent years. People were friendlier and there
was no fear. We could walk anywhere at night or day
without being molested. It was just a beautiful city. Of
course, we were young and in love. We walked everywhere—Washington Monument, Haines Point, and the mu-
seums, what have you. Then we moved out to 700 Rhode
Island Avenue, N.E., in another apartment. And here
again the rent for the apartment was just thirty dollars a
month. Thirty dollars a month for a furnished apartment.
Of course we had to buy our food and prepare it. We
lived here for a couple of years and had one child born
to us, our oldest, Janie. Then we moved up into a duplex
apartment, 2618 Fourth Street, N.E., up near the Catholic University. And there we stayed until we had three
children, in a one-bedroom apartment. We slept in a
folding bed put up during the day, in the front room. Had
the kids in one bedroom in two bunk beds. We had four
children before we moved. Two boys and two girls in
this one-bedroom apartment.

Finally, in 1953, I worked during my days off, Saturdays and Sundays, for years, and we saved one thousand
dollars cash. So we had one thousand dollars toward a
down payment on a house here. They were building some
little houses and I was looking around. We bought here
because it was close enough in and it had bus lines a block
away. Churches and schools within walking distance and
stores. We were too poor at that time to own a car. My
wife hadn't worked, and since we had the kids she
couldn't work. She had no special training anyway, other
than maybe a saleslady or something of this nature. So
we moved here and that was the beginning of a new life
for us. We had this little home. We bought it new. They
built five, right in this same area. We paid thirteen thousand five hundred dollars for the home. I put nine hundred fifty dollars down and that left thirteen thousand
dollars mortgage. Of course the home could be expanded;
it had the possibilities.

Well, the kids were happy here, they had a lot of freedom, although they still thought about the old days back

on Fourth Street, since they had made playmates there, and they had grounds around the Catholic University where they could play. It was quite open and they enjoyed that.

Well, when we moved to the new place, why the back yard was like a jungle, all trees and brush and stuff. I chopped this out and burned it, and gradually over the years I got the last tree out. I had a garden for several years, a vegetable garden in the back. A wonderful garden. I grew everything—beets, always had tomatoes, green beans, peppers. We didn't try anything which took too much ground, like corn, because of limited space.

The kids went through the local schools. And the oldest girl, when she graduated from elementary school, received a good citizenship award. One child in the whole school chosen for this award. A few years later my son came along and gets the citizenship award, too—a watch. Well, they all go on to high school. Had three of them there at once at one time. And then the three older ones go on to college. Had three in college at one time. They went to Maryland University. They were excellent students. They all had partial scholarships going out of high school and they all three worked during the summer. Two of the girls worked as clerk-typists with the government for at least two summers. The boy always found a job. They helped themselves. We furnished them with an extra car between the three of them and helped them some financially and gave them a place to sleep and food. But they did the greatest part themselves.

Well, they all did real well. The two girls won one honor after another. And the boy—he was the third in line, the girls were older—he comes along and he's president of this, that, and the other, all through college, leader of some group, and gets nominated to *Who's Who in American Colleges.* He graduated in the spring of 1968. So in the meantime he had *fished* for a scholarship. He wanted to be a lawyer, and he got a scholarship to Duke University.

So the kids all got through school pretty good. The fourth one, the boy, he finished high school. He didn't have the desire for higher education to the extent that the first three had. But he's smart and a good worker. He'll always have a job. He's twenty-one now and is living

in an apartment with another friend. Bought himself a
new car. He works as a salesman. Changes jobs fairly
often. I've had to make a few payments on this new car
he's bought, but for the main part he's taken care of it.

The fifth one, sort of our old-age baby, she's different.
She's twelve and we are enjoying her. She is the light
of our life. I'm teaching her to do the little things I missed
with the others. I've always been great for hunting and
shooting, yet my two boys were very little interested in
this aspect of things.

I go hunting during hunting season, both in Maryland
and Virginia. I get out every opportunity. I hunted in
Maryland this year. I did kill a deer in Maryland and I
didn't kill one in Virginia, although I went hunting on
several occasions.

I'm a great nature lover. As a young man I studied
wildlife, studied the varieties of wild flowers in particular
and where they grew. Bird study was always a hobby.
Tree formations. That all came from the Boy Scouts and
their nature book. I learned to identify practically all forest trees when I was young as well as most wild flowers
and birds. And this combined with a love of hunting,
it all goes together, and I get a lot more out of it than
most people would when they go hunting because I'm
not particularly discouraged if I don't bag anything. I've
had a good day. I feel that when I'm in the woods I'm
pretty much alone with my own thoughts, and it's quite
peaceful and it's been real worthwhile, because sometimes
you can collect your thoughts and reflect on the past and
future. . . .

Pete Dale's life style was quite structured. He got up at six
every morning, worked from eight until two in the afternoon
at the County Services Building, and returned home for a late
lunch. He spent his afternoons and evenings working on the
house and the yard or reading or watching TV. His wife,
Sally, cooked and kept house and was involved in church
work. Believing in strong discipline for their children, Pete
and Sally tried to maintain strict control over their children
until they finished high school. They both were very pleased
with the way their children had turned out.

Tony and Maria DeAngelo were like the Dales in that

they, too, kept an orderly, tidy house. They set strict rules for
their teen-age daughters and maintained a very routine life.
They were more active in community affairs, however, since
both Maria and Tony belonged to the local Citizens' Association, Democratic Club, and several clubs at the local Catholic
Church. Tony had been a city councilman and had published
a local newspaper. Maria bowled while Tony was quite active
in his fishing club. Like the Dales, the DeAngelos were
registered Democrats who voted in every election, though they
labeled their political views as conservative.

On the block next to the DeAngelos and Dales lived the
Martins, another routine-oriented, stable family. Ed was a
thirty-eight-year-old construction worker, who one evening
explained his daily routine to me—a routine not unlike many
such families:

> At five-thirty on the dot every morning, that is, during
> the week, we get up. Me and my wife at the same time.
> She goes about fixing things for the kids, their breakfast
> and getting them ready, and getting herself ready to go
> to work. And then I go about and I get my own breakfast
> and I fix my own lunch. And then at six-thirty our oldest
> daughter, who is thirteen, gets up. By this time my wife's
> got everything all straightened up and gotten herself
> ready to go. Then at seven my eleven-year-old son and
> nine-year-old daughter get up, and a little bit later our
> four-year-old boy gets up. My wife feeds them, gets them
> ready for school, especially the four-year-old who can't
> fix himself up too well, and they have breakfast.
>
> By that time I leave, 'cause I have to be at work by
> eight-thirty, and I work all over—in Rockville and some-
> times in Virginia and even way out near Baltimore in a
> place called Columbia City. I work for a big home
> builder. So I have to go, but at eight-thirty my daughter
> who goes to junior high school—she walks, it's not that
> far, and my son walks my little girl to school right up
> here—she leaves for school then.
>
> And then my wife leaves around nine. She doesn't have
> to be to work until nine-thirty. And she drops the kid off.
> Now at three-thirty the kids come home and they've got

chores to do. And it's very important that they do these
little things like clean the ash trays and straighten up.
And they get paid for this. The girl, she gets five dollars
'cause she washes dishes and makes up the beds and does
a lot. The oldest boy gets two dollars and fifty cents, and
the other one dollar and fifty cents. Of course the four-
year-old doesn't get an allowance, but we pay him when
he helps around. And if they don't do their work, you
better believe they're going to get docked. Their allowance is going to be less than it would ordinarily be. Like
it would be fifty cents less if for one day they forgot to
do what they were supposed to do.

Well, my wife gets home about five-thirty and I get
home about six. And let me tell you, that house is always
clean. There's nothing we have to do. And then we have
a big family dinner. A family dinner. All of us eat together every evening. And after dinner I work on the
house, play with the kids; sometimes we play horseshoes.
In the summer horseshoe games go to one or two in the
morning on the weekends. Throw football in the street.
Or the kids, they might go off to majorette practice, or to
play basketball in the gym, or to teen dances here on
Saturday.

Then at eight-thirty the youngest goes to bed; at nine
the nine- and eleven-year-old go to bed; at ten the oldest
girl goes to bed; and at eleven me and my wife turn in.
We always turn in together. One never goes to bed before
the other, and if we've had an argument during the day,
we make up. I never go to bed mad at my wife, she never
goes to bed mad at me, and I always kiss her good night.
Now, some people, they get in an argument, and they
don't make up at the end of the day, but I don't believe
in going to sleep if you're mad at each other. I never have
done it, and I never will do it.

On weekends I usually work on the house. See, the
house that we bought five years ago wasn't in all that
good a shape, so I've been working on it, bit by bit. I've
redone the basement, the living room, and the bedrooms.
I've practically done everything. You should see the living
room. I've got a brick wall, fireplace here, a speaker here
and a speaker here, and artificial flowers here. And I've
got a swirling ceiling and I've got parquet floors. And

all these materials I use, I haven't paid a cent for them. I get them from my job, see, like the parquet floors. And so we got the floors and we got the wall material, and I've expanded the living room, and I've worked on the basement. And it's taken pretty much of five years, working most of the time, to get the house into the shape it's in now. My wife helps me and the kids help me and we try to do things as a family as much as we can. . . .

The Dales, the DeAngelos, and the Martins were not hard living. On the contrary they lived a structured, routine, stable life. Though they had some marriage problems, health problems, and problems at work, their concerns were more community-oriented. They were worried about inflation, about losing the Vietnam war, about busing, about law and order. They were worried about certain types of people moving into their community: blacks and those they called "low-class whites." The life style of the Dales, the DeAngelos, and the Martins I call "settled living." The settled living families, rather than the hard living families, constituted the majority of families living in this particular area.

Also, some tension existed between the hard living and the settled living families in the area. Pete Dale wasn't the only one to express contempt for unstable, hard living white families. Mrs. Jackson, a stately woman in her sixties who had lived on Clay Street with her husband, a retired mailman, for almost fifty years, expressed a similar view:

> It's just not the same any more. The folks that are moving in. They just aren't like the old families who used to live here. I hate to admit it, but the neighborhood is going downhill—in fact it has been going downhill for the past ten or fifteen years. Good old families dying or moving to newer areas and lower-class people moving in.
>
> And it's not the colored I'm talking about. For the most part, the colored who have moved in have been good colored. It's some of these lower-class white families. They come from West Virginia and North Carolina and no telling where and just don't seem to care about the neighborhood. No sooner have they moved in—they are off again to someplace else. Strange people. I suppose

folks have to live somewhere, but, as I say, they aren't doing our neighborhood any good. Some of them are nothing but white trash. . . .

Mrs. Jackson did not know June and Sam or Bobbi and Barry or for that matter many of the families on her block. She and her husband associated with the DeAngelos and other older residents who lived throughout the community; and they had relatively few contacts with their immediate neighbors, most of whom she said she did not approve of. In her view, families like the Shackelfords and the Mosebys were not a positive asset to the neighborhood.

Like Mrs. Jackson, most of these settled families perceived a class difference between themselves and other white families living in the community. Making an "us-them" distinction, some expressed this in terms of "owner–renter," or "old-timer–newcomer" or "middle class–lower class," or, all too frequently, "good families–white trash." While the "lower-class" families were definitely in the minority, many people feared their numbers were increasing.

Moreover, what determined whether a person was "lower class" in the minds of the settled families was not his income, education, or general background but rather the kind of life style he led. The hard living life style was viewed by these families as being lower class. One of my neighbors who was a D.C. fireman defined what he meant by "lower class" or "white trash" as follows:

> I'll tell you what I mean by white trash. I mean a family that has lots of kids and the husband doesn't work, maybe is a drunkard and works part-time but not enough to get by and the kids just run wild. They don't have any respect for property, especially other people's property. They go outside without any clothes on; they urinate out in the front yard in plain view; they holler and scream and use cuss words every other word, and all other kinds of words; and just are a bad influence on other people's children. They keep dogs out in the yard and maybe junk cars and generally have no respect for property.
>
> But one thing about these families, they just don't stay around that long. I mean, they're on the move. They've

come from somewhere and are going somewhere else. They're drifters. They probably came from the mountains or the country or someplace, but they just don't stay here long. Either they get behind in their rent, and these land-lords in most cases will get rid of them as soon as they realize what kind of family they've got. And then they'll move on. Who knows where they go? Who knows where they'll end up? Just drifters.

The concept of a continuum is useful here. At one end of the continuum are the Shackelfords, an extremely hard living family, described to me by some people in the community as "lower class." At the other end are the DeAngelos and Dales, whose lives are orderly and stable. Many of these families are socially conscious with strong ambitions for their children. In the middle are the Mosebys, a family that lives hard and yet maintains some restraint. It was not so much June and Sam but rather June's children who were living hard during the year. Moreover, most people on Clay Street who knew the Mosebys described them as a typical, ordinary family, while no one ever described the Shackelfords as such.

On Clay Street and its surrounding area, then, there were two dominant life styles, hard living and settled living, with families gravitating toward one or the other. The hard living families tended to differ from the restrained living families in seven general aspects, which are the focus of the chapter that follows.

12

The Ingredients of Hard Living

Thus far I have presented three families that I suggest represent different types of blue collar families living on or near Clay Street. Further I have suggested that the concept of a continuum is useful in defining the range of differences between their life styles. At one end of the continuum, the Shackelfords represent a hard living family. At the other, the Pete Dales live a settled life. The Mosebys are somewhere in the middle. Finally I have suggested that from the viewpoint of many of the settled families, the difference between them and the Shackelfords is one of class. They consider themselves "middle class" or "working people" and the Shackelfords "lower class."

The purpose of this chapter is to examine some of the differences between them in more detail. There are seven general areas in which the hard living families and settled families are dissimilar:

1. *Heavy drinking.* Heavy drinking was a way of life on Clay Street. Pete Dale and Tony DeAngelo drank only occasionally. Many such families abstained completely.

2. *Marital instability.* Most of the hard living families I knew on Clay Street had had at least one previous marriage, with their current marriage being somewhat shaky. The Dales, Martins, and others had long-term, stable marriages.

3. *Toughness.* Hard living families used an abundance of profanity, talked a lot about violence, and generally acted tough in contrast to the more moderate approach to life of Pete Dale and his friends.

4. *Political alienation.* Few hard living families on Clay Street voted or held strong political views. They felt

government was unresponsive, corrupt at all levels, and irrelevant to their needs. The settled families voted, and while they expressed feelings of frustration, they felt they had a stake in society worth fighting for and preserving. They considered themselves conservative.

5. *Rootlessness.* The hard living families rented their homes and tended to move frequently from one place to another. Few felt they had roots anywhere. In contrast, the DeAngelos and their friends were homeowners and had lived for some time in the community.

6. *Present-time orientation.* The Shackelfords, for instance, were preoccupied with surviving from one day to the next without giving much thought to the future. Pete Dale and Tony DeAngelo were able to save a little money and were quite concerned about the future of their family and their community.

7. *A strong sense of individualism.* The hard living families described themselves as "loners," as their "own men," and liked to work alone. Few were active in community life or belonged to any groups. In contrast, the settled families belonged to groups, participated in community life, and rarely expressed such feelings of independence.

These seven basic differences constitute the ingredients of hard living. They are not exhaustive, nor should they be viewed as rigidly distinct categories. Obviously there is considerable interaction among the categories. At best they are intended to serve as focal points for illustrating a life style found in one particular blue collar neighborhood. In the following sections the titles of country and western songs are used as subheadings. They are songs that might be heard playing on Walt's radio or Sam's hi-fi and that articulate the essence of hard living.

Drinking: "My Rough and Rowdy Ways"

There was a member of our congregation who moved up here from South Carolina. Her husband had a good job and they had six kids and were buying a house. Then her husband starts to drink and running around, and the family stops coming to church. Next thing you know her husband has taken off with another woman and left his wife with six kids to feed. The family is destroyed, and it all started with the bottle. I've seen it happen again and again. And once they've started on the bottle, you lose them. Very few come back to church.

> REVEREND LITTLE, local Southern
> Baptist minister

Mr. Clark, Barry's ex-parole officer, commented on one particular blue collar neighborhood not far from Clay Street: "The folks that live over there," he said, "they are really something. For them drinking is a way of life. They work hard during the week, and they live for Saturday nights and the bottle. They would rather buy and fix up an old Cadillac than fix a hole in their roof. They aren't white trash—they're the lower-income whites, hard working, proud, ornery, but they're good people. If alcohol finally gets the best of them, they end up in our program. Beat up their old lady, slug their boss, occasionally try to pull off a petty theft. . . ."

For many on Clay Street, drinking had in fact become a way of life. It was for Barry, for June, for Sam, for Phyllis as well as various others: Phyllis's mother, Bertie, and her husband, Zeek Grizzard; Ted's second wife, Peg; Big John Higgins, who lived across the street from us and operated something resembling a halfway house for his cousins coming from the mountains; Barry's friends Mack, Kate, Al, and others.

When the men came home from work, they would usually carry with them a six-pack or two of beer and a half pint of whiskey and would spend the rest of the evening drinking and working on the house or the yard or the car or watching TV. Wives would usually drink along with their husbands. On weekends drinking would begin shortly after breakfast and continue until bedtime. If you stopped to chat with someone on his front porch, invariably you would end up having two or three beers.

Although for the most part drinking took place at home rather than in local bars or taverns, occasionally people would go to a local tavern. There were three distinct types of bars in the area: the city bar, the country or "hillbilly" bar, as it was sometimes called, and the club. The city bar had carpeting on the floor, a color TV, paintings on the wall, a male bartender, and it served food as well (usually having a varied menu). Waitresses wore very short barmaid dresses. Most of the music on the jukebox was pop, though the jukebox tended to be turned down low and rarely played. These bars were clean, but dimly lighted; and they tried to appear urbane and sophisticated. They attracted single workingmen in their twenties and thirties and older men getting away from their families. Patrons tended to come regularly and often in small groups. Although most of the patrons were men, a few were accompanied by wives or girl friends. I met few people in these bars who lived in the community; but those who did tended to be established residents. Drinking was heavy but controlled. Bookies frequented these bars on a regular basis taking bets on sporting events. Folks on Clay Street avoided these places. They were "dead," "no fun," "gyp joints."

Country bars were quite different. Wood floors were covered not with a carpet but with cigarette butts; and the furniture and tables were usually very plain. Bartenders were mostly women—not the sexy barmaid types but rather women in their forties, simply dressed in slacks, women who wore little make-up, strong women who could take care of themselves and outcuss any nasty drunk. These places were well lighted with wood-paneled or cement block walls, covered with beer advertisements and various mementos—autographed photographs of country and western stars, photographs of the employees' children, auto race posters, etc. Invariably there was a pool table to one side and several pin ball machines, and the juke blared country music. If you could get anything to eat there, it was no more than a hamburger. Single women came to these bars, often in groups of two or three; and no one dressed up. Women wore slacks, and most of the men wore work clothes, overalls, and grease-stained T-shirts. Often small children accompanied their parents. Some of these bars, such as the Bronco, were notorious for Friday and Saturday night fights, though no fights ever occurred when I happened to be in any of them. When folks on Clay Street went out for a drink, this was where they went.

The third kind of bar was the club. These clubs had their country and city varieties. What distinguished a club from a bar was that a club had live entertainment and a dance floor and was usually somewhat larger than a bar. Of all the clubs in the area, the Dixie Club was the most popular. Every night of the week it featured live country and western music and on the weekends was usually packed. Many women and men came stag. The men would wander over and ask the women to dance, then after the music stopped, retreat to their separate tables. Like the country bars, it had several pool tables, pin ball machines, women bartenders, was well lighted, and generally filthy. This is where Bobbi and Barry went for their one fling of the year and where Bobbi went alone upon occasion when Barry was drunk or gone. June and Sam did not go to the Dixie Club but to a similar club farther out in the country.

The city night clubs featured topless go-go girls and were the only establishments that were racially integrated. The motorcycle clubs such as the Night Raiders, Outlaws, and Bandits hung out at these clubs, which like the country music establishments were sparsely decorated and filthy (even grimier than the country music clubs). The younger people such as Les, Arlene, and Ted went here occasionally, though older white couples avoided these establishments.

Besides the clubs there were occasional country music dances sponsored by volunteer fire department auxiliaries. These affairs usually featured a local country music band and provided setups and beer. The Mosebys' best time of the entire year was at one of these affairs when the entire family celebrated Arlene's twenty-first birthday just before she started going with Lonnie.

In regard to drinking, as one neighborhood person put it, there were three types of people on Clay Street: "Them that don't drink, them that drink a lot, them that drink a helluva lot." The majority of families I knew fell into the middle category. These people, like June and Sam, made alcohol part of their daily routine, consuming a six-pack and half pint every evening. Like Sam the men did not drink until after work, when their wives would join them. While June drank during the day, she tried to conceal it until Sam came home. On Saturdays and Sundays, even though drinking usually began quite early, there was rarely much drunkenness. In contrast to "the drunks," the heavy drinkers were able to ration their drinking. This was the reason Sam always bought six-packs and half pints instead of larger quantities. He knew what he could drink and bought only that amount.

The difference between the heavy drinker such as Sam and "them that drink a helluva lot" was said to be self-control. The latter were those who were conspicuously drunk most of the time. While by no means a majority, there were quite a few such drinkers on Clay Street: Zeek and Bertie Grizzard, Carlyle, Big John Higgins, Barry and his friends. Because they were unable to control their drinking and because alcohol had contributed to the disintegration of their personal lives, these people were generally looked down on by everyone else. Sam, for instance, said about Barry: "Ain't no excuse for carrying on like he does. Now, I ain't got nothing against a man having a drink every now and then. But I don't mix working and drinking and I know when to stop. Barry ain't nothin' but a drunk."

Of course, a fine line separated these two groups. Many who called themselves heavy drinkers were labeled drunks by others. For most drunks, the transition from heavy drinker to a drunk was a slow one, which occurred gradually over a good many years. Some of the young people such as Ted's wife Peg, or Phyllis, were well on their way.

Another aspect of drinking associated with the drunks was the Saturday night binge. For a few people on Clay Street such as Zeek and Bertie Grizzard or several of the younger men, Friday or Saturday night was the time to let loose. While these people would drink a lot during the week, Friday or Saturday night was a special time, in their words, "to let it all hang out." The pattern varied. Zeek and Bertie, for instance, would drink until one or both passed out practically every weekend. Quite frequently an argument between them would develop; and before it was over, the police would be called in. Sunday morning Bertie would appear with a black eye or bruised arms talking apologetically about how she "tripped and fell and hurt herself" the night before. Few people could match the Grizzards, however. Most bingers went on wild drunks less frequently. People developed their own style. Bobbi Jean said her mother, for instance, would go on binges lasting several weeks after which she would go for months without drinking anything. Walt explained it by saying, "She had to do it to get everything out of her system, then she'd be okay."

The binges were the cause of much of the neighborhood violence and conflict. Marital fights often occurred when one or both partners had too much to drink. In the fall when one neighbor got drunk, he shot bullets through the walls of his apartment (fortunately no one was hurt). Ted's boss at the auto shop shot up his office one evening on a drunk. The year before Carlyle shot one of B.J.'s cousins who according to Carlyle was drinking too much of Carlyle's "goddamn whiskey." Toward the end of the summer, a young man barely twenty-two who was living with Grammaw's daughter poured kerosene over himself and set himself aflame, dying three weeks later. Most neighbors denied that it was a suicide. One man said, "It was just that he was rip-roaring drunk and took a dare from his brother. . . ."

Of all the bingers, Barry was the most notorious. Barry had been going on weekend binges ever since he was a teenager. In his younger years he reserved the binges only for the weekends. The older he got, the more frequent the binges became so that Bobbi could describe her husband as "being on one goddamn drunk after another." One of Barry's binges was a key turning point in their life together, according to Bobbi. It occurred several years before when Bobbi and Barry were buying a house. Bobbi told me what happened:

> This time Barry had been drinking on and off and going on binges and all that. He'd been gone for three or four days, and I didn't see him. I didn't know what he did. When he came back, he was sober, and so I could put up with him. We didn't have much furniture. And we were going to fix up the house 'cause it was ours. Barry

was working on it. We were painting together. This night, we were painting and everything was fine. Barry, he hadn't been drinking, and he was doing a good job painting. We were going to fix up a nice place. And the next morning we started again. Everything was fine.

Then Barry's friend Wade, he come over and Barry and Wade leave. So I left. Came back later in the afternoon and Barry was there painting.

I said, "Well, it's about time you got back."

Well, I must have said the wrong thing 'cause Barry looked at me and said, "You goddamn whore bitch. I'm going to kill you, you stay out of my way or I'm going to kill you."

And I could tell he meant it. He called me a bitch, and a common whore, and everything else. I mean, you name it and he called me that. I realized he was upset. I mean, he was really drunk. So I left. I went over to Mamma and Daddy's, and I told them that Barry was drunk something awful and had been real nasty to me and threatened me. They said that he'd probably pass out, wait awhile, and go back later. They said I ought to call the police. I thought about it and then decided not to do it. I should have, but I didn't do it.

So in the evening I decided to go back. I took the children. Praise you God Almighty, when I got there, there was Barry's stepdaddy and there was Wade's car. I went in the house and there was Barry. We didn't have no furniture in the living room except for one chair. Barry was sitting in that chair, and around him was a whole row of beer bottles. I mean surrounding his chair. Barry was sitting there in the middle of the room, by himself, surrounded by all these beer bottles, and he had two guns. A shotgun and a rifle. He was just sitting there. And his mamma and Blackie and Wade and Barry's son, they were all trying to persuade Barry to give them the guns. Wade, he tells it that Barry was threatening to kill himself. In fact, he tells me that Barry put a gun to his head and was going to pull the trigger.

I looked up, and sure enough, there was a big hole in the ceiling, and there is holes in the walls where the gun has gone off. Barry was going to kill himself but he didn't. He pulled the trigger and shot the walls instead.

Well, we all sat there and talked to Barry, and Barry seems like he's getting better. So Almeda and Blackie, they decide to leave and go home. Wade, he decides to leave and that leaves me and the children. So I got in the bathroom and get ready to take a shower. I was scared. I mean to tell you I was scared, so I gave Billy to Bubba, who was just a little fellow then, and told Bubba to hold Billy. And Cindy, she was just a little toddler.

So I go in and take a shower and Barry comes in, opens the door, and calls me all these names again. Says he's going to shoot himself and goes down in the basement. Well, I was really scared so I told the children to go to their room. And I went in the baby's room. I was going to fix him a bottle and I hear Barry stirring around downstairs. I don't know what he's going to do. So I was going to get the bottle and all of a sudden I hear a gunshot and a bullet come whizzing up through the floor. And the bullet almost hits Billy! Goes through his crib. God Almighty, strike me down if what I'm saying is not the truth! Strike me and my children down.

Well, I got real scared when this happens and we go next door. Run out of the house to our next-door neighbors and tell them. Of course, they heard the gunshot. So the fellow who lived next door, he comes over and is going to go downstairs and talk to Barry, see if he can persuade him. By this time I called the police. I called my folks and they told me to call the police. So they all go downstairs and talk to Barry. John, he stands at the top of the steps and starts talking and Barry doesn't answer. He's afraid Barry's already killed himself. So the police, when they get there, asked me to sign some papers before they can go down and get him. I signed the papers. When they got down there in the basement, Barry was gone. Hell, that sonofabitch had snuck out the window and climbed a forty-foot tree! Still had both guns. So then they called the fire department, ambulance, and started to rope off the neighborhood.

Well, you can imagine, people were coming out of their houses and crowding around. They had a road block, searchlights. Didn't take them long to find Barry. Wade found him. Wade had come back when he heard what happened. Blackie and Almeda, they'd come back. They'd thought about calling the police before. So Wade finds Barry up in the tree with his guns. The police convince Barry to come down, though he says he'll kill himself. They finally got him and took him to the police department. I went down there with him and you should of heard Barry talking to those cops. He was calling them bastards and motherfuckers, shit-asses, and everything. I heard him. I never heard anybody talk to policemen like Barry talked to them. But they locked him up.

Come the next day they had the trial, the hearing, or whatever you call it. Anyway, I got to go to court. And they call out Barry's name, this big old judge, he sits up there and calls out, "Barry Shackelford, Barry Shackelford, I understand you are a plasterer."

"Yes."

Course Barry's sober now, he's real humble now. He don't know what he's done.

And the judge says to Barry, "And I understand you get real *plastered,* too."

"Yeah," says Barry.

The judge calls me up and I tell the story, everything just the way it happened. "Okay, Barry Shackelford," he says, "I'm going to sentence you to three years in jail. And I'm going to put you on immediate probation for eighteen months."

So Barry, he comes home that afternoon. Now, if I knew what was right, I should have told the judge I didn't want him home and I would have had an automatic divorce. I didn't know that, but that's what I should have done. 'Cause I was afraid of him, afraid of what he would do. I was afraid he would do it again, I didn't know any better. I didn't know it. So Barry, he comes home. They took all the guns away from him. In fact, he is not supposed to have any guns now. Confiscated all the guns in the house. And then they put him in this alcoholic rehabilitation program and if he was to drink any, he'd have to go to jail. . . .

Why people drank was a matter of some concern on Clay Street. Baptist ministers were concerned about it. Social workers were concerned about it, and to a certain extent, folks themselves were concerned about it. One Sunday morning when both Zeek and Carlyle were recovering from hangovers, sitting on the curb watching a neighbor repair his car, Carlyle turned to Grizzard. "Grizzard," he said, "why does a man drink?"

"I'll tell you why," said Grizzard. "A man takes a drink because he's stupid. He don't know no goddamned better."

"Oh, that ain't right," said Carlyle.

"Okay," said Grizzard, "I'll tell you why. Man takes a drink to ease his mind. To ease the tension. That's why."

"Well, if that's why, how come it does him no good? I don't know nobody who drinking has done good to. Take me, for instance. Now, I've been drinking hard for God knows how long. And it ain't doing me no good. I'm beginning to get the shakes. It's not helping my tension none. It's giving me more tension."

Grizzard looked Carlyle in the eye and replied, "Carlyle, you got to be a man to hold your liquor."

For many of the men drinking was involved with strength, virility, and toughness. A man should be able to drink and drink a lot. Yet at the same time, both Grizzard and Carlyle acknowledged that other motivations were often present. It was an escape from problems. It was a means of coping. It was certainly this for June, who consumed liquor daily as the middle-class housewife consumes tranquilizers. "My bottle *is* my tranquilizer," June once told me. "If I didn't have it, I don't think I could make it through the day."

Others disagreed with June. Alcohol was not simply a way of coping but rather a way of getting the most out of life, of having fun. While alcohol might have its unpleasant side effects, it helped a person get some excitement and enjoyment out of a life that was otherwise pretty difficult. There was considerable bragging about drinking and episodes involved with drinking.

While there was some talk about why people drank, there was less talk about why people went on binges. "Things like that just happen," said Bobbi when describing one of Barry's binges. "That's just what happens when you're drunk." Husband and wife fights, bar fights, shoot-ups—these incidents were explained away by saying, "Well, of course, he was drinking, and . . ."

Unstable Marriages: "Your Good Girl's Gonna Go Bad"

> You know, in my whole life I've only known three people
> not counting my stepdaddy who were decent husbands—
> worked, paid their bills, didn't run around, and cared about
> their kids.
>
> BOBBI JEAN SHACKELFORD

Practically everyone I knew on Clay Street had been married before. Six couples had consensual marriages. (In five out of the six relationships, the woman had taken the man's name.) Many marital relationships remained shaky throughout the year. Bobbi was on the verge of leaving Barry; June seriously considered leaving Sam; Ruby was about to leave Randy; etc. Ted and Peg split up, as did Arlene and Les—eleven times! Marital relationships were the focus of considerable amounts of time, emotion, and energy. It was June's dominant concern over the year and to a certain extent Bobbi's as well, in contrast to the Pete Dales and Tony DeAngelos, who rarely talked about their marriages.

Many people acknowledged that marital stability was an indicator of where people stood in the community. A local police officer put it this way: "Well, there are basically two types of folks in this community: middle class and what you might call lower class. The middle-class folks, the working people, they never cause no trouble—law-abiding, upright, quiet. Now the lower class, they are different. We're all the time getting calls when husbands and wives get into fights, husband leaves, wife leaves, that sort of thing." Various other people—local ministers, school principals, local officials—characterized the "lower-class people" as having temporary, often tumultuous marital relationships. Stability was the goal of a settled life, and the most crucial aspect of stability was a stable marriage.

What impressed me most about Clay Street marriages was how quickly relationships seemed to change from one day to the next. One was never too sure whether Arlene and Les, Ted and Peg, Ruby and Randy, were back together or whether they were separated. Also, some marital relationships that seemed stable dramatically and suddenly dissolved. An extreme incident of "a good girl going bad" is the story of Tammy and Fred Jamison:

Over the summer Arlene had become quite close to Tammy, her old friend who was June's neighbor up the street. Tammy and her husband, Fred, had moved in during the winter. They owned a mobile home out in the country but had gotten into some trouble and had been unable to continue the payments. When they were first married, Arlene and Les lived in a mobile home and were Fred and Tammy's next-door neighbors. Fred and Tammy just happened to end up on Clay Street because Tammy was Big John Higgins's stepdaughter. When Tammy turned sixteen, she had married Fred, a thirty-year-old man from South Carolina who had been married and had an eight-year-old son, who was living with them for the summer. Fred, who was a house painter, was in a union and worked on large government projects.

Tammy at twenty-two was a strikingly beautiful woman. Since she had two small children, she spent most of her time doing household chores and watching her kids. She was at June's a lot, especially in the spring, but she never said very much. (When Phyllis was at June's, it was impossible for anyone besides Phyllis to say very much.) June was particularly fond of Tammy.

Fred was very hard to get to know, for he was never home. He worked late, would stop on the way home to have a few beers with the boys, and was often drunk by the time he got home.

Tammy and Fred's house was furnished with new furniture and they had many of the same tastes and possessions of Les and Arlene: color TV, stereo, a gun collection, etc. Fred had just purchased an outboard speedboat for fishing in the bay. As the Tupperware representative on the block, Tammy gave two Tupperware parties in the spring. I concluded that they were a stable young family, working hard to acquire a few material possessions—in many respects a family similar to Arlene and Les before Arlene started going with Lonnie.

Tammy was not only Arlene's confidante, she was a good friend to Les as well. When Arlene was staying with June and had not gone back to Les, she would spend most of her time with Tammy. Once Arlene told me that Tammy was the person who helped her decide to go back to Les. Les told me that Tammy was the person who helped him understand Arlene's reckless ways.

My only chance to get to talk with Tammy came during one of the tense moments when Arlene was off and Les was trying to decide what to do. When I saw him on Tammy's front porch, I wandered up and joined them. Les was saying, "I must be crazier than a goddamn fool to put up with all this stuff. I know Arlene ought to see a psychiatrist, but I ought to see one for putting up with it. I guess you might say, well, I'm trapped."

Tammy then said, "Well, I guess that puts me and you in the same boat, don't it?" Les laughed and Tammy continued, "My old man, he treats me just like Arlene treats you. And I'm trapped and I'd like to get away, but it looks like there's not a thing I'm able to do." When I asked her how long they'd been married, she said, "Six years. Ain't that a long time! Six years too many. I sure wish I weren't.

"You know what I'd like to be right now? Now don't you dare tell Fred. Don't you tell Fred I told you 'cause he can't stand motorcycles. But I'd like to be with the Bandits. That's a motorcycle club like the D.C. Outlaws. I left Fred awhile back and rode around for a while with the prez of that club. Oh, man, he's a tough guy. Long hair down to his shoulders, earrings, mustache, and goatee, and wears all them colors. Oh, man, he's my idea of tough, man, tough.

"My twin sister, she's been running with the D.C. Outlaws for so long—I mean, she's wild. She does lots of running with the bike clubs. Down in Austin, Texas, she's now running with the El Dorados. Her husband, he was even prez of one of them clubs. He was a D.C. Outlaw up here and then moved down to Texas and joined the El Dorados. But then a couple years back he got killed. When they found him, he'd been beat to death and then shot a couple of times with a shotgun. But that time he and Lou, my sister, they weren't going together. I mean, they were married but he was running around with somebody else's old lady, know what I mean? And that somebody else happened to be the prez of another bike club, and when he found out about it, he came after Denny, Lou's husband. Pretty brutal.

"That was a bad year. My mother died about a month apart from when Denny got shot up. But I have to admit"—she sighed—"I'd like to be riding right now on the back of one of them big bikes with the Bandits. That's freedom—riding on the back of a big bike. . . .

"But Fred, he don't go for that. He don't go for it at all. Fred likes to drink. In fact, he drinks two or three six-packs sometimes before he comes home. By the time he gets home he's so drunk he don't know what he's doing. He's drunk right now. He had a six-pack or so before he came home, and now he is gone. That's why I say I'm trapped, just like you, Les. Like a bird in a cage. Here all day. Can't leave because of the two kids."

"Yeah," said Les, "pretty bad."

"Sometimes I ask myself why I stay, why I hang around. Yet I know the reason. It's these two little people right here, my two children. You know the funny thing about it is my sister Lou, she and I are twins, identical twins, and sometimes when we go out to Sin City or Harry's—that's where the D.C. Outlaws and the other clubs hang out, like the Raiders—people will mistake me for Lou. Now that's embarrassing, 'cause Fred, he don't know what to do. They come up and put their arms around me, you know, that sort of stuff. And I have to tell them I'm Tammy, not Lou. Sometimes they don't believe me 'cause we look so much alike, and my sister, she's done lots of running and she's real wild.

"Yeah, you know, it's a thrilling thing, those motor-cycle clubs. It's really exciting and really a thrill. And it's rough, though. I know. Like when Denny was killed —that was over a year ago. Well, just this fall, his brother was killed. You might have read about it in the papers. He and a member of another gang were drinking at the same bar, and they were both getting sort of high. Denny's brother is sort of religious. The other guy was saying something like 'goddamn,' and Denny's brother, he asked him to quit cussing, quit using God's name that way, that he believed in God. And the other guy, he just pulled out a gun and blew Denny's brother's brains out. Killed him right then and said, 'If you're so goddamn religious, let's see if *you* rise again in three days.' That's what I mean when I say it's sort of rough. Denny's mother, losing her two sons like that all in a year's time, it's sort of hard on her. She has one more son. He likes bikes, too, but don't have much to do with the clubs. He stays clean."

This conversation struck me as extremely interesting both because it changed my image of Tammy—the contented housewife minding the kids and giving a Tupperware party—and because I had seen several bikes with swastikas on them in the neighborhood and had wondered whom they belonged to. Consequently, I was not shocked three weeks later when Fred came over to June's one evening, very upset, asking if we had seen Tammy. She had left her children with her half-sister, Marge, and had gone off with a guy in a blue '59 Chevy; and since Marge said she knew nothing about the guy, Fred thought June might know. June shook her head.

June nudged me after Fred took off in his truck. "I do know where she is, but I can't tell. See, Fred was supposed to go fishing this weekend, right? With guys from work. So Tammy—she had it all figured out—she was gonna go off with some of her friends, have a good time over the weekend. God knows, the poor child is cooped up all day like a bird in a cage. She needs to have a little fun. The problem was, Fred didn't go fishing after all."

"Oh, oh," said Sam and burst out laughing. "The goddamn shit is gonna hit the fan!"

June smirked and shrugged her shoulders. "Well, sometimes things don't work out as planned."

Tammy did not come back that night or the next or the next. What was funny at first began to cause June to have some anxiety, for no one knew where she was or if she was all right. Marge still had Tammy's children and had not heard from her.

Monday evening following Tammy's sudden departure, I was going out to one of the local taverns. Just as I was heading off about ten o'clock, Arlene and Les drove up, so I stopped and asked if they would care for a beer.

Les said, "Sure, and let's see if Fred wants to go. He was pretty down tonight and said something about going out."

So I parked the car and we walked up to Fred's. When we got up there, the house was in complete chaos. The two kids were running wild, dirt was caked on the rugs, chairs were turned over, and dishes were piled up in the sink. Fred was sitting in one corner with his head in his hands. B.J. was on the sofa along with Carl, Fred's next-door neighbor. They were sipping National beer. Billy-John was chasing Fred's son Terry; and Fay, his daughter, was sitting by herself watching TV.

Les said to Fred, "How about going over to Harry's for a beer?"

Fred didn't say anything. Big John Higgins, who was pretty well drunk by this time, started talking about going to the welfare and how hard he had to work to clothe and feed Billy-John and how he'd needed some help from the welfare. He wanted to be sure that I would take him next week. He went on and on about how hard he worked. (When he was drunk, Big John always wanted me to take him to the welfare.) This all seemed to go past Fred, who continued sitting with his head in his hands the whole time.

Later, when we walked out on the porch, Les said to me, "I don't think he's going to want to go to Harry's. But I'd like to go just to see if Tammy's there."

I asked, "Well, what is it with Tammy anyway? What's going on?"

"We don't know."

Arlene said the same thing. "We don't know what's going on. All we know is that she disappeared mysteriously on Friday. She didn't tell anyone—her sister, her kids—anything. We think that something bad might have happened to her. If she went to Harry's and got picked up, maybe she passed herself off as her sister or something and they found out. I don't know."

Les said, "But whatever it is, it could be pretty bad. I don't know. Do you know what a 'train' is? Well, it's a thing the D.C. Outlaws have. You know, when a girl goes with the D.C. Outlaws, everybody gets to bang her—you know what I mean—like she gets it by everybody. Well, that's what could have happened with Tammy. And I don't know, if she protested or something like that, they might have killed her. Who knows, anything could have happened. The Outlaws, you know how *they* are."

"How do you know she's with the D.C. Outlaws?"

Arlene said, "Well, the day before she left Tammy and

me, we were over there together at Harry's. A couple of
Outlaws walked up and Tammy passed herself off as her
twin sister and said she'd be back at nine that night. I
wasn't back at nine, and neither was she, but that's why
I think she might be with the Outlaws, though. Because
I could tell then she wanted to go with them, do anything, and pass herself off as her sister. You know, her
sister used to go with one of the D.C. Outlaws."

We decided to go to Harry's. I was sure he didn't
really expect to see Tammy and certainly I didn't.

Yet when we got there, a dozen big motorbikes were
out front. One guy, who had on a T-shirt with a swastika
on the back, was working on his bike. Several of the bikes
had swastikas painted on the side or back.

Arlene whispered, "The D.C. Outlaws! She might be
here."

Harry's must have been one of the nastiest places in
Washington. A topless, black go-go girl danced to recorded music. The one room was small and fairly
crowded and there were a good number of blacks.
Sparsely decorated with wooden tables and chairs and
very dark, the room reeked of vomit and the smell of
bad whiskey. The music blared. The topless go-go girl
danced unenthusiastically. As we looked for a table, we
passed by a large group of people in one corner. I
glanced over and saw that they had on denim jackets,
some with swastikas on the back. Most of the guys had
beards and long hair. Some of the girls were sitting in
their laps. I didn't think much about it until Arlene
punched Les and whispered, "There she is! It's Tammy!"

When we sat down, Tammy got up from her position
in the lap of one of the guys with a beard and T-shirt
and walked over, handed something to Arlene, exchanged a few words with her, looked over at me, and
said, "Bet you don't know what to think of me, do you?"

"Hell, I don't know what to think of anybody any
more."

She turned away with a sullen look on her face and
walked back.

I said, "Goddamn, I can't believe this."

She had handed Arlene a checkbook. Arlene had mentioned Fred was very concerned that she was writing
checks against their account.

Les leaned over and whispered to me, "Those are the D.C. Outlaws. They are watching everything we do. So watch it. Don't do anything rash, okay?"

"Are you kidding?" I sat back and watched the topless go-go girl.

Tammy looked like a different person. Her hair was not rolled up as it usually was but was falling freely over her shoulders. She had on an Indian headband, extremely tight pants, and a body shirt. I would never have recognized her if Arlene hadn't pointed her out.

After dancing, the go-go girl would walk over to the D.C. Outlaw table and sit in somebody's lap. They would embrace, and he would pinch her behind. She usually giggled or screamed.

Then one guy got up and yelled at the top of his voice, "Why am I so fucked up on Friday night?"

"It's not Friday night, you shithead, it's Monday night."

"Oh fuck!" His voice boomed above the sounds of the jukebox. With a full beard and hair that was well beyond shoulder length, he looked like the meanest and orneriest one of the whole group.

Arlene nudged me and said, "That's Arnie. That's who Tammy is with."

"He's got to be the worst of the group," I replied.

Les snapped, "Watch what you say! They might overhear us."

We had been there a little over half an hour when Arnie got up and said, "I'm tired of this shit. Let's move on."

All the guys got up, followed by the girls; and they began to file out. Arnie hollered over to one of the Outlaws who remained, "We'll be back in a few minutes. Keep the beers warm."

As Tammy walked out, she didn't look at us but motioned with her hand a feeble good-by.

I said, "Well, they're gone. Wonder where they're going?"

Les said, "They'll be back, but let's get out of here."

Before we had finished our beer, in walked Fred, Big John, and Carl. It hadn't been more than two minutes since the Outlaws left. They walked over to our table and sat down.

Fred said, "Have you seen her? Have you seen her? Was she here?" When Arlene and Les nodded, he grimaced and sat down.

Big John said, "I'll kill those bastards! They may look mean, but they ain't mean. I'll kill them." Big John was so drunk he could hardly stand up.

I remarked, "Those are about the meanest, nastiest-looking guys I've ever seen."

Carl said, "Well, they might look big and nasty, but they aren't any tougher than you or me. It's just a big image, a big put-on. All those beards, leather jackets, and so on, they just try to look tough. They really aren't that tough." (Carl was a 220-pound construction worker.) When I asked him what he thought Fred was going to do, he said the best thing Fred could do right now was to leave well enough alone. He had got his checkbook and that was one of the things he was most concerned about.

Les motioned me to go downstairs to the john with him. While we were down there, he suggested that we try to persuade Fred to leave because the Outlaws could come back anytime. When we got back upstairs, Les said, "Come on, Fred, let's go. I don't know what's going to happen; but it's best for you to go on home, have a few more beers, and go to bed."

When Fred reluctantly consented, we walked outdoors. At that point Big John wobbled over to one of the motorcycles belonging to one of the remaining Outlaws and mounted it. "Anybody want to go for a ride?" he hollered.

Les shouted, "You dumb bastard, get off the motorcycle! They'll kill you if they come outside and see you on that motorcycle."

Big John drawled, "Oh, I can take them on, I can take them on. Let them come out here."

Les said, "Oh my God, we're all going to get killed if we don't get out of here."

So we hustled Big John off. Big John, Carl, and Fred got in the truck, and the three of us got in my car and departed. When we left there were a number of other motorcycles in the parking lot, and more Outlaws were arriving.

On the way back when we passed Sin City, another topless go-go club, Arlene looked at it and exclaimed,

"Oh shit, those are the bikes! They're in Sin City!" Just at that point we saw Fred's truck make a sharp right turn and pull into the club parking lot. The three of us returned home.

Arlene's and Les's curiosity got the best of them; and after I returned home they got in Les's Camaro and headed back to Sin City. By the time they got there, the confrontation was over, but it had been handled peacefully. When Tammy saw Fred coming, she excused herself from the group, so Fred and Arnie never came face to face. Carl was able to control Big John, who kept snorting, "Let me at the sonofabitch."

When Fred asked Tammy why she had done it, she said, "Don't know. Crazy, I guess."

"Are you gonna stay with these guys?"

"No," she told him. "But I know I can't come home. So I'll stay with Marge and get a job." She handed Fred his credit cards and the second set of keys to the truck.

Fred told her he was filing for a divorce and would try to gain custody of the children by proving her an unfit mother. Tammy went back to the Outlaws; and Fred, Big John, and Carl departed with Arlene and Les.

Tammy did not leave the Outlaws as she had said. She did, however, appear in the neighborhood occasionally to "baby-sit" for the children. When Fred came home from work, she would leave. From then on, however, she refused to talk to anyone on Clay Street.

Many on Clay Street had had tumultuous marital experiences. June had left her first husband because of his drinking and said her second marriage was only for convenience. Sam's first wife had left him. Les's first wife left him. Helga left Ted. Ruby's first and second husbands left her. Bobbi Jean and Barry had similar experiences. In none of the cases was a separation or divorce agreed upon by both partners. Rather one partner left another or discovered that the other partner was cheating. As in the case of Arlene and Les or Fred and Tammy, the separations were usually dramatic. Bobbi Jean's experience, which follows, was not atypical:

We were sitting at this table right here. Mamma was talking to us. She said, "George"—that was my husband

—"I wish you wouldn't get married right now. Bobbi is sixteen. She hasn't made up her mind yet. She really does not know what she wants yet. And as far as you all getting married, I really am not as scared of you as I am afraid for her."

But nothing would do but to get married. And you can ask anybody, I mean anybody, I never did nothing, I never went no place. And when I found out that he was running around on me, I didn't want to believe it. And in fact it was his sister who called me and told me! She said, "Bobbi, I don't know whether you know it or not, but George has got an affair with this other girl named Mary."

Well, I had met her, because she lived next door to his sister, and when we would go out there, she would come out. But stupid me, I still didn't think anything about it. His sister told me that it started the day I went to the hospital to have Bubba; that day he went out to his sister's house and she had to go out. When she went out, her bed was all made up; and when she got back, it was messed up. She caught the two of them and they admitted it. And when she called me, she said, "Bobbi, I'll tell you where she's going to meet him and when and what time. He's going to meet her when she gets off from work. They will meet at Branch Avenue where she gets off the bus. Her stepfather usually picks her up, but she's made arrangements for him not to pick her up for a couple of hours."

So I made arrangements for Mamma and Daddy to watch Bubba, 'cause Bubba was a baby; but they didn't want to do it so I just walked out and left him. I caught a bus to the shopping center. His sister met me there at Peoples Drug Store, and we were setting there drinking a Coca-Cola when he drove up. I seen the car when he pulled up. Well, my temper was arousing, but I just left well enough alone because my sister-in-law said, "Just sit tight and see what happens."

The way she called it was the way it happened. She got off a bus marked Livingston. She got off the bus and walked over to the car. She reached over and kissed him. Oh, they were really embracing and I just sat there watching for a while. Well, I want to tell you, a little bit got too much for me, and I walked over to the car, on

her side, and I jerked the door open. And when I jerked
the door open, there he was having intercourse with
her right there in the broad daylight! And she was a tremendous woman. When I drew back my fist to hit her,
she said, "You better not hit me."

I says, "You two-bitten whoring bitch, don't tell me
what I will do!"

She says, "Well, you do, and you'll go to jail for hitting
a pregnant woman!"

Then I told him, "You better march your ass home
and you better get every goddamn piece of clothes
you've got in that house out." I caught a cab and went
on back to the house. Well, he wasn't there. When he got
there, I want to tell you, gray-green uniforms, army
khakis were flying out into the front yard. . . ."

Barry's experience was quite similar to Bobbi's. Like Bobbi,
Barry's first marriage ended when he discovered his wife had
a lover:

We were living in Maryland in a little house that we
were renting, and I was learning my trade as an appren-
tice. If it rains the construction workers don't go to work
because they know they can't work that day. When it
starts pouring down rain, the laborers that are making
up the mud for the plastering can't work. Once it starts
raining, hot damn, we're going home in another hour,
so let's get rid of this mud. We're due home at a certain
time, maybe stop off for a beer or something, but we're
due home at a certain time. If we get off at four or four-
thirty, we probably get home at six. But if we get
knocked off during the day or an hour after we start or
something, good chance to catch your old lady—that was
the joke.

Well, this one joke worked out for me in a sense. I
never caught her outright, but I caught her. It's just like
the old saying, I'm your friend, you know. I don't want
to do nothing to her but punch her. All the time you are
thinking that it's not true, but your gut is grinding 'cause
you know what your buddy's going to say or he wouldn't
be talking to you that way. And then he comes up and
says, "Your wife is cheating on you, and I know for a
fact, and I'm going to tell you about it, and if you get

mad at me, all right, but I'm your friend and I want you
to know."

Then you say, "Well, I want to hear it because nobody
else will tell me, everybody else will probably hear it but
me."

"Go home right now and catch her yourself."

Things are ringing in your head. Things like, "Damn
that bitch. . . ." So you got all this going on in your
head, and you're just waiting to get home, waiting for
the job to get done. All the time you're in shock. Then
after this job gets half done, or a quarter way, then you
think, you take a deep breath, and then you say to yourself, "It makes sense,"—but you won't believe it unless
you have proof.

So, instead of waiting, like you're supposed to, you go
home, walk in the door, go to your closet, get the single-
barreled shotgun and put a shell in it, you cock the handle back, and you say, "Now, baby, tell me about it."
That's what I did. I said, "I mean, you tell me about it,"
and it started like that.

She knew I was serious, she knew I was going to blow
her brains out, so she fell on the floor. Tears come to
her eyes.

I said, "I want to hear about it." And I said a
few words about remember such and such a day. She
thought I knew more than I knew, 'cause I never completed what I was saying.

She cried, "Please don't kill me."

I don't know what stopped me from blowing her
brains out. Course, I was learning a trade. I was going
into apprenticeship. I was trying to do the best I could,
and what else can you do? I really don't know what kept
me from killing her. I never cheated on her. I never
cheated at all. I know that I was late in coming home
sometimes and I would stop off and have a beer with the
boys, you know. But I wouldn't stay out late. It wasn't
nothing like I didn't know when to come home. There
was no reason. I didn't know the guy. I never had seen
him before. I asked her, I says, "Take me to his house."

She did. I had a .25 automatic. I put that in my pocket.
She directed me to his house. I knocked on the door and
his wife answered the door. Went in, sat down, she introduced us. He had two of the prettiest daughters that

you've ever seen. I could have blowed his brains out and he knew it. What my intention was was to tell his wife exactly what he was doing to my home, busting my home up. My son was seven months old at the time. He had screwed her four times in the six months' time—the first time she did it was at Mother's house on my mother's couch, and my baby was laying in the crib.

So when I was in that man's living room, sitting down, he was sitting over there and his wife was sitting over there and his children was playing on the floor. I didn't let myself say anything that messed up that home, but before I walked out that door, he knew why I was there. He knew. I mean, just from my feelings and from the way I looked at him. I know he knew it after that 'cause I know she talked to him later. I could have blowed his brains out right in front of his wife at a certain point, but I couldn't see myself. He done messed up one home. I won't mess up his.

A few months later Barry was the one who ran off with a woman named Jackie, whose husband was serving time in the state prison. They sold all her and her husband's possessions, bought a car, and headed off to Florida. They ended up living together for over two years, living off the land (selling junk and fruit), and finally going to Oklahoma:

> We met through her four-year-old son. I was sitting in one booth, and she was sitting in another with her daughter and some other girls. I went down there with the idea of having a good time, dancing, you know. The little boy comes walking around, saying a couple of words. I seen where he come from, and I give him a quarter to put in the jukebox. I said, "Ask your mamma if you can put this in the jukebox."
>
> He knew what I was saying, and he did, and she sent her daughter over to put the quarter in the jukebox. So when she put it in, I got up and asked one of the girls if she would like to dance. She said no. That shocked me 'cause I usually didn't have no problem, but this time I did. I was really shocked. So I asked Jackie to dance—of course I didn't know her name at the time—and she did.
>
> She said, "Don't bug me. I've got a whole lot on my mind."

Then I asked the other one to dance again and this time she did. We danced around. So my friend and myself, finally we moved into the one table with them after an hour of goofing off and dancing.

Then for some reason or other Jackie and I got together. We got to talking and it started right. It wasn't like she was trying to make me pull out everything I had in my pockets, 'cause she would pay for her own drinks. At the time she wasn't hurting. I mean, she had some money in her pocket. Anyway, after closing, we all decided to go to her house. I didn't have no place to go, really. I was sleeping in my car or out behind my friend's house. Her old man was in jail. I come on in the house and I feel funny, but I end up never leaving.

So we put two and two together. We both got the same problems, and so we say let's take them together. We did. We talked about her daughter and her stepson, and everything was good until the day we were gonna leave. We sold everything we could, furniture, car, everything. The daughter stole twenty dollars from me, 'cause I had it counted one time and know that.

Come time to go, the daughter disappeared. We searched and searched but we couldn't find her, so we left. Figured she might as well be grown-up anyway.

So we left for Florida, a new car, U-haul trailer, her son, and a Pekingese dog which every meal had to have a hamburger cooked rare.

But Barry's time came again to be on the receiving end. He was working as a plasterer when he introduced Jackie to his fellow worker, Clyde. Jackie used to accompany Barry hunting; but when she started refusing, he got suspicious. One hunting trip he returned home early to find Jackie gone:

> Instead of staying three days, I stayed two; and when I got home, she wasn't there, and her kid wasn't there either. So I waited in the bushes with my shotgun. I was going to blow her brains out. I just had an inkling of what was happening. I got the inkling because I asked my neighbors if maybe something had happened, if they were in the hospital or had an accident, and I went around to one of my friends and he says, "Barry, I saw your wife go in a car with Clyde, your friend."

So I waited across the street from where I was living. I had a friend with me and he thought I was crazy. He must have known something 'cause we were on the same hunting trip together; and when we came back early, he acted like he knew something, but he wouldn't tell me. So I waited and waited and waited. And finally here comes this car. They got out of the car and was walking towards the door. I raised up the gun and fired it. I missed, hit the side of the door. They run and jumped in the car. I jumped in my car and was chasing them but lost them.

I stayed away from the house all night 'cause the cops were wondering what was going on, and I didn't want to get in no trouble with them on account of it. I don't know how, but I didn't get in trouble. They never even come around the next day, 'cause the neighbors, they halfway knew what I was going to do. I didn't get into no trouble. I didn't see her again until a couple of weeks later. After she left I moved out, too, and moved in with a friend and was spending most of my time drinking.

One night I was by myself, and I went to find one of my friends. I did and we got in this little party and ended up going to this half-assed beer joint. I had my shoulder holster on with a .25 automatic. And we were drinking. I was cutting up and dancing, and it was hot, so I stepped outside for some air. I see her and this guy pulling in the lot. I get out of sight. Before he could get out of the car, I opened her side, and I pulled the gun and cocked it. They saw it and saw it was ready to fire. I pointed it right on her nose through to his head, and I said, "I'm going to blow your brains out."

I almost pulled the trigger, but I backed off, closed her door, handed her the gun, with the safety on. That's how much faith I had in her. I handed her the gun, run around on his side, yanked him out of the car, leaned him against the wall. She jumped out and grabbed at me. "Don't, don't, don't!" she hollered.

I picked up a cinder block while he was half unconscious and on the ground, and I put it up over the top of my head and was going to crash it down on his head. She pushed me, and it just missed his head, just by an inch or so.

People were gathering around the car. She and him got back in the car real quick and backed out. I jumped

on the car on his side. He had the door open, you know.
He backed out and then stopped. I grabbed hold of him
and he crammed on the gas and I slide down dragging
on the ground while hanging on the door. If he'd turned
his wheels he'd have run right over me, but he was going straight. I let go and the wheel went by right beside
me.

Later I found out when she and Clyde drove off, he
smacked her right in the mouth, thought that she'd set
him up so that I could get him, you know. And she got
locked up for attempted murder 'cause she damn near
beat him to death with the heel of her shoe, wanting to
get back to me.

Course we made up after that. But Jackie, she left my
ass once we got to Oklahoma. . . .

As in the case of drinking, the difficulties in marriage were
discussed upon occasion in the community. The local Southern Baptist preacher felt unstable marriages were part of an
over-all reckless approach to life. "These folks," he said,
"they just seem to live hard for the moment and seem to
want romance and plenty of action. They are self-centered.
When something doesn't go right or when a marriage gets
hard, then they get disappointed and try to find someone else.
It is all a vicious circle. . . ." A public health nurse felt that
many of the young people, especially those from unstable
families, went into marriages not really expecting them to last.
This was impressed upon her once when she discussed birth
control with a twenty-four-year-old mother of three. When
the nurse suggested the young woman might consider having
her tubes tied, the woman remarked, "Why, no. I would
never think of that now. You see, when I remarry I would
like to have some more children." The nurse remarked that
she said she was not aware that the woman was having marital
difficulties. "Oh no," the young mother replied, "I'm not having marital difficulties at all. But you know, most girls remarry
sooner or later."

Most people took a philosophical attitude regarding marriage. "Divorce is simply part of life," they would say; "that's
just the way things are." For instance, it was part of life for a
young married man or young married woman to want to have

an affair with someone else. Bobbi explained her attitude as follows:

> I tell you this—and so help me this is the truth—every woman, every woman wants to have her fling. Every woman that I know wants to have a fling and most women have a fling. It's just something about women, I don't know what it is. I don't know how men feel; whether men have that or not. But it's the woman's fling that's the important thing. I remember my mother telling me that.
>
> She said, "Bobbi"—this was before I got married— "Bobbi, one of these days you'll probably get married and have a family. And after you're married you're probably going to want to have a fling. You'll be attracted by a guy or a gang or a bunch of hoods and want to leave your children, your family. Leave everything you have and run off with these guys. This is what you're going to want to do. This is going to be your fling. But resist it, Bobbi. Don't do it. Be strong. Resist it."
>
> Well, I didn't. I had my fling and I'm glad I had it. My first husband was over there in Germany and had all his girls and everything, and he didn't give a damn. So I had my fling and I'm proud of it. The boy's name was Ronnie. I only had one child then, Bubba, and my mother could baby sit and I could work it out. But when you have more children and don't have anybody to help out, then it gets to be sort of a problem. But you ought to understand, all men should understand, that women really need to have this fling. I don't know what it is.
>
> It happened to me and it happens to most women, especially if they've been married five or six years and their husband don't care about them any more and don't treat them right. What do you expect when some guy comes around and pays you some mind? Hell, what do you expect? All women have to have it, they're all going to have their fling. And something else I believe. I don't believe you're a woman until you've had your fling. I really don't. . . .

June also expressed a philosophical attitude. "Marriage ain't no bed of roses," she said. "When will these young folks understand? Heartache is just part of life."

June's neighbor, Harry Cheek, expressed the ambivalence most people felt as well as anyone: "Well, it's too bad. Sure, I want my marriage to work out. But it didn't. And it doesn't for most folks around here. The way I see it, it's inherited. My granddaddy, he had it. He was married several times. My dad and mom, hell, they had it. And my children, they are going to have it, too. Divorces, separations, broken marriages. Hell, that's just the way life is. It just runs in the family. It's inherited."

Toughness: "The Fightin' Side of Me"

> Well, there's one thing about me as well as lots of folks around here. I don't take no shit off nobody. I don't let nobody shove me around. I'm a fighter.
>
> ALTON SHORT

Most of the people on Clay Street saw themselves as fighters in both the figurative and literal sense. They considered themselves strong, independent people who would not let themselves be pushed around. For Bobbi, being a fighter meant battling the welfare department and cussing out social workers and doctors upon occasion. It meant spiking Barry's beer with sleeping pills and bashing him over the head with a broom. For Barry it meant telling off his boss and refusing to hang the door, an act that led to his being fired. It meant going through the ritual of a duel with Al. It meant pushing Bubba around and at times getting rough with Bobbi.

June and Sam had less to fight about, though if pressed they both hinted that they, too, would fight. Being a fighter led Ted into near conflict with Peg's brothers, Les into conflict with Lonnie, Arlene into conflict with Phyllis at the bowling alley, etc.

For most people being a fighter was synonymous with being tough. The epitome of the tough guy was Larry, Arlene's boy friend for two days during the spring. In looking tough Larry was unsurpassed. Twenty-seven years old, he was six-foot-four, 234 pounds, all muscle. He had bulging biceps covered with tattoos and had long wavy blond hair, greased and combed in a ducktail with long sideburns. He appeared in the neighborhood one day, saying he was staying with Phyllis "for the time being," along with his pregnant wife and some of their children, who appeared occasionally in Phyllis's front yard.

Since Larry's car had been demolished—he told everyone he had a fancy Plymouth which supposedly was so fast the highway patrol had informed him he could not drive it on the highways—he drove Phyllis's car. When he drove, he invariably screeched off as if he were in a drag race. Although Larry said he was a foreman on a construction project, when he wasn't in Phyllis's apartment, he spent most of his time driving her car and drinking at the local bars.

I first talked to Larry at the Bronco, a local country bar. After he had finished shooting pool, he walked over to where I was, remarking he had seen me around, and we started up a conversation:

> When I asked him how he was doing, he replied, "Not too good, there's too many guys out to beat my ass. A guy has to watch out nowadays." I then asked him if he came to the Bronco often, to which he replied, "Ah—no, not too much. I used to come in here some, but—ah— last month they asked me not to come back after I got in the big fight."
>
> "The big fight?"
>
> "Oh, yeah, goddamn big fight. I like to tore this place up. I knocked over the goddamn chairs, busted some tables, almost knocked over a goddamn pool table. Busted the partition there between the pool table and the bar. Shit, it was some goddamn fight. I left eleven people on the goddamn floor. They asked me not to come back."
>
> "How did it get started?" I asked.
>
> "Well, see, me and my buddy, we were there watching them play pool. My buddy was next. These two damn Germans were playing, and they had this girl with them. These Germans worked over the Volkswagen place, and shit, they didn't know that much about pool. So you know, when you lose you get to step out and let the next guy play, the challenger play. Well shit, one of these Germans didn't want to step out, so my buddy comes up and says, 'I'm playing next.' The German says no and starts to push my buddy around. Well shit, I got up and

say, 'If you push my buddy around you're gonna deal
with me.'

" 'Oh yeah?' 'Yeah.'

"Now you see, I know karate and my hands are registered as lethal weapons. It's like carrying a gun. But I
can fight more than two people. Like if there was three
people, it wouldn't be against the law. But I can't fight
less than three people. So I got three of 'em to fight
me, both Germans and a friend of theirs. I had them on
their ass after about . . . oh . . . under a minute. They
were on the floor. Then these other folks that were
around, they joined in; and before it was all over, there
was all of them against me, and I left every one of them
sons of bitches on the floor."

"Do you get in fights often?"

"Ah . . . no, not too much. I mean, I could, but I
walk out of it 'cause I know I could kill just about anybody with my hands. And if I did, I'd be arrested, 'cause
as I say, my hands are registered. But I mean, I haven't
gotten in more than . . . oh . . . oh . . . two or three
fights in the last few months. I try to stay out of
fights. I got discharged from the service because of my
hands." Larry didn't elaborate on that. He continued:
"Yeah, well . . . you need a ride? I'm driving Phyllis's
car tonight. But I'm thinking of getting me another car.
In fact, I've done ordered it. It's a '71 GTO. It cost
eighty-five hundred dollars with everything on it. 'Cause
of that sonofabitch who wrecked my car. I was sitting
still, and he ran into my damn rear end and totaled my
car. So they're going to have to pay sixty-five hundred
dollars for it. Hell, I had the Plymouth then. A goddamn
nice Plymouth. I'd much rather have that old car than
this one, but I guess I'm going to get a pretty nice car
for my money."

This was my first encounter with Larry. On the way back
home in Phyllis's car he told me he had recently moved up
here from High Point, North Carolina. He said he didn't like
Washington much and wanted to go back home, but since it
was easier to find work here, he would probably stay.

"I like the Bronco," he said, "but I got . . . like I told
you, I got kicked out of there because of the fight. Now

the Dixie Club is pretty nice, too, but it's pretty rough. I mean, it's a lot rougher than the Bronco. Here, let me show you this." He opened the glove compartment and pulled out a .38 revolver, fully loaded with eight bullets. "I don't ever go to the Dixie Club without this. I mean, my hands are pretty good, but at the Dixie Club you need more than hands. I wouldn't go there without this gun. You never know what you're going to get into. . . ."

Two days later Larry was working on Phyllis's car (before doing construction work he said he had been a mechanic, in fact, "the best goddamned mechanic in High Point"). I was watching him work on the motor when he turned to me and said:

"Well, it happened again."

"What?" I asked.

"Another fight at the Bronco. Seems like every time I go up there I get in a goddamn fight. Yeah, goddammit, I got real drunk last night. I started drinking beer and vodka. And I went up to the Bronco and was playing some pool. I had my quarter there on the table—you put a quarter there when you're going to be next—and this sonofabitch tells me it's his quarter. I say, 'Goddammit, it's my quarter!' He says it's his quarter, so I say, 'Okay, you play.' Then he says, 'No, you play!' I says, 'Goddamn, I'm tired of this shit. There ain't nobody in this pool room can make me play. You or nobody else.' 'Oh yeah?' Three of his buddies get up out of the booth they were sitting at and say, 'Oh yeah? We think we can make you play.'

"I punched him in the stomach with a pool cue and told him to cram it up his ass, I don't want to fool around with him. So I start to leave. I don't want to get in no fight, I don't like fights. The sonofabitch grabs me by my collar, so I say, 'Oh shit, boys, we'll get this over with right now.' So I floored the sonofabitch. Three guys hopped up and I floored them. A couple other guys joined in and I knocked them out. Tore up some more chairs.

"You know, I think they're going to ban me from the Bronco. I went up there today and asked them if I was

barred from the Bronco and they said no. Margaret, the
barmaid, she's my friend, she says, 'No, we'd like to have
you back 'cause those three sons of bitches have been
asking for it. They've laid lots of guys. But they met their
match last night.' You see, people like to get in a fight
with me. Now I take care of myself. And those sons of
bitches, they're at places like the Bronco, the Dixie Club,
and they're looking for somebody to lay on their ass.
So I get lots of guys picking fights with me. Hell, just
two weeks ago a sonofabitch pulled a gun but I pulled
mine and said, 'Okay, shoot.' He didn't have guts
enough to shoot. I'd of blown his brains out. See, I'm
a pretty good shot. . . .

"But you know, fighting ain't a good thing. It ain't
a good thing, but goddammit, you got to stick up for
yourself, and you got to take care of yourself, and you
can't let nobody push you around. Once you start letting
somebody push you around, then other people are going
to start pushing you around. You got to stick up for your
rights. But if you can, you shouldn't get in too many
fights."

Larry lived on Clay Street for three weeks—until the police
located him and returned him to the state prison where he was
serving a twelve-year sentence for armed robbery and assaulting a police officer. He had escaped a few months before.

B. J. Higgins was generally acknowledged to be the toughest of the men in the neighborhood. One afternoon Bobbi,
Walt, and Al were talking about tough men when B.J.'s name
came up.

"Yep," said Bobbi, "that B.J. is the toughest of all,
and you know, there's only one family down there on
Clay Street that I can't stand. It's only one person. And
I'll tell you who it is, it's B. J. Higgins. That no-good sonofabitch, he's no good at all. He's dirt. That man is dirt."

Walt and Al both nodded. Walt said, "He sure is. He's
an ornery sonofabitch if I ever seen one."

"Yeah," said Bobbi, "he was run out of Port Royal,
Virginia, after getting in trouble with the police. It had
to do with an automobile accident he was involved in
as well as some other things. But he was smuggled up
here in a truck, and that's God's truth. Smuggled up in

a truck so he could get away from the police down there. They were after him. He was married to a wife, who was an invalid, but he beat her so bad that she finally left him. He came up here alone, but then his no-good relatives and cousins followed and moved in with him. Eight years ago he moved to the house on Clay Street. That was when he was living with Doris. Doris was never married to B.J.; she was married to Sonny Barren. But B.J. had it fixed so Sonny Barren could be put in a mental institution and he spent several years in Spring Grove. Doris had some money and B.J. got his hands on it. That's how he got started. When he gets drunk he shows rolls and rolls of bills, five hundred dollars and a thousand. Doris would have black and blue marks on her arms and ribs from where B.J. would beat her up. And they had a thing going when after payday, when B.J. would pay his workers for helping him clean bricks, Doris would buy whiskey and get the workers drunk. Get them so drunk they would pass out and spend the night there and Doris would go through their pockets and take all their money. This happened several times."

I asked, "Why didn't the workers get wise and call the police or get mad at B.J. or kill him or something?" They all shook their heads and said, "B.J.'s a rough man. He's a mean sonofabitch. He drives a hard bargain."

Walt said, "Another thing, that sonofabitch B.J. ain't paid no income tax in twenty-six years. God's truth, and he makes good money. He says he used to make as much as four to five hundred a week sometimes, cleaning bricks or having people work for him and paying them dirt wages or rolling them after he pays them. He's a mean fellow, that B. J. Higgins."

Bobbi said, "The way he treats the people who live with him, you wouldn't believe it. The way he treats those people. He's beat up several of them. Three of them died while we lived on Clay Street. Goose died. He lived there for a while. And a couple of others, I think they died because B.J. beat them up, that's why."

Al said, "Well, Goose died from cirrhosis of the liver, that's why he died."

Bobbi said, "Yeah, I guess that's right. But B.J. beats up those people. Take Steve. Steve hasn't died yet, but he

will. He's been there for a long time. Steve used to be one
of the best ice men around. Then a horse kicked him in
the head, and he ain't been the same since. And ever
since that day, B.J.'s been taking advantage of him. Now
he gets sixty-five dollars a month in welfare and B.J.
gets sixty of that and has got him so scared he'll do anything B.J. says. It's just pitiful. B.J. beat him up two or
three times. Beat his head in, kicked him down the
stairs. That B.J., he's a mean sonofabitch. A tough
motherfucker."

Bobbi then recalled an incident that happened at their
house two Christmases before. Barry was drunk, Al was
on his way to being drunk, but Christmas was going
pretty well. The kids had some toys and were playing
with them. Barry had passed out on the sofa. Steve was
there. Although he had been drinking, he was harmless
and was getting along fine with everyone else. About the
middle of the morning B.J. came in, shouting, "Where's
that sonofabitch Steve? I'm going to kill him!"

At that time Steve was asleep in the chair. B.J. went
over and hit him two or three times in the head, kicked
him in the groin, kicked him on the floor, and began
stomping him. Apparently Barry never woke up, but
Walt came downstairs and asked what was going on. B.J.
didn't say anything except, "I'm going to kill that sonofabitch! I'm going to kill him." Walt said if it had been
his house he would have shot B.J. for coming in and
beating up Steve for no reason at all. Steve got up in fear
and hobbled across the street to B.J.'s house.

"Well," said Bobbi, "Doris and B.J. lived together for
several years, but finally Sonny got out of the mental
institution; and when he came home, he and B.J. had
it out. Some fight. B.J. beat Sonny up so bad he had to
be rushed to the hospital. Doris registered him as her
brother rather than her husband. They forged all the
papers. Sonny never came out of the hospital. He died
the next week. . . .

"B.J. and Doris kept on a-fighting. He beat her so she
had a heart attack a couple of years ago. She came out
of the hospital but they kept on a-fighting, and a year ago
September Doris had a second heart attack and died.
The night before, B.J. beat the shit out of her. I saw
the black and blue marks on her arms and ribs. B.J.

killed her, that's who killed her. I know that sonofabitch did. I saw those marks. I know that's the reason she had a heart attack, and B.J. ought to be put in prison. But they said it was an accident. They said that she just had a normal heart attack. But all of us, all of us right around here know it was different.

"After Doris's death, May moved in with B.J. B.J. beats May as much as he beat Doris," Bobbi said. "Well, you know, as much as I hate that sonofabitch B. J. Higgins, I say it's May's fault for letting him do that to her. She doesn't have to put up with that shit. She doesn't have to take that off him. And yet she does and she keeps coming back. She's got money, and she's got a house down on the beach, she's got a well-known name, and yet she lets B.J. push her around. That ain't for shit. . . ."

While B.J. and Larry were extreme cases, most people tried to maintain an image of being tough. For most people this meant *talking* about how they could defend themselves if necessary, how strong they were, how they "never took no shit." For most people, toughness was only talk, and few actual fights or incidents occurred.

An important symbol of toughness was having a "tough" car. Les had a new Camaro with "four on the floor," a stereo tape deck, pin stripes, and a customized engine. Ted had a fancy new Cougar before it was repossessed, and Lonnie had a new Mustang Mach I which he raced in drag strip competition. Phyllis reluctantly purchased a Pontiac Firebird, saying that even though it had a raised rear axle and four on the floor, it really didn't have class. Up and down Clay Street invariably there were several fancy "tough" cars parked along the curb and usually a few older Mercuries and Fords jacked up on cinder blocks in people's front yards.

For some people, guns were another symbol of toughness. Many families kept guns in their home—mainly for hunting. One neighbor, however, Duane Ford, a truck driver, had an arsenal of hand guns, none of which were used for hunting. The afternoon when I first met him, Duane proudly exhibited his guns.

He picked up a gun that was resting on the end table beside the couch. "See this here," he said. "I keep it loaded all the time, and I keep it with me all the time. I always have a gun in my glove compartment, a gun on my person, and a gun beside my bed. I have a gun under my bed and my wife has a gun and they all are loaded all the time, except the shotgun under the bed is not loaded right now, but the others all are." He showed me the gun's cylinder, which contained six bullets. "You want to see a gun, let me show you this." He brought out what he said was a Magnum .44, the largest hand weapon available. It, too, was loaded.

When I asked him how long he'd owned these guns, he said he'd been carrying guns for about fifteen years. His wife, Ronda, then brought out her gun, which she kept loaded and by her bed at all times—a very small gun that she could hold in the palm of her hand quite easily. She said she'd been carrying this gun ever since the riots several years before. They said there hadn't been any accidents with the guns except once when a friend came by who didn't realize they were loaded and fired two shots, which went into the wall.

I asked him why he kept all the guns loaded. "Goddammit, an empty gun never killed nobody," Duane replied. "You can't shoot nobody with empty guns. I say if you don't keep it loaded there's no sense in having a gun. You never know when there's going to be another riot, you don't know when you're going to get jumped, when you're going to get robbed. Gotta have a gun. Gotta have a gun to protect yourself. Now I have a permit for mine. Lot of people don't, but I'm legal. I carry my permit. I've never gotten in no trouble. Just prepared, that's all."

A further aspect of toughness was sexual exploits. Various men had stories to relate regarding their various conquests. Many of the stories, like this one by Barry's friend Wade, had a similar ring:

Yeah, my kid brother comes up to me and he says, "You know, there's this nympho who just can't get enough of it. You know what I mean?" And he's been going over to her place and laying her, and he asked me to come along. We'd do some drinking and have a good time.

So I said, "Hell yes." I went over there and we had one hell of a good time. Drinking and fucking all night. Goddamn, it was fun! I mean, we were really laying it on, you know! And I asked my brother about this woman's husband. He says she's separated from her husband, has lots of boy friends, but don't have much to do with her husband.

Well, we were going at it, and all of a sudden we hear a knock at the door. A goddamn heavy knock, *bang, bang.* I asked my brother, "What in the shit is that?"

He looked at her and she looked at him and they say one thing, "Goddamn husband."

I said, "Oh shit, we have had it now! That sonofabitch is going to come in here, see us laying up with his old lady, and what the hell are we going to do?" I figured there's only one thing to do. I told my kid brother, "You open the door real fast." I mean, this sonofabitch is really beating on the door by now. "I'm going to lay that bastard one. I'm going to hit him one in the gut and knock him out. And we're going to haul ass over his body."

Okay, this is what we get ready to do. And he goes up and opens the door and I lay ass on that sonofabitch. Pound him one in the stomach, whack him one in the jaw, and haul ass over his body. But goddamn, if that sonofabitch wasn't a cop! He didn't have nothing to do with the woman. He was just going to ask her about her neighbor next door!

Some luck, we both hauled ourselves over that sonofabitch's body and there are two more cops waiting at the end of the walk. Their damn car's ready, the engine's going, and the door's open. They haul our asses in the back seat and take us down to the police station. Assaulting a police officer. And that ain't no easy sentence tagged on to that crime.

Well, we got us a lawyer and the lawyer comes in, sits down with us and the cop, and we explain the whole thing. And the lawyer says, "Look"—now I had a couple of kids by then and was happily married—"look, this guy thought you were the husband coming back and finding him knocking up his old lady, and he wanted to get out without getting into any trouble. Now you can understand that."

The policeman, he was real nice, he understood it. So they agreed to drop charges 'cause they knew it would really mess up my life and mess my marriage up and all that. So they dropped charges and both me and my kid brother, we got out. We weren't even in the damn jail more than a couple of hours. And my wife, to this day, she doesn't know about it or about most of the other chicks I've laid.

Al was frequently telling of his various exploits, such as this typical episode:

Back in the late forties or early fifties, I worked for Greyhound. And this night I was running around with this man and his wife. He was one of the drivers, too. And I marked off when he would be off. I knew he had a trip to Philadelphia. So I made arrangements with the dispatcher for a day off—which would give me an opportunity to get my work in and help him with his housework.

So I took off and went to her house after I seen him mark off to Philly. Got in the house and got in bed with his old lady.

About the time I'm doing my business, and her husband's business, her husband hit the door and said, "Let me in, it's cold out here."

"Oh my God!" So I got up, put my shorts on, grabbed my pants, my coat, my topcoat, didn't get my shoes on, and I headed for the window. It was on the first floor, and in the back of the house was a coal house. Well, I hopped out on the coal house roof. It went in, and I went in, and there me and the coal were together. They had one of those wooden latches on the door on the outside to keep the door shut.

"What's all that damn noise?" he shouted.

"It's them dogs, they're out there again," she said. I finally got the latch off the door and just as I got out a cab came along. I got in that cab and had my clothes still hanging on my arm. The cab driver said, "Man, you had to leave quick." I told him what happened and he laughed and took me on home. I put my clothes on in the cab as best I could. When I got home, I looked in the mirror, and I looked like the blackest nigger in town. But I got away. He never did get wise.

The image cultivated by and large was of the tough *guy* rather than the tough gal, though women were far from sweet and servile. They, too, were strong and tough. Bobbi, for instance, boasted of cussing out Barry or pulling a knife on the guy who got fresh with her in the laundromat. She, like June and most of the Clay Street women, could match her husband swear word for swear word and would not let herself be pushed around. Married to "an ornery so and so," she said she had to be tough to survive.

At age thirty-one, Bobbi had been through many difficult experiences: an early marriage, divorce, giving birth to six children, the death of two of her children, poverty, poor health, and Barry's alcoholism and violence. "Take me," Bobbi once told me. "If I wasn't a fighter I'd never of made it, not to say that I've really made it now. . . ." June and Sam told me almost the same thing. Life was essentially very hard, they said. You had to make it on your own without a lot of help from other people. Consequently, in order to "get through" a person had to be tough, he had to be able to fend for himself, he had to be willing and able at times to fight.

In the same breath Bobbi described herself as a fighter, she added, "But shit, folks around here talk a big game, but really they ain't so tough. Not *underneath* they ain't."

Underneath the tough image, I found most folks on Clay Street compassionate and sensitive. Underneath the coarseness and hardness, Bobbi's compassion for Barry and her children came through again and again as did Barry's love for Bobbi. Similarly, underneath much of the rough exchange of words between June and Sam, June's eyes would twinkle and Sam would smile, thus transforming the harsh words to mean their opposite. When June would holler at the bowling alley to Sam, "Okay, big Daddy, you really socked it to 'em. One pin that time! Old fat ass is having trouble lifting the ball," and Sam would return her encouragement by giving June the

finger, this was not a hostile or mean exchange. The smiles
and the laughs changed everything.

Alienation: "I'm a Lonesome Fugitive"

> President Nixon? Fuck him. That's all I got to say. . . .
> Course I never thought about it all that much. He's probably
> doing the best he can with what he's got.
>
> BARRY SHACKELFORD (His sole political
> comment of the year)

People on Clay Street weren't particularly concerned about
politics and did not choose to articulate why. They would
usually just shrug their shoulders and say they weren't interested or didn't know anything about it. If they would say anything, it would be something like, "Hell, they are all a bunch
of crooked politicians anyway. . . ." Politicians were considered dishonest, could be bought off, and had only their own
interests or power in mind.

Most of the people did not vote or express much concern
with politics. Les was typical: "You know," he said, "I never
voted, never registered, and never will. Politics is a waste of
time because it's all the big wheels making deals to screw the
little guy. And all politicians are the same. It really don't make
no difference who you vote for. Sure, I like Wallace, and if I'd
voted, I would've voted for him. He says what he thinks.
But I don't vote." This kind of attitude, not identifying
with the political process, in fact, viewing it as detrimental to
their own interests, was the dominant attitude on Clay Street.

Barry's friend, Wade, expressed his feelings this way:

> Well, I'll tell you one thing about our country the way
> it is now. First of all, you talk a lot about the little man.
> You hear this all the time—the politician is going to be
> for the little man. Some folks think there is a chance that
> the little man can have his lot improved, that there will
> be people in power who really care about us. But I know
> there's not a damn bit of truth in that. 'Cause I know
> there's one thing and one thing only that speaks in this
> country and that's money. Money is power and power
> is money. And the guys that have money, they're the

ones that tell the rest of us what to do. Just look around. Rockefeller, Lyndon Johnson, Lady Bird Johnson, the Kennedys. You find me somebody in power who don't have money or who don't speak for those people who have money. That's the way it is, and that's the way it's always going to be, and more or less the way it has been. So I just don't give a damn.

While many on Clay Street considered themselves nominal Democrats, few were registered or took the time to vote because, as June described it, "There are too many other things on my mind. I just don't have the time, and besides it don't really make a difference nohow."

Yet though few people took an active interest in politics, most people felt there was a lot wrong with society that politics could address itself to—were politics not so corrupt and controlled by the rich for the rich. The following conversation occurred at the Shackelfords one afternoon in the spring:

> Walt started it off by saying, "You read the paper today? That sonofabitch Reagan out there in California? Did you hear that? The paper says that he don't pay no income taxes and he's going to eliminate all the welfare programs. That's the goddamnedest thing I've ever heard! I think Reagan is no good. But I just can't believe that he don't pay no income taxes. I mean, I know he don't, that no-good sonofabitch. And he's cutting off welfare. Ain't that some shit?"
>
> Alton Short said, "That's right. People got to live. Hell, he don't pay no taxes, and he's cutting off money from all the poor people. And Nixon, that sonofabitch, he's cutting down welfare and the health program and the food stamps. I tell you, we live in a fucked-up world."
>
> I said, "What do you think of the May Day demonstrations downtown? The kids, they are ones who are trying to do something to change things. They're against the Vietnam War and against all the cutbacks in welfare. And they say they're doing what they can to see things changed."
>
> Bobbi jumped in. "You know, I agree! And I'm thinking, what they did to those demonstrators, locked them up and everything, if they called for a big demonstration this weekend, goddammit, I'd like to go down there. I

sure as hell would. I mean, I ain't no goddamn hippie and I don't believe in all they're doing, but I think what's going on right now is full of shit."

Sitting back in his chair and staring out the window, Walt agreed, "It sure is, it sure is."

Bobbi said, "What I hear on the news is that they're going to close down the whole goddamn city. Well, close it down, Jack, close it down!"

"That's right. I heard that, too," added Walt.

Bobbi said, "Well, that's something. I hope they **do.** I hope they close down the whole goddamn city. Put so many kids in jail they overflow, they don't have no more jails. And I'll go down there, too. There's going to be some action, that's what I hear. There is going to be some real action."

Bobbi continued scrubbing the floor, and after a pause I asked everyone, "If you could change things in this country, what would be the first thing you'd do?"

Al immediately responded, "Well, I think we ought to have a nigger for President."

I said, "Come on, now, you're putting me on!"

Al said, "That's right. I ain't shitting. I mean a nigger for President. I mean, the niggers got it worse than the white folks, right? I mean the ghettos and all that, that's where the real poverty is. Hell, ninety per cent of the niggers in this country are poor. Get a nigger in there, and at least he'll have some feeling for what it is to be poor. He'd understand it; he's probably been poor himself. So I say, if you want to have somebody who will really do something to change things, get a goddamn nigger in there. Hell, I'd vote for the sonofabitch! I hate to say it, but I would. 'Cause I think there would be some changes if you get somebody in there that knows what's wrong with the country and knows what's needed. And I say you might as well get a nigger."

I asked Bobbi and Walt if they would vote for a black person.

Bobbi said, "I would. I would indeed. I'd vote for Mayor Washington for mayor if I lived in D.C. I think he's a good man, and there are lots of colored people I'd vote for. Now, there are lots I wouldn't vote for. It depends on the man."

Walt nodded. "That's what I say, it depends on the man. But I'd vote for a nigger. Hell yes. I'd vote for a nigger just as soon as I'd vote for a white person if that nigger knew what was happening."

I asked, "Well, who do you think would be a good black President?"

Al said, "Well, I don't know."

"What would you think about Martin Luther King if he were alive?"

Al said, "Well, he's the one. I'd vote for him. I think he'd make a goddamned good President. But that sonofabitch is dead now."

Bobbi said, "I'd vote for him, too." Walt agreed that King would have made a good President.

Of course not all hard living folks on Clay Street would have agreed with Alton Short's solution to the current problems. Most people saw blacks as a threat to their somewhat tenuous position in society. At the same time, however, most people sensed that something was wrong. The Shackelfords were destitute and had known extreme poverty as had many people on Clay Street. Several families had relatives and friends back in North Carolina or West Virginia who were poor. More important, even those who were relatively well off —like June and Sam—realized that their situation could change for the worse at any time. These families feared they would fall back into poverty if something were to happen to the breadwinner. The reason the Shackelfords were poor was that Barry could not work due to his health problems and drinking problems. Though the welfare did provide emergency aid, the help they received was hardly enough to get them on their feet. Others feared the same thing might happen to them.

Most people, however, did not make a connection between their own problems and the failure of government programs. On the contrary, the dominant feeling was against government intrusion into the lives of people. They valued independence and self-reliance, they said, and did not want government help. Most people said they wanted to succeed or fail on their own. At the same time, they realized that a government of sorts was located on Capitol Hill. This government was taxing their earnings and spending their money. In their view it was giving what they had to others—mainly the black poor—less deserving than themselves. Why shouldn't they get their fair share? This feeling of ambivalence about government and their relationships to it led most people to conclude the entire political process was irrelevant to their needs. They said the best thing for them to do was to live their lives the best way they could and "leave well enough alone."

Alienation was something the hard living people shared with many of their stable, home-owning neighbors, though for the settled families, alienation took a different form. Like Alton, most of these people felt the workingman was not getting his fair share, but unlike Alton, they thought the cause for the problems had to do with blacks and white liberals. The settled people had worked hard to secure a modest place in the world. In contrast to many of the hard livers they *had* a place. They had homes, stable families, steady jobs. They had a stake in society that they feared was slowly being taken away from them by liberal elitists and given to the poor, the blacks, and the "lazy bums on welfare." Consequently, most of these people voted, and voted against liberal Democrats. With them, too, of course, Wallace was popular, and those who voted Republican did so mainly because Republicans were the lesser of two evils. One home-owning neighbor expressed his feelings as follows:

> Yeah, some folks say I'm a stupid shit because I do vote. I know it's useless, but I do it anyway. Last election I voted for Nixon over Wallace 'cause I knew Wallace didn't have a chance of winning. I kinda like Agnew, though, 'cause he tells it like it is, calls a spade a spade. But I hate that bastard, Nixon. He ain't done nothing for me or the country or anything else. Now, Wallace, he's okay with the niggers, you know. He'd probably stop us from having a race war and all that, he knows what to do in that regard, but Agnew, he's pretty good, I think, all the way around. But I ain't got no use for Nixon. I ain't got no use for the Kennedys, for the Johnsons. I hate Humphrey's guts. He's a pansy —little-wise-ass-sonofabitch, that's what I call him. But I do vote. I know it's dumb, don't make no difference.

But I go ahead and do it. You might say I voted for Nixon 'cause I thought I had less to lose.

While I heard this view expressed often by home-owning families, there were a few people in the community who were extremely right wing. Some of these people talked about a communist take-over of the country, "communist domination of the coloreds," and communist control of the local schools. For these people even Richard Nixon was too left wing. My exposure to their political views came one evening after dinner at the local Southern Baptist Church:

> After the meeting broke up, people stood around in groups and chatted. On my way out I spoke to Mrs. Little, the peppy director of the Sunday morning choir and wife of the minister. She asked me how my study was going and exactly what I was doing. When I tried to explain briefly what it was all about, she responded, "Well, you know, I read the *Post* sometimes. But my favorite newspaper is the *Star* because I think the *Post* is too biased, liberal communist. I don't like it except for Jack Anderson. Now, I like Jack Anderson, he's all right."
>
> I did not know what prompted this kind of response, as I had said nothing about news media. But with this comment, she was off and running.
>
> She was a very small lady, about five feet tall, with gray hair, and she spoke with a delightful South Carolina accent. Though the conversation that followed centered on topics that were anything but charming and gracious, she never raised her voice nor spoke with any bitterness; and she always maintained her composure.
>
> "Well," she said, "I just believe that that Washington *Post* is a disreputable paper. They do not report the news. They only report what they want to report and with this very, *very* liberal viewpoint, which a lot of people don't agree with, like me. Now take Nicholas von Hoffman, for instance."
>
> "Nicholas von Hoffman," I said. "Do you like him?"
>
> "Oh my goodness! Nicholas von Hoffman? Oh, he's Satan himself! Nicholas von Hoffman is a communist! I'm sure of it. I don't know it for a fact, but he must be by the way he writes. He is Satan himself, and I simply cannot understand how a newspaper like the Washington

Post could allow somebody like that to write on their staff. That man has problems. He is degenerate. Oh, it is just shocking! But at least I'll say one thing for the *Post*. They have Jack Anderson on their staff and he tells it like it is. He calls a spade a spade. And he knows; he has the feeling of what's going on in our government.

"Listen, let me tell you, we must be aware of what's going on. Most people, most well-intentioned, well-meaning people just do not know. But we are now at a crisis like we have never faced before. Our country is at a turning point. Either the communists are going to take it, or we're going to save it for democracy and freedom. But the two forces, the Satanic force and the God force, are battling, and it's up to us Christians now to man the watch, to do something, to keep the communists from taking over our country, because, well, they've got the schools, they've got some churches, they've got the mental health institutes. Take this recent panel on pornography. Communist, yes, communist. I know it's communist because of what they said. They said it was okay, okay, for adults to see pornographic literature or films or anything else. They actually said that this was all right. That's why I know that this was a communist plot. It's in all levels of government, Republican as well as Democrat, but especially in the Democratic party. They are everywhere.

"Now the reason I know this is because of what I've read in a few key books and listened to a few key people. Now come to our library. I'd like to show you these books. I'd like for you to check them out. We have a complete selection of these books in our library."

She and the church librarian then took me to the church library and showed me several books. The church librarian was nodding her head with every word Mrs. Little uttered, saying, "Oh yes . . . yes indeed."

"The communists are everywhere and we as Christians must fight. If we don't fight today, tomorrow we won't be around to say anything." The librarian then pulled out the following books: *God's Smuggler,* by Brother Andrew; *Tortured for his Faith,* by Harlan Poppav; *Death of a Nation,* by John A. Stormer. Finally she said: "You must read these two immediately. After you read them your life will never be the same. Here's one, *None Dare*

Call It Treason, by John Stormer. This is what moved me, this is what really enabled me to see the light. And another one, *Communist America: Must It Be*, by Billy James Hargus. You must read these two books." She gave me the library cards, I filled them out, and she placed the books in my hand, gripping my hand firmly and saying, "In two weeks these books will be due. Please try to read them during that time." I thanked her and told her that I had an open mind and that if I didn't agree with the books at least I would promise to read them.

As we walked outdoors, Mrs. Little reminded me again not to forget to read the books, because they were very, very important and one could not be the same after he had read them. It would open up a whole new world of thinking; it would show people what was really happening to our government. "Now, look, take the peace movement, quote, 'Peace Movement,' because that's not really what it is. You know the symbol, the little round circle with the thing in it, the sign inside that, do you know what that is?" I told her no. "It is an ancient symbol, an ancient antichrist symbol. It's always been an antichrist symbol. It stands for the broken cross. It's the symbol of the Satanic forces, the forces of paganism and evil and barbarism and communism. That's what it stands for. I know this for a fact, it's always been a symbol as long as the cross. It stands for the antichrist. That's what that is, and that's why that symbol is so powerful. That's why it has control over these young people. You see, the communists have gained control over their minds. And that's what the communists try to do, is get control over the young people's minds. And the problem, the real tragedy, is that in this country they have succeeded and people are sitting back and not doing anything about it. People in the churches, even. In fact, as I said before, communists are everywhere! Besides being in the government and in the churches and in the schools, they've even gotten to our music. Rock music, hard rock music is written by communists. Because they know that those sounds, you know, that go against each other, turn people against authority and God. They know this and that's why they wrote it and sent it over here. It's the communists who have written our rock music and the young people have been misled. They like that music, which just proves my point

—that the communists have gained control over the
minds of our youth.

"Take sex education, for instance. Here is an obvious
communist plot to bring sex out into the open to destroy
the values of a free society. I've been to these meetings
about sex education and let me tell you, it is horrible.
They openly talk about sex in the schools! Oh . . . I get
so upset when I think about all that's happening and
about how little we're doing about it.

"Now, take the race question. Racism and all that that
you hear about. Now, you see the colored people are
really nice people. If you treat them nice, they'll treat
you nice. You reap what you sow and it works with colored just as it does with whites. There are good colored
and there are bad colored. And it's because the church
really hasn't been Christian and hasn't loved one another
and our colored brethren that things are so bad today.
Now all these militants, they are really bad. But there
are good colored people who are Christians and who talk
about love and brotherhood."

"You mean people like Dr. Martin Luther King?" I
asked.

"Oh my goodness, my goodness no. Oh no. No. The
colored people are good people, some of them. Some of
the colored are good people. . . ."

While Mrs. Little represented something of an extreme
position, some of the people I met at the Baptist Church and
in various community meetings tended to state similar posi-
tions. Most of the ministers in the area, for instance, described their congregation as "very, very conservative." The
mayor and members of the city council quite frequently
lamented the unfortunate "liberal influence" in government.
For the most part, the people who tended to be active politically were conservative and proud of their conservatism. For
them, most Republicans were too liberal.

Most people on Clay Street found themselves caught in the
middle. Since Clay Street was not a slum and since most families were making enough to get by, life in some respects was
better than it had been in the past. Yet at the same time, they
felt powerless and helpless to do much about what they per-

ceived as threats to their neighborhood and to their position
in society. Many people feared losing what little they had.
Since the settled families generally had more at stake and
more to lose than the hard living families, they tended to be
more concerned, more politically active, and more conservative.

Alienation on the part of hard living families ran deeper
than political views. It was expressed in their hostility toward
the church, professional people, government officials, and representatives of the government, such as the police. It was expressed in hostility toward college students and other groups
who appeared to "have made it" or were "making it"—the
boss, white collar workers in general, "rich folks."

Few people on Clay Street attended church because church,
like most other institutions, was said to be corrupt and a
waste of time. Most people considered themselves religious;
but to get religion you did not need to go to church. As far as
Les was concerned, for instance, churches were only out to
get your money.

Most people, like Wade, felt that people who went to
church were hypocrites. But he added:

> Now my wife, she's different. See, she . . . she believes
> in all this shit. She believes in politics and she believes in
> religion. You tell her that there is so much corruption
> and graft and all this shit that exists, and she'll say it's not
> true. 'Cause she's not that way herself. She's sort of pure
> and all that. Well, anyway, a lot of it has to do with
> religion. She's big on this Nazarene religion stuff. Now
> I don't have no use for that. I think the church is full of
> hypocrites, too, and they're as corrupt as everything else.
> You tell me what the wealthiest institution is in the whole
> world. Hell yes, everybody knows it, it's the goddamn
> Roman Catholic Church. And what are they doing with
> their money? Hell, they're sitting on it! They ain't giving
> it to people who need it. That's what I mean by corrupt.
> You talk about the Baptists and the Church of the Naza-
> rene getting up there and talking about smoking and
> drinking, how bad it is. Hell, after church is over, you
> know those ministers go up there and light up a cigarette
> and have a swig of gin. Goddamn, they all are a bunch of

hypocrites! I don't have no use for church. Now, I believe in God and all that, but I don't believe there is such a thing as a God that has long hair and a beard and all, shit, like they believe in church. I think He's maybe a being or something like that, but I mean, I don't believe it's a person. That's the kind of shit they believe in those churches. So I don't go. I mean, if there's a big event or something I'll go to satisfy my old lady, but the church is as crooked as everything else, and I ain't got no use for it.

Besides the church and preachers, professional people were generally suspect. Of all professional people, lawyers were the most disliked. Most of the people on Clay Street at one time or another had made use of a lawyer usually in getting a divorce or in trying to get a husband to pay support. Most of the people had had unpleasant experiences and/or felt they were overcharged. June's experience in trying to get support from her first husband was not uncommon:

> Well, my first husband ran out so I did what all women have to do, go to a lawyer. All it cost to sign a warrant was five dollars but for a woman without a husband that's a lot of money. And the five dollars goes to those damned lawyers who don't give a damn anyway. I paid the five dollars three times and nothing ever happened. It's all a big racket. . . .

Ted felt that his lawyer had deceived him when he was trying to get a divorce from Helga. Since those who had not had bad experiences themselves had heard about friends having bad experiences, most people were wàry of going to lawyers. After all, most politicians were lawyers. Hank Jones, who sold ice cream and lived on the next block, expressed the general distrust of lawyers as well as anyone. He was talking about all the crime in Washington and what he considered the breakdown of the court system:

> And the reason—I tell you the reason it's so bad is because of the goddamn court system. The courts let people go. You can't do anything. They never caught any of the people that robbed me. Not a single one. They don't care about bringing justice. There's no justice in this country. There never will be as long as the people

who are running this country don't know a goddamn thing about how people live. It's these lawyers, these goddamn elitist lawyers who think they know everything. All they know is each other. They went to the same prep school, they went to the same super-duper Ivy League college and they went to the same country club and they know the same people. They don't know anybody else but these same people who do all this big-shot stuff. You know, these elitist things, schools and clubs, and all that. And that's all the people they associate with and then they come into court and how they supposed to know what's right and wrong? How they supposed to know how to decide something?

That's the way it is all over government. These people who don't know how the common man, the workingman, the guy who's out here just living, trying to make a go of it, don't know how we live. That's the man who's running our government and why we're in such a goddamn mess today. And I tell you another thing, they're all crooked. You show me a lawyer who says he's not crooked, and I'll show you a liar. That's the way it works. I know, I've seen these guys operate. This guy calls up Bill and says, "Bill, I'll meet you at the club for lunch today." They'll have lunch and say, "Now look, we've got this client, right? I've got this client. He's suing your client. Let's you and me work something out on the side so we both get a lot of money and the clients get screwed. Okay?" Well, that's the way it works.

Next to lawyers and politicians, doctors were generally the most criticized. Duane Ford, for example, was quite hostile toward doctors and for good reason. "Doctors will screw you every time," he told me. "Prescribe medicine for you you don't need and then charge you double for not helping you one goddamn bit." When Duane told me this, he was almost completely blind and unable to work. Though he had been undergoing treatment from various doctors for over six months, he was still blind, and no one knew what the cause of his blindness was. Duane said one doctor said it had something to do with lead in his blood (Duane had painted cars for over twenty-five years), but workmen's compensation refused to pay. Duane had gotten a lawyer but felt the lawyer

was not any good. Though he had not worked for over six
months and had Medicaid, one doctor had billed him for
$278 and was now threatening to call a collection agency
since Duane could not pay. The doctor refused to accept
Medicaid. One morning Duane called me in desperation:

> What am I going to do? What the hell am I going to
> do? That sonofabitch doctor didn't do any two hundred
> and seventy-eight dollars' worth of work on me. Big shot,
> wears long hair, hippie clothes. Said, "Look, man, this
> man, that man." Boy, oh boy, I've had it with this guy!
> And now they're going to take me to court. Well, let 'em
> take me to court. 'Cause I ain't going to pay, I ain't going
> to pay one cent. I'd go to jail before I pay. He came
> in a couple of times and said, "Look, man, look, man,"
> then walked out. Thinks he's some sort of big shot. Well,
> let them take me to court. . . .

Like Duane, most people had reasons for their prejudices
toward professionals. Bobbi, of course, had similar experiences
with some of her doctors. Carlyle had had so much trouble
with doctors sending collection agencies after him, he said he
would just as soon die as go to a doctor. Because of experiences like these, there tended to be a very real barrier between
the people on Clay Street and the professionals they were often forced to deal with.

Of course, not all their experiences were unpleasant. Bobbi
had doctors she liked very much, who did much to help her
family, and whom she was quite fond of. Duane Ford said he
liked one of his doctors; and others had had good as well as
bad experiences with various professional people and expressed fondness and appreciation for these professionals as
individuals. Nevertheless, people tended to feel that as a rule
one had to be very careful in dealing with professional people. One was never too sure when he was getting help or when
he was being taken. The attitude they expressed was quite
similar to an attitude I have heard middle-class or professional
people express toward auto mechanics: "You just can never
be sure any more when you take your car to get repaired.
Maybe the mechanic will fix it, maybe he'll charge you for
work he didn't do or do work the car didn't need. . . ."

There was also some animosity toward government workers, especially welfare workers, since most families who for
one reason or another had to deal with the welfare department had had their share of unpleasant experiences. For no
reason Barney was considered ineligible for the Aid for the
Permanently or Totally Disabled and was reinstated only after
June finally got through to a caseworker, who admitted
there had been a mix-up. Practically every month Walt's check
went to the wrong address or was late; and Bobbi, who had
to wait in long lines to be recertified for stamps, detested the
way she was treated by the welfare workers. A young woman
down the street from June was informed she was no longer
eligible for AFDC because she had not filed proper papers
regarding her husband's whereabouts. Those people receiving
welfare all said they would much rather work. They hated
the stigma attached to welfare, and they hated what they had
to go through to get welfare. "It's better than starving," Bobbi
said, "but not much better. If it wasn't for the kids, I don't
know if I would keep on going down there."

The negative experiences people had with politics, government, and professional people also occurred in many of their
other dealings with the larger society. One family subscribed
to several magazines through a magazine club, which, although it failed to send the family three of the six magazines,
was threatening to get a collection agency after the family for
not paying. Other families had had some trouble with encyclopedia salesmen, insurance salesmen, and others who
came door-to-door. Many had been "taken" by loan sharks or
pawnbrokers. People tended to think they were buying something they weren't or failed to get what they thought they
bought. Rather than get involved with a lawyer "who probably wouldn't do you any good anyway," most people accepted
these difficulties as inevitable. "After all," they would say,
"just about everything is crooked anyway."

Barry and Bobbi had an experience getting taken when
they were buying their house. Like most couples, they wanted
to buy a house and settle down. Walt had allowed them to
take over payments on a house he and Bobbi's mother were
living in, and for a while things for Bobbi and Barry were

going all right. They bought new furniture and a new washing machine—naturally, all on credit—and were managing to meet most of the monthly payments. However, as the bills gradually began to pile up, Bobbi and Barry found themselves in a bind. Bobbi described what happened:

> You see, Barry and I were buying the house. We had two mortgages on it. One was with Security Exchange and the other was with Equitable Mortgage. And our payments were a hundred thirty a month. Barry got to drinking, couldn't keep the payments up. Mostly it was that we went into debt way over our heads. We went and bought new furniture after Mom and Daddy moved out, a new TV, we bought a washing machine. We had aluminum siding put on. And we were so far in debt, like, you pay fifty dollars here and fifty dollars there. We just couldn't keep up all the payments. And then we heard this thing they were advertising where you go to this company and you pay them so much money and they'll take care of your bills for you.
>
> Anyway, they set up a plan where we was to pay them so much a week and they would take care of our bills. If any bill collector called or anything else, they would take care of it. It was fifty dollars a month. They'd take care of our aluminum siding payments, they'd take care of our furniture payments. And they promised that nobody would call us in regard to our bills. So we were paying the damn people that money and the first thing you know we were getting calls from this person and that person. . . . They weren't getting paid and they were going to sue us, and they were going to do this and that! So Barry went over there and we come to find out they ain't done a damn thing! We're giving them money and they ain't doing nothing. We gave them about four hundred dollars, and they didn't pay any of those bills.
>
> So stupid us, we didn't think there was anything we could do. I wanted to do something, but Barry said, "No, ain't nothing we can do." And then this was when our aluminum siding got behind two months. First thing you know the FHA calls me and tells me they're going to put a foreclosure on our house. Like I ain't got enough headaches! They made an appointment for Barry and me to go

up there and see them. So we went up there and the FHA man wanted to know how come we hadn't made no payments. Barry told them we'd been paying these people. So, we didn't pay them no more money, but we never did get our money back either.

We figured we couldn't make the payments on nothing, and it just seemed like everything was crowding in. We had a gas bill around a hundred dollars. They cut the gas off. Oh, I went to stay with Daddy with the kids, and Barry went down to his mother's and stayed down there. We left everything in the house when they cut the gas off. And then Barry's mother gave him the money to put the gas back on, which we did, but we were so far back we couldn't catch up. And Barry, he really didn't give a damn. After Daddy paid three hundred dollars at one time and bought all new venetian blinds and everything for the house, Barry just . . . he just gave up. This is what he said to me, "I got too many bills on my back, and I just want to get rid of the whole stinking mess." We owed on our car, we owed a loan, we owed for furniture, we owed the house payment, we owed the hospital. We just had so damn many bills on us that it was pitiful and we done socked out all that money to this company and they ain't done nothing to help us. Nothing. And Barry was just to the point where he didn't give a damn. The man that we had our notes with, Security Exchange, came over and told us he was going to have us put out. And that scared Barry off.

They come and got my washing machine before Christmas, before anything happened. I only had to pay thirteen dollars a month on it. I had a girl call me and tell me some months later that by legal rights they had no business to take that out and that if I wanted that machine back she would get it back for me. She said that they were supposed to have sent me a letter informing me that they were going to take the thing back, which they never did.

So we said, bullshit, get the goddamn hell out of this place. We threw up our hands and walked out of that goddamn house and never came back. Hell, we left just about everything we had in that house. We didn't want to see the place again. And we never heard from the

FHA people or anybody else. They got our house and everything in it. I guess they sold it or something. People said we was crazy because the house, well hell, was worth fifteen thousand, and we never saw a penny of it. And of course we lost our credit. And now we can't get a loan anywhere. Well, that was how we blew it.

Although many families had had various experiences dealing with the larger society, experiences in which they felt they had gotten a bad deal, few had suffered as blatant an injustice as had Barney, Sam's forty-two-year-old younger brother.

June at first described Barney as "sort of mentally retarded," but I soon learned he was diagnosed as a paranoid schizophrenic, who was incapable of working and who had spent eleven years in the state prison for the criminally insane. In the spring Barney explained why he spent those years in prison:

> You see, I got in trouble with the Army in 1946. I was home on leave, and then I got AWOL and ran out of money and wanted to get back to my camp. I was staying with my sister, Flora, at the time—Flora and her first husband. He was drinking and I was trying to find out how to get back, back to my camp. And so we decided to go and try to rob an inn, you know, a hotel. And we did that, but they caught us. My handprint. I cut my hand and I left my handprint on the door and they tracked me down. All we got was seventy-two fifty. But that was enough. The Army gave me a bad-conduct discharge and then turned me over to the civilian authorities and they gave me five years. And I served five years in the state prison. It was like a nightmare. I mean the days just dragged on and on. There wasn't nothing to do. That was the first time I ever robbed anything.
>
> After I got out, I moved in with my sister and worked on her farm, then did some farming work for big farms up in New York State. Then I was an elephant boy with the circus for a while.
>
> Then in 1954, Roy, this friend of mine, asked me to break into a store with him. He got caught, and since he

was mad at me for not going with him, he swore I helped
him. And you see, I couldn't prove that I wasn't with
him. I didn't have no alibi. And because I had a record,
they got me and didn't get him and they gave me five
years. But I didn't do it. I didn't go with him. I told him
I didn't want to go. I guess that's why he was mad at me.
I don't know. But he got turned loose, and I got five
years at the state institute. I was sentenced to five years
but I got eleven.

You see, once you get in there it's hard to get out.
They've got these doctors and stuff and they say they're
supposed to help you. They have group therapy and they
give you things to do, and when your case comes up
every three years, the doctors, they get up and talk against
you and say how you haven't been helped and how you
need to stay there longer. That's what happened to me.
Each time I'd get up and tell my side of the story and the
doctors would get up and tell their side of the story and
the jury, you know who they listen to, they listen to the
doctors, 'cause the doctors, they're professionals, and me,
well, what am I to know?

I got a lawyer, but the lawyer, he never contacted my
folks or my family and there was never nobody to testify
for me. You see, I was a "defective delinquent," or
something like that, and that's what the institute is for,
defective delinquents. Guys go there for a year and end
up doing eleven or twelve or fifteen. They can't get out.
There's no way to get out. And there are people there for
all kind of crimes—murder and robbery—and they're all
thrown in together. And some of them get lost in there
and never get out. But finally I went to court and I had
a lawyer who contacted June and Sam, and Flora and
Mary and them—they were all there. And they got on the
stand and they talked. They said I wasn't as bad as the
doctors said I was.

Oh, I was fighting like hell to get out of there. I mean
I was fighting like hell. I'd been there eleven years. The
doctors would say this guy's not ready to face society.
Sam and June said that I was. And that did it. For the
first time my family could come. For the first time there
was somebody to get up and speak for me. The first time,
the jury they listened and said that I was right and the

doctors were wrong. You see, I'd written home before, but the word somehow never got around. . . .

Barney's experience only confirmed what many people believed anyway: Society was no damn ˜good. It was controlled by the rich and the powerful who made decisions to help themselves, not the common man. But the world was just this way, most people agreed. There wasn't much you could do to change it. Of course, you could fight it as an individual; and most people, like Barney, did. But few expected things to change or be any different.

While Barney's experience with justice was an extreme case, many people on Clay Street had had problems resulting in what they called "getting screwed." For this reason, few people thought twice about "getting back." For instance, hot merchandise was plentiful on Clay Street. At Christmas, June and Sam gave Sammy a five-speed chopper bike, listing at seventy-five dollars but for which they paid a "friend" thirty dollars. Les gave Phyllis a twenty-one-inch color TV in exchange for a new high-powered automatic rifle, both of which were hot. Les said about half of everything in their house was stolen; and even after Phyllis got convicted for shoplifting, she kept bringing home quantities of questionable merchandise, usually giving most of it away. One afternoon Phyllis was particularly upset because all of the clothes she brought home fit other people better than they fit her. Although few disclosed how they came upon the hot merchandise, they would usually take pride in getting an especially good deal. Having this merchandise was in no way considered dishonest.

My first week on Clay Street I met a young man who without knowing me or anything about me, volunteered with some pride how he increased his regular income:

> "I make a hell of a lot of goddamn money! Like I made sixteen thousand last year, and I'd only been working with this company a year and a half. Working for the Pepsi Cola Company as a salesman, deliveryman, delivering Pepsi Cola."

I said, "Well, that's a lot of money, sixteen thousand."

"Yeah, I made about eight thousand salary, and I stole about eight thousand."

"Oh?"

"Yeah, that's the only way to make a living up here, you earn half and you steal half. Everybody does it. Yeah, I'd been working about a year at some job for about one thirty-five an hour, worked on a milk truck, kept coming up short. See, I was from the South. You know how it is in the South, nobody knows anything. I got up here and I expected people to be straight, and somebody, some guy in this milk company, clued me in. He said, 'Listen, man, keep your eyes open. You'll see how the rest of us make our money. Gotta learn to take a little bit out. Take your share. You work hard, don't you? You take out your cut.' So, that's what I started doing. I saw you could get away with it on a milk truck, and somebody told me it was even a better deal working for Coca-Cola, Pepsi Cola, so I started working a year and a half with Pepsi Cola, and man, I've been rolling it in. Eight thousand. Yeah. Extra, that ain't bad, is it?"

"No," I said, "that's not too bad. How do you go about doing something like that?"

"Well, all you do is don't sell your customer everything you say you're selling, and you charge him for it. Hell, nobody ever counts. Say you're delivering fifty crates of Pepsis, and you leave forty-five. Let's see, now, five dollars a crate, that's twenty-five dollars in your pocket. Hell, nobody knows the difference. Customers don't ever care, especially the big customers, they hardly ever count. If they do count, you say, 'Oh, I made a mistake, sorry.' You know, everybody does it. It's nothing to it. I'm always going to stay in this business, I tell you, I'm always going to stay in sales. That's where the money is going to be made, in sales. It's that way in every business. I just quit Pepsi Cola. I ain't going to work there any more. I'm thinking about getting me another job. I'm thinking about Seven-Up, but I tell you, I made some good money working for them."

Breaking the law did not necessarily carry a stigma. No one looked down on Barney or Larry because they had served time, or Phyllis when she was convicted of shoplifting. On the contrary, serving time or having a run-in with the law was something some men bragged about. Al, for instance, had served time on more than one occasion and talked about these experiences with considerable enthusiasm. He said he prided himself on being a number one troublemaker, or "bad ass," as he called himself. When he left Washington, he met up with a guy who told Al how easy it was to write bad checks:

> Well, I had never wrote a bad check in my life. But one day he says, "I'll show you how easy it is." He had a daughter about twelve or thirteen, and he carried her as a front for himself; and he cashed about five to six hundred dollars' worth of checks that day. To me that looked like easy money so I thought I'd try my hand at it. At the time I was going with a girl from Florida, who was a registered nurse; and I wasn't making big money. I had an old Chevrolet car. I told her about the setup. She said try it. So I went off that day, her and I, looking well kept; and I didn't have no problems at all. That day I think I got in fifty dollars, something like that. What we would do is go to a bank and get a bankbook, in my own name. I didn't think I could forge anybody else's name complete with driver's license, registration card, etc. I'd go into a store and write out a check and tell them I'd just moved into the neighborhood. I'd find a house that was for sale and give that address, saying I'd just bought a house around here. He was looking at her rear end, he wasn't looking at me or my goddamn check. So first thing you know he'd say, "Why certainly, I'll take your check. What do you want?" I'd write a check for fifteen dollars and buy five dollars' worth of groceries.
>
> About that time I'd picked myself up an Oldsmobile, a big one. I had so many groceries, her and I, and so much money, that the car was full, and the back end was sagging down in this big ninety-eight Olds. Found someplace to sell the groceries.
>
> But that finally caught up with me. I had some real bad luck. I had written checks for seven thousand dollars in Virginia and Maryland. We decided to break off for a while and spend the money. So I went down for a brand-new Oldsmobile, and I paid cash for it. We decided to

start off for Florida. The fellow who had been running checks with me, he was in a Pontiac in back of me. So I wanted a drink. There wasn't no need to write a bad check no more. It's just—it had gotten in my blood by then and there was this big grocery store. I didn't need no groceries and I didn't need no money. But I just had that feeling that I had to hang another one. So I went in the store, wrote off another check, got some groceries, and went back to the car. When we got into Richmond, we checked into a motel. Meantime, I had a picture of her and I've got all this goddamn money, bunches of hundred-dollar bills. So I put the money behind the picture in the frame and put the picture in a foot locker. I had three or four traveling bags and she had luggage herself. Went down to this tourist motel and him and his daughter got a cabin; and this girl and me messed around for a while, and me and her went off.

When I come back to the tourist camp, I found that he had took off with all of my luggage, all of her luggage, everything, all the money. I had just two hundred dollars in my pocket. So we figured we had enough to get to Florida. And maybe we'd catch him on the way down there. So we were heading down the Petersburg Pike; and a tractor trailer, loaded down with something, swung out of a driveway, and his left front wheel drove right up onto the right front wheel of my car. The tractor turned over on the car. It killed her and busted me all up. I didn't know it, but my insurance was no good in that part of Virginia because I had been arrested one time a while back for driving drunk.

So I didn't get nothing for the car. My insurance company paid ten thousand dollars to her family, but the trucking company blamed me and gave me a year in jail for involuntary manslaughter. I wasn't supposed to drive in that area, see. It was his fault, the trailer jackknifed. But anyway, they blamed me for it, and 'cause of my record I didn't have a chance.

In the meantime, I'm wanted in Maryland and Virginia for bad checks. So they put me in a cell and by myself. Next morning I go to court. He said he would give me fifteen days on each check, to run concurrently, which means fifteen days would clean the whole thing. So I did fifteen days for seven thousand dollars' worth of bad checks.

On the twelfth day I was in, they called me up right after lunch and put me in isolation. Maryland had a hold on me. A smart cop up there says, "I know you're going to sign these extradition papers."

"I am, like hell," but I signed them to come to Washington and I ended up serving three years, those bastards!

"The world screws you, so you screw the world. If you can take your cut and not get caught, go to it, Jack," one person once explained to me. "Everybody is dishonest; the only difference is some of us get caught." This is not to imply that people on Clay Street participated in wide-scale crime. To my knowledge they did not. What is important is that they condoned what stealing did take place and did not place a stigma on those who got caught. Most important, they perceived buying hot goods as "getting a good deal" or a "fair deal." Furthermore, they never stole from each other but from "big shots"—employers, department stores, the government.

Because of various run-ins people had with the police, or "the law" as Grammaw called them, there was a general disrespect for law enforcement officers as well as for other representatives of the Establishment such as politicians, professionals, and social workers. Police, like politicians, were considered corrupt. Often people would make such statements as, "For a cop, he ain't so bad," or "Well, what do you expect from a cop?" or "He's just another stupid, dumb-assed cop. . . ." While Clay Street was in a community that had its own nine-man local police, few people on the street had anything good to say about the police force. Most people said that it, like most police departments, was no good.

At the same time, many of the police officers were known by name; many lived in the community and many were generally well liked. And in handling marital squabbles or drinking cases, they often knew the people involved and managed to cool the situation without making arrests. For instance, at least several police officers knew Barry and on more than one occasion responded to a complaint by suggesting that Barry and his friends not make "quite so much noise." Usually Barry would comply. Barry said he liked two of the policemen especially.

In other words, hostility was expressed toward police on general terms as representatives of the Establishment; but in this particular neighborhood, because many of the policemen were neighbors, they were viewed as individuals first and policemen second. Some were disliked and some were liked. They weren't seen as being much different from anyone else, no better and no worse. For this reason, the police who acted "uppity" or like "snot noses" were the most despised. The breakdown in communications between the people and the police one finds in many ghetto areas was not present on Clay Street. On Clay Street the police *were* the people, with many of the same foibles and problems that everyone else had.

Although there was some ambivalence on the part of the hard living families on Clay Street as to their place in contemporary American society, the feelings of being alienated tended to surface quite regularly. They were not part of middle America or the "silent majority," allegedly content with preserving the status quo. Rather they were the forgotten Americans—people who felt isolated and left out, people who felt scorned and looked down on by whites more affluent than themselves. Called "rednecks" by white liberals and by many of the professionals they occasionally came in contact with, they felt confused and bewildered as to who they were. Moreover, they were accused by the press and by onlookers of being "racists" and "bigots" only because in their view they did not want their local school closed or because they were wary of blacks moving in or were afraid of losing their jobs to blacks. They did not understand this hostility toward them. They did not understand why they were considered the obstacle to "progress." They did not understand why they could not receive decent treatment from government and receive adequate legal help and medical attention at reasonable costs.

Many people expressed to me that all they wanted to do was live their own lives, that they really did not want help, but when times got tough, they felt cheated and ignored by gov-

ernment. "All government wants to do is help niggers," Bobbi
said, "but what about us? Why doesn't anyone care about
us white folks? It just ain't right. It's one helluva world."

Rootlessness: "I'm Moving On"

> This is our house. But I wouldn't say as what we're set-
> tled here permanently.
>
> BARRY SHACKELFORD

Few hard living families on Clay Street considered themselves permanently settled. Relatively speaking, June and
Sam, who had lived in their apartment four years, were among
the senior residents. Yet June and Sam were not rooted by
any means, for June in fact talked frequently about leaving
Sam. Besides June's intention of leaving, there was little talk
about the future.

Bobbi and Barry, of course, were not settled either. They
were forced out of one house and had no plans for the future
except for Bobbi's desire to leave Barry. In their eight years
of marriage they had lived in ten houses. They started off in
Bobbi's parents' apartment near the Shackelfords' current
residence, then moved to a large apartment in an old house
a few blocks away. Then they moved into the house Walt
bought and assumed payments. These moves occurred during
the first year of their marriage. They lived in the house they
were buying for two years, then walked out on it and moved
into another apartment. When Bobbi's mother died, they
moved in with Walt for a few months after which they set off
to Richmond where they lived for a year and a half. When
they returned, they spent a few months living with Barry's
father, then located on Clay Street where they lived for a year
and a half. Regarding their plans to remain in their current
house, they had none. During the summer Bobbi was sure
they were going to be evicted any day, at which time they
would have to move on.

The house the Shackelfords vacated on Clay Street became
occupied almost immediately by a large family who had just
moved from West Virginia. The husband worked as a meat
cutter for a local supermarket and the wife sold Sarah Coven-

try jewelry. After living on Clay Street for several months, one morning they mysteriously packed all their belongings and disappeared. (Among other things, they left with orders for several hundred dollars' worth of jewelry, which they never delivered.) The house was then rented to another large family whom few people got to know before the wife took three of their six children and disappeared.

Jack, a truck driver, moved out during the year after living on Clay Street just fourteen months. He said that he hated city life and found a place farther out in the country. Fred and Tammy Jamison moved into Jack's house, having previously lived in a mobile home in the country, which they had to give up after getting behind in their payments. After Tammy ran off with the D.C. Outlaws, Fred was considering moving again. The Grizzards moved three times over the course of the year; and during the summer Phyllis and Granny moved out to unknown whereabouts. Larry's stay, of course, was the shortest of all, only three weeks.

Arlene and Les, during their five years of marriage, had lived briefly in an apartment in D.C., then in a mobile home in the country (where they met Tammy and Fred), then in an apartment on Clay Street, and for the last three years in a house in a newer suburb. But toward the end of the summer when Arlene was with Lonnie, Les was talking about giving up the house and "cutting loose." Ruby and Randy lived in three different houses over the year; and when at the end of the summer they had separated, Ruby was living temporarily with Herb, Dora's ex-boy friend, along with Lonnie and Arlene. And Ted started the year off living with Peg on her first husband's farm. He moved to West Virginia, came back, and returned to West Virginia. He lived with June and Sam for a while, Peg's uncle for a while, Les and Arlene for a while. Ted even lived with Phyllis for a few days. One was never sure who was living where or with whom.

Other families came and went on Clay Street without my getting to know them. Of the ones who stayed, however, few saw their present location as permanent. Rather, they were staying there "for the time being" and were uncertain of their future plans.

Younger men and women who prided themselves on their mobility, when they became older, often sought stability and security. Some people, such as Sam, were able to achieve some security. Others were not. Phil Gray, for instance, lived in the neighborhood and worked for the city, cleaning the streets and collecting garbage. One afternoon when we were talking, Phil explained his predicament:

Well, I'll tell you about me. I don't make a goddamn. I make two forty an hour. That's what I make, and I'm thirty-eight years old. Now, how in the hell can a man live on that? How in the hell can a human being live on that wage? It ain't easy! It's not that I'm not trying to better myself. I've just finished getting back from the job training down there on Route One. Those sons of bitches tell me that I'm too old to be retrained. And that's not the first time I've been told that. I've been told this too many goddamn times. That I'm too old. I'm thirty-eight years old and twenty-six is their goddamn cutoff. Shit. Thirty-eight years old, and I can't get another job. Why don't they give a man a chance? That's all I want is a chance. I'm ready to settle down. Hell, I've had twelve jobs, something like that. I'm ready to settle down. I want a trade, something I can stick with and make—you know, and go somewhere with, and make more than two forty an hour ten years from now. That's all I want. Now is that asking too much? Just tell me, is that asking too much?

Shit, I've got three kids, but I can't support them. They are in foster homes. I had to farm them out. I don't even know really where they are. And I tell you, it's been bothering me. I wouldn't tell anybody that, but it's been bothering me, that's what. It's really been getting to me lately. I told myself, I don't want to see happen to them what's happened to me. I want to see their lives made into something, and I don't have a say in how they are brought up. I want them to get religion, that's what I want to see. I want to see them brought up in a religious home, and let me tell you, that's not happening. They ain't getting religion. And the same thing that is happening to me is going to happen to them. And there ain't a damn thing that I can do about it. I want to make enough money so that I can support them and help them, help them make something of their lives. I'd also like to get me a decent car so I could go somewhere and live in a house that is worth a goddamn. That's all I want.

And two forty an hour, shit. Well, I tell you, I've been with this motherfucking job for two years. Two years. Well, I couldn't take no more of this shit so I quit two weeks ago and I set out to get me a new job, anything. Well, I'm back now, 'cause I couldn't get me anything, nothing. There just ain't nothing for a feller like me.

Phil Gray, like many on Clay Street, had moved from job to job and from apartment to apartment. Because his employment was unsteady, he was unwilling and unable to commit himself to living in one place. For many, the impermanence of their place of residence was interrelated with impermanence in other aspects of their lives. In other words, instability in one area usually contributed to instability in another. For instance, a job loss often intensified marital strain, leading to separation or divorce. Marital strain often led to more drinking, days missed from work, and a job loss. A separation usually meant both partners went in search of new homes, giving up past friendships. A job loss meant failure to pay the rent, an eviction, more marital strain, etc.

Another factor affecting rootlessness was that most of the people on Clay Street never felt much at home living in a city and did not want to think of themselves as permanently settled there. This was not so much the case with people like June and Sam or Bobbi, who, although born in the South (except for Sam), had lived many years in the D.C. area. But it was true of Barry, who wanted to build his own house in the country, and Walt, who wanted "to get back to the land," and many of the families from West Virginia, such as Grammaw, who finally did return to West Virginia.

Though many people remarked that someday they were going to return "down home," few in fact ever did; and when they returned, life proved to be harder than in the Washington area. Barry, Bobbi, and Walt tried going back to Richmond, but it didn't work out. They did not have the job contacts. Carlyle was continually talking about going back to Virginia where his family owned some land, but few people took him seriously. Les said he wanted to go back to West Virginia but knew he would have to work in the mines. What talk there was was mainly talk and nothing more. Most realized that the reason they left home was because life wasn't so good there either.

Many people had relatives who still lived in the South or in the mountains. Sam had a nephew in Florida whom they visited and a sister living on a farm near Manassas, Virginia. Bobbi had cousins living outside Richmond. Most of Carlyle's family lived in Virginia. Ronda Kraft's family lived in Staunton, Virginia, and Duane had a son living in Alabama. Wade had brothers and sisters in the Virginia mountains. Many of Grammaw's children and grandchildren lived in the Beckley, West Virginia, area. Les's parents and one of his brothers lived in Beckley. What family ties existed were toward the rural South or the mountains.

Yet few people on Clay Street felt close to their families. They rarely saw their brothers and sisters, even the ones who lived in the Washington area; and most had some brothers and sisters whom they had not seen for years and did not know if they were dead or alive. For one thing, most were from broken marriages themselves. Also, since they were the ones who for one reason or another left home, they said they felt different from the brothers and sisters who stayed behind. Many described themselves as "black sheep" compared to others in their family. The general pattern seemed to be for families to scatter, with some children remaining on the farm, some settling in the Washington area and others locating out West, moving to northern industrial cities, or just disappearing altogether. While some nostalgia remained for home, there was no real "home" to return to and there were few close family who remained. The people were, in a very real sense, rootless.

There were several side effects of this rootlessness. One had to do with the nature of personal relationships that these people tended to form. There were two basic responses to lack of permanence. One was that a family tended to make few neighborhood contacts and stayed to themselves. This was the case with both families who moved into the Shackelfords' house on Clay Street. Few people knew anything about them. As June said, "They more or less stick to themselves." However, this was perfectly acceptable on Clay Street. Few people resented a family who remained aloof, unless the family tended to look down their noses at their neighbors. A condescending family, commonly referred to as "snot noses," was the worst kind of family to have around. But if a family did not act as if it were superior and still did not wish to participate in neighborhood social life, that was all right. People could be themselves and do their own thing on Clay Street.

Besides the approach of withdrawing from neighborhood contacts, there was another approach—forming very close personal relationships very quickly. Among the hard living families I knew best, this was the basic pattern.

Before I went into the community I was warned by one sociologist that I would have a very difficult time being accepted, that working-class people were very closed, family-oriented, and quite suspicious of strangers. On Clay Street nothing could have been further from the truth. Our first day there, June poured us a pitcher of water, and a few hours later I was joining them in a game of lawn darts. That evening when neighbors dropped over and their children stopped by, we were treated like old friends. "What beer I got here in the fridge is yours," said Sam, "you're always at home here." Acceptance from then on was no problem.

And this was the way it was for most people moving in. Until proven otherwise, a new neighbor was a friend. Phyllis had lived on the block for only a few weeks when she announced that she had adopted June and Sam as her "real parents." After that she spent most of her time at June's. No one seemed to consider this unusual. It was as if they had known each other for years.

Larry showed up in the neighborhood, having met Phyllis at the Bronco the evening before. He moved into her apartment and later was joined by his wife. They all seemed to be close friends after knowing each other only a few days. No one seemed to think it unusual. Over the course of the year such close relationships tended to form between others—Les and Ted; Les and Phyllis; the Shackelfords and Mack and Kate;

Duane, Ronda, and Grammaw; June and Tammy; June and Linda; etc.

Yet while the relationships formed very quickly and were intense, they often ended just as abruptly. When Bobbi moved just a block away, she saw few of her neighbors with whom she felt very close—June, B.J.'s mother, Jack's wife. When Larry disappeared, no one even mentioned it. I had to ask what happened to him to find out. June answered very matter-of-factly, "Oh, him, he's back in jail."

When Phyllis finally left the neighborhood at the end of the summer, she said she would be coming back; but in fact she returned only a couple of times. When Grammaw left for West Virginia, everyone seemed to accept it as inevitable, and there was little talk about it after her departure. When Tammy left Fred for the D.C. Outlaws and withdrew from neighborhood life, no one said much or thought much about it. The transitory nature of human relationships seemed to be an accepted fact. The feeling was that you have a close friendship, but when it's over, it's over. This is the way life is.

While I was astonished that Bobbi could terminate a life-long relationship with Al or that Al and Barry could go through the ritual of a duel, no one else seemed to think this highly unusual. When Arlene and Ruby moved into the home of a man they hardly knew, no one seemed surprised, nor was anyone surprised that Phyllis and Les, or Ted and Les, or Mack and Barry could be best friends one week and claim they hated each other the next. No one seemed to think it unusual that Duane and Ronda and the Mosebys, who used to be great friends, no longer spoke to each other. (June and Sam said the reason was that Duane and Ronda had become snobs.) And so it went. New people would appear in the neighborhood, be treated like old friends, and disappear without further mention. Lifelong friends would suddenly become enemies.

These relationships were friendships rather than sexual relationships, but the same pattern prevailed here as discussed in the section on marital instability. Ted had known Peg only a short while before they were married; Anita, only two weeks before he asked her to marry him. Arlene was sure she was going to marry Lonnie, having known him only a few weeks. These relationships, too, often had a pattern of forming very quickly and intensely and stopping abruptly. Suddenly, for one reason or another, you were no longer friends, lovers, or husband and wife. Human relationships were warm and intense but not permanent.

Another side effect of rootlessness had to do with the nature of community participation. Few hard living people belonged to any formal groups or clubs. They rarely attended church, PTA, or belonged to civic or social clubs. A few such as June and Sam were members of a bowling league, though the Mosebys both expressed their misgivings about participating in such a rigid and formal activity. Arlene said the reason she did not think of joining anything was that she did not want to get tied down. June and Bobbi Jean both had similar views —they had too much on their minds and too many other things to do besides go to meetings. That kind of participation just did not make any sense to them.

Similarly, there was relatively little interest in local community affairs. The following incident occurred early in the fall:

> Shortly before noon, when I noticed that Sam was out changing the oil in June's car, I wandered out to talk to him. Soon Sam's neighbor, Mr. Cates, and Carlyle had wandered up, and Arlene and Les pulled up in Arlene's VW. So as Sam, Les, Mr. Cates, Carlyle, and I stood around talking, a Chevy station wagon drove up and stopped in front of us, and out stepped the town mayor. He walked over to Mr. Cates and casually mentioned that he was doing what he could to get the junk removed from the yard across the street. (There was an old car, some bedsprings, and some other odds and ends accumulating.) Mr. Cates said that he knew the guy who owned the house and that he was simply using the vacant lot as a place to store and sell the junk. The mayor remarked that it was against zoning regulations, and besides, it was a disgrace to the neighborhood. Sam and Carlyle shrugged their shoulders. After assuring Mr. Cates that he was working on the problem, the mayor looked at Mr. Cates and said, "Tuesday's the big day, Fred."

Fred said, "Yeah, Tuesday. Election day, I guess I'll have to vote."

Repeating how important it was for people to vote, the mayor hopped in his car and pulled off.

As soon as he left, Sam asked, "Who was that sonofabitch anyway?"

Fred Cates laughed, saying, "Who was he? He's the mayor! That's who he is."

"Goddamn! You mean we got a mayor in this town?"

"Hell yes, we've got a mayor. And that was him. Mayor Jackson."

Carlyle said, "Well, I've never heard of him."

Les shook his head and said, "Well, I never heard of him either, but course I don't live here."

Sam said, "Well, I'll be goddamned. A mayor. Goddamn. And that sonofabitch was the mayor!"

Few took an active interest in community affairs, but there were exceptions. One issue aroused the interest of June and Bobbi and even Sam—the closing of their neighborhood school. During the early fall, the county school board decided the elementary school that served Clay Street should be closed down and its students merged with a larger school several blocks away. They said their decision was based on two considerations: (1) that it was more desirable from an economic standpoint to expand the newer elementary school rather than remodel the neighborhood school which was old and in need of repair and (2) that it was more desirable from a social standpoint to merge the two schools thus creating a more even racial balance. (The school serving Clay Street had a 10 per cent black enrollment while the newer school had about 20 per cent.) Consequently, the school board announced their plans and called for a public hearing.

When the word reached Clay Street about the closing of the school, people were furious, including June and Bobbi. "They can't do it," June said. "That's a wonderful school and we won't let them close it." Both June and Bobbi turned out for the public hearing as did most of their neighbors who had school-age children. The protest was so strong throughout the community that the County Commission eventually vetoed the school board's decision.

The hard living families were not against community involvement per se. It was just that they felt few community issues affected their lives and few community groups offered them much. The school issue was a different matter. Both Bobbi and June liked having a school within walking distance and were willing to join the fight to keep the school open.

Present-Time Orientation: "Today Is That Tomorrow"

Freedom is riding on the back of a big bike.

TAMMY JAMISON

Life on Clay Street was intense, episodic, and preoccupied with the present. Arlene left Les "for Lonnie and a good time." Tammy left Fred for about the same reasons. Most people seemed to be involved almost entirely with immediate day-to-day problems of living, especially problems having to do with human relationships.

Some families were present-time oriented out of necessity. The Shackelfords, for instance, were practically overwhelmed with the task of making it through the day. Continually faced with the problems of getting the children fed, taking care of Walt, paying the overdue bills, Bobbi had little time to think about the future. The future seemed unpredictable, uncertain, and not very promising. Most of the time it was safer and more realistic to try not to think about it at all. "After all," Bobbi once told me, "sure, I'd like to change things. I'd like to leave that old sothead. I'd like to move into a nicer place with more room. But if there ain't no place to go, how am I gonna do it?"

Bobbi was in many respects imprisoned. Though she was not happy with her current situation, she could see no viable way of changing it. The social worker suggested to Bobbi that she should weigh alternatives. The solution, the social worker concluded, was for her to leave Barry. The problem was that no housing was available for Bobbi to move into and, equally important, Bobbi loved Barry. She was trapped. Since there was little she felt she could do to affect her own future, it did not make sense to her to try to "plan ahead" or "choose alternatives." At one point Bobbi told me she had opened a small savings account to put money in so that she would have enough to pay the first month's rent when she left Barry. The next week Bobbi withdrew the entire $13.57 to buy milk and food.

For the Shackelfords every day was a new crisis that had to be dealt with, leaving no time to deal with the future. This was not the case with June and Sam, who had sufficient income to avoid the daily crises of the Shackelfords. Consequently, both June and Sam were more concerned about the future, especially about their retirement. Since Sam did not have a pension plan at work, June tried to put a little into savings each month. At the same time, since her children were continually needing financial assistance, June was unable to save very much. "Everything is okay now with us moneywise," she said. "But if anything was to happen to Sam, like if he was to lose his job or something, we'd be back in the poorhouse. So I try not to think too much about it. . . ." For June and Sam, too, the future was uncertain and it was easier not to give it a great deal of thought. During the spring, when June said she had decided to leave Sam for good, this added another dimension of uncertainty. "That's why we don't buy a house," she said. "We're too old and things are always so up in the air."

While one aspect of a present-time orientation toward life had to do with a general uncertainty about the future combined with an abundance of daily problems, another aspect had to do with a philosophy of getting the most out of life now. Alton Short was a strong proponent of the "live for today" attitude. One day at the Shackelfords he was talking about how he believed in investing his money in houses and lots.

"Oh," I said, "you mean real estate."

"Shit no, man," Al replied, to the delight of Barry and Bobbi, "whore *houses* and *lots* of whiskey." On another occasion he commented, "The way I see it you got to live hard now, 'cause the devil's gonna get you when you die and you're gonna burn in hell."

People like Alton, Arlene, Larry, Lonnie, and Mack bragged about their hard living. As far as they were concerned, the future was now. Saving, planning for the future, and self-denial were associated with a dull, unexciting life. Whatever rewards these sacrifices might yield were not worth the effort. Rather "you should live now before the devil gets you."

At least this was the philosophy some people expressed upon occasion. At other times, however, practically everyone expressed a completely different view. Barry, for instance, who bragged about "raising more hell" and being "the meanest, orneriest so and so around," also frequently expressed feelings of personal failure. What he wanted to do more than anything else was settle down and live a stable life. His dream was to buy some land out in the country, build a house, and feed and clothe his children. Mack talked about wanting to stop drinking and get a job; Bobbi talked about how she wanted more room so she could keep a good house; and June talked about how more than anything else she wanted Sammy to finish high school. Ted's dream was to rid himself of Peg, marry a good girl, and have a stable job. In the midst of her leaving and returning to Les, Arlene kept saying how she wanted to save her marriage, how she wanted children, and how she wanted to be a good wife.

In other words, while occasionally people bragged about dramatic, intense experiences, at the same time these people did not consciously pursue a hard living, intense life. On the contrary, the hopes and dreams they expressed to me were more frequently for just the opposite—to settle down and live a stable life. The gap between thought and action, however, was quite apparent in the course their lives took during the year. While people said they wanted one thing, they tended to do almost the exact opposite. For instance, from listening to Bobbi talk about cleaning her house and getting her children ready for school, often I was impressed by how her speech—except for the occasional punctuation with four-letter words—could be interpreted as sounding like the speech of the stereotype housewife. Her life style, however, was a far cry from the stereotype. While Arlene said she wanted to be a "good girl," she did just the opposite.

While the gap between words and deeds was great, so was the gap between their dreams and their ability to achieve these dreams. Most people considered themselves "ordinary, typical

Americans" and as such were entitled to all the things "ordinary, typical Americans" were entitled to—the ranch house, the fancy car, the color TV, the dish washer. Young families, especially, were quite conscious of the need to have these symbols of being a typical American. Arlene and Les had all these things, as did Tammy and Fred. The first thing Ted talked about after his engagement to Anita was getting new furniture. Bobbi and Barry once were buying a house. The problem was, however, that acquiring these symbols came at quite an expense for many of these families, an expense that, among other things, created excessive strain on marital relationships. Monthly payments were such that there was no money left for anything else. This, combined with other problems at home or at work, was often enough to cause an Arlene or a Barry or a Tammy to say: "The hell with it. I can't take this shit no more. I'm cutting loose and having my fun now." Given the fact that by playing by the rules it often seemed impossible to be an "ordinary, typical American," people opted for a life style almost exactly the opposite of what they said they wanted —an intense life style, dramatic and present-time oriented.

Individualism: "Pride in What I Am"

> Yep, I've had some hard times in my life, but I'll tell you this—I ain't no worse and I ain't no better than the next guy.
>
> CARLYLE JAMES

The hard living families on Clay Street had a strong sense of individualism. They valued independence and self-reliance. Most people called themselves "loners," having little use for clubs or organizations. "I like to do things *my* way," Carlyle James told me, "even if it means taking just a little longer." In short, the hard livers were not organization men.

Individualism manifested itself in various aspects of their lives: in the clothes people wore (Barry's trademark was his red stocking cap and plaid shirt; Sam's, his blue work shirt; Les's, his western shirts); in the language they used; in the cars they drove (Barry's beat-up truck and homemade camper, Sam's dented New Yorker, Les's pin-striped Camaro). Individualism was particularly strong in regard to their attitudes toward work. For the most part, the hard living men shunned factory work, which they considered dull and routine. Viewing themselves more as craftsmen, they were proud of their abilities and skills. Sam, for instance, was quite proud of his skill as a front-end mechanic. Upon occasion June referred to him as a "master technician," the wording that appeared on a gold-plated set of tools Sam was awarded "for excellent work." Sam would blush and reply, "Shit, I ain't no goddamn 'master technician,' just an old front-end man—but a pretty good one." Similarly, Bobbi described Barry's work as "interior decorating." Barry would say, "Well, Bobbi calls me an interior decorator. Actually, I'm sort of a Jack-of-all-trades—plasterer, painter, carpenter, paper hanger—you name it and I'll do it." Wade described himself as a "helluva fine cabinetmaker"; Duane Ford, a "damn good car painter." Even Carlyle James called himself a "Jack-of-all-trades" rather than a janitor, which some people might have called him.

In other words, the men had skills, which both they and their wives were proud of. Of course, there were some— like Les or Ted or Randy—who lacked skills. Most of these men at one time or another hinted they would rather be doing something else. Ted said he regretted leaving the telephone company. Randy wanted to learn how to be an electrician, and Les remarked several times that he wished he could do something else besides drive a truck. Having a skill was an important goal, which most young men tried to pursue.

Crazy Ed, "Les's friend from the West Virginia caves," as June called him, was a young man who at age seventeen came to Washington with no skills. By the time he was twenty-two he was an accomplished welder, making as much as seven dollars an hour. He took several weeks off every year during hunting season to return to West Virginia to hunt and trap. One day at June's, Ed described how he was able to learn a trade:

> Ah shit, I came up here four years ago. Hadn't finished high school. Just seventeen years old. I knew I had to get me a job, so I went to work for a big lumber company. Told them I was a maintenance man. Shit, I didn't know nothing about maintenance. I didn't know

nothing about anything. They had all this machinery
and construction stuff. I told them I knew how to take
care of it. Shit, I didn't know how to do that. But hell, I
knew I had to learn how to do something. So they hired
me. And all the time I was there, see, I just watched this
welder. I knew welders made good money and so I
watched him work, and I'd say, "Hey, man, how do you
do that?" and he'd show me, and I'd say, "Let me try,"
and he'd show me how to do it.

Hell, I wasn't doing no maintenance, not very much.
I was watching the sonofabitch welder all the time. And
he let me weld more and more, and hell, I learned how
to weld. And shit, as soon as I learned enough how to
weld, I quit that goddamn job. I went to work for another place. They asked me what I could do, and I said
I was a welder.

"How do we know you're a welder?"

"I don't know if I can weld as good as you city dudes,
but shit, I can weld! Had my own truck back in West
Virginia."

So they said, "Hell, come on. We'll give you a try."

Well, I wasn't the best welder then, but I learned how
to be a pretty good goddamn welder. Made some mis-
takes at first, but goddamn, I wasn't there but four or five
months, and I was welding like a sonofabitch. But I realized there wasn't a helluva lot of money to be made
there as a welder so I said I'd go to work for a goddamn
steel company and really make me some money. So shit,
I left that place and went to work for a goddamn steel
company, and I get paid seven dollars and two cents an
hour, on federal jobs, and we do mostly federal jobs.
Seven oh two an hour! Goddamn. And they know I'm
a good welder now, so I work for four or five months
and save me up some money and go down to West Virginia. Then I come back and work some more, and they
haven't fired me yet. They tell me, "We know that you
can find another job; we'll keep you on as long as you do
good work for us."

And I said, "Shit yes, I'll work for you as long as you
don't give me a hard time."

Like Crazy Ed, many of the men were self-made. They had
dropped out of school very early, usually after the eighth or

ninth grade, and had managed to learn a skill, like Ed, by using their wits.

Duane Ford, who was in his mid-fifties, had started off like Ed. He grew up in a small town on the border of Tennessee and Alabama, quitting school after the eighth grade. After doing odd jobs farming, truck driving, and working at gas stations, at age twenty-four he came to Washington. He worked for a few years in a service station when one day a friend gave him some advice. Duane said he would never forget what the man told him: "Listen, sonny, if you are gonna make it in this city or anyplace, you got to get yourself a job that you can do well. Now, take me, I'm a painter; and 'cause I can paint, if some sonofabitch pushes me around, I can quit and work for somebody else. You got to get you a job you can do so nobody pushes you around." Duane learned to be an automobile painter and painted automobiles for twenty-five years.

Having a job skill was important because the work itself was more rewarding than unskilled work, because the jobs paid more, and because a skill gave a person more independence. Most men, for instance, expressed the desire to be their own boss. For this reason subcontracting was popular. Barry, when he worked, was his own boss. Though Sam worked for a Dodge dealer, being a specialized mechanic meant he had a certain amount of independence. Other jobs such as plumbing, electrical repair, and even truck driving were popular because they allowed some independence. The least desirable jobs were factory jobs or jobs where you had to take orders all day and had no freedom. Sam, for instance, was proud of the fact that he could talk back to the boss if he felt like it. "The sonofabitch won't fire me, 'cause he knows he can't find anybody as good as me. I want to call the goddamn shots. I don't want some lousy foreman telling me when I can shit or piss."

Les's friend Bobby expressed a similar view, relating the following incident:

> Now, the guy I work for, that's something, man, he's got his own business. Let me tell you, that's something to have your own business because you can tell people

off. Like just yesterday, some guy comes in and says,
"Hey, I want a fan belt."

And I said, "Okay, here's a fan belt."

And he said, "Well, will it work?"

I said, "Well, I don't know. I guess it will work. Why
not? We sell it, it should work."

"Well, what I mean, will it stay on?"

"Well yeah, it should stay on."

"Well, what I mean is, will it flap?"

Al, the boss, comes up and says, "What is that you
said?"

And the man said, "The fan belt. Are they any good,
the ones you sell here?"

"Goddamn sonofabitch. If you don't like our fan belt,
just cram it up your ass. Get the hell out of our store."

That man, he didn't say nothing. And I said, "Goddamn sonofabitch, get the hell out of our store. You
heard what he said."

The man just shook his head and walked out of the
store. Al treats a lot of people like that. Like just yesterday, day before yesterday, got a telephone call. Guy said
he wanted to return a part. Said it was defective. Second
defective part he'd bought. Al heard about it. "Let me
have that goddamn telephone." Picks it up, says, "Sonofabitch, a defective part, is it? You don't like anything
you buy in this goddamn store. Let me tell you something. You take your business elsewhere. We don't want
it."

Now, that's the guy who is his own boss. That's what
I call really making it.

Arlene expressed a similar attitude. In fact, when she was a
cashier at the supermarket, she got fired for telling off a customer who got smart with her (though when the union complained, she later was rehired). "I just don't like to take any
shit off people. If they talk to me mean, then I talk to them
mean. You got to stick up for yourself."

Wade felt this way, too:

Not taking any shit off anybody. Now, that's one thing
I believe in more than anything else. I won't lick anybody's ass for anything. I'm in business for myself. I

work when I want to on what I want to. I do what I want to, and I don't have to take any crap off anybody else. And if I ever did, if I ever had to brown-nose to get where I wanted to go, I'd say the hell with it. I'd quit. I wouldn't do it. I don't have to do it. I guess I'm lucky. But most of the folks in this country, they do. They have to ass-lick to get where they're going. But I don't believe in that, and I'd take the lowliest goddamn job in society before I'd do that. And I'm damned proud and happy with the job I got. I ain't got no complaints in that regard. I ain't got no complaints. I consider myself pretty goddamn lucky. I'm proud of my work; I do what I want to do when I want to do it. I go where I want to go when I want to leave. I don't have to take no shit off nobody. And that's what I call having a pretty lucky job.

Carlyle, who as a janitor found himself in one of the lowest paying jobs, believed in this philosophy as much as anyone else. "You know," he said, "I think a guy should do what he wants to do. That's what I want to do and what I've tried to do. Okay, so I got to take orders from the super and the owner. Okay, but I don't let 'em push me around. I don't let 'em give me no shit." It was not so much what kind of work you did, although that did make a difference. Rather it was the attitude you had toward your work and your employer. Most people said they would quit or change jobs or take a reduction in pay before they would let a boss or foreman push them around.

Duane Ford led the neighborhood in this regard. Before his eyes went bad, he was skilled as an auto painter who could easily get another job when he got fed up. "Yep," he said, "I used to average four or five jobs a year. If I didn't like the boss, I'd tell him to go to hell and walk out. I don't take no lip." When Duane could no longer paint, he found himself in a difficult situation, though he was finally able to get a job as a truck driver and in three months had changed jobs three times.

Since work was important to most of the men, those who were unable to work had a particularly difficult adjustment. For instance, when Zeek Grizzard hurt his back on a construction job, he found himself drinking more and more. The

following conversation occurred one afternoon in the fall
when Zeek, Carlyle, and I were sitting on Carlyle's stoop:

> "You know," said Zeek, "it's been six weeks since I
> touched any work. Six goddamn weeks, and I haven't
> done a damn thing. Six goddamn weeks. Seems all there
> is to do around this goddamn place is to drink."
> "Jesus, has it been that long?" asked Carlyle. "That's
> a long time."
> "Goddamn right it's a long time, and all I've been
> making is eighty-one dollars a week on unemployment.
> A man can't live on eighty-one dollars a week. Shit, I
> wish they'd get this thing solved. Those bastards owe me
> forty-five thousand. They damn well aren't out to pay it
> quick, but it ain't the money that bothers me."
> "Hell," said Carlyle, "making eighty-one dollars a week
> ain't so bad. I make only sixty dollars a week."
> "Well, it's not the money I'm after. It's my work. I
> just don't feel right without my work. I don't know what
> to do with myself. It's not like me to drink like this. I
> usually don't drink when I've got work to do. But with-
> out my work, hell. I don't know what I'm going to be
> able to do. The doctor said he doesn't know if I'm going
> to be able to work again. Goddamn, I'm fifty-six years
> old. I've got some work left in me. . . ."
> "Yeah," said Carlyle, "I know what you mean. A man's
> got to work."

Since doing "man's work" was important for most men,
there was some contempt expressed for both white collar workers, who really didn't work anyway, and people on welfare.
In regard to white collar work, Crazy Ed expressed most
people's sentiments when, upon finding out I worked for the
government, he replied derogatorily, "Oh, I see, you're a pencil pusher." When I replied that wasn't exactly what I did, he
remarked, "Well, that's what most of them dudes do." On
several occasions Sam commented, "I wouldn't work in no
office for nothin'. Sit at a desk and push some paper around
and then on Saturday you got to go and play golf for exercise.
Hell with it. I get my exercise on the job!" According to one
neighbor, *all* government white collar workers were on "glorified relief."

There was even greater hostility expressed toward those "on relief." Most people believed that everyone should work and that government welfare was wrong. Those receiving welfare, however, usually meant those *blacks* receiving welfare rather than those whites. The fact that few were willing to admit was that the welfare system was often part of their own lives as well. Barney and Mack both received welfare for being permanently and totally disabled. Ruby and Bobbi and Linda received AFDC. Walt received welfare as well as social security. At the end of the summer Phyllis had applied for emergency welfare, as did Duane Ford before he got a job as a truck driver. And of course, the welfare department was the Shackelfords' main source of income during the spring. Once when I asked Barry what he thought about welfare, he replied, "Good God, where would Bobbi and my kids be without it?"

Those families not receiving welfare usually expressed their disapproval of those who did. Les said he thought it was terrible that Ruby was on welfare. Yet for her, as for Les's sister in West Virginia, welfare was not something permanent in Les's view. Rather it was only some "temporary help, to help get them through." The Shackelfords certainly did not view their financial problems as permanent. Once Barry's arm got better and once he got back to work, then welfare would no longer be necessary. Welfare in general was considered bad; and in general those who did not work were considered bad, but not so with specific individuals. Bobbi, Barry, Ruby, Barney, even Mack—these people were different. These people needed some temporary relief.

The apparent inconsistency in the attitudes regarding work and welfare is illustrative of their basic way of viewing the world which distinguished between the general rule and the individual or specific case. Hard living folks on Clay Street had opinions on practically everything—politics, religion, race, national and world affairs. Often they would make sweeping generalizations such as "Everyone on welfare is a bum," or "Niggers ought to go back to Africa," or "Politicians are all crooked," or "Never met an honest preacher." When it came to a specific individual, however, people tended to judge him on his own merits. Here their basic personal, individualistic approach to life prevailed over their feelings about things in general.

Nowhere was this individualistic approach to life more apparent than in their views on class and race. In regard to class, most people agreed that most politicians, white collar workers, executives, professionals, and government officials were at best highly suspect of being purely out for their own interests. At worst the "big boys" were a definite evil force in society. At the same time, George Wallace, a politician, really "tells it like it is," a given employer might be a "great guy," and certain doctors or lawyers, "wonderful people."

In other words, exceptions were as prevalent as the rule. A given personality or individual could be admired and accepted regardless of his social position, just so long as he seemed to be an "okay guy." Being an "okay guy" meant among other things having a likable personality, being honest, kind, and unpretentious. The worst kind of person was a snob, or "snot nose" as Bobbi called them—"somebody who says my shit don't stink, that sort of thing. . . ."

June and Bobbi were both sensitive to being looked down on. June said, "Us folks around here, we're just folks, you know what I mean, just plain folks. Nothin' special. And the way I see it, people are all the same everywhere. It don't make no difference; people are people. It's all the snobs and snot noses who think they are big shots. That's what messes everything up."

June's philosophy of accepting people affected her attitude toward some of the neighborhood who might be considered deviant or strange. These people were "just folks," too, according to June, and should be treated as such. Although Barney created problems for June, she loved him and made him feel a part of the family. While she described him as being mentally retarded or "a little bit off," she and others in the neighborhood did not treat him as if he had a stigma. There were two other men Barney's age, who obviously had mental problems; but both men held jobs and were accepted and liked by the people on Clay Street. One of the men spent many hours on Sam's porch drinking Sam's beer. When I remarked to June that he seemed a little different, she replied: "Well, maybe he ain't all there, but he is a real nice fella." Although Grammaw's fifty-year-old son was retarded, a neighbor across the street had given him a job installing insulation; and, like Barney, he was liked. "We call him Shifty," said Sam, " 'cause he shifts his beer from one hand to the other every time he walks past our house, but he's okay, he's all right."

People were generally tolerant of each other. Even though Sam complained about Phyllis, she remained a fixture in the Moseby household and an omnipresent figure in the neighborhood. People's complaints about Phyllis usually had to do with her personality rather than her lesbianism. In June's words, "What she does with her sex life is her business, not mine." When an occasional disturbance would occur between Bertie and Zeek Grizzard or between B.J. and May Jones, no one said too much about it. "Live and let live," people would say. "What goes on at their house is their business, not mine." As mad as June and Les and Sam got at Arlene, they tolerated her behavior. As mad as Bobbi got at Barry, she didn't leave. As mad as she got at Mack and Kate, she continued lending them sugar. People got mad at each other and expressed their feelings openly. But they made up and they put up with each other through many trying circumstances. Also, old people were not institutionalized but were kept in the home where they were expected to carry their load (indeed, in the case of Walt or Granny, they carried more than their load). On Clay Street a person was accepted as long as he was willing to accept other people and do his part. One neighbor put this very well:

> You know, one thing I like about this neighborhood is the way folks are just folks. Take Carlyle, for instance. Here's a guy who is a janitor, a maintenance man, and yet he's just part of the neighborhood. Nobody looks down on him. Nobody says, "Hey, look. That's a janitor." Carlyle can go anywhere and talk to anybody and is accepted just as a person who lives here. He's just one of the folks. That's what I like about this neighborhood—you're just one of the folks no matter who you are.

Individualism also applied to the question of race. Tolerance was true here as well in many respects, though the issue was complex. On the one hand, admittedly, the people on Clay Street were racists. They used the word "nigger" frequently and talked about "how them niggers are trying to take over everything." They perceived blacks as a very real threat to their jobs, to their neighborhood, and to their position in society. Because of their strong language and of the vocal protests on the part of a few people in the area, the people in their community were described to me by various outsiders—school planners, sociologists, city planners, etc.—above all else as being racists. Quite often the phrase "racists/rednecks" would be used. "Oh, the people who live *there*, well, if you don't mind living with racists/rednecks it will probably be okay," as if this term accurately characterized the entire character of the community.

Granted, the people on Clay Street talked about "how the niggers have ruined Washington," how they didn't like "nigger work" (mindless work), how they didn't like to see "all them niggers laying around and living on welfare." This kind of language bothered me and I am not condoning it. At the same time, however, Sam worked and ate his lunch alongside blacks at his job, blacks he referred to as "good colored, damn nice guys I have a lot of respect for." One of Sammy's best friends was black, and he spent as much time in the Moseby household as did Sammy's white friends. No one ever said anything about it. June carried two black children to school every day when she drove Sammy and did not consider this unusual. Bobbi's son, Billy, came home one day and told his mother he had a new girl friend. When Bobbi found out the little girl was black, she laughed but said nothing more about it. Throughout the year Bobbi praised Cindy's teacher for being such a good teacher. "I really think she is a wonderful person," Bobbi said. "I love that woman." Later in the year when I went with Bobbi to pick up Cindy, I was surprised to discover the woman was black. Barry and Walt both worked with blacks, many of whom they referred to as "damn good guys." Practically every day of the year black children played with white children on Clay Street, with usually about a fourth of the children being black, ranging from preschoolers to teens; and only on one occasion did I hear any racial comments. (Bertie Grizzard was drunk and wanted to know "which nigger hit my car with a football." Zeek Grizzard came out of their apartment, kicked her behind, and dragged her indoors. That was that.)

There is no question that some tension existed between these people on Clay Street and the blacks they saw moving into their neighborhood and competing for their jobs. Yet at the same time tolerance applied here as it did in other areas of their life—tolerance for particular individuals. Everyone made the distinction between "nigger" and "good colored." "Nigger" was like "them welfare people," "crooked politicians," etc.; it applied to a general class of people whom they perceived as a threat to their way of life. But within this class, it was not considered unusual to find decent people. In the case of blacks, decent people tended to be the people they worked with or lived next door to, people whom they called "good colored."

Though people tended to make the distinction between the general rule and the specific case, they seemed to pay far more attention to the specific case in their actual behavior. Personalities were extremely important, and many people tended to view structures and systems in terms of personalities. For instance, Bobbi saw the hospitals her family entered in terms of the doctors and nurses who helped them. She saw the welfare system in terms of the receptionist and her caseworkers. The school system was her children's teachers. In politics issues were far less important than individual personalities. The news people talked about, or expressed much interest in, had to do mainly with individuals—personalities and human interest stories.

Because people were accustomed to dealing with persons rather than with impersonal bureaucracies, they often had difficulties in dealing with large government agencies, large corporations, etc. Dealings with the welfare department were particularly difficult for the Shackelfords, for instance, because until the late spring, when Bobbi was assigned a caseworker, there was no one person concerned about her family and no one person she could go to for help. Various people asked me during the year to help them write letters to collection agencies, doctors, magazine companies, etc., with which they were having problems. Had I not been around to write the letters, they said they would probably have just let things go. Quite frequently people expressed dismay at legal and bureaucratic problems that prevented them from getting unemployment insurance, workmen's compensation, or Medicaid. Often, rather than try to battle a system they could not understand, they decided to quit trying. "The hell with it," said Duane Ford, "if I can't get the workmen's compensation, the hell with it. The government will screw you every time."

Many expressed this kind of frustration throughout the year. They felt it was of little use for a lone individual to battle such an enormous and impersonal system. Rather, as June put it, "You just got to live life the best way you can and just try not to worry about all that mess."

Conclusion

The local junior high school auditorium was about half full. A pretty young blond woman dressed in a pink mini-skirt was standing behind the podium on the stage. Seated behind her were several older men dressed in dark suits. Flowers covered the stage, and hanging from the ceiling behind the podium was a large neon cross.

The young woman spoke with a southern drawl, softly and sincerely, as those in the audience listened attentively. "Yes, as I said before, I can't possibly give my testimony in thirty minutes, 'cause I've done so many bad things in my life, it would take a week to tell them all. You see, I was a run-around. Nothin' but a run-around. I was married but I just wasn't happy. I didn't find in marriage what I wanted. You see, I wanted more than anything else to have a good time. I liked dancing and honky-tonks. Of course at that time I didn't care about church or about Jesus. So I left my husband and my two children and went to work at a bar. I broke just about every commandment there was to break. I was living a life of sin." The stone silence of the audience was broken only by an occasional squeal from an infant and the waving of fans in the humid summer air. The woman continued. "Well, I went on like this for months. I thought I was really having fun until one day I looked in the mirror in the ladies' room in the back of the club where I worked and I saw myself. I saw myself as God saw me and I was so ugly I ran to the phone to call my husband and I pleaded for him to take me back. He said he would, but you've got to understand, it was not the first time I'd left him. I'd done this many times before. . . ." The woman went on to say that after she returned life was still difficult until one day several months later

when her husband was in Vietnam and her baby was sick and
her basement flooded, in desperation she went to a neighbor
for help. "On the coffee table at the neighbor's house was a
Bible," she said, "and my neighbor—her name was Jane, I'll
never forget it—Jane said, 'Here, read this Bible and go to
church with me tomorrow.' I did. And that day, in that church
service, I saw Jesus. It was like Jesus drilled into my skull and
made a hole to let out the steam. That day the demons left
and I have not been the same since. Now my life is totally
different. . . ."

Watching the men and the women in the audience nod at
the end of practically every sentence, I could not help thinking of Arlene and Ruby. The kind of behavior she was describing sounded very much like Arlene's behavior and the religious
experience very similar to Ruby's. Earlier in her testimony she
had mentioned that she had been married before but that that
didn't work out because her husband loved the bottle more
than her. I thought of Bobbi. She concluded her testimony
saying that now her life was straightened out. Her second
marriage had been saved. Neither she nor her husband drank.
They owned their house. Her children were doing well. She
even mentioned that her bowling average had steadily increased ever since she convinced her fellow members to put
the letters PTLJS on their uniforms—standing for "Praise the
Lord, Jesus Saves."

From one perspective, her testimony can be interpreted as
an example of a change from hard living to a restrained, settled life. For her, as for Ruby, Jesus was the answer. Her
conversion to Christianity provided her with a means of rec-
onciling opposing forces in her life, forces that were making
her feel like a pressure cooker. "I was just a reckless run-
around and life didn't make much sense." The nods from
the audience suggested they, too, understood what she meant.

For a number of settled, church-going families, a conversion
to Christianity had radically affected their life styles. Several
families informed me that they used to be "hell raisers, run-
arounds, sorta wild," in their prechurch days. These were
people who had known hard living but who had come to live

a stable, orderly life. The church—especially the Pentecostal Church—offered hard living folks one possible channel for making the transition to settled living.

While religious conversion experiences were the most dramatic, there were other less spectacular ways of changing one's "reckless ways." The most prevalent way was for individuals to "outgrow" hard living. Les, for instance, said he was ready to settle down because he was older, had been around, and had had his fun. The main problem with Arlene, he said, was that she was still too young and had not got it out of her system. When individuals became older, the tendency was to become more settled. June and Sam, for instance, were considerably more settled than their children.

A change in other areas could affect over-all stability as well. When Ted finally got rid of Peg and met Anita, suddenly he began to think of marriage, settling down, and buying furniture. Had Barry been able to stop drinking and work consistently, his relationship with Bobbi might have been more stable. Perhaps someday they would have been able to buy that little place in the country they both dreamed of. In other words, to change from a hard living life style to a settled life style was not impossible. A change in one area—religion, marriage, work—often affected the other areas. Indeed, as in the case of Arlene, Ted, and Tammy, it could affect change in either direction.

Hard living was among other things a way of rebelling against the life circumstances one found himself in. It was as if the individual concluded consciously or unconsciously that there was little to be gained from "fitting in," or from saving for the future. Whatever the future held, it was not worth making the sacrifices. Rather, a person should live for the present and get the most out of life now. If something happened to change those life circumstances—that is, when the individual felt he did have a stake in society, that the future was promising, that there was a place for him—then there was a tendency to save, to be more cautious, to live a more restrained life.

In Arlene's case, for instance, the choice was whether she wanted to live a settled life with Les or have her fun with

Lonnie. She had chosen the former. She had her own car, a color TV, a house; but there was little money left over for anything else. As June put it, something was missing. "Arlene's just not the type to stay home all day and keep house," June said. "She needs something more." Tammy, like Arlene, was not the type to stay home all day. She loved her kids, she said, and she liked the material possessions Fred had bought her, but in her view she was like a prisoner in her own home. Fred was rarely home, spending his off hours drinking with the boys. Tammy rarely left home, since she had no car and had few outside interests. She took it as long as she could. Then she took off with the Outlaws.

Arlene and Tammy rebelled against a life style that was too restrained. They rebelled against a future that seemed to offer nothing besides more of the same. For them it wasn't worth it. June and Bobbi both understood Arlene and Tammy. June once described Tammy as being "cooped up." Bobbi saw Tammy's leaving as a "woman's fling, something every woman would do sooner or later."

For some, hard living was rebellion; for others, it was running away from life's problems. Barry admitted to me on several occasions that he drank more when he had a lot on his mind. "When I'm sober," he said once, "I start thinking about the bills and the job I got to finish and the goddamn truck's bad clutch and that I don't got no driver's license or auto insurance and Bobbi and the kids and the groceries and all and shit—I just got to go across the street and get me some beer." Bobbi told me there was so much she had to cope with, she could never let herself think much about the future. She had to live pretty much each day at a time.

In any event, the episodic, intense life style of these people was essentially an unconscious response. Few people articulated their motives or talked much about how they wanted to live hard. On the contrary, practically everyone at one time or another expressed the desire to settle down, to live moderate, restrained lives. Hard living was in many respects an unconscious response to the pressures and difficulties involved in trying to settle down.

Practically all of the hard living people on Clay Street had close relatives whom they described as "settled," or "well-to-do." Sam had two brothers who owned "nice new brick homes," who had not been divorced, who had steady jobs. Similarly June's sister in Virginia had been married to a farmer for over twenty years and was an enthusiastic member of the Church of God. Bobbi's cousins in Virginia were all "well-to-do," in fact "snot noses," according to Bobbi. And some of Barry's home-owning cousins were stable and upright.

Also many of the settled families mentioned they had brothers or sisters who were "black sheep" or "lost," sisters they had lost track of, or brothers who had gotten into trouble—such as Pete Dale's lost brother, who had spent time in prison.

In other words, the hard living families on Clay Street did not represent a distinct class or group of people, but rather a variation of life styles within the white working class. They were those brothers and sisters who for one reason or another did not settle down. They were the ones who "didn't make it." They were the ones who had marriage problems, drinking problems, perhaps had been in trouble with the law. Yes, their life styles differed considerably from those of their stable brothers and sisters; but while the stable families could point their fingers saying "shame, shame," they also said, "There but for the grace of God go I."

In describing Clay Street, Grammaw's grandson, Buddy, who had lived for a while on Clay Street but had returned to West Virginia, had this to say:

> You know, they are a bunch of drunks up there. A bunch of riffraff, really disgusting. You know, those people up there, it's just terrible the way they act and behave. Just terrible. And the thing that bothers me most is that people see these people, folks from West Virginia, up in Washington, and they think everybody from West Virginia is like that. Well, nothing could be further from the truth, nothing. It just so happens that most of the people who go to Washington from West Virginia are no good. The people who can't make it at home, sort of the lower-class people, they're the ones that leave home. I say good riddance, let them go. But once they get to a place like Washington they make a big mess and don't behave themselves, and everybody thinks that everybody

else from West Virginia is just like they are. That's the bad thing about it all. Well, I don't have any use for those people. The whole thing is rather disgusting.

In describing those families as "no-goods," Buddy was talking about his aunts and uncles and cousins. Unlike them, he got a scholarship to college and became a schoolteacher.

Finally, there was considerable ambivalence on the part of most hard living individuals about their own lives and their place in society. Most of the time June, Sam, Bobbi, and others would talk about themselves with pride. They had lived their own lives, in Barry's words, "the way we damn well pleased." They did not have to make any apologies to anyone. They were ordinary Americans, just plain folks.

At other times, however, they became more introspective. Bobbi and Barry, for example, were not making it. By their own admission their lives were painful and difficult and filled with far more unhappiness than pleasure. Barry was a failure as a husband, father, and breadwinner. In comparison to most of the other families, the Shackelfords found themselves close to the bottom of the ladder. "I'm living in hell," Barry would say frequently when he was drunk, "but I don't know how to get out. . . ." Not "fitting in" or "giving in" had its price, and the price was often high.

Even June and Sam at times expressed regret about their lives. "I just don't want my kids to have the miserable life I've had," June said. "Yet I see the same thing happening." Sam rarely talked about his life except to say, "It ain't all that much. I just don't want to think that much about it."

Others on Clay Street occasionally referred to themselves as "the other half" or "black sheep." Yes, they had been individuals and had led their own life, but for this they had paid a price: broken families, little security, few close family ties, drinking problems, etc. When I asked June if she could live her life over again, would she live it the same way, she paused for a moment, then shook her head. "I don't know," she sighed, "I just don't know."

In this book I have not tried to deal explicitly with the societal causes influencing the hard living behavior on Clay

Street. I have not stated the social causes behind family instability, drinking, alienation, rootlessness, etc. The reasons lie beyond the scope of my data. I am able to suggest that had Barry's father not been an alcoholic, had Barry gotten along with his stepfather, had he not had such an unstable childhood, had he liked school, had his first marriage worked out, etc., then things would have been different. But this does not explain why many people on Clay Street came from broken families, why so few had remained in school, why so many were heavy drinkers or alcoholics. In each case it is relatively easy to guess at the social-psychological reasons for that particular individual's living hard or another individual's choosing settling down, but this tends to obscure the problems having to do with structural and cultural forces. We can say, If only Arlene could have had a baby, if only Barry could have stopped drinking, if only Ted had never met Peg. . . . Raising these questions, however, does not answer the questions why these things happened to the people on Clay Street in the first place.

At the other extreme is the temptation to explain all behavior with sweeping societal generalities. One academic friend responded to my anecdotes on Clay Street by saying, "Oh, I see. These people are rednecks. Well, it is an obvious adjustment problem having to do with rural to urban migration. When you put hillbillies in the city, this is what happens." Another person remarked that it had to do with the class structure. As members of the oppressed working class, these people were taking out their frustrations and hostilities on themselves and each other rather than on their employers. Bobbi's social worker remarked that the main reason for such "reckless, unstable" behavior was a kind of self-perpetuating family instability. A community organizer suggested it had to do with the impermanence and instability of the job market.

I have chosen not to go beyond my observations and suggest what the "real underlying causes" are that foster hard living. My task has been more limited—documenting this life style and suggesting reasons the people themselves give for such behavior. June put it better than anyone else: "You can call us what you want to, but folks around here, hell, we're just plain folks. We got problems like everybody else. Maybe the difference is we don't try to shove 'em all into some closet. That's 'cause we ain't too proud to admit we're just folks." Above all else, the people on Clay Street were "just folks," and their humanity expressed itself in every aspect of their lives. With its many inconsistencies, paradoxes, and contradictions, the humanity of June, Sam, Bobbi, and Barry prevents me from neatly packaging them into a sociological bundle of theories about the social structure of working-class subculture. On the contrary, for me it is quite difficult to see them as anything but themselves. Their humanity touched me, my wife, and my child. For having known them and experienced life with them, I will always be grateful.

Epilogue

I kept in touch with both the Shackelfords and the Mosebys during the year following my stay on Clay Street. For both families life continued in pretty much the same vein.

In the fall Barry left Bobbi for three weeks when he went off to Richmond for a good time with his boss and two women. Bobbi tried futilely to find another apartment during that time; and when Barry returned, she boarded the door shut to try to keep him out. Barry tore the door down. When Bobbi called the police, she was informed that since the lease was in Barry's name, there was nothing they could do. Since Barry continued to drink heavily and work sporadically, their financial situation did not change.

As for the children, Cindy did somewhat better in school, though her ear continued giving her problems. In the spring Billy had an ear operation identical to the operation Cindy had. Bubba made the honor roll in the junior high. He was placed in a special work-study program, which involved going to school in the mornings and working in the afternoons at a car wash near his home.

In June Walt Walters died. He developed gangrene in his leg, went into the hospital for surgery, and never came back home. Bobbi said that he seemed to be doing a whole lot better, then all of a sudden—about ten days after the operation—his heart stopped and he died. She said the doctors told her a clot in his leg went to his heart. Walt was almost sixty-six. The year before, when he celebrated his sixty-fifth birthday, I remember Walt shaking his head and saying, "You know, I never thought I'd live to be sixty-five. . . ." He never regained his eyesight.

Kate died that year. So did her father. Mack disappeared from the neighborhood. In all, Bobbi said she knew eight people in the neighborhood who died. "It was just one of them bad years for dying," she said.

Bobbi finally had her long awaited hysterectomy in the spring of the year. I happened to be visiting on Clay Street two days after she had returned home from her operation. She was in particularly bad spirits that day since Barry was quite drunk and the day before he had hit her in the stomach. When I asked her about any possible malignancy, she shrugged her shoulders, saying, "Well, I don't think there is none. But frankly, I don't know because the doctors ain't told me a thing."

In the fall of 1972 we moved back to Washington; and though we no longer lived on Clay Street, we were able to maintain a close relationship with the Shackelfords. After Walt's death, Barry stopped drinking for a while, "making a real good effort," said Bobbi, "to do better." He did, however, get into an argument with the driver of a pickup truck—while Barry and the other driver were both stopped for a red light —and proceeded to bash the driver over the head with his hammer. The other driver was rushed to the hospital where he received twenty-seven stitches. Barry was arrested and charged with assault with a deadly weapon. In a few days Barry was allowed to go free when the other party—who apparently was drunk at the time—failed to appear for the trial.

During the summer Cindy developed kidney stones due in part, Bobbi said, to too much calcium consumption. She underwent surgery in November and was forced to miss most of the school year. Bobbi remained very worried about Cindy, fearing that more surgery would be required. The doctors had informed her that one of Cindy's kidneys was not functioning at all and that severe problems were involved in the functioning of the other.

In October the landlord, Mr. Brant, informed the Shackelfords he no longer wanted them living in his apartment. Since they never received any formal notice of eviction, they did not take him seriously until the day before Thanksgiving when Mr. Brant appeared with the county sheriff and four "moving men." Bobbi said the sheriff gave her exactly seven minutes to get dressed and get all her possessions together after which time they shoved her and Cindy, who was asleep on the bed, down the stairs and began throwing their furniture down after them. Most of their things were destroyed, including an old bureau and a mirror that was the only possession Walt left behind. "Them moving men even tried to take my Thanksgiving turkey," said Bobbi. "Told me, 'Lady, you don't need no goddamn turkey—you ain't got no place to eat it!' and they all started laughing."

The Shackelfords stayed with B. J. Higgins for a week, with Alton Short for a week, and lived in various houses Barry was painting—houses that lacked heat or hot water. When I returned home from a business trip the first week in January, Embry informed me that Bobbi had called and told her that for the last week, all the Shackelfords—including the three dogs—had been sleeping in their car. The temperature had been in the teens and a blizzard was expected.

So we invited the Shackelfords to stay with us. During the nine days they lived at our house, I tried every conceivable channel to try to find them a house—various "hot lines" and "crisis calls," the Red Cross, the Salvation Army, practically every apartment house in the county, apartment-finding services, churches, the welfare department, the public housing authority, even the congressman's district office. No one could help. There were few vacancies, and those apartments that had available units refused to rent to large families or charged upward of $250 a month. The Shackelfords were accepted for public housing, but over three hundred "needier" families were ahead of them in line.

In desperation we went to a mobile home park and put a deposit down on a $2,500 used mobile home. The deal fell through when the welfare department reneged on an agreement to contribute $250 in "emergency housing money" toward the $750 down payment. The caseworker informed me, "Sir, my supervisor and I feel that a mobile home is an unsuitable living environment for a lower-income family. . . ."

"But," I screamed over the phone, "the alternative is sleeping in their goddamned car!"

"I'm sorry, the decision is final," she said.

Later I was informed that if I acted in such an impolite manner again, the Shackelfords would only be hurt.

In spite of my futile efforts to find them a place, the Shackelfords finally found a house through the help of some friends —an older frame house in poor condition in a predominantly black suburb. They loved the house and the neighborhood, and by some miraculous good fortune their credit was approved for a "rent with the option to buy" agreement. When Barry departed, the last thing he said was, "I'm starting over a new leaf. I'm buying me a house. I'm gonna start all over again. . . ."

As for the Mosebys, life was a mixture of the good and the bad. Ted and Anita got married in the fall and had a Catholic church wedding followed by a reception at the NCO club at the navy base. After the wedding they moved into an apartment on Clay Street, and Ted started working two jobs to try to pay for their new furniture and their new Vega.

The following fall Anita and Ted separated when Anita ran off with another man. Ted hurt his back on the job and was unable to work during the winter of 1972–73. Arlene and Les finally got a divorce, which became final in December, and Arlene continued living with Lonnie off and on, spending much of her time at Fred's house up the street, minding his children. In the fall Arlene became pregnant with Lonnie's child. Fred's wife, Tammy, who ran off with the D.C. Outlaws, never returned.

Les lost his job around the first of December and went back to West Virginia. He lost so much time from work, his boss finally asked him to "retire." Because his boss liked Les, he was allowed to receive his company pension, which—combined with unemployment—enabled him to not have to work for a while. He still had his house and was renting it out in hopes of someday returning to the Washington area. According to June, he was finished with truck driving and wanted to become a carpenter.

Ruby and Randy got back together after having to split up at the end of the summer when they could not find housing. Randy had found a job building boats, and they were able to rent another cottage on the Chesapeake Bay. June said that

Ruby wasn't on her religious kick so much any more but that she still sent her kids to Sunday school.

For June and Sam the big event was that the Dodge dealer Sam worked for closed down in November and Sam had to find another job. After a couple of weeks without work, he finally got a job as a mechanic for another Dodge dealer on the beltway; but he did "line" work rather than front-end work and brought home on the average a hundred dollars less per week. Though he was unhappy with the work and the working conditions, there were no openings for Dodge front-end specialists anywhere in the D.C. area. In March he was hurt on the job lifting a back seat out of a car and had to miss two weeks from work. In June's words, their current financial situation was "passable but a little shaky."

As for the other members of the household, Sammy entered the first grade and hated it, according to June; and of course, Barney was still there. In the winter Phyllis returned after breaking up with Dora, and she and Granny temporarily moved in with Arlene and Lonnie up at Fred's house.

In the spring Sam and June purchased adjacent cemetery lots, costing over $1,400. "It's a helluva lot of money," June said, "but why not? We decided to go ahead and get 'em next to each other. . . ."

Epilogue 1991

"Guess what!" I said with excitement, talking to Bobbi Jean. "I just got a call from a book publisher, and they are going to put out a reprint of the book." "The book" as it had become known on Clay Street had become to Bobbi Jean a minor irritant in recent years because it was no longer in print, and she couldn't give it to friends who kept asking for it.

"Well, it's about goddamn time! What I keep telling you is we gotta write another one. Joe, there is so much that has happened..."

So much has happened. In fact, having maintained fairly close contact with Bobbi Jean over the last twenty years, I am convinced that I could have picked any year during this period — any year — and there would have been a story. It would not have been exactly the same story, but there would have been a story.

Twenty years ago Bobbi was thirty-one and Barry thirty-four. In 1990 Bubba, her oldest son, is thirty-three and Cindy, her daughter, twenty-seven. The second generation is just about the same age as their parents were in 1970. What would the story be like today focusing on the second generation?

As I am writing this, I realize that I am two years older than June was when we moved to Clay Street. And some of June's grandchildren are older now than I was when we lived on Clay Street. What would the story be like today focusing on the third generation?

Here are the facts.

The Shackelfords

I suspected that when Barry finally died — and we all recognized that he was a marked man — it would be something spectacular. There was an article referencing his death that made the front page of the

Washington Post on Memorial Day weekend 1975.

It was a beautiful day and Barry had decided to take his three smallest children and a neighborhood friend on an overnight camping adventure. Barry had been drinking heavily, but since he always drank heavily, I doubt that this was necessarily a factor in what happened. They had borrowed a small outboard motor boat and had planned to put the boat in the river where he and I had fished so many times a few years before. The river was located only a few blocks from their house and resembled more than anything else a large uncovered sewer. About a mile downstream — where they were planning to camp — was a deserted overgrown area used mainly as a dumping ground for beat-up cars and garbage.

They put the boat in the water around noon. Naturally the boat, which was packed to the gunwales with gear, was overloaded. When the fourth child boarded and they pushed off toward the center of the stream, it was too much. The boat capsized.

Now one of the things that Barry was proudest of was his ability as a swimmer. I recall one of his stories, told admittedly when he was in one of his drunken moods of exuberance, about when he swam across the Chesapeake Bay or at least a portion of it. When Barry came to the surface, he realized that only three of the four kids were bobbing in the water. All three were clinging to the overturned boat. No one was wearing a life preserver, but there were two preservers floating in the water. The missing child was a little girl, a friend of Cindy's, who could not swim at all. Barry dove for her twice without luck. On the third try he brought her up gasping for breath.

"It's all right, honey, it's gonna be all right," he said as he managed to get a preserver around her. Those were his last words. Just as he got the preserver around her, Barry's head went under water, and he never came up again.

People on shore were so concerned about the children that no one paid much attention to Barry. Two fishermen jumped in the water and pulled out the screaming children and dragged the overturned boat to shore. Then they realized that Barry had disappeared.

This account of his death was told to me by Bobbi Jean, who heard it from the children and from several witnesses on shore. She was not there at the time but rushed to the scene when she heard the news. She called the police, who arrived about a half hour later. The police brought with them a small outboard motor boat and spent about an hour cruising up and down the river. After finding no trace of Barry, they departed saying that they would return the next day with more equipment.

Bobbi Jean was hysterical. She spent the rest of that day and evening pacing up and down the banks of the river looking in vain for the body of her husband.

The next day the county police did not return. Bobbi Jean did not know what to do. She frantically called them to find out what was happening. She was told that county police did not have proper dredging equipment and that there was nothing that could be done.

She then called the District of Columbia police. They told her that they understood her problem, that they did have proper dredging equipment but that the scene of the accident was not in their jurisdiction.

Frankly, I do not know to what extent Bobbi Jean was exaggerating or failed to understand the situation. I still find it hard to believe that she was treated this way by the police. Since I was not there myself, I heard the story from her point of view. It turned out that I was out of town with my family for the long Memorial Day weekend and did not hear from Bobbi Jean until the following Tuesday, three full days after the accident. However, I do know that on that Tuesday no police had been to the area except on Saturday, the day of the accident and that Bobbi Jean was in a state of hysteria.

Just as I had almost persuaded a reporter at the *Post* to run another story to shame the police into action (their first story, published on Sunday was about the fact that six people, including Barry, drowned that day in the Washington area), the body was discovered about a mile downstream, almost in the exact location where they had planned to go camping. Bobbi Jean said that the body was bloated beyond recognition.

The autopsy was never done. She was informed by one medical authority that before the hospital could undertake an autopsy, she would have to put up a cash deposit since she had no insurance. In addition, they told her the body was too decomposed for an autopsy to reveal anything anyway.

Barry's funeral occurred about a week later; and, frankly, I was surprised to see such a large turnout. About fifty people attended, most of whom I had never seen before, people who I presumed were relatives. Barry's mother had managed to persuade her preacher, a self-styled evangelist in the tradition of the early Oral Roberts, to conduct the service. His eulogy turned out not to be a eulogy at all but rather a fire-and-brimstone sermon aimed at converting many in the congregation who he presumed were just like Barry.

"If you all don't stop your drinking, your running around, your reckless ways," he shouted leaning over the pulpit, "the same thing is gonna happen to you as what happened to this man here." He went on and on, raving and fuming about the evils of alcohol, gambling, running around, and other assorted sins. There was a considerable amount of squirming in the congregation. I could not believe that he had the gall to use Barry's death to promote his own pet sermon topic in such a crass and insensitive manner. I could see Bobbi Jean stone faced in the front row.

After he had gone on for about twenty minutes, he glanced at his watch and abruptly stopped. There was an uneasy pause for a moment, then his voice lowered almost to a whisper.

"Now take Barry here," he said slowly, gesturing to the coffin, "take old Barry. Now I'm not worrying about old Barry going to hell because I happen to know for a fact that the day before he died, he found Jesus." He stopped, then concluded, "Now let us pray. . ."

For a split second the entire congregation seemed to stop breathing. After twenty minutes of if-you-don't-live-right-you're-gonna-go-to-hell-too hollering, there was a great deal of rumbling. All of a sudden everyone was in stunned silence. "What? What did he say?" I whispered to my wife. I noticed other people were whispering to each other the same thing.

The funeral service quickly concluded and Barry was buried. After the service I could not keep from rushing up to Bobbi Jean to ask her about Barry's conversion.

"What happened, what happened?" I asked eagerly. "When did Barry find Jesus?"

"Never," said Bobbi Jean. "The preacher just said that shit 'cause he didn't want to make me feel bad."

And so ended the life of Barry Shackelford, dying mysteriously in an act of heroism. Yet because of some mix-up, which I still do not understand, the police did not even dredge for his body. The hospital would not perform an autopsy without a cash deposit, and the preacher used Barry to promote his own message. The exploitation and abuse which plagued Barry all his life were present even to the very end. It occurred to me sometime later that the way Barry died symbolized his entire life — his recklessness, his courage, his inability to fit in, his alienation and exploitation. Even the newspaper which ran the front page article about the various drownings misspelled Barry's name almost beyond recognition. "Poor old Barry." I heard someone comment at the funeral, "For him nothing went right."

Not long after Barry's death, Bobbi Jean moved in with a man old enough to be her father. He left his wife of 40 years for Bobbi Jean and they moved into a mobile home located in the country near the Chesapeake Bay. Then sometime later, the kids joined them — and the Shackelfords' dogs, cats, and other pets. This proved to be too much for the old man who moved out to rejoin his wife.

The next man in her life was a tough, burly construction worker with a leather-like face, a hearty laugh and a strong temper. After living together for about six months they decided to get married. Three weeks after the marriage he went into a drunken rage and beat up Bobbi. She called the police the next day to report him only to discover that her new husband had broken bond and was wanted by the police for several counts of theft and armed robbery. He immediately left town, and I do not believe they have seen each other since. She divorced him and took back the name of Shackelford which she still uses.

In 1979 she took up with Gene Autry, a glass cutter, whom she is still with. He is in the glazers' union, is regularly employed, seems to care a great deal about Bobbi Jean and the children and has provided stability that Bobbi Jean never knew during her previous marriages.

Except for the last five years, during which time Bobbi has had three heart attacks — one quite serious — she has been employed most of the time. Much of the time she has held two jobs. For a long period she worked two or three nights every week — all night — assembling newspapers. During the day she has worked as a department store sales clerk, office clerk, paint salesperson and assistant resident manager, a job which she had for several apartment complexes. She has never earned much more than the minimum wage; however, by combining her income with Gene Autry's income, her family has been much better off financially than during the Clay Street year. I do not believe that she has received any federal or state payments throughout the period except from Barry's Social Security and from time to time food stamps and Medicaid. For the last five years they have lived in a mobile home, which they are buying, in a mobile home park about 20 miles from Washington.

As for the children, Bubba was the first to grow up and leave home. He graduated from the local high school in a graduation ceremony that symbolized for me a triumph of the human spirit. No one had given him any chance of making it; but thanks to one teacher who took special interest in him, Bubba walked down the aisle to the shouts and cheers of all the Shackelfords and assorted friends. No one was more proud than Bobbi Jean, who exclaimed that this was the best day of her life. I found myself drying a tear now and then throughout the ceremony.

Bubba by all accounts has been a success story. Though it took him a few years to settle down and find a permanent job, he was finally able to land a union job working for one of the major newspapers in the area where he has been employed for about 15 years as a mailer. He has worked his way up to an assistant foreman.

Bubba got married about the same time he started working in the union (in a big church ceremony which Embry and I attended) and now has four children — all boys — ranging in age from two to 10. His wife, Kathy, has worked off and on, between children, and currently works full time as an accounting clerk for a large bank. She works during the day, and he works on the night shift so that they won't have to hire a baby sitter. They bought a house about two years ago — a two-story older house, which they are slowly fixing up, in a middle income suburb not too far from Clay Street.

In a sense Bubba and his wife have joined the ranks of the settled families — a nice house in the suburbs, a car, a truck, a steady job — but at a price and on shaky enough ground so that any significant adversity could push them over the edge. They now need both incomes to get by; and if for some reason one of them cannot work — and this happened a few months ago when Bubba's hand was caught in a paper assembly machine and he had to miss a considerable amount of work — times get real tough. "It's kinda like a roller coaster," Bubba told me. "You think you're fine, then boom, something happens and you don't know how you're gonna manage."

And times have not always been stable. Several years ago the pressure got to be too much and Bubba moved out and Kathy moved back in with her mother. "I just hadn't sowed my wild oats," said Bubba, "but this girl who I lived with, when she joined this church and started speaking in tongues, then I moved out and came back home to Kathy."

Cindy, the second oldest — and the first child of Barry and Bobbi Jean — is now twenty-seven and a very pretty young woman — though extremely thin due I suspect in part to the kidney problem which was already a problem the year we were on Clay Street and has plagued her ever since. Having missed so much school due to her illness, Cindy never was able to catch up and never finished high school. When she was sixteen she gave birth to a little girl, Amy, who is now eleven. Steve, the 18-year-old father of the child had spent most of his young life in foster homes and juvenile institutions. He was at the hospital when Amy was born and lived with the Shackelfords off and on for about two years. He and Cindy had broken up for a period of time — about a year — when Steve's body was found along side a lonely country highway. The circumstances surrounding Steve's murder are still murky although one of his friends was later convicted and sentenced.

Cindy took Steve's murder very hard. It was a long time before she went out again with a man; and since that time, she has lived with Bobbi Jean almost all of the time. I am not aware of Cindy's ever having a job though she says when Amy gets a little bigger she will try to find one.

Though Cindy went for years without a serious boyfriend, she has one now — Fred, a handsome blond construction worker — who has moved in with Cindy in the Shackelford's mobile home. Cindy and Fred are engaged to be married though no date is set.

Like his sister, Billy also had difficulties with school and dropped out before he finished high school. He left home fairly early — in his teens — and moved in with an older man, Warren, who runs a small construction subcontracting business and with whom Billy still lives. Though I have never seen the house, it is reported to be "real nice and in a real nice neighborhood."

Working off and on for Warren and doing other construction jobs, Billy has been employed most of the time. He has a naturally charming personality, is friendly and warm, and inherited the artistic and poetic side of Barry's personality. Though his life has been far from easy, he gives you the impression of being on top of things. "Yeah," Bubba said, "Billy has been through some hard times but he really has his shit together. He's doing great now.''

And Littlebit—now called by his real name, Lyman—is by all accounts "just like Barry." This description is generally said with affection, remembering Barry's good qualities, but also with the recognition that Lyman has a wild streak.

Lyman was the second Shackelford child to finish high school and the graduation ceremony was as moving as that of Bubba's. It was held in a large high school auditorium with the graduating class seated on the gym floor and parents and supporters seated in the grandstand. It seemed almost every graduate had his or her own cheering section. When the person's name was called to come forward to receive the diploma, their cheering section would scream loudly, clap, and wave. With all the Shackelfords present including extended family and friends, Lyman got one of the loudest ovations of all.

Since his high school graduation, which occurred in 1985, Lyman has worked off and on mainly in construction and still lives at home. He is tall, thin and handsome and looks very much like his brother Billy—both of whom actually look astonishingly like their father. It is ironic that of all the Shackelford children, the one who seems most influenced by Barry is Lyman, the child who was the youngest. Recently he showed me his room and with pride pointed to several items that were Barry's—a gun, a kerosene lamp, deer hoofs—and an old photo of Barry in his red hunting shirt and stocking cap. Lyman is the only Shackelford child who takes off time every fall to go deer hunting and he has more hunting trophies to show than anyone else. "It is true," he told me, "that I was only eight and a half when my dad died but I remember him and I admire him and he has had more influence on my life than anyone else." Like Barry, Lyman is a heavy drinker but at this stage of his life, his drinking does not appear to be out of control.

When I visited the Shackelfords recently to pull together this epilogue, it was a Sunday afternoon and the Redskins were playing San Francisco. In addition to the Shackelford clan (except for Bubba and his family), several other young men and women in their twenties were present— friends of the children. As usual, I was greeted like a long lost member of the family—it had been about a year since I had seen them—with the usual hugs and embraces. The young adults were drinking beer and cheering and groaning at the appropriate times during the football game. The mood was relaxed, upbeat and enthusiastic—every young person present had on the jersey of his or her favorite NFL team (which included, to my surprise, various teams besides the Redskins) — with lots of high fives, laughter and stomps on the floor. Collectively, a great deal of money was riding on the various games being played that day; and when other football scores were announced, there would be more cheers and groans.

I sat at the kitchen table with Bobbi Jean and Gene, neither of whom drink anymore, watching the game out of one eye and chatting about what was going on in their lives. Bobbi Jean was most concerned about her own health. She showed me a letter from her doctor written after her third heart attack stating she could no longer work. Despite the letter, she complained, she had been unable to receive disability benefits. She said she is very weak and realizes that she should stop smoking but it is so hard to do. She said she was also concerned about her children — the fact that, except for Bubba, they really haven't settled down and that their future is so uncertain — especially Cindy and Amy. "What would happen to them if I was to die?" she sighed, looking at Cindy and Amy sitting together on the couch.

Gene, who was sitting at the table with us quietly sipping non-alcoholic beer, pulled out a dead bolt lock that goes inside a door and handed it to me. "Hey look at this," he said, "when I retire from the union — which I hope will be soon — I'm gonna open up my own business as a locksmith."

"Won't that be great!" exclaimed Bobbi Jean, "his own business! And Steve — Cindy's fiance — he's gonna start his own plumbing business too." Always the optimist, I thought to myself, how does she do it?

I departed later in the afternoon following a tremendous thunderstorm. Wind had made the mobile home shake, and hail had pelted the tin roof sounding like gravel being dumped from a truck. As the rain tapered off to a drizzle, Bobbi Jean stood on the front porch and waved good bye; and though she looked much older than she did twenty years ago, I could picture her as she looked then waving to us when we left Clay Street twenty years earlier.

The Mosebys

I have not maintained as close ties with the Mosebys primarily because June died less than a year after the book was published. June was a relatively young woman — 48 years old. While her death — apparently caused by cirrhosis of the liver — was mourned by all who knew her, people did not react as they would have if a young person had died prematurely. By Clay Street standards, June was not young. Though she was full of life and energy, she did not look young, act young or think of herself as young. She was a grandmother and proud of it. She was the elder stateswoman of the neighborhood. Her death was accepted with the pain and remorse that accompany the loss of an aging parent or loved one — as something very sad but inevitable.

Hard living folks seem to die young. Barney died at age 52 a few years after June's death (he was no longer living with Sam and had been placed in a group home for disturbed adults). Barry died at age 37 and many of the minor characters encountered died before they reached 60.

Yet many also survived and one survivor was Sam. Never one who liked living alone — June always complained that if she died Sam could never take care of himself — Sam quickly rebounded and renewed a relationship with his first wife, who moved into his Clay Street apartment within a year after June's death. Just as Bobbi Jean's next marriage lasted only briefly, the relationship was over almost before it began, leaving Sam and Sammy to take care of each other in their Clay Street apartment. Several years later, Helen moved in. She was another old girlfriend whose personality was surprisingly like June's — warm, outgoing with wit and a sense of humor. Helen and Sam are still together living — "happy as can be" according to Sam — in a mobile home in the foothills of the Blue Ridge mountains between Richmond and Charlottesville, Virginia. Sam bought ten acres of land with June's insurance money and he and Helen moved there ten years ago when he retired. Sam is now 72.

Though I have not seen where Sam lives, June's son Ted described it this way: "You drive for miles up a lonely dirt road, then you come to a farm house. You go up the driveway to the farm house, then past the farm house into a field. Then you follow a cow path for a long ways and come to a stop sign in the middle of a field. Just beyond the stop sign is Sam's mobile home. When I asked Sam what the hell is a stop sign doing out in the middle of nowhere, he just threw his head back and laughed, "Don't want nobody to miss our house!" Sam bought the property because his sister lived in the area. He told me over the phone he has never been happier.

Of all June's children, we were closest to Arlene. Frankly, I would not have bet anything that Lonnie and Arlene would be together after twenty years. A year after we left Clay Street, Arlene and Lonnie got married; and they moved with their infant daughter to Orlando, Florida where jobs for electricians were supposedly abundant. While Lonnie did not find a stable job as an electrician, he did finally settle into a permanent job as a security guard in Disney World and will soon be eligible to retire with a pension.

From Ted's description, their life has been a series of ups and downs and their relationship tumultuous. Their daughter—now in her late teens—is more or less on her own and, according to Ted, has been hard to handle. Two years ago Arlene and Lonnie got a divorce, then after 18 months were remarried. A few weeks after their remarriage, Arlene was hit by a car while walking in the parking lot of a McDonald's restaurant. Her back was hurt, but I gather she has recovered with no serious lasting problems. The good news was that she received a $500,000 insurance settlement—over $350,000 net to her—which she and Lonnie used to purchase a house in Pompano Beach. Arlene has worked off and on—when they needed extra money—but has not had a career.

Ruby and Randy are also still together. According to Ted, their life has been pretty much the same—living from hand to mouth, "down country" in a house next to the volunteer fire department in a little village on the Chesapeake Bay. Their oldest son, a career soldier, is a staff sergeant in the Army. He is married, has several children and is already thinking about retirement. Their middle son was killed tragically in an automobile accident last year. According to Ted, his life had been troubled and he had had some problems with the law. Except for Sammy, all June's children were present for the funeral which was the closest thing they have had to a reunion. All the other children of Ruby and Randy have settled in the country, and the youngest just got married this summer. Ted couldn't recall whether any of Randy and Ruby's children had finished high school.

Of all the children of both families, the only person who has become "middle class" is Ted. He and his wife, Paula, live in a three-bedroom split level house in an attractive Virginia suburb where houses in 1990 sold for $250,000 and up. (Ted was quick to point out that they were renting their house.) Ted is currently regional sales manager of a large plumbing supply company in the area and has been in management positions in the plumbing supply business for over 15 years. He married Paula about two years ago, after living with her for a few years. She is a waitress in a restaurant located near Ted's business — where they met. Paula's 15-year-old daughter from a previous marriage lives with them (an older son lives with his father).

Ted proudly showed me an autographed photo of President Reagan, addressed to him personally and given to him by Senator Dole whom Ted once helped with a plumbing problem. He also showed me a copy of "Who's Who in Alexandria" where he is listed as a prominent businessman. Bowling trophies line the mantle of the rec room fireplace — including the horses ass trophy we won when we bowled together in 1970. He and Paula bowl now in a league once a week, and he assured me they do much better than we did in 1970.

There was a Bible on the kitchen table — obviously worn and used. Paula and her daughter attend the Baptist Church in the neighborhood regularly, though Ted doesn't go much.

Ted's personality is still the same — low key, soft spoken and modest. He said he stopped drinking years ago. The year June died, his father also died and from that year on there was really not that much to hold the family together. He has not seen his half brother Sammy for over eight years.

Sammy, now age 25, is one member of the family I was worried about. I had heard from Bobbi Jean that Sammy had had a hard time following June's death and that during high school he had moved out of the house on Clay Street and was living on his own. Bobbi Jean didn't think that he had finished high school. I learned from Ted that Sammy was currently living in the volunteer fire house in the Clay Street neighborhood. From talking to Ted, it was obvious that Sammy was not close to any of his half brothers or sisters.

I tracked Sammy down at the volunteer fire department where he was still living. I had talked to him on the phone to set up a time to get together. When I arrived there that evening, it was dusk. A woman in her mid-20s was standing in front of the building. She was pretty with blond hair and was smiling. As I got out of the car and walked toward the fire department, she walked up to me and said, "You must be Joe, and I bet you are looking for Sam." We walked back into the fire department between two large fire engines into a back room where there was a coffee pot, a large television and two or three overstuffed sofas in what otherwise was a fairly drab room. "He's here, Sam, he's here!" Out of a back room appeared a young man, about six feet tall with a round face and short hair. He was wearing a blue T-shirt and jeans and had grease on his hands and arms suggesting he had just come from work. He smiled and stretched out his hand saying, "Joe, it's great to see you. How are you?"

"Do you remember me?" I asked.

"Well, I don't remember you, but I sure know who you are and I know all about the book."

"Have you read the book?"

"Well no; not yet but I know about it, and I'm real glad to see you."

He then introduced me to the young woman, Jan, his fiancee. The wedding is scheduled for June 16—eight months away. Jan grew up on Clay Street and still lives there with her family, about a block from where we lived. She graduated from Catholic high school and is a secretary for a federal government agency where she has worked for over six years.

We then sat down on the sofa. The TV was playing, and young men dressed in jeans wandered in and out of the small room getting coffee and cokes. A two-way radio was blaring in the background, and we were interrupted a couple of times by what I thought were fire alarms but obviously were not since no one budged. Sammy was warm, friendly and self-confident. His bride-to-be seemed very interested in our conversation and nodded approvals from time to time.

When I asked about what happened after his mother's death, Sammy said, "Well, it is hard to talk about. I don't remember much about my mom at all. The main thing I remember is that I was the one who found her dead. I woke up in the morning and went over to her and she didn't move. I remember shaking her, and I remember how strange she looked—almost blue—and there was some blood coming out her mouth. I remember screaming, running and hanging onto the neighbor's door and not letting go.

"Then after my mom died, my dad took up with his first wife for awhile but that didn't work out. Then he and I lived together and that was all right. We got along pretty good just the two of us—just us two men. Then when I was about 11, Helen moved in and that was awful. It might not have been so bad but Helen brought her grandson. Now he was an A-B student, and I was a C-D student. He couldn't do anything wrong, and I couldn't do anything right. From the outset Helen didn't have any use for me. I tried as best I could, but it got to the point when I was about 16 that I just couldn't take it any more and so I left. My dad had to choose between me and Helen. He loved Helen so he chose her, and that put me pretty much on my own. I didn't have a place to live, so I went to the volunteer fire department, and I've been here pretty much ever since, off and on. Sometimes I lived with friends, but most of the time I've been here. Of course it's not so nice but the price is right—it doesn't cost me anything.

"Of course being a C-D student and having kind of a hard time during those years, I just didn't do too well in high school. I got my dad's permission to drop out, and then I had to find some way to support myself. I had an odd job here, an odd job there, mainly working minimum wage. I had a whole bunch of jobs. I had one job working in a nursing home as a maintenance man, but that didn't work out. Of course, since I didn't have to pay rent, it wasn't too bad, but I did have to eat. Sometimes I didn't eat a whole lot—in fact I was real thin in those days. But then I finally ended up with a good job working for a big plumbing company, where I've been for about the last four or five years. They sent me to plumbing school. I've done my apprenticeship. I've got my license and now I'm just opening up my own plumbing contracting business with Jan's brother."

Jan was listening with great interest and seemed to be very proud of Sam's accomplishments. It dawned on me while he was talking, however, that this young man had been pretty much on his own for almost ten years. I felt very bad that Embry and I had not been able to help Sammy when he needed it.

He went on to say that he had been reconciled with his father once his father and Helen had moved down to the country and that every year for the past few years he has gone down to visit during hunting season. He is planning to go this fall, hopefully within a week or two.

"Yeah,' he said, "It was hard for awhile. I just didn't get along

with my dad. We just didn't seem to understand each other when Helen
and her grandson moved in, mainly because our little house wasn't
big enough for the four of us. I remember when he and Helen decided
to move to the country. He gave me a car and gave me a little money
left over from my mom's social security, and he gave me the Clay
Street apartment. The car just wasn't right, and the money didn't last
very long, and I only stayed in that apartment for a few months. But
all that's behind us now. Me and Jan are going to get married soon.
We are looking for a house to buy right here in this neighborhood.
I'm getting ready to start my own business. And me and my dad —
well, we get along now. Even Helen seems to like me.''

The experience seeing Sammy was bittersweet. I couldn't help
thinking how proud June would be of her son starting his own business
and settling down with Jan, who at least from her appearance, seems
to be a very "settled living" person. And at the same time how sad
she would be about the situation following her death: little Sammy —
the one person in the world she lived for — having to fend for himself
at such an early age.

The Neighborhood

Clay Street looks the same as it did in 1970. The apartment house
adjacent to our house is slightly more run down but otherwise the houses
look almost like they did twenty years ago. The chain link fences,
beware of dog signs, pick-up trucks, camper vans, cars on cinder blocks
and temporarily abandoned tricycles are still there. Most houses are
in fairly reasonable shape, but dotted throughout the community are
run down houses with debris littering the small front yards.

I was astonished to discover that the asking price for several typical
two-story homes in the area ranged from $80,000 to $120,000, still
well below the Washington area median of over $200,000 in 1990 but
nonetheless high — I thought — for their age, size and condition.

The commercial areas also look pretty much the same though one
notorious area of pawn shops and honky tonks was removed several
years ago (part of an urban renewal program) to make way for a strip
shopping center. Several store front gospel churches have recently
opened up in the area.

What has changed is the racial and ethnic diversity of the people who live on Clay Street. The homes occupied by families like the Mosebys and Shackelfords have been taken, more often than not, by black, Hispanic and Asian families.

We knew that change was coming in 1970 but what is surprising is the gradual nature of the change and the fact that it has occurred generally without incident. In 1970 the area defined as the study area contained about 14,300 people, 95 percent of whom were white. In 1980, the population had dropped to about 12,700 with a white population of just under 64 percent. In 1990 the total population remains about the same but the white population is estimated at just under 44 percent (as of this writing the official 1990 census figures had not been published). The vast majority of the new people moving in are black though there are some Asians and Hispanics as well.

The change is obvious as one drives through the community. Black families now live in the houses where several Clay Street families lived including both houses occupied by the Shackelfords that year. Black children can be seen playing in the street directly in front of our house as well as an occasional Vietnamese or Hispanic child. The change was also evident at the high school graduation ceremonies of Bubba and Littlebit. At Bubba's ceremony, about 30 percent of the graduating class were black; at Littlebit's ceremony, about 30 percent were white.

I do not know how the current residents who are white feel about the racial and ethnic change that has occurred. Of the four small towns in the area, there have been a few elected black public officials but only a few (one of the small communities, however, has had a black mayor eight of the last twelve years). "Most people don't like it all that much," said one neighborhood resident, "but what the hell are you gonna do about it?" Sammy and Jan both complained that the Clay Street neighborhood had gone down hill. It was not as safe as it used to be, and there were several known crack houses in the area. Some streets no longer had any white families remaining.

What I do know is that the county in which Clay Street is located — the blue collar county in the Washington area — has been the most racially integrated county in the region. While some neighborhoods have changed quickly from all white to all black, a surprising number — including Clay Street — continue to be racially integrated. It is one of those unsung small success stories that somehow never seem to get written about in newspapers or magazines.

In terms of incomes, families in the neighborhood are considerably worse off relative to the overall Washington area and to the state now than they were in 1970. In 1970 the median household income was just under $9,500 compared to a Maryland median of just under $12,000 or about 78% of the median. In 1980 the median income was just under $14,000 in contrast to a state median of about $25,000 or 56% of the state median. The percentage is estimated to be slightly better in 1990 — about 60 percent with median incomes of $30,000 compared to a state median of over $49,000.

Most people have jobs — often two to a household — and though the jobs are not always stable nor do they usually pay well, people do not have trouble finding work. The continued strong economy and sustained growth in the Washington area from 1970 to 1990 created numerous job opportunities, especially in construction and service related jobs. If the Washington economy experiences a serious recession — as appears likely as of this writing times will be harder; and many of the folks on Clay Street will be the first to feel the pinch. I think particularly of the eight or nine young people sitting in the small living room of Bobbi Jean's mobile home cheering the Redskins. Every one of the young men was involved in construction in one way or another. If new construction is sharply curtailed (as is now happening), where will they be this time next year?

The Book

I am continually asked how the families reacted once the book was published. Just as I was astonished to find the openness and warmth on Clay Street, I was equally astonished by the Shackelfords' and Mosebys' reaction to the book.

Once I knew it was going to be published, I let each family know immediately what was going to happen and also worked out an arrangement whereby each shared in the book's proceeds. In my view, this was no big deal and the right thing to do, given the circumstances. Each family got approximately ten percent of the revenues over a ten-year period, an amount which was not particularly large but which provided a little cushion. Following June's death, I put the Moseby's share into a savings account in Sammy's name. This was according to her wishes should anything ever happen to her. The reprinting of the book made me remember the long dormant savings account which I was able to access and deliver a cashier's check to Sammy. It was not for the college education that June hoped Sammy would get, but I think she would be pleased to know it would be used to help get his plumbing business going.

I do not know to what extent the financial arrangement affected the families' acceptance of the book—it probably had more to do with my own guilt than about their reactions—but in any event it was not long before Bobbi Jean was complaining that the book could not be found in any of the local bookstores—not at Dart Drug, Peoples Drug or anywhere—and was telling me I should be doing more to promote it.

I was most worried about June, given her general sensitivity about what I was doing and her mixed feelings about her own situation in life. After she had had a week or so to read her copy, I called her up and with some reluctance asked the inevitable question. "Well, what do you think?"

June paused for a moment then sighed. "Well, I think Ruby said it better than anyone else. Joe Howell, don't he write purty, but goddamn, don't he tell it like it is!"

Two other events stand out in my mind about reactions to the book. The first was a phone call I got from an irate woman whose husband was a minor character in the book. She said she was going to hire a lawyer and sue me because "not a goddamn thing I said about her husband was true." When she gave me an example of how I had maliciously misrepresented the facts, I said, "Now wait a minute, which character do you think your husband was?"

When she told me, I burst out laughing. "That's not your husband, your husband was really..."

She was silent for a moment then said, "No shit," hung up the phone and that was the last I heard from her.

The other call was more troubling. "Are you the Joe Howell who wrote the trashy book *Hard Living on Clay Street?*" came a woman's voice, obviously very angry.

"Yes," I said, bracing myself for what was coming next.

"Well, you're talking to Bobbi Jean Shackelford."

I did not recognize the voice. It was clear it was not the voice of *my* Bobbi Jean Shackelford.

"You're who?"

"I'm Bobbi Jean Shackelford, goddamn it! And I'm gonna sue your ass for a lot of money."

I still had not made the connection but the point was slowly getting through.

"You mean that's your name—Bobbi Jean Shackelford?" I stuttered, "Your real name?"

"Jesus," came the reply with the tone of "Boy, this guy is *really* stupid."

I was silent. Stunned is more like it. I had worked so hard to come up with unusual names which somehow captured the real person's personality but were different. I seemed to have come too close for comfort on this one.

It got worse. "Look, sonofabitch, I live in the neighborhood and I know who you really wrote about—and she knows me—so I know it's not me, but what I want to know is how come you used *my name?*"

Now this was too much. Live in the neighborhood? Impossible.

"If you don't believe it, call [the person you wrote about] and ask her. She'll tell you. But what I want to know is..."

I mumbled something like "pure chance, luck." I meant bad luck.

She went on to say that she really wasn't all that worried but more curious than anything. After all, she was not at all similar in *any* way to the woman I had written about except that her husband—whose name, thank God, was not Barry—did like to take a drink from time to time and to play the horses.

I immediately placed two calls—first to "my" Bobbi Jean who told me she did know a woman with that name who did live in the general neighborhood. The reason she didn't mention it to me before was that she just didn't think that much about it. I couldn't believe it, but what difference did it make now anyway?

The second call was to Doubleday, the original publisher. The person I talked to found the coincidence amusing and said she would check it out with a lawyer and call back if it was a problem but not to worry. "After all," she said, "It's hard to come up with a name that somebody in the world doesn't have." I found that thought reassuring. Neither Doubleday nor the "real" Bobbi Jean Shackelford ever called me back.

The book was more controversial among the settled living families.

These people were as kind to me as the hard living families and were generous with their time. Some felt betrayed that I had chosen to focus my book on the "atypical" few families which, in their view, were not representative of their community. To many of these people I became persona non grata. One person told me that my book was the second worst thing ever to happen to this community in all of its history. The first was *The Exorcist*, which allegedly occurred in a house located in the same community only blocks from Clay Street. (Interestingly the movie was filmed mostly in Georgetown and neither my book nor *The Exorcist* mentioned the community by name.)

The Author

The other question I often get is what has happened to me, the author. Several people have remarked that the most curious thing about the entire book is that there was this almost invisible person whose personality and whose age (most people were mildly surprised that I was so young — 28 at the time) remained somewhat obscure as the lives of these people unfolded. I was, they point out, like a fly on the wall.

After finishing up the year with the Clay Street project, I then had to find a "real" job. I will never forget my first job interviews. Since Embry had landed a good job in the public health field in Washington, I agreed to cast my lot in the Washington job market. As big as that metropolitan area was, certainly I could find something. Though I had just finished the *Clay Street* manuscript, at that point I did not have a publisher nor, for that matter, any assurance whatsoever that there would ever be a real "book."

The Clay Street experience had actually been something of a diversion along a career path, albeit a rather crooked and winding career path, which at this point in life I felt I needed to pursue in earnest. I had had graduate training for both the Episcopal ministry — which I with the help of my Bishop had determined I was grossly unsuited for — and urban planning. For lack of other options, I chose urban planning.

I was more attracted to the consulting side of urban planning than the government agency side since a job with a consulting firm seemed to be more diverse and less structured. The most probable job opportunity was with a well respected Washington area planning firm, one of whose principals was a prominent graduate of the University of North Carolina Planning School, my alma mater.

My interview went something like this:

> *Prominent alumnus*: "So exactly what did you do when you worked on the research project with F. Stuart Chapin?"
>
> *Me*: "My wife and I lived in this blue collar neighborhood and I've written a manuscript which I hope to get published."
>
> *Him* (mildly curious): "And what does your manuscript say?"
>
> *Me*: "Well it's about the day-in day-out lives of two struggling blue collar families. It's about how their lives unfolded, what happened to them and how they got by."
>
> *Him* (now puzzled): "It's about what?"
>
> I tried again, somewhat more feebly.
>
> *Him* (clearly irritated): "And what, I pray tell, has this to do with anything and what use is it to anybody, anytime or any place?"
>
> I swallowed hard trying to think of something.
>
> *Him*: "It is precisely this kind of irrelevant shit that is indicative of what is wrong with the University of North Carolina, with what is wrong with the planning profession and what is wrong with the government!"

He went on for a while longer, but I was in such a state of shock and humiliation that I do not remember what he said. Needless to say, I did not get the job.

The second job interview was with a young man in a three-piece suit — also a job opening with a consulting firm but this firm had more of a real estate orientation than a planning or urban policy orientation as did the other firm. I dreaded the thought of working for a real estate consulting firm. A real sell out. But after several weeks in Washington and no promises yet for a job, I was beginning to get less choosey. I decided I would not mention anything about my manuscript or what I had been doing for the last two years except when asked say "urban research."

After the usual preliminaries, my interview with him went something like this:

Him: "So what the hell *have* you been doing these eight years after college?"

Me: "Graduate school and urban research."

Him: "How old are you?"

Me: "30."

Him: "Take a hard look at yourself in the mirror. You are 30, applying for an entry level job. I'm executive vice president of this entire company. I'm 29 — you're 30. Buddy, you got a long way to go to catch up."

That was the end of that interview which I left absolutely furious. I swore I would never — never — work for such an arrogant jerk.

Three days later I got a formal job offer from the company. I accepted it and never once regretted the decision.

The decision, however, did send me along a career path which was related neither to academia (I have been occasionally referred to as "Doctor Howell," which, of course, is not the case) nor to urban social policy, if indeed there is such a thing. The career path was related to urban development — specifically housing development — and that essentially is what I have been doing for the last twenty years. My job with the consulting firm lasted two years, after which I spent several years with the Episcopal Church in Washington developing low income housing for the elderly, then as a developer for a large national low income housing development firm. The bottom fell out of the low income housing business in 1980 when virtually all federal low income housing development incentives were eliminated. After teaching real estate development at George Washington University for a semester (which did produce my only other book — one on developing low income housing) I opened up my own firm in 1981 and have been there ever since. The firm has expanded and contracted over the years — we were up to over 20 persons at one time — and has focused primarily on developing housing for poor folks and for old folks. My wife, Embry, has worked most of her career for a health care consulting firm and will receive her Ph.D. in health policy in the spring. We have two children, a son (the toddler on Clay Street) who is now in college and a 16-year-old daughter in high school.

Looking back at the lives of the people on Clay Street, it is not possible to avoid thinking about my own life and how it has been

changed by that experience. Like so many experiences of this nature —
the Peace Corps experience is probably the best example — the one
who really benefits is the visitor to the foreign land. While Clay Street
was not foreign like, say, Africa or South America, in some respects
it was and still is another country, as far as many Americans are
concerned. In any event, I truly was the beneficiary. To be able to
share the lives of the people on Clay Street for one year was indeed
the opportunity of a lifetime. For this I will remain forever grateful.

Appendix

NOTES ON METHODOLOGY

While the particular method one chooses in participant observation varies according to the researcher, who must adapt an approach to fit his own style and circumstances, most participant observation studies consist of four separate phases. These phases might be called *making friends, being where the action is, putting it all down,* and *putting it all together.* If the researcher fails in any of these four areas, he is unlikely to produce a viable study. What follows are my thoughts concerning how I undertook each of these four phases in this study of working-class families.

Making Friends

It is only too obvious that without the trust and acceptance of the people he is studying, the participant observer will have very little to observe. The acceptance problem, therefore, is the first obstacle that must be overcome before much else can happen. The problem is in essence: How is he going to make friends?

In my case I had three things going for me. I lived in the neighborhood, I had a southern accent, and I had a family. Taken together these things made me more understandable, less threatening, and easier to accept, for they established something I had in common with most people in the community.

It was by chance that we lived where we did. Since my job description called for my living somewhere in the study area, the project director, Stu Chapin, and I visited the area about six weeks before I was to move into the community. Driving through the area looking for "for rent" signs or centrally located apartment houses, we happened upon a vacant apartment on the ground floor of a duplex the third place we came to. Had this apartment not been available—someone else had already forfeited a deposit on the unit just two days before—we would probably have had to settle for an apartment in one of the massive garden apartment complexes on the edge of the study area. Since these garden apartments contained many students and young white collar families and had a very high rate of turnover, it would have been extremely difficult to get to know families such as those who lived on Clay Street. We were lucky.

Living in the neighborhood was important because most personal relationships were family- or neighborhood-oriented, and people were generally wary of outsiders, who were usually thought to be either bill collectors or salesmen. My friendship with the Mosebys, for example, was predicated on the fact that I lived next door to them. The day we arrived in our U-Haul van, June brought us over a huge pitcher of ice water and some cookies from Sammy's birthday party, which was in progress. From that moment on we were friends, simply because June considered any next-door neighbor a friend until proven otherwise. From then on, practically every day, we would borrow sugar or milk or laundry money from June; or she would borrow something from us or wander over to share some of the latest gossip.

Most people in the neighborhood tended to see me first of all as a neighbor and secondly as a person on some incomprehensible research project. Since I was a neighbor, however, the particular job I had was forgivable. Because I lived in the community I had as legitimate a right as anyone else to drink beer on my front steps, to stroll my son down the sidewalk, to stop and talk with a friend, to attend church services and community meetings. I was not just another outsider.

My relationship with the Shackelfords was also tied to my living in the neighborhood, although they moved to an apartment two blocks from ours. Bobbi could still drop in when coming down to retrieve her kids and I could stop by to say hello on my way to the post office, bank, or corner market. Since most neighborhood interaction was on a casual, informal basis, no one ever made plans to see anyone else. People just dropped by, and dropping by would have been extremely difficult had I not lived in the neighborhood.

As a neighbor I did what most neighbors were expected to do. I helped out when I could. Helping out for me consisted of giving people rides when they needed transportation, lending money, and writing letters to bill collectors, magazine companies, or doctors for people who felt they were being abused. During the fall, when I accompanied June to the welfare department with Barney, I gained the reputation of being able to "work miracles with the welfare." In fact my only miracle was intimidating the welfare workers by my appearance—coat, tie, empty brief case—to treating June and Barney fairly and with respect. People seemed to appreciate my helping out, however, for though the things I did were small and often insignificant, they communicated that I cared and that I wanted to become involved. Finally, as a neighbor, I not only gave help, I received help from people as well. For instance, Sam repaired a friend's car for free; Barry repaired some broken furniture; the Mosebys gave me a movie projector. Most important, however, the people shared with me their lives. Being a neighbor on Clay Street meant give and take.

A second thing I had in my favor was a southern accent and North Carolina license plates. Many of the people in the neighborhood were from the South or had relatives living in the South. Occasionally someone would pull up in front of my house if I happened to be outside and ask what part of North Carolina I was from. "Well goddamn" would come the reply. "Chapel Hill. Hell, I'm from outside of Raleigh!" Many people in the community identified with the South and liked to think of themselves as Southerners even if it had been years since they had been "down home." As one person put it, "Hell, man, if you are a Southerner, you can't be all bad." When I told people I was brought up in Nashville, Tennessee, this was even better. "What's the Opry really like?" people would ask. "Goddamn, if it's the last thing I do, I'm gonna get to the Opry. . . ."

Being married and having a small child were also very important in my being accepted. Being a "family man" meant that I was not an obvious threat to the men, who were gone all day. Because Embry and Andrew were often with me when I was with Bobbi and June, Barry and Sam had less reason to feel threatened. In fact Barry told me that if I had not been a family man, he would have "blowed my brains out then and there" when he came home and found me drinking coffee with Bobbi. It was not just *I* who was a friend of Bobbi's but rather *our family* that was close to Barry and Bobbi's family. It was our family that bowled with the Mosebys. On Clay Street, people did things as families. Most activities were co-ed. No adult peer groups existed. Had I been single, I would not have fitted in as easily.

Also, children were very important on Clay Street. While the ideal child should be seen and not heard (or in Clay Street language, "should keep his ass outa his daddy and mamma's way"), families were expected to have children. Since we had a young child—Andrew was only three months old when we arrived—we were a normal, young family. Moreover, Andrew became something of a mascot on the block in that he was the youngest child on the block (at least until the spring) and was omnipresent. Practically every day he would crawl over to June's—with Embry following in pursuit—or Embry and I would carry him with us up to Bobbi's. People would invariably greet us with, "How's the baby?" or "Bring the baby over sometime," or "My, ain't he getting to be a big little feller!" Andrew was far more popular in the community than either Embry or I.

Being married was important not only because it helped me be accepted but also because in her own right Embry played an extremely important role in the project. She was very much a participant in the life of the community and passed on to me a great deal of information that people told her. Quite frequently when I would be at a community meeting or off somewhere, Embry would be home socializing and later would record her own observations and insights, many of which are included in this book. In many respects it was a joint effort. My friends were her friends. We did many of the same things and shared insights and compared observations. The study is in many ways as much her work as it is mine.

For the reasons I have just discussed, I found the acceptance obstacle to be much less difficult than I had anticipated. People were not cold, aloof, and hostile as I had been told by some sociologists they would be. Rather they were friendly, warm, and open. This is not to imply, however, that acceptance was assured from the outset or that I ran into no problems whatsoever. For one thing there were many on Clay Street—not to mention those in the surrounding area—whom I did not get to know. Doubtless some of these may have been suspicious, cold, aloof, etc. For example, I got to know few homeowners on Clay Street, mainly because the homeowners tended to look down on the renters, of which I was one. The homeowners I did get to know I met through community meetings. And these people tended to think of me as a university researcher first and a resident second, nor did they know my friends on Clay Street. Therefore, while I was accepted, I was by no means accepted by all the people. Such is one of the chief drawbacks of participant observation. One's sample is not necessarily representative of all the people who live in a study area.

Secondly, even among my closest friends, there was always some ambivalence about who I was and what I was doing in the community. My hair was a bit long; we had a large abstract modern painting and lots of books in our living room; we bought a Toyota automobile during the year. We had friends who lived in *downtown* Washington, D.C., who occasionally came for dinner, etc. Our life style in many respects was different from theirs. And to top it all off, I worked for a university and had a job that was beyond anyone's comprehension. At various times I would be reminded of these differences, usually just when I was beginning to think I was really "one of the boys." To my great horror and embarrassment, June once introduced me as "our neighborhood spy." Then she laughed and said, "But that's okay. You're harmless. You're a friendly neighborhood spy." At other times she would comment, "Okay, I *really* got something for your book this time." Though I was accepted, I was accepted not just as "one of the boys," but for who I was, namely, someone working for a university, trying to understand people in that community.

At times I felt guilty about my role in the community and never completely resolved certain ambivalent feelings of my own. In many respects I was just another exploiter. I was being paid by a university to pry into the lives of people who, in all likelihood, would never be helped by anything we did. People were taking me into their trust and sharing their lives with me for which they would receive quite little in return.

To allay these feelings, I would tell myself that my ends were not malicious. While no one would be helped, changing all names of people and places would insure that no one would be hurt either. Also, I was honest with people. I told everyone from the outset what I was doing and why I was in the area. If they did not like what I was about, they did not have to co-operate. The fact that everyone knew I was a "friendly neighborhood spy" made these feelings of guilt somewhat easier to take, though the feelings remained with me throughout the study.

I suppose the thing I felt most uneasy about was my not going to work like most of the other men. Some of my neighbors half seriously referred to me as being on "glorified relief," though they were quick to point out that most people who worked for the government were on "glorified relief." Because this label hit a little close to home, I tended to avoid being conspicuously present during the day when most men were away at work. In other words, between nine and five during the week, I would try to stay indoors or in somebody's home or try to arrange an interview with someone, rather than standing around or sitting on my front porch waiting for something to happen, as I frequently did after five o'clock or on weekends. At one point I considered working in a potato chip factory nearby but decided against it, I think wisely, because I could not have worked and observed neighborhood life at the same time.

In the final analysis acceptance problems in participant observation are more often than not due to the researcher's own hang-ups. My not having a regular blue collar job, for instance, was not perceived by others as a barrier to my being accepted. It was my own hang-up. If I had had two blue collar jobs, it would not have made me more acceptable. Few people really cared what I did. The most important thing was that I cared about them and was willing to become involved with their problems. I had time and I was willing to listen. This was what was most important.

Being Where the Action Is

Once a participant observer feels he is accepted by people in the community, then he is faced with the problem of being in a situation where he can continue to learn and collect valuable data. In other words, he must try to be where the action is.

The approach I decided to follow consisted of two types of involvement—an involvement with families on my block and an involvement with community groups and community activities. As is apparent in this book, my involvement with families was far more productive and occupied most of my time and energy. This was due in part to a conscious decision on my part. I felt I was learning much more and collecting more valuable, "unique" data by staying with the Shackelfords and Mosebys than by my involvement with community groups. It was also due in part to accident, for I became involved with these families and by December could not have become uninvolved even if I had wanted to.

In regard to my community involvement, I tried to attend as many meetings, join as many clubs, and do as many "typical" things as possible. I attended most local council meetings and most meetings of the local Democratic Club. I joined the Citizens Association and also a fishing club. Often accompanied by Embry and Andrew, I attended Sunday services at every church in the study area (eight in all, with a special emphasis on the Southern Baptist and the Pentecostal). And, of course, Embry and I bowled with June and Sam every Sunday evening for something like thirty-six consecutive weeks. I also stopped in most of the local bars and ate in most of the local restaurants.

These community involvements were important in two respects. First of all, they gave me some perspective for interpreting the in-depth material I was gathering from my involvement on Clay Street. In these meetings, for example, I was continually reminded that the hard living families were a minority in the area. Secondly, it gave me an opportunity to get to know stable, home-owning families who were not as easy to get to know on Clay Street. Actually I was able to develop good relationships with a number of these families such as the DeAngelos and the Dales, though I decided to concentrate on the hard living families, about whom I felt much less was known.

The vast portion of my recorded data, however, was a result of my involvements with my immediate neighbors. In all I got to know twenty-five families who lived on or near Clay Street (and sixty-six families throughout the larger area); but of these, I knew only two quite well. I was not worried that I knew few families to the extent I knew the Shackelfords and Mosebys because I was convinced the other families were not significantly different from the life styles represented by these main families, and I found I did not have the extra time to spend anyway. I chose to pursue getting in-depth material from two families and using the other families for breadth and perspective.

My approach differed in regard to each of the two families. June Moseby more or less played the role of a typical informant. Through her and her family, I was able to catch a glimpse of neighborhood life. Since she was at the center of neighborhood activity, I would usually learn from her everything that

was going on. Embry and I kept in touch with June on a daily
basis, stopping by to borrow laundry money or chasing after
Andrew. My general method was to spend at least some time
with the Mosebys practically every day. Most of the time
Embry or I would not stay long, usually only a few minutes,
long enough to catch up on what was happening in the neighborhood or with her family. Some days, however, if a lot was
going on, we might end up spending half a day.

The Mosebys tended to look upon my work as a neighborhood study. Consequently June would talk quite a lot about
what was going on in the neighborhood but was somewhat reluctant to talk about herself. And Sam was even more reserved. Since I was their friend, they wanted to co-operate
in helping me with my work, though some ambivalence remained on their part as to exactly how they fitted into my
study.

In contrast, Barry and Bobbi Jean both realized that they
were a central focus of my study. When I was at their house,
they knew I was there, among other things, to learn about
them. They seemed more willing to talk about themselves and
their problems, even to the extent of recording their life histories—an action that June was extremely reticent to undertake. Furthermore, where the Mosebys saw me first of all as a
neighbor, I felt almost as if I were a member of the Shackelford family. Quite frequently I would end up spending
practically an entire day with them. I worked, fished, and
hunted with Barry. I gave Bobbi rides to the doctor's or to the
welfare department. I spent hours and hours, just sitting,
drinking coffee or beer, and listening. If I didn't see her, invariably Bobbi would call Embry or me and talk to us on the
phone, filling us in on what crises had occurred in her household. While I probably spent almost as much time with the
Mosebys, my relationship with them was not as intense. They
did not depend on me as did Bobbi and Barry, nor did they
reveal as much about themselves.

Trying to be where the action was for both families consisted primarily of my trying to spend as much time with them
as possible. Since so much of what happened was unplanned,
I was never too sure what to expect. This fact made my work
both interesting and frustrating. In the mornings, for instance,
when I would set off to the Shackelfords, I would usually have
a feeling of anticipation, saying to myself, "Well, here goes
another adventure. Who knows what will happen today?" At

the same time, on many days nothing happened. No one would be home. Bobbi Jean would have to leave early to take someone to the doctor. Barry would be in an angry mood and not want to socialize. I soon learned that above all else participant observation requires patience. I had to meet people on their terms and adjust accordingly. I had to wait for the action. I could not initiate it myself. But when I was patient and stayed around long enough, I usually found I had seen or heard more than I could possibly remember.

Because it was impossible to know what would happen on a given day, it is difficult to say what constituted a "typical" day in my work. I tended to use weekday mornings for recording observations I had failed to record the preceding evening, for going over notes, or for determining what I needed to do that particular day. Toward midmorning Embry or I would usually drop by June's or I might wander up to the Shackelfords'— at which point what happened the rest of the day was anyone's guess. Toward the end of my stay I used the mornings for more formal interviews with community leaders, elected officials, and professionals involved in the area.

During the first part of my stay, I tried to eat lunch at the various restaurants in the community but found this to be unproductive, since most of the clientele were outsiders who only worked in the area. I also frequented most of the bars and taverns, which I found relatively unproductive for the same reasons. The people I met at the bars tended to be outsiders whom I rarely saw again.

The most productive hours for neighborhood observations were usually between the hours of four-thirty and nine o'clock in the evening. During this time when the weather was warm, I tried to be outside as much as possible. Embry and I would stroll with the baby, I would work in the yard, or stroll down the block ostensibly to buy something at the store. Almost always I ended up stopping to talk with someone. After dinner we would sit out on our porch, play lawn darts at the Mosebys', or sit on the Mosebys' porch, listening to the ball game and drinking beer. The weekends were like the evenings. I would try to remain out of doors, just hanging around, talking and listening.

Many weekday evenings I would attend community meetings, which usually started at eight. Since I found most of the meetings dull in contrast to the vibrant street life on Clay Street, during warm weather I tended to stay home more and attend fewer meetings. Also most Sunday mornings we attended one of the local churches. The time in between hanging around or going to meetings was usually spent recording conversations and observations.

One of the difficulties involved in a participant observation study is that one is never too sure when he is working and when he is relaxing. For this reason Embry and I found it very important to leave the neighborhood at least one or two times a week when, to the amazement of most of our neighbors, we would go into Washington to see friends, go to a movie, or have dinner.

Putting It All Down

The next phase of participant observation consists of recording one's observations of what is going on. In this phase the participant observer is faced with a number of crucial tasks. He must be able to figure out what is happening; he must be able to determine what is worth remembering about it; he must remember it long enough to record it; and, finally, he must be able to record the observations accurately and vividly. The tool that I found invaluable in recording my observations was a tape recorder. I depended on the tape recorder almost entirely; and without it, I venture to say this particular study would have been quite different.

I rarely carried a tape recorder with me. Rather, after talking with June or Bobbi or "being in some action," I would return home where I would record on tape what happened. Though I never took notes during an observation or conversation, once by myself I would try to jot down a few words or phrases to help me remember later. Living in the community allowed me to go home for lunch or dinner or leave temporarily, during which time I would do my tape recording. Quite often I would record four or five separate times a day. I found that if I waited until the next day, I had trouble remembering many of the details. The rules I tried to follow throughout my stay were, therefore: Record as soon after the event as possible and record as much of what happened as possible.

For me this particular method seemed to work. During a bull session at the Shackelfords, for instance, I would concentrate very hard and try to take in what was happening. Then I might excuse myself and go into the bathroom where

I would jot down some key words. Later in the day when I would return home, I would immediately go to my desk and look over my notes. Next I would write out a more thorough outline of who did and said what. Then I would sit at the desk for a few moments and try to put myself back into the event, trying to visualize the experience. Then I would turn on the tape recorder and let myself go. I could see Barry sitting at the table with a beer in his hand and hear him speak, "Goddamn, I'm fixing to catch me one helluva big catfish this afternoon. . . ." The words came freely, and I found I was sounding very much like Bobbi or Barry or Walt themselves sounded. Unconsciously I would even mimic their accents and take on their mannerisms. I found myself shouting, whispering, and occasionally almost weeping into the tape recorder. Had I not recorded soon after the experiences and had I not thrown myself into it, I am sure I would have never captured the dialogue to the extent that I did. I enjoyed recording in this fashion, and I never really got tired of it.

Once I would finish a tape I would send it to Chapel Hill where it would be transcribed. I was particularly fortunate in having someone in Chapel Hill, Linda Killen, who not only could make sense out of the tapes and type accurate transcripts but also organized much of the material into paragraphs and sections. Her ability as an interpreter, typist, and later critic and editor made her an essential part of the team and freed me from having to worry about organization when I recorded. When she finished transcribing, she would mail copies of the transcripts to me as well as to my colleagues, Robert Zehner and Stuart Chapin, who would read the transcripts, make suggestions, and monitor my progress. Particularly useful were biweekly conferences I had with Ruth Landman, head of the Department of Anthropology at American University, who also read the transcripts and gave me some very useful suggestions. The sessions with Dr. Landman enabled me to do some preliminary analysis and reflection and helped me gain some perspective on the data.

The net result of all this was two thousand pages of transcribed observations. These observations constituted my data and were waiting for me upon my return to Chapel Hill.

Besides recording my own observations, I used the tape recorder directly for recording life histories. Barry recorded four tapes—much of what pertains to him in Part Three; Bobbi, two tapes; and various others—Alton, Bubba, Walt,

June—recorded portions of tapes. I found recording life histories to be extremely difficult, however. Barry would consent
to record only when he was drunk and finally reached a point
—when he got to his life with Bobbi—when he would not go
any farther. Bobbi could never free herself from her children
or record in private (Barry always recorded in his truck),
and June and Sam refused to record at all. June tried twice
but became very tense and nervous, so I decided not to force
her. Since most of the people did not like recording and
seemed to resent me for it, I did not pursue it as I had
intended. The understanding seemed to be: As long as you
accept us and deal with us where we are, we'll co-operate; but
if you try to manipulate us to playing your game, we can only
do so much. I respected their feelings and gave up on trying
to get full life histories. (The Pete Dale history included in
Chapter 11 was relatively successful, however.)

To my knowledge, no one knew that I was recording my
observations on a tape recorder. Since no one asked me, I did
not volunteer the information, for I felt it would just make
them self-conscious and ill at ease. This was one of the two
secrets I kept from people—the other being the fact that I was
reimbursed for bowling as a "business expense."

Finally, I conducted a number of informal open-ended interviews with community leaders, school principals, social
workers, public health nurses, city planners, elected officials,
and ministers. In these interviews I would take extensive
notes, from which I would later record a summary of the interview. Though I ended up with several hundred pages of
transcribed interviews, I used little of this material directly
in this monograph. While I found it to be helpful in providing
perspective and in forming my interpretation of much of my
data, by comparison the dialogue was lifeless and dull.

Putting It All Together

In September when I returned to Chapel Hill I had staring
me in the face six volumes containing over two thousand
pages of transcribed observations. The first thing I did was to
read through the transcripts one time, making notes and jot-
ting down ideas as I read. Next I went back through the
material again, this time organizing it according to the people, families, or groups the material was about. Since several
copies of the transcripts were available, I used the "cut and

paste" method to set up separate files on the Shackelfords, Mosebys, Kate and Mack, Phyllis, B. J. Higgins, Carlyle James, etc., as well as files on bowling, taverns, community groups, churches, and interviews with outsiders. I then read through each of these files, making a chronological outline of what each person or family did over the course of the year and making notes concerning daily activities and routine. Completing this exercise enabled me to see more clearly the families as units and to see differences and similarities between various life styles.

Having gone through these files, I then returned to the original transcripts and read through them again, this time organizing the material according to topical subject matter. I made an index listing the data as it pertained to the following topics:

1. Background data
2. Health
3. Work
4. Welfare
5. Housing
6. (Other) Family problems
7. Friends and social networks—
    attitudes about others
8. Consumption patterns and habits
9. Family relationships, child rearing
10. Goals and aspirations
11. Religion and world view
12. Fears
13. Politics, justice, and equity
14. Education
15. Race
16. Episodes
17. Activities (off work, recreation)
18. Environmental perceptions
19. Ethics, morals, values
20. Finances
21. View of self—
    others' view of them
22. Moving behavior
23. Time
24. Views on change
25. Community issues and problems

Going over the material in this fashion gave me a better idea of the material as a whole and certain common themes that were present in the data. After I had finished indexing and rereading the material according to topics, it was close to Thanksgiving, I had read through the material five times, looking at it from three perspectives, and had practically memorized the transcripts.

The key decision I faced at that time was what approach I should take in writing up the material. I had two options. One, I could do something along the order of a conventional participant observation study, discussing the material according to certain general topics—work, child rearing, family relationships, political views, etc. If I had decided on this approach, I would have established a hard living/settled living typology and then discussed how the life styles differed in regard to the various topics. The advantage of this approach was that it was analytical, representative, and inclusive. The problem was that it was dull. Nor did it involve the use of much of the original transcripts I had taken such pains to record. For this reason, I opted for a less conventional approach, telling the story of the lives of two families over the course of one year. While this approach was less analytical, narrower, and less representative of the entire study area, it made use of material that I felt could best communicate who these people were. The transcripts far surpassed anything I could say about these people sitting in my office in Chapel Hill. Once in Chapel Hill, my thoughts and sentences sounded more and more like those of an academician and my descriptions of the people became less convincing and less real. Therefore, I opted "for telling it like it is," piecing together my transcripts with only minor editing and revising. Once I made this decision to use my transcripts directly in the text, taking a chronological view seemed the most natural approach.

The final monograph, of course, was something of a compromise between the two approaches—Parts One and Two being almost entirely chronological transcript material and Part Three organizing around certain general themes. Even in Part Three, however, I drew almost exclusively from the transcripts themselves. At the risk of being too anecdotal, I felt that the episodes and examples that I included in Part Three embodied life style and expressed the themes far better than anything I could say.

This particular book is the result of the methodology that I

have outlined here. It is by no means the only way a participant study of the people in the area could have been done.
There is no right or wrong way to go about participant
observation. Each participant observer must find a style and
approach that work for him. There are, however, six basic
rules that, as a now seasoned participant observer, I would
like to pass on to anyone who is so fortunate as to find himself "getting paid to do nothing." All are based on common
sense:

1. *Be honest about who you are and what you are
    doing.* You need not tell more than is asked for,
    but if you are ever caught lying, you are
    finished.

2. *Be yourself.* Don't try to overidentify or be "one
    of the boys." Chances are you will be less threatening to the people you are studying if you are a
    little different from them anyway. This way you
    are not competing with them.

3. *Be involved with people.* Don't worry about getting too involved with people and their problems.
    If you remain aloof and detached, you are not
    truly a participant. Don't be afraid of expressing
    your feelings. A participant observer is first of all
    a participant.

4. *Record every day as soon after the observation as
    possible.* This is where the observation part comes
    in. Try to be as thorough and as systematic as
    possible. But above all, don't let up here even
    when it becomes dull and boring. This is the essence of your data.

5. *Be patient.* If you are around people and accept
    them and are willing to listen, you will hear and
    see more than you know what to do with. But it
    takes time and patience.

6. In your analysis *stick to your data,* don't go beyond what you have seen or heard. As June would
    say, "No bullshit."